CICERO

XX

LCL 154

CICERO

DE SENECTUTE
DE AMICITIA
DE DIVINATIONE

WITH AN ENGLISH TRANSLATION BY

WILLIAM ARMISTEAD FALCONER

HARVARD UNIVERSITY PRESS

CAMBRIDGE, MASSACHUSETTS

LONDON, ENGLAND

First published 1923
Reprinted 1927, 1930, 1938, 1946, 1953, 1959, 1964, 1971, 1979,
1992, 1996

ISBN 0-674-99170-2

Printed in Great Britain by St Edmundsbury Press Ltd,
Bury St Edmunds, Suffolk, on acid-free paper.
Bound by Hunter & Foulis Ltd, Edinburgh, Scotland.

CONTENTS

PREFACE

WHILE my uncle,[1] then in his eighty-first year, was confined to his room by a serious illness, he received a letter of consolation from a friend, who quoted from Shuckburgh's translation of the *De senectute*. This quotation, though short, brought solace and cheer to the invalid and made him eager to hear more of Cicero's views on old age, and, as a result, he asked me to bring him the essay in the Latin and read it to him. Twenty years had passed since I had read the tractate at the University of Virginia under my revered old professor, Dr. Wm. E. Peters, and hence my rendering at sight must have done violence to the original in many places; but just as 'honour peereth in the meanest habit,' so the light of Cicero's genius was not wholly obscured by the medium through which it passed. At any rate, when I had finished, my uncle begged me—more, I think, for my good than for his own pleasure—to write out a translation of the entire treatise. I pleaded that my Latin was too rusty and that my judicial duties did not leave me leisure for such a task. He replied that my Latin would brighten with use and that an hour or

[1] Gen. H. B. Armistead, of Charleston, Ark.; b. 1832 in Fauquier Co., Virginia; Secretary of State of Arkansas, 1892-1896.

PREFACE

half-hour spent upon it now and then would not be missed and would afford me needed recreation. In his earnestness he exacted a promise which his death a few months later made only the more sacred. And so, on the trains as I went about the circuit, in hotels at night after trying cases all day, and in odd moments at home, I strove to redeem that promise. After several revisions a translation was completed and put into type.

My version had passed from hand to hand for two or three years with no thought of publication, when my poet-friend Brookes More asked permission to show it to his brother, Dr. Paul Elmer More of Princeton University, who brought it to the attention of Dr. Edward Capps, the American Editor of the L.C.L. At Dr. Capps' suggestion it was sent to the Senior Editor in England. After another revision it was accepted by him for publication and an invitation given to translate also the *De amicitia* and the *De divinatione*. Four years have gone by since this work was begun. It has been carried on amid many interruptions. Ill-health and, more often, the prior claims of professional and official duties have made the task an arduous one; and yet, because of these studies in classical learning and my contact with great scholars, living and dead, no other period of my life has brought me so much pleasure of mind and soul: *qua voluptate nulla certe potest esse maior.*

WILLIAM ARMISTEAD FALCONER.

Fort Smith, Arkansas, U.S.A.,
March 15, 1922.

CATO MAIOR DE SENECTUTE

INTRODUCTION TO THE
CATO MAIOR

1. CICERO AS A WRITER OF PHILOSOPHY

IN his youth, in preparation for a public career, Cicero devoted himself with ardour and success to the study of philosophy, and, during the whole of an exceptionally busy life, spent all his spare moments in reading and in the society of the learned. As a relaxation from public employment he produced in 55 B.C. his *De oratore*, in 54 his *De republica* and in 52 his *De legibus*. His choice of literature as his chief pursuit was due to political causes.

In January 49 B.C., after twelve months as governor of Cilicia, Cicero returned to Italy to find his country in the midst of civil war. Long hesitating which side to embrace, he finally gave his support to Pompey. After the battle of Pharsalus, in August 48, Cicero decided that further resistance to Caesar was useless and, in October, went to Brundisium, remaining there virtually a prisoner until September 47, when Caesar granted him an unconditional pardon. Although treated by the dictator and his friends with great respect, Cicero held proudly aloof from any active participation in a government which he regarded as a tyranny.

2

When, by Caesar's complete dominance of the courts and the Senate, Cicero had been excluded from those activities in which he had spent thirty brilliant and laborious years, he was forced to find some other outlet for his tireless energy of mind and body. Full of grief for the downfall of the Republic, harassed by debt and struggling under an almost intolerable weight of domestic sorrows, he turned to the writing of philosophic books as the surest relief from trouble and as the best means of serving his country. Early in 46 B.C., he withdrew from Rome to the quiet of his country places, and in that year published *Paradoxa, Partitiones oratoriae, Orator, De claris oratoribus*, and, probably, *Hortensius*. In February 45 the death of his adored and only daughter drove him into a frenzy of writing in an effort to forget his grief. In an incredibly short time he produced, in the years 45 and 44, *Consolatio, De finibus, Tusculanae disputationes, De natura deorum, Cato Maior, De divinatione, De fato, De gloria, De amicitia, Topica*, and *De officiis*. The *De officiis*, finished in November, closed his literary career.

2. Date of Composition

In a letter to Atticus written on May 11, 44 B.C. (*Ad Att.* xiv. 21), Cicero speaks of the *Cato Maior* as then already written. In the *De divinatione* it is referred to as a recent work. It followed the *De natura deorum* which was not completed until late in August 45. While there can be no certainty as to the exact time of composition the probability is that it was written between

December 15, 45 and January 3, 44 B.C. It was not fully revised, however, until July 17, 44 (*Ad Att.* xvi. 3).[1]

3. TITLE

Cicero once refers to this essay as *O Tite, si quid* (*Ad Att.* xiv. 11), from its initial words; once as *De senectute* (*De div.* ii. 3), and twice as *Cato Maior* (*Lael.* 4; *Ad Att.* xiv. 21). Its full title is *Cato Maior de senectute*.

4. DEDICATION TO ATTICUS

The *Cato Maior* and the *Laelius* are both dedicated to TITUS POMPONIUS ATTICUS, who was born at Rome in 109 B.C. His friendship with Cicero began in childhood and continued until Cicero's death in 43 B.C. From about 88 to 65 B.C., Atticus lived in Athens, devoting himself to the study of Greek philosophy and literature. He wrote Latin verses, which are highly commended by his biographer Cornelius Nepos, Roman *Annales*, a genealogical history of Roman families and a history in Greek of Cicero's consulship. He died in 32 B.C., at the age of 77, highly esteemed by the Emperor Augustus Caesar and by the leading Romans of his day. More than 400 letters from Cicero to him are extant to prove the rare intimacy and deep affection existing between these two remarkable men.

---

[1] That the reference in this letter is to *Cato Maior* and not to *De gloria* is clear from the context; besides, the *De gloria* had been sent to Atticus six days before (*Ad Att.* xvi. 2).

DE SENECTUTE

5. Time of the Dialogue and its Interlocutors

The discussion is supposed to occur in the year
150 B.C., between Cato, then 84, Scipio, then 35,
and Laelius,[1] then about 36.

Marcus Porcius Cato, who was born at Tusculum in 234 B.C., served under Fabius Maximus as
a private soldier in the campaign against Hannibal
in Campania in 214, and as a military tribune in the
siege of Tarentum in 209. He was elected quaestor
in 204, plebeian aedile in 199, praetor in 198, and
consul in 195. In 194 he celebrated a triumph for
his victories in Spain.

In the war against Antiochus he was on the staff
of the consul Marcus Acilius Glabrio, and distinguished himself at the Battle of Thermopylae in
191. In 184 he was censor with Flaccus and began
his struggles against the lax morals of the day.
He degraded seven senators, and exerted all his
power to stem the tide of luxury and extravagance.
Going as an envoy to Carthage in 157, he returned
full of alarm at its prosperity and always thereafter,
it is said, concluded every speech with the words
ceterum censeo delendam esse Carthaginem. He died
in 149. In addition to his ability as a farmer,
soldier, statesman and orator, Cato had consider-
able literary talent. He published 150 speeches,
a book of witticisms, a treatise entitled *De re
rustica*, works on legal subjects and a history of
Rome from its foundation to the year 150 B.C.,
entitled *Origines*.

Publius Scipio Africanus Minor was born about
185 B.C. He was the son by birth of Lucius Aemilius

---

[1] For a sketch of Laelius see *Lael.* Introd, pp. 104-105.

Paulus, and the son by adoption of Publius Cornelius Scipio, son of Africanus the Elder. He was a great student and a patron of Greek and Roman letters, and numbered among his intimate friends Polybius, the Greek historian; Panaetius the Stoic, and the Roman poets Lucullus and Terence. At the age of seventeen he fought under his father Paulus at Pydna, and in 151 B.C. was military tribune in Spain. In 148, though only a candidate for the aedileship, he was elected consul. As consul a second time he destroyed Carthage in 146. Thirteen years later, in his third consulship, he captured Numantia. His death occurred in 129 and was due, it was thought, to violence. Carbo, the popular leader, was suspected of having strangled him in his bed as he slept. According to the evidence of Cicero and Polybius (*Hist.* xxxii. 9-16), Scipio was one of the purest and noblest men in history.

6. Greek Sources of the *Cato Maior*

Cicero, in the letter of dedication of the *Cato Maior*, refers to Aristo Cius as the author of a treatise on old age, and he may have drawn upon that author in writing his own treatise. In Chapters 2 and 3 the conversation between Cephalus and Socrates in Plato's *Republic* is closely followed. Chapters 17 and 22 contain passages from Xenophon's *Oeconomicus* and *Cyropaedia*. In the form of the dialogue Cicero adopted the method of Aristotle rather than that of Plato, to avoid the frequent and continuous exchange of question and answer, and to permit one speaker, after a few

remarks from the other interlocutors, to give a connected discussion.

7. MANUSCRIPTS, EDITIONS AND TRANSLATIONS

The best MSS. of the *Cato Maior* are : P (at Paris), 9th or 10th century ; L (at Leyden), 10th century ; B (at Munich), 12th century ; R (at Zurich), of uncertain date ; E (at Berlin), 12th century ; S (at Munich), 11th century.

The present text is eclectic, following most closely that of J. S. Reid, but with such readings adopted from the editions of Müller, Bennett and others as seemed preferable. The critical notes of Reid and Müller and the interpretative notes of Reid and Bennett have been consulted with great profit in the preparation of the translation.

For an extensive bibliography of this essay the reader is referred to the excellent edition of Frank Gardner Moore. Of the many translations consulted the best, in the opinion of the present translator, in their order of merit, are those of Shuckburgh, Edmonds, and A. P. Peabody.

My grateful acknowledgements are due to Prof. Bechtel of Tulane University, and to Prof. Henry Strauss and Dr. J. L. Hancock of the University of Arkansas for a critical reading of the manuscript, and to my friends Mr. Brookes More of Hingham, Mass., and the late Judge Jesse Turner of Van Buren, Ark., for many helpful suggestions and criticisms.

[We now have in the Budé series the edition and French translation by P. Wuilleumier, Paris, 1955. P. Venini also has published *De Senectute*, Turin, 1959.]

M. TULLI CICERONIS

CATO MAIOR

DE SENECTUTE

I. O Tite, si quid ego adiuero curamve levasso
quae nunc te coquit et versat in pectore fixa,
ecquid erit praemi ?

Licet enim mihi versibus isdem affari te, Attice,
quibus affatur Flamininum

ille vir haud magna cum re, sed plenus fidei,

quamquam certo scio non, ut Flamininum,

sollicitari te, Tite, sic noctesque diesque,

novi enim moderationem animi tui et aequitatem,
teque non cognomen solum Athenis deportasse, sed
humanitatem et prudentiam intellego. Et tamen
te suspicor isdem rebus quibus me ipsum interdum
gravius commoveri, quarum consolatio et maior est
et in aliud tempus differenda.

---

¹ Ennius, *Annales*, lib. x., words addressed by an
Epirote shepherd to Titus Quinctius Flamininus, then
(198 B.C.) engaged in war with Philip of Macedon, and here
applied by Cicero to his lifelong friend, Titus Pomponius
Atticus.

² Referring to the existing political situation. See Introd.
p. 3.

MARCUS TULLIUS CICERO

CATO THE ELDER

ON OLD AGE

I. O Titus, should some aid of mine dispel
   The cares that now within thy bosom dwell
   And wring thy heart and torture thee with pain,
   What then would be the measure of my gain ? [1]

For, my dear Atticus, I may fitly speak to you in these self-same lines in which,

> That man
> Of little wealth, but rich in loyalty

speaks to Flamininus. And yet I am perfectly sure that it cannot be said of you, as the poet said of Flamininus,

> You fret and worry, Titus, day and night,

for I know your self-control and the even temper of your mind, and I am aware that you brought home from Athens not only a cognomen but culture and practical wisdom too. Nevertheless I suspect that you, at times, are quite seriously perturbed by the same circumstances [2] which are troubling me ; but to find comfort for them is too difficult a task to be undertaken now and must be deferred until another time.

9

Nunc autem visum est mihi de senectute aliquid
2 ad te conscribere, hoc enim onere, quod mihi
commune tecum est, aut iam urgentis aut certe
adventantis senectutis et te et me ipsum levari
volo ; etsi te quidem id modice ac sapienter, sicut
omnia, et ferre et laturum esse certo scio. Sed
mihi, cum de senectute vellem aliquid scribere, tu
occurrebas dignus eo munere, quo uterque nostrum
communiter uteretur. Mihi quidem ita iucunda
huius libri confectio fuit, ut non modo omnis abster-
serit senectutis molestias, sed effecerit mollem etiam
et iucundam senectutem. Numquam igitur laudari
satis digne philosophia poterit, cui qui pareat omne
tempus aetatis sine molestia possit degere.

3 Sed de ceteris et diximus multa et saepe dicemus :
hunc librum ad te de senectute misimus. Omnem
autem sermonem tribuimus non Tithono, ut Aristo
Cius, parum enim esset auctoritatis in fabula, sed
M. Catoni seni, quo maiorem auctoritatem haberet
oratio ; apud quem Laelium et Scipionem facimus
admirantis, quod is tam facile senectutem ferat,
eisque eum respondentem ; qui si eruditius videbitur disputare quam consuevit ipse in suis libris,
attribuito litteris Graecis, quarum constat eum per-
studiosum fuisse in senectute. Sed quid opus est
plura ? Iam enim ipsius Catonis sermo explicabit
nostram omnem de senectute sententiam.

---

[1] Cicero was then 62, Atticus 65.

However, at the present, I have determined to write something on old age to be dedicated to you, for I fain would lighten both for you and for me our common burden [1] of old age, which, if not already pressing hard upon us, is surely coming on apace; and yet I have certain knowledge that you, at all events, are bearing and will continue to bear that burden, as you do all others, with a calm and philosophic mind. But when I resolved to write something on this theme you continually came before my mind as worthy of a gift which both of us might enjoy together. To me, at any rate, the composition of this book has been so delightful that it has not only wiped away all the annoyances of old age, but has even made it an easy and a happy state. Philosophy, therefore, can never be praised as much as she deserves, since she enables the man who is obedient to her precepts to pass every season of life free from worry.

Now on other subjects I have said much and shall often have much to say; this book, which I am sending to you, is on old age. But the entire discourse I have attributed, not to Tithonus, as Aristo of Ceos did, (for there would be too little authority in a myth), but, that I might give it greater weight, I have ascribed it to the venerable Marcus Cato; and I represent Laelius and Scipio, while at his house, expressing wonder that he bears his age so well, and Cato replying to them. If it shall appear that he argues more learnedly than he was accustomed to do in his own books, give the credit to Greek literature, of which, as is well known, he was very studious in his later years. But why need I say more? For from now on the words of Cato himself will completely unfold to you my own views on old age.

4   II. Scipio. Saepe numero admirari soleo cum hoc
C. Laelio cum ceterarum rerum tuam excellentem,
M. Cato, perfectamque sapientiam, tum vel maxime
quod numquam tibi senectutem gravem esse senserim, quae plerisque senibus sic odiosa est, ut onus
se Aetna gravius dicant sustinere.

Cato. Rem haud sane, Scipio et Laeli, difficilem
admirari videmini. Quibus enim nihil est in ipsis
opis ad bene beateque vivendum, eis omnis aetas
gravis est ; qui autem omnia bona a se ipsi petunt,
eis nihil potest malum videri quod naturae necessitas
afferat. Quo in genere est in primis senectus, quam
ut adipiscantur omnes optant, eandem accusant
adeptam[1] ; tanta est stultitiae inconstantia atque
perversitas. Obrepere aiunt eam citius quam putas-
sent. Primum quis coegit eos falsum putare ? Qui
enim citius adulescentiae senectus quam pueritiae
adulescentia obrepit ? Deinde qui minus gravis
esset eis senectus, si octingentesimum annum agerent,
quam si octogesimum ? Praeterita enim aetas
quamvis longa, cum effluxisset, nulla consolatione[2]
permulcere posset stultam senectutem.

5   Quocirca si sapientiam meam admirari soletis,
quae utinam digna esset opinione vestra nostroque
cognomine, in hoc sumus sapientes, quod naturam
optimam ducem tamquam deum sequimur eique
paremus ; a qua non veri simile est, cum ceterae
partes aetatis bene discriptae sint, extremum actum

---

[1] adeptam *other MSS.*; adepti *LE, Bait., Müller.*
[2] consolatione *EI, Halm.*; consolatio *LP, Momms., Bait.*

---

[1] Cato was called *sapiens*, Cic. *Lael. 2. 6.*

II. Scipio. When conversing with Gaius Laelius here present, I am frequently wont to marvel, Cato, both at your pre-eminent, nay, faultless, wisdom in matters generally, and especially at the fact that, so far as I have been able to see, old age is never burdensome to you, though it is so vexatious to most old men that they declare it to be a load heavier than Aetna.

Cato. I think, my friends, that you marvel at a thing really far from difficult. For to those who have not the means within themselves of a virtuous and happy life every age is burdensome; and, on the other hand, to those who seek all good from themselves nothing can seem evil that the laws of nature inevitably impose. To this class old age especially belongs, which all men wish to attain and yet reproach when attained; such is the inconsistency and perversity of Folly! They say that it stole upon them faster than they had expected. In the first place, who has forced them to form a mistaken judgement? For how much more rapidly does old age steal upon youth than youth upon childhood? And again, how much less burdensome would old age be to them if they were in their eight hundredth rather than in their eightieth year? In fact, no lapse of time, however long, once it had slipped away, could solace or soothe a foolish old age.

Wherefore, if you are accustomed to marvel at my wisdom—and would that it were worthy of your estimate and of my cognomen [1]—I am wise because I follow Nature as the best of guides and obey her as a god; and since she has fitly planned the other acts of life's drama, it is not likely that she has

13

tamquam ab inerti poeta esse neglectum. Sed tamen necesse fuit esse aliquid extremum et, tamquam in arborum bacis terraeque fructibus, maturitate tempestiva quasi vietum et caducum, quod ferendum est molliter sapienti. Quid est enim aliud gigantum modo bellare cum dis nisi naturae repugnare ?

6 LAELIUS. Atqui, Cato, gratissimum nobis, ut etiam pro Scipione pollicear, feceris, si, quoniam speramus, volumus quidem certe, senes fieri, multo ante a te didicerimus quibus facillime rationibus ingravescentem aetatem ferre possimus.

CATO. Faciam vero, Laeli, praesertim si utrique vestrum, ut dicis, gratum futurum est.

LAELIUS. Volumus sane, nisi molestum est. Cato, tamquam longam aliquam viam confeceris, quam nobis quoque ingrediendum sit, istuc, quo pervenisti, videre quale sit.

7 III. CATO. Faciam ut potero, Laeli. Saepe enim interfui querellis aequalium meorum, pares autem vetere proverbio cum paribus facillime congregantur, quae C. Salinator, quae Sp. Albinus, homines consulares, nostri fere aequales, deplorare solebant, tum quod voluptatibus carerent, sine quibus vitam nullam putarent, tum quod spernerentur ab eis, a quibus essent coli soliti ; qui mihi non id videbantur

---

[1] *Cf.* Plato, *Rep.* 328 E. Cicero almost translates the words there addressed by Socrates to the aged Cephalus.

[2] Both were younger than Cato.

neglected the final act as if she were a careless playwright. And yet there had to be something final, and—as in the case of orchard fruits and crops of grain in the process of ripening which comes with time—something shrivelled, as it were, and prone to fall. But this state the wise man should endure with resignation. For what is warring against the gods, as the giants did, other than fighting against Nature?

LAELIUS True, Cato, but you will do a thing most agreeable to us both—assuming that I may speak for Scipio, too—if, since we hope to become old (at least we wish it), you will, long in advance, teach us on what principles we may most easily support the weight of increasing years.

CATO. To be sure I will, Laelius, especially if, as you say, it is going to prove agreeable to you both.

LAELIUS. Unless it is too much trouble to you, Cato, since you have, as it were, travelled the long road upon which we also must set out, we really do wish to see what sort of a place it is at which you have arrived.[1]

III. CATO. I will do so, Laelius, as well as I can. For I have often listened to the complaints of my contemporaries (and according to the old adage, " like with like most readily foregathers "), complaints made also by the ex-consuls, Gaius Salinator and Spurius Albinus,[2] who were almost my equals in years, wherein they used to lament, now because they were denied the sensual pleasures without which they thought life not life at all, and now because they were scorned by the people who had been wont to pay them court. But it seemed to me

15

accusare, quod esset accusandum. Nam si id culpa senectutis accideret, eadem mihi usu venirent reliquisque omnibus maioribus natu, quorum ego multorum cognovi senectutem sine querella, qui se et libidinum vinculis laxatos esse non moleste ferrent nec a suis despicerentur. Sed omnium istius modi querellarum in moribus est culpa, non in aetate. Moderati enim et nec difficiles nec inhumani senes tolerabilem senectutem agunt, importunitas autem et inhumanitas omni aetati molesta est.

8 LAELIUS. Est, ut dicis, Cato ; sed fortasse dixerit quispiam tibi propter opes et copias et dignitatem tuam tolerabiliorem senectutem videri, id autem non posse multis contingere.

CATO. Est istuc quidem, Laeli, aliquid, sed nequaquam in isto sunt omnia ; ut Themistocles fertur Seriphio cuidam in iurgio respondisse, cum ille dixisset non eum sua, sed patriae gloria splendorem assecutum : " nec hercule," inquit, " si ego Seriphius essem, nec tu, si Atheniensis,[1] clarus umquam fuisses." Quod eodem modo de senectute dici potest ; nec enim in summa inopia levis esse senectus potest, ne sapienti quidem, nec insipienti etiam in summa copia non gravis.

9 Aptissima omnino sunt, Scipio et Laeli, arma senectutis artes exercitationesque virtutum, quae in omni aetate cultae, cum diu multumque vixeris,

---

[1] *LE add* esses *after* Atheniensis.

---

[1] Seriphos, an island of the Cyclades group, a symbol of smallness and insignificance.

that they were not placing the blame where the blame was due. For if the ills of which they complained were the faults of old age, the same ills would befall me and all other old men : but I have known many who were of such a nature that they bore their old age without complaint, who were not unhappy because they had been loosed from the chains of passion, and who were not scorned by their friends. But as regards all such complaints, the blame rests with character, not with age. For old men of self-control, who are neither churlish nor ungracious, find old age endurable ; while on the other hand perversity and an unkindly disposition render irksome every period of life.

LAELIUS. What you say is true, Cato ; but perhaps some one may reply that old age seems more tolerable to you because of your resources, means, and social position, and that these are advantages which cannot fall to the lot of many.

CATO. There is something in that objection, Laelius, but not everything. For example, there is a story that when, in the course of a quarrel, a certain Seriphian[1] had said to Themistocles, " Your brilliant reputation is due to your country's glory, not your own," Themistocles replied, " True, by Hercules, I should never have been famous if I had been a Seriphian, nor you if you had been an Athenian." The same may be said of old age ; for amid utter want old age cannot be a light thing, not even to a wise man ; nor to a fool, even amid utmost wealth, can it be otherwise than burdensome.

Undoubtedly, Scipio and Laelius, the most suitable defences of old age are the principles and practice of the virtues, which, if cultivated in every period

mirificos ecferunt fructus, non solum quia numquam
deserunt, ne extremo quidem tempore aetatis, quamquam id quidem maximum est, verum etiam quia
conscientia bene actae vitae multorumque bene
factorum recordatio iucundissima est.

10   IV. Ego Q. Maximum, eum qui Tarentum recepit,
senem adulescens ita dilexi, ut aequalem. Erat
enim in illo viro comitate condita gravitas, nec
senectus mores mutaverat. Quamquam eum colere
coepi non admodum grandem natu, sed tamen iam
aetate provectum. Anno enim post consul primum
fuerat quam ego natus sum, cumque eo quartum
consule adulescentulus miles ad Capuam profectus
sum quintoque anno post ad Tarentum. Quaestor
deinde quadriennio post factus sum, quem magistratum gessi consulibus Tuditano et Cethego, cum
quidem ille admodum senex suasor legis Cinciae de
donis et muneribus fuit. Hic et bella gerebat ut
adulescens, cum plane grandis esset, et Hannibalem
iuveniliter exsultantem patientia sua molliebat ;
de quo praeclare familiaris noster Ennius :

> unus homo nobis cunctando restituit rem ;
> noenum[1] rumores ponebat ante salutem;
> ergo plusque[2] magisque viri nunc gloria claret.

11   Tarentum vero qua vigilantia, quo consilio recepit !
Cum quidem me audiente Salinatori, qui amisso

----

[1] noenum *Lachmann* ; non enim MSS.
[2] plusque *Bernays* ; postque MSS.

----

[1] This law was proposed by M. Cincius Alimentus in
204 B.C. and prohibited lawyers from receiving fees from
clients and the rich from receiving gifts from the poor for
services. Cato's irrelevant digression here is a happy
illustration of Cicero's art in impressing us with Cato's age.

of life, bring forth wonderful fruits at the close of a long and busy career, not only because they never fail you even at the very end of life—although that is a matter of highest moment—but also because it is most delightful to have the consciousness of a life well spent and the memory of many deeds worthily performed.

IV. I was as fond of Quintus Fabius Maximus, who recovered Tarentum, as if he had been of my own age, though he was old and I was young. For there was in him a dignity tempered with courtesy, and age had not altered his disposition ; and yet when I began to cultivate him he was not extremely old, though he was well advanced in life. For he had been consul for the first time the year after I was born ; and when he was in his fourth consulship I was a mere lad, and set out as a private soldier with him for Capua, and five years later for Tarentum ; then, four years after that I became quaestor, which office I held while Tuditanus and Cethegus were consuls, and he, at that very time, though far advanced in age, made speeches in favour of the Cincian law [1] on fees and gifts. Though quite old he waged war like a young man, and by his patient endurance checked the boyish impetuosity of Hannibal. My friend Ennius admirably speaks of him thus :

> One man's delay alone restored our State :
> He valued safety more than mob's applause ;
> Hence now his glory more resplendent grows.

Indeed, with what vigilance, with what skill he recaptured Tarentum ! It was in my own hearing that Salinator,[2] who had fled to the citadel after

[2] Cicero blunders here, for it was M. Livius Macatus, a relation of Salinator, who held the citadel, Livy xxvii. 34. 7.

oppido fugerat in arcem, glorianti atque ita dicenti,
" mea opera, Q. Fabi, Tarentum recepisti " ; " certe,"
inquit ridens, " nam nisi tu amisisses, numquam
recepissem." Nec vero in armis praestantior quam
in toga ; qui consul iterum, Sp. Carvilio collega
quiescente, C. Flaminio tribuno plebis, quoad potuit,
restitit agrum Picentem et Gallicum viritim contra
senatus auctoritatem dividenti ; augurque cum esset,
dicere ausus est optimis auspiciis ea geri, quae pro
rei publicae salute gererentur ; quae contra rem
publicam ferrentur, contra auspicia ferri.

12   Multa in eo viro praeclara cognovi, sed nihil
admirabilius quam quo modo ille mortem fili tulit,
clari viri et consularis. Est in manibus laudatio,
quam cum legimus, quem philosophum non contem-
nimus ? Nec vero ille in luce modo atque in oculis
civium magnus, sed intus domique praestantior.
Qui sermo, quae praecepta ! Quanta notitia antiquitatis, scientia iuris auguri ! Multae etiam, ut in
homine Romano, litterae : omnia memoria tenebat
non domestica solum, sed etiam externa bella. Cuius
sermone ita tum cupide fruebar, quasi iam divinarem, id quod evenit, illo exstincto fore unde dis-
cerem neminem.

13   V. Quorsus¹ igitur haec tam multa de Maximo ?

---

¹ quorsus *other* MSS.; quorsum *L.*

---

¹ Gaius Flaminius was popular tribune in 232 B.C. when
this law was enacted. It provided for the settlement of
citizen farmers on public lands, and resembled somewhat
the American homestead laws. Cicero gives the date
here as in the second consulship of Q. Fabius Maximus,
i.e. 228 B.C.

losing the town, remarked to him in a boasting
tone : " Through my instrumentality, Q. Fabius, you
have recaptured Tarentum." " Undoubtedly," said
Fabius, laughing, " for if you had not lost it I should
never have recaptured it." But, indeed, he was not
more distinguished in war than in civil life. While
consul the second time, unaided by his colleague
Spurius Carvilius he, as far as he could, opposed
the people's tribune Gaius Flaminius who was
endeavouring to parcel out the Picene and Gallic
lands,[1] contrary to the expressed will of the senate.
And, although an augur, he dared to say that whatever was done for the safety of the Republic was
done under the best auspices, and that whatever
was inimical to the Republic was against the auspices.

Many are the remarkable things I have observed
in that great man, but nothing more striking than
the manner in which he bore the death of his distinguished son, a former consul. The funeral oration
delivered by him on that occasion is in general
circulation, and, when we read it, what philosopher
does not appear contemptible ? Nor was it merely
in public and under the gaze of his fellow-citizens
that he was great, but he was greater still in the
privacy of his home. What conversation ! What
maxims ! What a knowledge of ancient history !
What skill in augural law ! He had also read much,
for a Roman, and knew by heart the entire history,
not only of our own wars, but of foreign wars as well.
I was, at that time, as eager to profit by his conversation as if I already foresaw what, in fact, came
to pass, that, when he was gone, I should have no
one from whom to learn.

V. Why, then, have I said so much about

21

Quia profecto videtis nefas esse dictu miseram fuisse talem senectutem. Nec tamen omnes possunt esse Scipiones aut Maximi, ut urbium expugnationes, ut pedestris navalisve pugnas, ut bella a se gesta, ut triumphos recordentur. Est etiam quiete et pure atque eleganter actae aetatis placida ac lenis senectus, qualem accepimus Platonis, qui uno et octogesimo anno scribens est mortuus, qualem Isocratis, qui eum librum, qui Panathenaicus inscribitur, quarto nonagesimo anno scripsisse dicit vixitque quinquennium postea; cuius magister Leontinus Gorgias centum et septem complevit annos, neque umquam in suo studio atque opere cessavit. Qui, cum ex eo quaereretur cur tam diu vellet esse in vita, " nihil habeo," inquit, " quod accusem senectutem." Prae-
14 clarum responsum et docto homine dignum !

Sua enim vitia insipientes et suam culpam in senectutem conferunt, quod non faciebat is, cuius modo mentionem feci, Ennius :

> sic ut fortis equus, spatio qui saepe supremo
> vicit Olympia, nunc senio confectus quiescit.

Equi fortis et victoris senectuti comparat suam ; quem quidem probe meminisse potestis ; anno enim undevicesimo post eius mortem hi consules, T. Flamininus et M'. Acilius, facti sunt ; ille autem Caepione et Philippo iterum consulibus mortuus est, cum ego quinque et sexaginta annos natus legem

---

[1] Not necessarily to be taken literally; but meaning that he had not abandoned the writing of books. Plato is said to have died at a marriage-feast (Diog. Laert. iii. 2).

[2] Laelius and Scipio, at the death of Ennius, were respectively seventeen and sixteen years old.

Maximus? Because you surely realize now that it would be monstrous to call unhappy such an old age as his. And yet, not every one can be a Scipio or a Maximus and call to mind the cities he has taken, the battles he has fought on land and sea, the campaigns he has conducted, and the triumphs he has won. But there is also the tranquil and serene old age of a life spent quietly, amid pure and refining pursuits—such an old age, for example, as we are told was that of Plato, who died, pen in hand,[1] in his eighty-first year; such as that of Isocrates, who, by his own statement, was ninety-four when he composed the work entitled *Panathenaicus*, and he lived five years after that. His teacher, Gorgias of Leontini, rounded out one hundred and seven years and never rested from his pursuits or his labours. When some one asked him why he chose to remain so long alive, he answered: " I have no reason to reproach old age." A noble answer and worthy of a scholar!

For, in truth, it is their own vices and their own faults that fools charge to old age ; but Ennius, of whom I spoke a while ago, did not do this, for he says :

> He, like the gallant steed that often won
> Olympic trophy in the final lap,
> Now takes his rest when weakened by old age.

He is comparing his old age to that of a brave and victorious horse. You both may recall him distinctly,[2] for it was only nineteen years from his death until the election of the present consuls, Titus Flamininus and Manius Acilius, and he did not pass away until the consulship of Caepio and Philip (the latter being in his second term), at a time when I, at sixty-five, spoke publicly for the Voconian

Voconiam magna voce et bonis lateribus suasissem.[1]
Annos septuaginta natus, tot enim vixit Ennius,
ita ferebat duo quae maxima putantur onera, paupertatem et senectutem, ut eis paene delectari videretur.

15 Etenim, cum complector animo, quattuor reperio
causas cur senectus misera videatur : unam, quod
avocet a rebus gerendis ; alteram, quod corpus faciat
infirmius ; tertiam, quod privet omnibus fere voluptatibus ; quartam, quod haud procul absit a morte.
Earum, si placet, causarum quanta quamque sit
iusta una quaeque videamus.

VI. A rebus gerendis senectus abstrahit. Quibus ?
An eis, quae iuventute geruntur et viribus ? Nul-
laene igitur res sunt seniles, quae vel infirmis corporibus animo et mente administrentur ? Nihil ergo
agebat Q. Maximus, nihil L. Paulus, pater tuus, socer
optimi viri fili mei ? Ceteri senes, Fabricii Curii
Coruncanii, cum rem publicam consilio et auctoritate
defendebant, nihil agebant ?

Ad Appi Claudi senectutem accedebat etiam ut
16 caecus esset ; tamen is, cum sententia senatus
inclinaret ad pacem cum Pyrrho foedusque faciendum,
non dubitavit dicere illa, quae versibus persecutus
est Ennius :

> quo vobis mentes, rectae quae stare solebant
> antehac, dementis sese flexere viai ?

ceteraque gravissime, notum enim vobis carmen est,

---

[1] suasissem *other MSS.*; suasisset *P*; suasi sed *Forch.*,
Müller.

---

[1] This law, named from its author, Voconius Saxa,
tribune of the plebs, passed in 169 B.C., provided (1) that no
one enrolled as having 100,000 *asses* (about $1,000) should
make a woman his heir ; or (2) leave to another a sum
greater than the heirs would receive.

law,[1] with loud voice and mighty lungs. But he at seventy—for Ennius lived that long—was bearing the two burdens which are considered the greatest—poverty and old age—and was bearing them in such a way that he seemed almost to take a pleasure in them.

And, indeed, when I reflect on this subject I find four reasons why old age appears to be unhappy : first, that it withdraws us from active pursuits ; second, that it makes the body weaker ; third, that it deprives us of almost all physical pleasures ; and, fourth, that it is not far removed from death. Let us, if you please, examine each of these reasons separately and see how much truth they contain.

VI. " Old age withdraws us from active pursuits." From what pursuits ? Is it not from those which are followed because of youth and vigour ? Are there, then, no intellectual employments in which aged men may engage, even though their bodies are infirm ? Was there, then, no employment for Quintus Maximus ? And none, Scipio, for your father Lucius Paulus, the father-in-law of that best of men, my son ? And those other old men, like Fabricius, Curius, and Coruncanius — were they doing nothing, when by their wisdom and influence they were preserving the state ?

To the old age of Appius Claudius was also added blindness ; yet when the sentiment of the senate was inclining towards peace and an alliance with Pyrrhus, he did not hesitate to say what Ennius has thus put into verse :

Your minds that once did stand erect and strong,
What madness swerves them from their wonted course ?

—and so on, in most impressive style. But you are

et tamen ipsius Appi exstat oratio. Atque haec ille egit septemdecim annis post alterum consulatum, cum inter duos consulatus anni decem interfuissent censorque ante superiorem consulatum fuisset, ex quo intellegitur Pyrrhi bello grandem sane fuisse, et tamen sic a patribus accepimus.

17 Nihil igitur afferunt qui in re gerenda versari senectutem negant, similesque sunt ut si qui gubernatorem in navigando nihil agere dicant, cum alii malos scandant, alii per foros cursent, alii sentinam exhauriant, ille clavum tenens quietus sedeat in puppi; non faciat ea, quae iuvenes; at vero multo maiora et meliora facit. Non viribus aut velocitate aut celeritate corporum res magnae geruntur, sed consilio auctoritate sententia, quibus non modo non orbari, sed etiam augeri senectus solet.

18 Nisi forte ego vobis, qui et miles et tribunus et legatus et consul versatus sum in vario genere bellorum, cessare nunc videor, cum bella non gero. At senatui quae sint gerenda praescribo et quo modo; Carthagini male iam diu cogitanti bellum multo ante denuntio, de qua vereri non ante desinam quam illam exscisam esse cognovero. Quam palmam

19 utinam di immortales, Scipio, tibi reservent, ut avi relliquias persequare, cuius a morte tertius hic et tricesimus annus est, sed memoriam illius viri omnes

familiar with the poem, and, after all, the actual speech of Appius is still extant. It was delivered seventeen years after his second consulship, although ten years had intervened between the two consulships and he had been censor before he was consul. Hence, it is known that he was undoubtedly an old man at the time of the war with Pyrrhus, and yet such is the story as we have it by tradition.

Those, therefore, who allege that old age is devoid of useful activity adduce nothing to the purpose, and are like those who would say that the pilot does nothing in the sailing of the ship, because, while others are climbing the masts, or running about the gangways, or working at the pumps, he sits quietly in the stern and simply holds the tiller. He may not be doing what younger members of the crew are doing, but what he does is better and much more important. It is not by muscle, speed, or physical dexterity that great things are achieved, but by reflection, force of character, and judgement; in these qualities old age is usually not only not poorer, but is even richer.

But perhaps it seems to you that I who engaged in various kinds of warfare as private, captain, general, and commander-in-chief, am unemployed now that I do not go to war. And yet I direct the senate as to what wars should be waged and how; at the present time, far in advance of hostilities, I am declaring war on Carthage, for she has long been plotting mischief; and I shall not cease to fear her until I know that she has been utterly destroyed. And I pray the immortal gods to reserve for you, Scipio, the glory of completing the work which your grandfather left unfinished! Thirty-three years have passed since that hero's death, but each succeeding

excipient anni consequentes. Anno ante me cen-
sorem mortuus est, novem annis post meum consulatum, cum consul iterum me consule creatus esset.
Num igitur, si ad centesimum annum vixisset,
senectutis eum suae paeniteret ? Nec enim excur-
sione nec saltu, nec eminus hastis aut comminus
gladiis uteretur, sed consilio ratione sententia, quae
nisi essent in senibus, non summum consilium
maiores nostri appellassent senatum. Apud Lace-
20 daemonios quidem ei, qui amplissimum magistratum
gerunt, ut sunt, sic etiam nominantur, senes. Quod
si legere aut audire voletis externa, maximas res
publicas ab adulescentibus labefactatas, a senibus
sustentatas et restitutas reperietis.

Cedo qui vestram rem publicam tantam amisistis tam cito?

sic enim percontantur[1] in Naevi poetae Lupo.[2]
Respondentur et alia et hoc in primis :

proveniebant oratores novi, stulti adulescentuli.

Temeritas est videlicet florentis aetatis, prudentia
senescentis.

21 VII. At memoria minuitur. Credo, nisi eam exer-
ceas, aut etiam si sis natura tardior. Themistocles
omnium civium perceperat nomina ; num igitur

---

[1] ut est *after* percontantur *in* MSS., *generally omitted by editors.*
[2] Lupo *Ribbeck, Bennett, Mommsen* ; Ludo MSS.

---

[1] *Senatus*, an assembly of *senes*, or elders.
[2] The citizens of Athens (native males, over 20, having the franchise) were then probably about 20,000.

year will receive his memory and pass it on. He died in the year before I was censor, nine years after I was consul; and while I was holding the latter office he was elected consul for the second time. If, then, he had lived to his hundredth year, would he be repenting of his old age? No, for he would not be employing his time in running and in leaping, or in long-distance throwing of the spear, or in hand-to-hand sword-play, but he would be engaged in using reflection, reason, and judgement. If these mental qualities were not characteristic of old men our fathers would not have called their highest deliberative body the "senate."[1] Among the Lacedaemonians, for example, those who fill their chief magistracies are called " elders," as they are in fact. And indeed, if you care to read or hear foreign history, you will find that the greatest states have been overthrown by the young and sustained and restored by the old.

> How lost you, pray, your mighty state so soon?

for such is the question put in a play entitled the *Wolf*, by the poet Naevius. Several answers are given, but the one chiefly in point is this:

> Through swarms of green, declaiming, silly lads.

True enough, for rashness is the product of the budding-time of youth, prudence of the harvest-time of age.

VII. But, it is alleged, the memory is impaired. Of course, if you do not exercise it, or also if you are by nature somewhat dull. Themistocles had learned the names of all the citizens of Athens [2] by heart; do you think, then, that after he became

censetis eum, cum aetate processisset, qui Aristides
esset Lysimachum salutare solitum ? Equidem non
modo eos novi qui sunt, sed eorum patres etiam et
avos, nec sepulcra legens vereor, quod aiunt, ne
memoriam perdam ; his enim ipsis legendis in
memoriam redeo mortuorum. Nec vero quemquam
senem audivi oblitum, quo loco thesaurum obruisset.
Omnia quae curant meminerunt, vadimonia constituta, quis sibi, cui ipsi debeant.

22 Quid iuris consulti, quid pontifices, quid augures,
quid philosophi senes ? Quam multa meminerunt !
Manent ingenia senibus, modo permaneat studium
et industria, neque ea solum claris et honoratis viris,
sed in vita etiam privata et quieta. Sophocles ad
summam senectutem tragoedias fecit ; quod propter
studium cum rem neglegere familiarem videretur,
filiis in iudicium vocatus est, ut, quem ad modum
nostro more male rem gerentibus patribus bonis
interdici solet, sic illum quasi desipientem a re
familiari removerent iudices. Tum senex dicitur
eam fabulam quam in manibus habebat et proxime
scripserat, Oedipum Coloneum, recitasse iudicibus
quaesisseque num illud carmen desipientis videre-
23 tur, quo recitato sententiis iudicum est liberatus.
Num igitur hunc, num Homerum Hesiodum Simo-

---

[1] Lysimachus was the father of Aristides the bitter enemy
of Themistocles ; hence there is pointed humour in the
question.

old he was wont to address as Lysimachus one who in fact was Aristides ? [1] I, for instance, know not only the people who are living, but I recall their fathers and grandfathers, too ; and as I read their epitaphs I am not afraid of the superstition that, in so doing, I shall lose my memory ; for by reading them I refresh my recollection of the dead. I certainly never heard of any old man forgetting where he had hidden his money ! The aged remember everything that interests them, their appointments to appear in court, and who are their creditors and who their debtors.

And how is it with aged lawyers, pontiffs, augurs, and philosophers ? What a multitude of things they remember ! Old men retain their mental faculties, provided their interest and application continue ; and this is true, not only of men in exalted public station, but likewise of those in the quiet of private life. Sophocles composed tragedies to extreme old age ; and when, because of his absorption in literary work, he was thought to be neglecting his business affairs, his sons haled him into court in order to secure a verdict removing him from the control of his property on the ground of imbecility, under a law similar to ours, whereby it is customary to restrain heads of families from wasting their estates. Thereupon, it is said, the old man read to the jury his play, *Oedipus at Colonus*, which he had just written and was revising, and inquired : " Does that poem seem to you to be the work of an imbecile ? " When he had finished he was acquitted by the verdict of the jury. Think you, then, that old age forced him to abandon his calling, or that it silenced Homer, Hesiod, Simonides, Stesichorus, or

31

niden Stesichorum, num quos ante dixi Isocraten
Gorgian, num philosophorum principes, Pythagoran
Democritum, num Platonem Xenocraten, num postea
Zenonem Cleanthen, aut eum, quem vos etiam
vidistis Romae, Diogenen Stoicum coegit in suis
studiis obmutiscere senectus? An in omnibus
studiorum agitatio vitae aequalis fuit?

24 Age, ut ista divina studia omittamus, possum
nominare ex agro Sabino rusticos Romanos, vicinos
et familiaris meos, quibus absentibus numquam fere
ulla in agro maiora opera fiunt, non serendis, non
percipiendis, non condendis fructibus. Quamquam
in aliis minus hoc mirum est, nemo enim est tam
senex qui se annum non putet posse vivere; sed
idem in eis elaborant, quae sciunt nihil ad se omnino
pertinere:

> serit arbores, quae alteri saeclo prosint,

25 ut ait Statius noster in Synephebis. Nec vero
dubitat agricola, quamvis sit senex, quaerenti cui
serat respondere: "dis immortalibus, qui me non
accipere modo haec a maioribus voluerunt, sed etiam
posteris prodere."

VIII. Et melius Caecilius de sene alteri saeculo
prospiciente, quam illud idem:

> edepol, senectus, si nil quicquam aliud viti
> adportes tecum, cum advenis, unum id sat est,
> quod diu vivendo multa quae non volt videt.

---

[1] From Caecilius's comedy, *Plocium.*

Isocrates, and Gorgias (whom I have mentioned already), or any of those princes of philosophy Pythagoras, Democritus, Plato, and Xenocrates, or Zeno and Cleanthes of a later time, or Diogenes the Stoic, whom you both have seen at Rome ? Rather, did not activity in their several pursuits continue with all of them as long as life itself ?

But come now—to pass over these divine pursuits —I can point out to you Roman farmers in the Sabine country, friends and neighbours of mine, who are scarcely ever absent from the field while the more important operations of husbandry, as sowing, reaping, and storing the crops, are going on. Although this interest of theirs is less remarkable in the case of annual crops,—for no one is so old as to think that he cannot live one more year—yet these same men labour at things which they know will not profit them in the least.

> He plants the trees to serve another age,

as our Caecilius Statius says in his *Young Comrades*. And if you ask a farmer, however old, for whom he is planting, he will unhesitatingly reply, " For the immortal gods, who have willed not only that I should receive these blessings from my ancestors, but also that I should hand them on to posterity."

VIII. And the same Caecilius, in writing of the old man making provision for a future generation, spoke to better purpose than he did in the following lines :

> In truth, Old Age, if you did bring no bane
> But this alone, 'twould me suffice: that one,
> By living long, sees much he hates to see.[1]

33

Et multa fortasse quae volt, atque in ea, quae non volt, saepe etiam adulescentia incurrit. Illud vero idem Caecilius vitiosius :

> tum equidem in senecta hoc deputo miserrimum,
> sentire ea aetate eumpse esse odiosum alteri.

26 Iucundum potius quam odiosum ! Ut enim adulescentibus bona indole praeditis sapientes senes delectantur, leviorque fit senectus eorum qui a iuventute coluntur et diliguntur, sic adulescentes senum praeceptis gaudent, quibus ad virtutum studia ducuntur ; nec minus intellego me vobis quam mihi vos esse iucundos. Sed videtis, ut senectus non modo languida atque iners non sit, verum etiam sit operosa et semper agens aliquid et moliens, tale scilicet, quale cuiusque studium in superiore vita fuit. Quid, qui etiam addiscunt aliquid, ut et Solonem versibus gloriantem videmus, qui se cotidie aliquid addiscentem dicit senem fieri. Et ego feci, qui litteras Graecas senex didici, quas quidem sic avide arripui quasi diuturnam sitim explere cupiens, ut ea ipsa mihi nota essent, quibus me nunc exemplis uti videtis. Quod cum fecisse Socraten in fidibus audirem, vellem equidem etiam illud, discebant enim fidibus antiqui, sed in litteris certe elaboravi.

27   IX. Ne nunc quidem viris desidero adulescentis,

---

[1] From the play called *Ephesio.*

[2] Quoted by Plutarch, *Sol.* 31 γηράσκω δ᾽ ἀεὶ πολλὰ διδασκόμενος.

[3] *Cf.* Plato, *Menexenus*, 235 ε ; id. *Euthydemus*, 272 ο.

Possibly, also, many things he likes ; and as for things one does not wish to see, even youth often encounters them. However, this other sentiment from the same Caecilius is worse :

> But saddest bane of age, I think, is this :
> That old men feel their years a bore to youth.[1]

A pleasure, rather than a bore, say I. For just as wise men, when they are old, take delight in the society of youths endowed with sprightly wit, and the burdens of age are rendered lighter to those who are courted and highly esteemed by the young, so young men find pleasure in their elders, by whose, precepts they are led into virtue's paths; nor indeed do I feel that I am any less of a pleasure to you than you are to me. But you see how old age, so far from being feeble and inactive, is even busy and is always doing and effecting something— that is to say, something of the same nature in each case as were the pursuits of earlier years. And what of those who even go on adding to their store of knowledge ? Such was the case with Solon, whom we see boasting in his verses that he grows old learning something every day.[2] And I have done the same, for in my old age I have learned Greek, which I seized upon as eagerly as if I had been desirous of satisfying a long-continued thirst, with the result that I have acquired first-hand the information which you see me using in this discussion by way of illustration. And when I read what Socrates [3] had done in the case of the lyre, an instrument much cultivated by the ancients, I should have liked to do that too, if I could ; but in literature I have certainly laboured hard.

IX. I do not now feel the need of the strength

35

is enim erat locus alter de vitiis senectutis, non plus
quam adulescens tauri aut elephanti desiderabam.
Quod est, eo decet uti et quidquid agis[1] agere pro
viribus. Quae enim vox potest esse contemptior
quam Milonis Crotoniatae? Qui cum iam senex
esset athletasque se exercentis in curriculo videret,
aspexisse lacertos suos dicitur illacrimansque dixisse,
"at hi quidem mortui iam sunt." Non vero tam isti,
quam tu ipse, nugator, neque enim ex te umquam
es nobilitatus, sed ex lateribus et lacertis tuis. Nihil
Sex. Aelius tale, nihil multis annis ante Ti. Coruncanius, nihil modo P. Crassus, a quibus iura civibus
praescribebantur, quorum usque ad extremum
spiritum est provecta prudentia.

28   Orator metuo ne languescat senectute, est enim
munus eius non ingeni solum, sed laterum etiam et
virium. Omnino canorum illud in voce splendescit
etiam nescio quo pacto in senectute, quod equidem
adhuc non amisi, et videtis annos. Sed tamen est
decorus seni sermo quietus et remissus, facitque persaepe ipsa[2] sibi audientiam diserti senis composita[3]
et mitis oratio, quam si ipse exsequi nequeas, possis
tamen Scipioni praecipere et Laelio. Quid enim est
29 iucundius senectute stipata studiis iuventutis? An
ne illas quidem viris senectuti relinquimus,[4] ut

---

[1] agis *Reid*; agas *MSS.*
[2] persaepe ipsa *other MSS.*; per se ipsa *L, Müller.*
[3] composita *edd.*; compta *MSS., Müller.*
[4] relinquimus *other MSS.*; relinquemus *L, Müller.*

---

[1] By the old Roman custom these lawyers gave audience
in the early hours of the day to all who chose to consult
them on legal questions.

[2] *Canorum . . . splendescit* is a mixed metaphor—the first
word appeals to the ear, the second to the eye; literally,
"a clarion-like ring which gives it brilliancy."

of youth—for that was the second head under the
faults of old age—any more than when a young man
I felt the need of the strength of the bull or of the
elephant. Such strength as a man has he should use,
and whatever he does should be done in proportion
to his strength. For what utterance can be more
pitiable than that of Milo of Crotona ? After he
was already an old man and was watching the
athletes training in the race-course, it is related that,
as he looked upon his shrunken muscles, he wept
and said : " Yes, but they now are dead." But not
as dead as you, you babbler ! For you never gained
renown from your real self, but from brute strength
of lungs and limb. Of a far different stamp were
Sextus Aelius and Titus Coruncanius of ancient
times, and Publius Crassus of a later date, by
whom instruction in jurisprudence [1] was given to
their fellow-citizens, and whose skill in law continued
to the very last gasp.

The orator, I fear, does lose in efficiency on account
of old age, because his success depends not only
upon his intellect, but also upon his lungs and
bodily strength. In old age, no doubt, the voice
actually gains (I know not how) that magnificent
resonance [2] which even I have not lost, and you see
my years ; and yet the style of speech that graces
the old man is subdued and gentle, and very often
the sedate and mild speaking of an eloquent old man
wins itself a hearing. And although one cannot
himself engage in oratory, still, he may be able to
give instruction to a Scipio or a Laelius ! For what
is more agreeable than an old age surrounded by the
enthusiasm of youth ? Or do we not concede to
old age even strength enough to instruct and train

37

adulescentis doceat, instituat, ad omne offici munus
instruat ? Quo quidem opere quid potest esse prae-
clarius ? Mihi vero et Cn. et P. Scipiones et avi tui
duo L. Aemilius et P. Africanus comitatu nobilium
iuvenum fortunati videbantur, nec ulli bonarum
artium magistri non beati putandi, quamvis con-
senuerint vires atque defecerint.

Etsi ipsa ista defectio virium adulescentiae vitiis
efficitur saepius quam senectute ; libidinosa enim
et intemperans adulescentia effetum corpus tradit
30 senectuti.[1] Cyrus quidem apud Xenophontem eo
sermone, quem moriens habuit, cum admodum senex
esset, negat se umquam sensisse senectutem suam
imbecilliorem factam quam adulescentia fuisset.
Ego L. Metellum memini puer, qui, cum quadriennio post alterum consulatum pontifex maximus
factus esset, viginti et duos annos ei sacerdotio praefuit, ita bonis esse viribus extremo tempore aetatis,
ut adulescentiam non requireret. Nihil necesse est
mihi de me ipso dicere, quamquam est id quidem
31 senile aetatique nostrae conceditur. X. Videtisne,
ut apud Homerum saepissime Nestor de virtutibus
suis praedicet ? Tertiam enim aetatem hominum
videbat, nec erat ei verendum ne vera praedicans de
se nimis videretur aut insolens aut loquax. "Etenim,"
ut ait Homerus, " ex eius lingua melle dulcior fluebat
oratio ; " quam ad suavitatem nullis egebat corporis

---

[1] senectuti *Reid* ; senectutis MSS.

---

[1] Cyrus the Elder, Xen. *Cyropaedia*, viii. 7. 6. But other
authorities (Herod. i. 24, Lucian, *Charon*, 30) say that
Cyrus died in battle with the Scythians.
[2] *e.g. Iliad*, i. 260 ; vii. 124 ; xi. 668.
[3] *Iliad*, i. 247.
[4] *Iliad*, i. 249.

young men and equip them for every function and
duty ?   And what more exalted service can there
be than this ?   For my part, Scipio, I used to consider Gnaeus and Publius Scipio and your two grandfathers, Lucius Aemilius and Publius Africanus,
fortunate in being attended by throngs of noble
youths ; and no teachers of the liberal arts should
be considered unhappy, even though their bodily
vigour may have waned and failed.

And yet, even that very loss of strength is more
often chargeable to the dissipations of youth than
to any fault of old age ; for an intemperate and
indulgent youth delivers to old age a body all worn
out. For example, Cyrus,[1] in Xenophon, in that
discourse which he delivered when he was very
old and on his death-bed, says that he had never
felt that his old age was any less vigorous than his
youth had been.   I remember that in my boyhood I
saw Lucius Metellus, who, four years after his second
consulship, became Chief Pontiff and held that
sacred office for twenty-two years, and I recall
that he enjoyed such great vigour of body to the end
of his days that he did not feel the loss of youth.
I need say nothing of myself in this connexion,
though to do so is an old man's privilege and permitted to one of my age.

X. Do you not observe in Homer how, time and
again, Nestor proclaims his own merits ?[2] For he,
at that time, was looking on the third generation of
men,[3] yet he did not fear that, in speaking the truth
about himself, he would appear to any great extent
either odd or loquacious. For as Homer says,
" Speech sweeter than honey flowed from his
tongue " ;[4] and this sweetness had no need of

viribus. Et tamen dux ille Graeciae nusquam optat
ut Aiacis similis habeat decem, sed ut Nestoris, quod
si sibi acciderit, non dubitat quin brevi sit Troia
peritura.

32 Sed redeo ad me. Quartum ago annum et octogesimum : vellem equidem idem posse gloriari quod
Cyrus, sed tamen hoc queo dicere, non me quidem
eis esse viribus, quibus aut miles bello Punico aut
quaestor eodem bello aut consul in Hispania fuerim
aut quadriennio post, cum tribunus militaris depug-
navi apud Thermopylas M'. Glabrione consule ; sed
tamen, ut vos videtis, non plane me enervavit, non
afflixit senectus : non curia viris meas desiderat, non
rostra, non amici, non clientes, non hospites. Nec
enim umquam sum assensus veteri illi laudatoque
proverbio, quod monet mature fieri senem, si diu
velis senex esse. Ego vero me minus diu senem
esse mallem quam esse senem ante quam essem.
Itaque nemo adhuc convenire me voluit cui fuerim
occupatus.

33 At minus habeo virium quam vestrum utervis.
Ne vos quidem T. Ponti centurionis viris habetis :
num idcirco est ille praestantior ? Moderatio modo
virium adsit et tantum quantum potest quisque
nitatur, ne ille non magno desiderio tenebitur virium.
Olympiae per stadium ingressus esse Milo dicitur,
cum umeris sustineret bovem : utrum igitur has
corporis an Pythagorae tibi malis viris ingeni dari ?

---

[1] *i.e.* Agamemnon, *Iliad*, ii. 371.
[2] For these events in Cato's life and their dates see
Introduction.
[3] This was some man famous for his strength in Cato's
day, but of whom we know nothing more.

physical strength ; and yet the illustrious Grecian chief [1] never prays for ten men like Ajax. but for ten like Nestor, and he doubts not that, if he had them, Troy would speedily be destroyed.

But I return to myself. I am in my eighty-fourth year and would that I myself could boast as Cyrus did ; but still I can say this much : that while I am not now, indeed, possessed of that physical strength which I had as a private soldier in the Punic War, or as a quaestor in the same war, or as commander-in-chief in Spain, or when as military tribune four years later I fought the war out at Thermopylae under the command of Manius Acilius Glabrio ; [2] yet, as you see, old age has not quite unnerved or shattered me. The senate and the popular assembly never find my vigour wanting, nor do my friends, my dependents, or my guests ; for I have never assented to that ancient and much-quoted proverb, which advises : " Become old early if you would be old long." For my part I would rather not be old so long than be old before my time. Accordingly, I have so far never refused an audience to anyone who wished to consult me.

But it may be said that I have less strength than either of you ; but I reply that you, for your part, have not the strength of the centurion Titus Pontius [3]; is he, for that reason, more excellent than you ? Only let every man make a proper use of his strength and strive to his utmost, then assuredly he will have no regret for his want of strength. It is said that Milo walked the length of the race-course at Olympia, carrying an ox on his shoulders. Which, therefore, would you prefer should be given to you—the physical powers of Milo, or the mental powers of

41

Denique isto bono utare, dum adsit, cum absit, ne
requiras : nisi forte adulescentes pueritiam, paulum
aetate progressi adulescentiam debent requirere.
Cursus est certus aetatis et una via naturae eaque
simplex, suaque cuique parti aetatis tempestivitas
est data, ut et infirmitas puerorum et ferocitas
iuvenum et gravitas iam constantis aetatis et senectutis maturitas naturale quiddam habet, quod suo
tempore percipi debeat.

34 Audire te arbitror, Scipio, hospes tuus avitus
Masinissa quae faciat hodie nonaginta natus annos :
cum ingressus iter pedibus sit, in equum omnino
non ascendere ; cum autem equo, ex equo non
descendere ; nullo imbri, nullo frigore adduci ut
capite operto sit ; summam esse in eo corporis
siccitatem, itaque omnia exsequi regis officia et
munera. Potest igitur exercitatio et temperantia
etiam in senectute conservare aliquid pristini roboris.

XI. Ne sint[1] in senectute vires : ne postulantur
quidem vires a senectute. Ergo et legibus et
institutis vacat aetas nostra muneribus eis quae non
possunt sine viribus sustineri. Itaque non modo
quod non possumus, sed ne quantum possumus
35 quidem cogimur. At multi ita sunt imbecilli senes,
ut nullum offici aut omnino vitae munus exsequi

[1] ne sint *R, Reid* ; non sunt *LBIS, Müller.*

Pythagoras ? In short, enjoy the blessing of strength while you have it and do not bewail it when it is gone, unless, forsooth, you believe that youth must lament the loss of infancy, or early manhood the passing of youth. Life's race-course is fixed; Nature has only a single path and that path is run but once, and to each stage of existence has been allotted its own appropriate quality ; so that the weakness of childhood, the impetuosity of youth, the seriousness of middle life, the maturity of old age—each bears some of Nature's fruit, which must be garnered in its own season.

I think, Scipio, that the news reaches you of the daily activities of your grandfather's friend and host Masinissa, now ninety years old ; that when he begins a march on foot, he never mounts a horse, and when he sets out on horseback he never dismounts ; that no rain or cold, however great, can induce him to cover his head ; and—such is the extreme wiriness of his body—that he in person performs all the duties and functions of his kingly office. It is possible, therefore, for a man by exercise and self-control, even in old age, to preserve some of his original vigour.

XI. But, grant that old age is devoid of strength ; none is even expected of it. Hence both by law and by custom men of my age are exempt from those public services which cannot be rendered without strength of body. Therefore, we are not only not required to do what we cannot perform, but we are not required to do even as much as we can. Yet, it may be urged, many old men are so feeble that they can perform no function that duty or indeed any position in life demands. True, but

possint. At id quidem non proprium senectutis
vitium est, sed commune valetudinis. Quam fuit
imbecillus P. Africani filius, is qui te adoptavit, quam
tenui aut nulla potius valetudine ! Quod ni ita
fuisset, alterum illud exstitisset lumen civitatis ; ad
paternam enim magnitudinem animi doctrina uberior
accesserat. Quid mirum igitur in senibus, si infirmi
sunt aliquando, cum id ne adulescentes quidem
effugere possint ?

Resistendum, Laeli et Scipio, senectuti est eiusque
vitia diligentia compensanda sunt, pugnandum tamquam contra morbum[1] sic contra senectutem, habenda
36 ratio valetudinis, utendum exercitationibus modicis,
tantum cibi et potionis adhibendum, ut reficiantur
vires, non opprimantur. Nec vero corpori solum
subveniendum est, sed menti atque animo multo
magis. Nam haec quoque, nisi tamquam lumini
oleum instilles, exstinguuntur senectute. Et corpora
quidem exercitationum defetigatione ingravescunt,
animi autem exercitando[2] levantur. Nam quos ait
Caecilius " comicos stultos senes," hos significat
credulos obliviosos dissolutos, quae vitia sunt non
senectutis, sed inertis ignavae somniculosae senectutis. Ut petulantia, ut libido magis est adulescentium quam senum, nec tamen omnium adulescentium, sed non proborum, sic ista senilis stultitia,
quae deliratio appellari solet, senum levium est, non
omnium.

37 Quattuor robustos filios, quinque filias, tantam

---

[1] morbum *MSS.* ; morborum *Müller.*
[2] exercitando *other MSS.* ; exercendo *LER.*

---

[1] Scipio Africanus, the Elder, was the first luminary.
[2] From his lost play *Epiclerus.* For the line in full see
De amicitia 99.

that is not peculiar to old age; generally it is a characteristic of ill-health. Note how weak, Scipio, was your adoptive father, the son of Publius Africanus! What feeble health he had, or rather no health at all! But for this he would have shone forth as the second luminary [1] of the state; for to his father's greatness of intellect he had added a more abundant learning. What wonder, then, that the aged are sometimes weak, when even the young cannot escape the same fate?

But it is our duty, my young friends, to resist old age; to compensate for its defects by a watchful care; to fight against it as we would fight against disease; to adopt a regimen of health; to practise moderate exercise; and to take just enough of food and drink to restore our strength and not to over-burden it. Nor, indeed, are we to give our attention solely to the body; much greater care is due to the mind and soul; for they, too, like lamps, grow dim with time, unless we keep them supplied with oil. Moreover, exercise causes the body to become heavy with fatigue, but intellectual activity gives buoyancy to the mind. For when Caecilius speaks of "the old fools of the comic stage," [2] he has in mind old men characterized by credulity, forgetfulness, and carelessness, which are faults, not of old age generally, but only of an old age that is drowsy, slothful, and inert. Just as waywardness and lust are more often found in the young man than in the old, yet not in all who are young, but only in those naturally base; so that senile debility, usually called "dotage," is a characteristic, not of all old men, but only of those who are weak in mind and will.

Appius, though he was both blind and old, managed

domum, tantas clientelas Appius regebat et caecus et
senex; intentum enim animum tamquam arcum habebat nec languescens succumbebat senectuti. Tenebat
non modo auctoritatem, sed etiam imperium in suos :
metuebant servi, verebantur liberi, carum omnes
habebant ; vigebat in illa domo mos patrius et
38 disciplina.[1]   Ita enim senectus honesta est, si se ipsa
defendit, si ius suum retinet, si nemini emancipata
est, si usque ad ultimum spiritum dominatur in suos.
Ut enim adulescentem in quo est senile aliquid, sic
senem in quo est aliquid adulescentis probo, quod
qui sequitur, corpore senex esse poterit, animo
numquam erit.

Septimus mihi liber Originum est in manibus ;
omnia antiquitatis monumenta colligo ; causarum
illustrium, quascunque defendi, nunc cum maxime
conficio orationes ; ius augurium pontificium civile
tracto ; multum etiam Graecis litteris utor ; Pytha-
goriorumque more, exercendae memoriae gratia,
quid quoque die dixerim audierim egerim commemoro
vesperi. Hae sunt exercitationes ingeni, haec cur-
ricula mentis ; in his desudans atque elaborans
corporis viris non magno opere desidero. Adsum
amicis, venio in senatum frequens ultroque affero res
multum et diu cogitatas easque tueor animi, non

---

[1] in illa domo patrius mos et disciplina *Müller* ; in illo
animus patrius et disciplina *Reid, Moore*.

four sturdy sons, five daughters, a great household, and many dependents; for he did not languidly succumb to old age, but kept his mind ever taut, like a well-strung bow. He maintained not mere authority, but absolute command over his household; his slaves feared him, his children revered him, all loved him, and the customs and discipline of his forefathers flourished beneath his roof. For old age is honoured only on condition that it defends itself, maintains its rights, is subservient to no one, and to the last breath rules over its own domain. For just as I approve of the young man in whom there is a touch of age, so I approve of the old man in whom there is some of the flavour of youth. He who strives thus to mingle youthfulness and age may grow old in body, but old in spirit he will never be.

I am now at work on the seventh volume of my *Antiquities*. I am collecting all the records of our ancient history, and at the present moment am revising all the speeches made by me in the notable causes which I conducted. I am investigating the augural, pontifical, and secular law; I also devote much of my time to Greek literature; and, in order to exercise my memory, I follow the practice of the Pythagoreans and run over in my mind every evening all that I have said, heard, or done during the day. These employments are my intellectual gymnastics; these the race-courses of my mind; and while I sweat and toil with them I do not greatly feel the loss of bodily strength. I act as counsel for my friends; I frequently attend the senate, where, on my own motion, I propose subjects for discussion after having pondered over them seriously and long; and there I maintain my views in debate, not with

corporis viribus. Quas si exsequi nequirem, tamen
me lectulus meus oblectaret ea ipsa cogitantem,
quae iam agere non possem ; sed ut possim facit
acta vita. Semper enim in his studiis laboribusque
viventi non intellegitur quando obrepat senectus :
ita sensim sine sensu aetas senescit nec subito fran-
gitur, sed diuturnitate exstinguitur.

39 XII. Sequitur tertia vituperatio senectutis, quod
eam carere dicunt voluptatibus. O praeclarum munus
aetatis, si quidem id aufert a nobis, quod est in
adulescentia vitiosissimum ! Accipite enim, optimi
adulescentes, veterem orationem Archytae Tarentini,
magni in primis et praeclari viri, quae mihi tradita
est cum essem adulescens Tarenti cum Q. Maximo.
Nullam capitaliorem pestem quam voluptatem corporis hominibus dicebat a natura datam, cuius
voluptatis avidae libidines temere et ecfrenate ad
40 potiendum incitarentur. Hinc patriae proditiones,
hinc rerum publicarum eversiones, hinc cum hostibus
clandestina colloquia nasci ; nullum denique scelus,
nullum malum facinus esse, ad quod suscipiendum
non libido voluptatis impelleret ; stupra vero et
adulteria et omne tale flagitium nullis excitari aliis
illecebris nisi voluptatis ; cumque homini sive natura
sive quis deus nihil mente praestabilius dedisset,
huic divino muneri ac dono nihil tam esse inimicum

---

[1] *i.e.* the *lectulus lucubratorius,* used when reading or
the like.

strength of body, but with force of mind. But even
if I could not perform these services, nevertheless,
my couch [1] would afford me delight while reflecting
on the very things that I lacked the strength to do.
However, the fact that I can do them is due to the
life that I have led. For the man who lives always
amid such studies and pursuits as mine is not aware
of the stealthy approach of age. Thus employed
his life gradually and imperceptibly glides into old
age, and succumbs, not to a quick assault, but to a
long-continued siege.

XII. We come now to the third ground for abusing
old age, and that is, that it is devoid of sensual
pleasures. O glorious boon of age, if it does indeed
free us from youth's most vicious fault! Now
listen, most noble young men, to what that remark-
ably great and distinguished man, Archytas of
Tarentum, said in an ancient speech repeated to me
when I was a young man serving with Quintus
Maximus at Tarentum : " No more deadly curse,"
said he, " has been given by nature to man than
carnal pleasure, through eagerness for which the
passions are driven recklessly and uncontrollably
to its gratification. From it come treason and the
overthrow of states ; and from it spring secret and
corrupt conferences with public foes. In short,
there is no criminal purpose and no evil deed which
the lust for pleasure will not drive men to undertake. Indeed, rape, adultery, and every like
offence are set in motion by the enticements of
pleasure and by nothing else ; and since nature—
or some god, perhaps—has given to man nothing
more excellent than his intellect, therefore this
divine gift has no deadlier foe than pleasure ; for

41 quam voluptatem. Nec enim libidıne dominante temperantiae locum esse, neque omnino in voluptatis regno virtutem posse consistere.

Quod quo magis intellegi posset, fingere animo iubebat tanta incitatum aliquem voluptate corporis, quanta percipi posset maxima ; nemini censebat fore dubium quin tam diu, dum ita gauderet, nihil agitare mente, nihil ratione, nihil cogitatione consequi posset. Quocirca nihil esse tam detestabile tamque pestiferum quam voluptatem, si quidem ea, cum maior esset atque longior, omne animi lumen exstingueret. Haec cum C. Pontio Samnite, patre eius, a quo Caudino proelio Sp. Postumius T. Veturius consules superati sunt, locutum Archytam Nearchus Tarentinus hospes noster, qui in amicitia populi Romani permanserat, se a maioribus natu accepisse dicebat, cum quidem ei sermoni interfuisset Plato Atheniensis, quem Tarentum venisse L. Camillo Ap. Claudio consulibus reperio.

42 Quorsus hoc ? Ut intellegeretis, si voluptatem aspernari ratione et sapientia non possemus, magnam esse habendam senectuti gratiam, quae efficeret ut id non liberet quod non oporteret. Impedit enim consilium voluptas, rationi inimica est, mentis ut ita dicam praestringit oculos, nec habet ullum cum virtute commercium.

Invitus feci ut fortissimi viri T. Flaminini fratrem L. Flamininum e senatu eicerem septem annis post

---

[1] 321 b.c.

[2] That is, in 349 b.c. when Plato was 79 years old and too old, it is thought, to have visited Italy. The date of his last visit is usually given as 361.

[3] This was done while Cato and L. Valerius Flaccus were censors, in 184 b.c. Titus Flamininus was consul in 192,

where lust holds despotic sway self-control has no
place, and in pleasure's realm there is not a single
spot where virtue can put her foot.

" Imagine," he begged, to make his meaning
clearer, " imagine a person enjoying the most
exquisite bodily pleasure to be had. No one will
doubt, I think, that such a man, while in the midst
of this enjoyment, is incapable of any mental action,
and can accomplish nothing requiring reason and
reflection. Hence there is nothing so hateful and
so pernicious as pleasure, since, if indulged in too
much and too long, it turns the light of the soul into
utter darkness." My Tarentine host Nearchus, who
remained steadfast in his friendship to the Roman
people, told me that, according to tradition, Archytas
uttered these words while conversing with Pontius the
Samnite, father of the man who defeated the consuls
Spurius Postumius and Titus Veturius at the Caudine
Forks.[1] Indeed he further told me that Plato the
Athenian was present and heard Archytas deliver this
discourse, and, upon investigation, I find that Plato
did come to Tarentum in the consulship of Lucius
Camillus and Appius Claudius.[2]

Now, why did I quote Archytas ? To make you
realize that if reason and wisdom did not enable us
to reject pleasure, we should be very grateful to old
age for taking away the desire to do what we ought
not to do. For carnal pleasure hinders deliberation,
is at war with reason, blindfolds the eyes of the mind,
so to speak, and has no fellowship with virtue.

It was a disagreeable duty that I performed in
expelling [3] Lucius Flamininus from the senate, for

hence seven years intervened between the consulship and the
expulsion of Lucius Flamininus from the senate.

quam consul fuisset, sed notandam putavi libidinem.
Ille enim cum esset consul in Gallia exoratus in
convivio a scorto est ut securi feriret aliquem eorum
qui in vinculis essent, damnati rei capitalis. Hic
Tito fratre suo censore, qui proximus ante me fuerat,
elapsus est, mihi vero et Flacco neutiquam probari
potuit tam flagitiosa et tam perdita libido, quae cum
probro privato coniungeret imperi dedecus.

43　XIII. Saepe audivi e maioribus natu, qui se porro
pueros a senibus audisse dicebant, mirari solitum C.
Fabricium quod, cum apud regem Pyrrhum legatus
esset, audisset a Thessalo Cinea esse quendam
Athenis qui se sapientem profiteretur, eumque dicere
omnia quae faceremus ad voluptatem esse referenda.
Quod ex eo audientis M'. Curium et Ti. Coruncanium optare solitos ut id Samnitibus ipsique Pyrrho
persuaderetur, quo facilius vinci possent cum se
voluptatibus dedissent. Vixerat M'. Curius cum
P. Decio, qui quinquennio ante eum consulem se
pro re publica quarto consulatu devoverat : norat
eundem Fabricius, norat Coruncanius, qui cum ex
sua vita tum ex eius quem dico Deci facto iudica-
bant esse profecto aliquid natura pulchrum atque
praeclarum, quod sua sponte expeteretur[1] quodque

---

[1] expeteretur *Reid*; peteretur MSS.

---

[1] *Cf.* Livy xxxix. 42. 7, xxxix. 43. 2.
[2] *i.e.* Epicurus, who claimed to be not only φιλόσοφος but
σοφός.

he was a brother of that most valiant man, Titus
Flamininus, and had been consul seven years before;
but I thought that lust merited the brand of infamy.
For, when in Gaul during his consulship, at the
solicitation of a courtesan at a banquet, he beheaded
a prisoner then under condemnation for some
capital offence.[1] While his brother, my immediate
predecessor, was censor, Lucius escaped punishment,
but Flaccus and I could by no means approve of
conduct so flagrant and abandoned, especially when
to his crime against an individual he added dishonour
to the state.

XIII. I often heard from my elders—who, in turn,
said they, when boys, had heard it from old men—
that Gaius Fabricius used to marvel at the story told
him, while an envoy at the headquarters of King
Pyrrhus, by Cineas of Thessaly, that there was
a man[2] at Athens who professed himself "wise"
and used to say that everything we do should be
judged by the standard of pleasure. Now when
Manius Curius and Tiberius Coruncanius learned
of this from Fabricius they expressed the wish that
the Samnites and Pyrrhus himself would become
converts to it, because, when given up to pleasure,
they would be much easier to overcome. Manius
Curius had lived on intimate terms with Publius
Decius who, in his fourth consulship, and five years
before Curius held that office, had offered up his
life for his country's safety; Fabricius and Coruncanius also knew him, and they all were firmly
persuaded, both by their own experience and
especially by the heroic deed of Decius, that assuredly
there are ends, inherently pure and noble, which
are sought for their own sake, and which will be

spreta et contempta voluptate optimus quisque sequeretur.

44 Quorsum igitur tam multa de voluptate ? Quia non modo vituperatio nulla, sed etiam summa laus senectutis est, quod ea voluptates nullas magno opere desiderat. Caret epulis exstructisque mensis et frequentibus poculis. Caret ergo etiam vinulentia et cruditate et insomniis. Sed si aliquid dandum est voluptati, quoniam eius blanditiis non facile obsistimus, divine enim Plato " escam malorum " appellat voluptatem quod ea videlicet homines capiantur ut pisces, quamquam immoderatis epulis caret senectus, modicis tamen conviviis delectari potest. C. Duellium M. F., qui Poenos classe primus devicerat, redeuntem a cena senem saepe videbam puer ; delectabatur cereo[1] funali et tibicine, quae sibi nullo exemplo privatus sumpserat : tantum licentiae dabat gloria.

45 Sed quid ego alios ? Ad me ipsum iam revertar. Primum habui semper sodalis—sodalitates autem me quaestore constitutae sunt sacris Idaeis Magnae Matris acceptis—epulabar igitur cum sodalibus, omnino modice, sed erat quidam fervor aetatis, qua progrediente omnia fiunt in dies mitiora. Neque enim ipsorum conviviorum delectationem volup-

---

[1] cereo *Manutius, Mommsen* ; crebro MSS.

---

[1] κακοῦ δέλεαρ, *Timaeus*, 69 **D**.
[2] *i.e.* in 204 **B.C.**

pursued by all good men who look on self-gratifica-
tion with loathing and contempt.

Why then, do I dwell at such length on pleasure ?
Because the fact that old age feels little longing
for sensual pleasures not only is no cause for reproach,
but rather is ground for the highest praise. Old
age lacks the heavy banquet, the loaded table, and
the oft-filled cup ; therefore it also lacks drunken-
ness, indigestion, and loss of sleep. But if some
concession must be made to pleasure, since her
allurements are difficult to resist, and she is, as Plato
happily says, " the bait of sin," [1]—evidently because
men are caught therewith like fish—then I admit
that old age, though it lacks immoderate banquets,
may find delight in temperate repasts. Gaius
Duellius, son of Marcus, and the first Roman to win a
naval victory over the Carthaginians, was often seen
by me in my childhood, when he was an old man,
returning home from dining out, attended, as was
his delight, by a torch-bearer and flute-player—an
ostentation which as a private citizen he had assumed,
though without precedent : but that much licence
did his glory give him.

But why speak of others ? Let me now return
to myself. In the first place I have always had my
club companions. Moreover, it was in my quaestorship [2] that clubs in honour of Cybele were organized,
when the Idaean worship was introduced at Rome,
and therefore I used to dine with these companions—
in an altogether moderate way, yet with a certain
ardour appropriate to my age, which, as time goes
on, daily mitigates my zest for every pleasure. Nor,
indeed, did I measure my delight in these social
gatherings more by the physical pleasure than by

tatibus corporis magis quam coetu amicorum et
sermonibus metiebar ; bene enim maiores accubitio-
nem epularem amicorum, quia vitae coniunctionem
haberet, " convivium " nominaverunt, melius quam
Graeci, qui hoc idem tum " compotationem," tum
" concenationem " vocant, ut, quod in eo genere
minimum est, id maxime probare videantur.

46 XIV. Ego vero propter sermonis delectationem
tempestivis quoque conviviis delector, nec cum
aequalibus solum, qui pauci admodum restant, sed
cum vestra etiam aetate atque vobiscum, habeoque
senectuti magnam gratiam, quae mihi sermonis
aviditatem auxit, potionis et cibi sustulit. Quod si
quem etiam ista delectant, ne omnino bellum in-
dixisse videar voluptati, cuius est fortasse quidam
naturalis modus, non intellego ne in istis quidem
ipsis voluptatibus carere sensu senectutem. Me
vero et magisteria delectant a maioribus instituta
et is sermo, qui more maiorum a summo adhibetur
in poculo, et pocula, sicut in Symposio Xenophontis
est, minuta atque rorantia, et refrigeratio aestate
et vicissim aut sol aut ignis hibernus. Quae quidem
etiam in Sabinis persequi soleo conviviumque vicino-
rum cotidie compleo, quod ad multam noctem quam
maxime possumus vario sermone producimus.

---

¹ Cicero thus translates συμπόσιον and σύνδειπνον.
² *i.e.* banquets which began early and shortened the
business day ; the phrase usually suggests something of a
debauch.
³ Referring to the *arbiter bibendi*, or *rex*—also called
magister—convivi. The word " toast-masters " as used in
the United States is the exact equivalent of the Latin. They
were appointed with due ceremony even at public banquets.
⁴ *Cf.* Xen. *Symp.* 2. 26.
⁵ Noted for their simple habits.

the pleasure of meeting and conversing with my friends. For our fathers did well in calling the reclining of friends at feasts a *convivium*, because it implies a communion of life, which is a better designation than that of the Greeks, who call it sometimes a " drinking together " and sometimes an " eating together," [1] thereby apparently exalting what is of least value in these associations above that which gives them their greatest charm.

XIV. For my own part, because of my love of conversation, I enjoy even " afternoon banquets," [2] not with my contemporaries only, very few of whom now remain, but also with you and with those of your age ; and I am profoundly grateful to old age, which has increased my eagerness for conversation and taken away that for food and drink. But if there are any who find delight in such things (that I may by no means seem to have declared war on every kind of pleasure, when, perhaps, a certain amount of it is justified by nature), then I may say that I am not aware that old age is altogether wanting in appreciation even of these very pleasures. Indeed I find delight in the custom established by our forefathers of appointing presidents [3] at such gatherings ; and in the talk, which, after that ancestral custom, begins at the head of the table when the wine comes in ; and I enjoy cups, like those described in Xenophon's *Symposium*,[4] that are small in size, filled with dew-like drops, cooled in summer, and, again, in winter, warmed by the heat of sun or fire. Even when among the Sabines [5] I keep up the practice of frequenting such gatherings, and every day I join my neighbours in a social meal which we protract as late as we can into the night with talk on varying themes.

47   At non est voluptatum tanta quasi titillatio in
senibus. Credo, sed ne desideratio quidem ; nihil
autem est molestum quod non desideres. Bene
Sophocles, cum ex eo quidam iam affecto aetate
quaereret, utereturne rebus veneriis, " di meliora ! "
inquit ; " ego vero[1] istinc sicut a domino agresti ac
furioso profugi." Cupidis enim rerum talium odiosum
fortasse et molestum est carere, satiatis vero et
expletis iucundius est carere quam frui ; quamquam
non caret is, qui non desiderat ; ergo hoc non
desiderare dico esse iucundius.

48   Quod si istis ipsis voluptatibus bona aetas fruitur
libentius, primum parvulis fruitur rebus, ut diximus,
deinde eis, quibus senectus, etiam si non abunde
potitur, non omnino caret. Ut Turpione Ambivio
magis delectatur qui in prima cavea spectat, delectatur tamen etiam qui in ultima, sic adulescentia
voluptates propter intuens magis fortasse laetatur,
sed delectatur etiam senectus, procul eas spectans,
tantum quantum sat est.

49   At illa quanti sunt, animum tamquam emeritis
stipendiis libidinis ambitionis, contentionum inimicitiarum, cupiditatum omnium secum esse secumque,
ut dicitur, vivere ! Si vero habet aliquod tamquam

---

[1] ego vero *PL*[2], *Halm, Bait.* ; libenter vero *L*[1]*BIRS,
Müller.*

---

[1] *Titillatio* is Cicero's rendering of the Epicurean word
γαργαλισμός.
[2] Plato, *Rep.* 329 в ἀσμενέστατα αὐτὸ ἀπέφυγον ὥσπερ
λυττῶντά τινα καὶ ἄγριον δεσπότην ἀποφυγών.

But it may be urged that, in old men, " pleasure's tingling," [1] if I may so call it, is not so great. True, but neither is their yearning for pleasures so great, and, moreover, nothing troubles you for which you do not yearn. It was an excellent reply that Sophocles made to a certain man who asked him, when he was already old, if he still indulged in the delights of love. " Heaven forbid ! " he said. " Indeed I have fled from them as from a harsh and cruel master." [2] For to those who eagerly desire such things the want of them is perhaps an annoyance and a trouble ; but to those who are sated and cloyed with them it is more pleasant to be in want of them than to possess them ; though, indeed. a man cannot " want " that for which he has no longing, and therefore I assert that the absence of longing is more pleasant.

But granting that youth enjoys pleasures of that kind with a keener relish, then, in the first place, as I have said, they are petty things which it enjoys ; and, in the next place, although old age does not possess these pleasures in abundance, yet it is by no means wanting in them. Just as Ambivius Turpio gives greater delight to the spectators in the front row at the theatre, and yet gives some delight even to those in the last row, so youth, looking on pleasures at closer range, perhaps enjoys them more, while old age, on the other hand, finds delight enough in a more distant view.

But how blessed it is for the soul, after having, as it were, finished its campaigns of lust and ambition, of strife and enmity and of all the passions, to return within itself, and, as the saying is, " to live apart " ! And indeed if it has any provender, so to

59

pabulum studi atque doctrinae, nihil est otiosa
senectute iucundius. Videbamus[1] in studio di-
metiendi paene caeli atque terrae Gallum familiarem
patris tui, Scipio. Quotiens illum lux noctu aliquid
describere ingressum, quotiens nox oppressit cum
mane coepisset! Quam delectabat eum defectiones
50 solis et lunae multo ante nobis praedicere! Quid
in levioribus studiis, sed tamen acutis? Quam
gaudebat Bello suo Punico Naevius, quam Truculento
Plautus, quam Pseudolo! Vidi etiam senem Livium,
qui, cum sex annis ante quam ego natus sum fabulam
docuisset Centone Tuditanoque consulibus, usque ad
adulescentiam meam processit aetate.

Quid de P. Licini Crassi et pontifici et civilis iuris
studio loquar aut de huius P. Scipionis, qui his paucis
diebus pontifex maximus factus est? Atque eos
omnis, quos commemoravi, his studiis flagrantis
senes vidimus. M. vero Cethegum, quem recte
"suadae medullam" dixit Ennius, quanto studio exerceri in dicendo videbamus etiam senem! Quae sunt
igitur epularum aut ludorum aut scortorum voluptates cum his voluptatibus comparandae? Atque
haec quidem studia doctrinae, quae quidem pruden-
tibus et bene institutis pariter cum aetate crescunt,
ut honestum illud Solonis sit, quod ait versiculo

---

[1] mori *before* videbamus *in the* MSS., *omitted by most editors.*
For mori *Bennett conjectured* exerceri, *cf. infra* § 50.

---

[1] *Cf.* Cic. *Brutus* 58.

speak, of study and learning, nothing is more enjoyable than a leisured old age. Scipio, I used to see your father's intimate friend, Gaius Gallus, engaged in the task of measuring, almost bit by bit, the heavens and the earth. How often the morning sun has surprised him working on some chart which he had begun at night! and how often night has surprised him at a task begun at the break of day! How much joy he took in telling us, long in advance, of eclipses of the sun and moon! And what of those men occupied in studies which, though not so exacting, yet demand keenness of intellect? How Naevius used to revel in his *Punic War*! and Plautus in his *Savage* and *Cheat*! I myself saw Livius Andronicus when he was an old man, who, though he brought out a play in the consulship of Cento and Tuditanus, six years before I was born, yet continued to live until I was a young man.

Why need I speak of the zeal of Publius Licinius Crassus in pontifical and civil law, or of that of the present Publius Scipio, who was elected Chief Pontiff only a few days ago? And yet I have seen all these men whom I have mentioned, ardent in their several callings after they had grown old. Then too, there was Marcus Cethegus, whom Ennius justly styled " the marrow of eloquence." [1] What enthusiasm I saw him also display in his public speeches, although he was an old man! Therefore, how can the pleasures of feasting, plays, and brothels be compared with the pleasures which these men enjoyed? But theirs was a zeal for learning, and this zeal, at least in the case of wise and well-trained men, advances in even pace with age; so that there is truth in what Solon says in a certain bit of verse,

61

quodam, ut ante dixi, senescere se multa in dies addiscentem, qua voluptate animi nulla certe potest esse maior.

51 XV. Venio nunc ad voluptates agricolarum, quibus ego incredibiliter delector, quae nec ulla impediuntur senectute et mihi ad sapientis vitam proxime videntur accedere. Habent enim rationem cum terra, quae numquam recusat imperium nec umquam sine usura reddit quod accepit, sed alias minore, plerumque maiore cum faenore ; quamquam me quidem non fructus modo, sed etiam ipsius terrae vis ac natura delectat. Quae cum gremio mollito ac subacto sparsum semen excepit, primum id occaecatum cohibet, ex quo occatio quae hoc efficit nominata est ; deinde tepefactum vapore et compressu suo diffundit et elicit herbescentem ex eo viriditatem, quae nixa fibris stirpium sensim adolescit culmoque erecta geniculato vaginis iam quasi pubescens includitur ; e quibus cum emersit, fundit frugem spici ordine structam et contra avium minorum morsus munitur vallo aristarum.

52 Quid ego vitium ortus satus incrementa commemorem ? Satiari delectatione non possum, ut meae senectutis requietem[1] oblectamentumque noscatis. Omitto enim vim ipsam omnium quae generantur e terra, quae ex fici tantulo grano aut ex acini vinaceo

---

[1] requiem *L* ; requietem *other* MSS.

---

[1] The real derivation is from *occa = rastrum*, " a hoe."

already mentioned, that, as he grew old, he learned many things every day ; and surely there can be no greater pleasure than the pleasures of the mind.

XV. I come now to the pleasures of agriculture in which I find incredible delight ; they are not one whit checked by old age, and are, it seems to me, in the highest degree suited to the life of the wise man. For these pleasures have an account in the bank of Mother Earth who never protests a draft, but always returns the principal with interest added, at a rate sometimes low, but usually at a high per cent. And yet what I enjoy is not the fruit alone, but I also enjoy the soil itself, its nature and its power. It takes the scattered grain of wheat within its soft, upturned breast, hides it from sight at first—(it is hidden by harrowing,[1] derived from a word meaning " to hide ")—then, having warmed it with the heat of its embrace, expands it and from it brings forth a verdant blade, which, supported by fibrous roots, and maturing by degrees, stands erect upon its jointed stalk, enfolded in a sheath, when now, so to speak, it has arrived at man's estate ; and, when it has emerged from the sheath, the ear comes to view with its grain in ordered rows and protected by a palisade of spikes against the attacks of the smaller birds.

Why should I mention the origin, cultivation, and growth of the vine ? But, that you may know what affords the recreation and delight of my old age, I will say that vine-culture gives me a joy of which I cannot get too much. For I pass over the inherent force of all those things which are generated from the earth—a force that, from the tiny fig-seed, or grape-stone, or from the smallest seeds of other

63

aut ex ceterarum frugum aut stirpium minutissimis
seminibus tantos truncos ramosque procreet ; mal-
leoli plantae sarmenta viviradices propagines nonne
efficiunt ut quemvis cum admiratione delectent ?
Vitis quidem quae natura caduca est et, nisi fulta
est, fertur ad terram, eadem, ut se erigat, claviculis
suis quasi manibus quidquid est nacta complectitur,
quam serpentem multiplici lapsu et erratico, ferro
amputans coercet ars agricolarum, ne silvescat sar-
53 mentis et in omnis partis nimia fundatur. Itaque
ineunte vere in eis quae relicta sunt exsistit tamquam
ad articulos sarmentorum ea quae gemma dicitur, a
qua oriens uva se ostendit, quae et suco terrae et
calore solis augescens primo est peracerba gustatu,
dein maturata dulcescit vestitaque pampinis nec
modico tepore caret et nimios solis defendit ardores.
Qua quid potest esse cum fructu laetius, tum aspectu
pulchrius ?

Cuius quidem non utilitas me solum, ut ante dixi,
sed etiam cultura et natura ipsa delectat : admini-
culorum ordines, capitum iugatio, religatio et pro-
pagatio vitium, sarmentorum ea, quam dixi, aliorum
amputatio, aliorum immissio.

Quid ego irrigationes, quid fossiones agri repas-
tinationesque · proferam, quibus fit multo terra
fecundior ? Quid de utilitate loquar stercorandi ?
54 Dixi in eo libro, quem de rebus rusticis scripsi. De
qua doctus Hesiodus ne verbum quidem fecit, cum

fruits and plants, can produce such mighty trunks and boughs. Are not the results obtained from mallet-shoots, sprouts, cuttings, divisions, and layers enough to afford wonder and delight to any man? The vine which droops by nature and falls to the ground unless it has support, raises itself by its finger-like tendrils and enfolds in its embrace the props that hold it up; and as it turns and twists with many a varying course the skilful gardener with his pruning knife checks its growth lest it run to wood and spread too far. So, in early spring, the branches which are left at every joint bring forth a bud, from which the grape, offspring of this bud, appears, growing with the moisture of the earth and the heat of the sun; and though at first it is very bitter to the taste, it afterwards becomes sweet as it ripens; and, enwrapped in foliage, it has no lack of tempered warmth and turns aside the more ardent glances of the sun. What, I ask, can be more delicious to the taste or more alluring to the eye?

Indeed it is not only the utility of the vine, as I said before, that gives me joy, but I find joy also in its culture and very nature; in the even-spaced rows of stakes, with strips across the top; in the tying up of the branches; in the propagating of the plants; in the pruning of some branches (to which I have already referred), and in the leaving of others to grow at will.

Why need I allude to the irrigation, ditching, and frequent hoeing of the soil, whereby its productiveness is so much enhanced? Why need I discuss the advantage of manuring, already dealt with in my book on agriculture? This is a matter about which the learned Hesiod, though he wrote on agriculture,

de cultura agri scriberet. At Homerus, qui multis ut mihi videtur, ante saeculis fuit, Laerten lenientem desiderium, quod capiebat e filio, colentem agrum et eum stercorantem facit. Nec vero segetibus solum et pratis et vineis et arbustis res rusticae laetae sunt, sed hortis etiam et pomariis, tum pecudum pastu, apium examinibus, florum omnium varietate. Nec consitiones modo delectant, sed etiam insitiones, quibus nihil invenit agri cultura sollertius.

55 XVI. Possum persequi permulta oblectamenta rerum rusticarum, sed ea[1] ipsa quae dixi sentio fuisse longiora. Ignoscetis autem, nam et studio rerum rusticarum provectus sum, et senectus est natura loquacior, ne ab omnibus eam vitiis videar vindicare. Ergo in hac vita M'. Curius, cum de Samnitibus, de Sabinis, de Pyrrho triumphavisset, consumpsit extremum tempus aetatis ; cuius quidem ego villam contemplans, abest enim non longe a me, admirari satis non possum vel hominis ipsius continentiam 56 vel temporum disciplinam. Curio ad focum sedenti magnum auri pondus Samnites cum attulissent, repudiati sunt ; non enim aurum habere praeclarum sibi videri dixit, sed eis qui haberent aurum imperare. Poteratne tantus animus efficere non iucundam senectutem ?

Sed venio ad agricolas, ne a me ipso recedam. In agris erant tum senatores, id est senes—si quidem aranti L. Quinctio Cincinnato nuntiatum est eum dictatorem esse factum, cuius dictatoris iussu magister

---

[1] ea *other* MSS. ; haec *L.*

has not one word to say. But Homer, who, I believe,
lived many generation earlier, represents Laërtes
as soothing his sorrow at the absence of his son
in cultivating his farm and in manuring it, too. Nor
does the farmer find joy only in his cornfields,
meadows, vineyards, and woodlands, but also in
his garden and orchard, in the rearing of his cattle,
in his swarms of bees, and in the infinite variety of
flowers. And not only does planting delight him,
but grafting also, than which there is nothing in
husbandry that is more ingenious.

XVI. I might enlarge upon all the many charms
of country life, but I realize that I have already said
too much. However, forgive me if I go on, for my
farmer's zeal has carried me away ; besides, old age
is naturally inclined to talk too much—and this I
say in order not to acquit it of every fault. Well,
then, it was in this sort of life that Manius Curius
passed his remaining years after he had triumphed
over the Samnites, the Sabines, and Pyrrhus ; and,
as I gaze upon his country house (for it is not far
from mine), I cannot sufficiently admire the frugality
of the man or the spirit of the age in which he
lived. When the Samnites had brought him a great
mass of gold as he sat before the fire, he declined
their gift with scorn ; " for," said he, " it seems to me
that the glory is not in having the gold, but in ruling
those who have it." Think you that such a mighty
soul could not make old age happy ?

But, lest I wander from my subject, I return to the
farmers. In those days senators (that is, *senes* or
" elders ") lived on farms—if the story is true that
Lucius Quinctius Cincinnatus was at the plough when
he was notified of his election to that dictatorship

equitum C. Servilius Ahala Sp. Maelium regnum
appetentem occupatum interemit. A villa in senatum arcessebatur et Curius et ceteri senes, ex quo
qui eos arcessebant viatores nominati sunt. Num
igitur horum senectus miserabilis fuit, qui se agri
cultione oblectabant? Mea quidem sententia haud
scio an nulla beatior possit esse, neque solum officio,
quod hominum generi universo cultura agrorum est
salutaris, sed et delectatione quam dixi, et saturitate
copiaque rerum omnium, quae ad victum hominum,
ad cultum etiam deorum pertinent, ut, quoniam haec
quidam desiderant, in gratiam iam cum voluptate
redeamus. Semper enim boni assiduique domini
referta cella vinaria, olearia, etiam penaria est,
villaque tota locuples est, abundat porco haedo agno
gallina, lacte caseo melle. Iam hortum ipsi agricolae
"succidiam alteram" appellant. Conditiora facit
haec supervacaneis etiam operis aucupium atque
venatio.

57 Quid de pratorum viriditate aut arborum ordinibus
aut vinearum olivetorumve specie plura dicam?
Brevi praecidam. Agro bene culto nihil potest esse
nec usu uberius nec specie ornatius, ad quem fruen-
dum non modo non retardat, verum etiam invitat
atque allectat senectus. Ubi enim potest illa aetas

in which, by his order, his master of the horse,
Gaius Servilius Ahala, seized Spurius Maelius and
put him to death for attempting to secure regal
power. It was from the farmhouse that Curius and
other old men were summoned to the senate, and
for that reason those who notified them were called
viatores, or travellers. Well, then, was there cause
to pity the old age of these men who delighted in
the cultivation of the soil? For my part, at least,
I am inclined to think that no life can be happier
than that of the farmer, not merely from the standpoint of the duty performed, which benefits the
entire human race, but also because of its charm
already mentioned, and the plenty and abundance
it gives of everything that tends to the nurture of
man and even to the worship of the gods; and since
certain people delight in these material joys, I have
said this that I may now make my peace with
pleasure. For the provident and industrious pro-
prietor always has his store-room and cellars well
filled with oil and wine and provisions; his entire
farmhouse has an air of plenty and abounds with
pork, goat's meat, lamb, poultry, milk, cheese, and
honey. And there is his garden, which the farmers
themselves term " the second flitch." Hawking
and hunting, too, in leisure times, furnish the sauce
for these dainties.

Of the verdure of the meadows, the even rows of
trees and the beauty of the vineyards and olive
groves why should I speak at length? I will be
concise. Nothing can be more abounding in usefulness or more attractive in appearance than a well-
tilled farm, and to its enjoyment old age not merely
offers no obstacle, but even entices and allures.

aut calescere vel apricatione melius vel igni, aut
vicissim umbris aquisve refrigerari salubrius ? Sibi
58 habeant igitur arma, sibi equos, sibi hastas, sibi
clavam et pilam, sibi natationes[1] atque cursus ; nobis
senibus ex lusionibus multis talos relinquant et
tesseras ; id ipsum ut[2] lubebit, quoniam sine eis
beata esse senectus potest.

59　XVII. Multas ad res perutiles Xenophontis libri
sunt, quos legite, quaeso, studiose, ut facitis. Quam
copiose ab eo agri cultura laudatur in eo libro, qui
est de tuenda re familiari, qui Oeconomicus inscribitur ! Atque ut intellegatis nihil ei tam regale
videri quam studium agri colendi, Socrates in eo
libro loquitur cum Critobulo Cyrum minorem, Persarum regem, praestantem ingenio atque imperi
gloria, cum Lysander Lacedaemonius, vir summae
virtutis, venisset ad eum Sardis eique dona a sociis
attulisset, et ceteris in rebus communem erga
Lysandrum atque humanum fuisse et ei quendam
consaeptum agrum diligenter consitum ostendisse.
Cum autem admiraretur Lysander et proceritates
arborum et directos in quincuncem ordines et humum
subactam atque puram et suavitatem odorum qui
afflarentur ex floribus, tum eum dixisse mirari se
non modo diligentiam sed etiam sollertiam eius a
quo essent illa dimensa atque discripta ; et Cyrum
respondisse : " atqui ego ista sum omnia dimensus,
mei sunt ordines, mea discriptio ; multae etiam
istarum arborum mea manu sunt satae." Tum

---

[1] natationes *MSS.* ; venationes *Reid.*
[2] ut *Reid, Bennett*; utrum *codd., Müller, Moore*; unum *P.*

---

[1] Xen. *Oecon.* 4. 20.

[2] *i.e.* arranged thus ⋰⋱⋰ : *cf.* Virg. *Georg.* ii. 277.

For where else can the old man find more genial
warmth of sun or fire, and, on the other hand,
where, in summer time, can he more healthfully
cool himself with shade and running streams?
Let others, then, have their weapons, their horses
and their spears, their fencing-foils, and games of
ball, their swimming contests and foot-races, and
out of many sports leave us old fellows our dice and
knuckle-bones. Or take away the dice-box, too,
if you will, since old age can be happy without it.

XVII. Xenophon's writings are very instructive
on many subjects and I beg you to go on reading
them with studious care. With what copious
eloquence agriculture is lauded in his book entitled
The Householder, which treats of the management
of estates! To show you that Xenophon regarded
nothing more befitting royalty than zeal in husbandry,
let me recall the incident [1] in the same book, related
by Socrates in a conversation with Critobulus.
Cyrus the Younger, a Persian prince, eminent
for his intelligence and the glory of his rule, was
visited at Sardis by Lysander the Spartan, a man
of the highest virtue, who brought presents from the
allies. Among other courtesies to Lysander while his
guest, Cyrus showed him a certain carefully planted
park. After admiring the stateliness of the trees,
regularly placed in quincunx rows,[2] the clean and
well-cultivated soil, and the sweet odours emanating
from the flowers, Lysander then remarked: "I marvel
not only at the industry, but also at the skill of the
man who planned and arranged this work." "But
it was I," Cyrus answered, "who planned it all;
mine are the rows and mine the arrangement, and
many of those trees I set out with my own hands."

Lysandrum, intuentem purpuram eius et nitorem
corporis ornatumque Persicum multo auro multisque
gemmis, dixisse : " recte vero te, Cyre, beatum ferunt,
quoniam virtuti tuae fortuna coniuncta est ! "

60　　Hac igitur fortuna frui licet senibus, nec aetas
impedit quo minus et ceterarum rerum et in primis
agri colendi studia teneamus usque ad ultimum
tempus senectutis. M. quidem Valerium Corvinum
accepimus ad centesimum annum perduxisse, cum
esset acta iam aetate in agris eosque coleret, cuius
inter primum et sextum consulatum sex et quadraginta anni interfuerunt. Ita quantum spatium
aetatis maiores ad senectutis initium esse voluerunt,
tantus illi cursus honorum fuit ; atque huius extrema
aetas hoc beatior quam media, quod auctoritatis
habebat plus, laboris minus.

61　　Apex est autem senectutis auctoritas. Quanta
fuit in L. Caecilio Metello, quanta in A. Atilio
Calatino ! In quem illud elogium :

> hunc unum plurimae consentiunt gentes
> populi primarium fuisse virum.

Notum est totum carmen[1] incisum in sepulcro. Iure
igitur gravis, cuius de laudibus omnium esset fama
consentiens. Quem virum nuper P. Crassum, pontificem maximum, quem postea M. Lepidum eodem
sacerdotio praeditum vidimus ! Quid de Paulo aut

---

[1] totum carmen *LBV* ; *other MSS. omit* totum.

After gazing at the prince's purple robe, the beauty of his person, his Persian costume adorned with much gold and many precious stones, Lysander said : " With good reason, Cyrus, men call you happy, since in you good fortune has been joined with virtue."

And this good fortune, therefore, we old men may enjoy ; nor does age offer any hindrance to our pursuit of other activities, and especially the cultivation of the soil, even to the very end of old age. For example, there is a tradition that Valerius Corvinus, after passing the ordinary span of life, lived on his farm and cultivated it, and continued his pursuit of agriculture to his hundredth year. Forty-six years intervened between his first and sixth consulships. Thus, so much space of time as by our forefathers' reckoning marked the beginning of old age, just that space was the course of his public honours ; and the last period of his life was happier than the middle span, because his influence was greater and his labours were less.

But the crowning glory of old age is influence. How great was the influence of Lucius Caecilius Metellus ! How great, too, was that of Aulus Atilius Calatinus, for whom this epitaph was made :

> All peoples say of him who lieth here :
> He was his country's very foremost man.

But the entire epitaph is known because it is inscribed upon his tomb. Deservedly weighty, then, was his influence, since all men united in his praise. What heroic qualities I saw not long ago in Publius Crassus, the chief pontiff, and in Marcus Lepidus, his successor in that priestly office ! And what shall

73

Africano loquar, aut, ut iam ante, de Maximo?
Quorum non in sententia solum, sed etiam in nutu
residebat auctoritas. Habet senectus, honorata
praesertim, tantam auctoritatem, ut ea pluris sit
quam omnes adulescentiae voluptates.

62 XVIII. Sed in omni oratione mementote eam me
senectutem laudare, quae fundamentis adulescentiae
constituta sit. Ex quo efficitur id, quod ego magno
quondam cum assensu omnium dixi, miseram esse
senectutem quae se oratione defenderet. Non cani
nec rugae repente auctoritatem arripere possunt, sed
honeste acta superior aetas fructus capit auctoritatis

63 extremos. Haec enim ipsa sunt honorabilia, quae
videntur levia atque communia—salutari appeti
decedi assurgi deduci reduci consuli, quae et apud
nos et in aliis civitatibus, ut quaeque optime morata
est, ita diligentissime observantur. Lysandrum Lace-
daemonium, cuius modo feci mentionem, dicere aiunt
solitum Lacedaemonem esse honestissimum domi-
cilium senectutis; nusquam enim tantum tribuitur
aetati, nusquam est senectus honoratior. Quin
etiam memoriae proditum est, cum Athenis ludis
quidam in theatrum grandis natu venisset, magno
consessu locum nusquam ei datum a suis civibus,
cum autem ad Lacedaemonios accessisset, qui, legati
cum essent, certo in loco considerant, consurrexisse
omnes illi dicuntur et senem sessum recepisse;

---

[1] *i.e.* instead of being able to refer to the actions of earlier
years.

I say of Paulus, and of Africanus, and of Maximus, of whom I have spoken before ? These men had power, not only in their speech, but in their very nod. Surely ·old age, when crowned with public honours, enjoys an influence which is of more account than all the sensual pleasures of youth.

XVIII. But bear well in mind that in this entire discussion I am praising that old age which has its foundation well laid in youth. Hence it follows— as I once said with the approval of all who heard it— that that old age is wretched which needs to defend itself with words.[1] Nor can wrinkles and grey hair suddenly seize upon influence ; but when the preceding part of life has been nobly spent, old age gathers the fruits of influence at the last. For those very things, that seem light and trivial, are marks of honour—the morning visit, being sought after, being made way for, having people rise at one's approach, being escorted to and from the forum, being asked for advice—civilities most scrupulously observed among us and in every other state in proportion as its morals are good. Moreover, Lysander, the Spartan, of whom I just now spoke, is reported to have said more than once that in Sparta old age has its most fitting abode ; because nowhere else is so much deference paid to age and nowhere else is it more honoured. For example, there is a story that when an old man entered the theatre at Athens during the dramatic performances, not one of his countrymen in that vast crowd offered him a place ; but when he came to the special seats occupied by the Lacedaemonians and assigned to them because they were ambassadors, all of them arose, it is said, and invited him to sit down. After

75

64 quibus cum a cuncto consessu plausus esset multiplex
datus, dixisse ex eis quendam Atheniensis scire quae
recta essent, sed facere nolle.

Multa in nostro[1] collegio praeclara, sed hoc, de
quo agimus, in primis, quod, ut quisque aetate
antecedit, ita sententiae principatum tenet, neque
solum honore antecedentibus, sed eis etiam, qui
cum imperio sunt, maiores natu augures ante-
ponuntur. Quae sunt igitur voluptates corporis cum
auctoritatis praemiis comparandae? Quibus qui
splendide usi sunt, ei mihi videntur fabulam aetatis
peregisse nec tamquam inexercitati histriones in
extremo actu corruisse.

65 At sunt morosi et anxii et iracundi et difficiles
senes. Si quaerimus, etiam avari; sed haec morum
vitia sunt, non senectutis. Ac morositas tamen et
ea vitia, quae dixi, habent aliquid excusationis, non
illius quidem iustae, sed quae probari posse videatur:
contemni se putant, despici, illudi; praeterea in
fragili corpore odiosa omnis offensio est; quae tamen
omnia dulciora fiunt et moribus bonis et artibus,
idque cum in vita tum in scaena intellegi potest ex
eis fratribus qui in Adelphis sunt. Quanta in altero
diritas, in altero comitas! Sic se res habet: ut
enim non omne vinum, sic non omnis natura vetustate coacescit. Severitatem in senectute probo, sed

---

[1] nostro *BS*, *Reid*, *Bennett*; vestro *L²*, *Müller*, *Mommsen*.

---

[1] Only the consuls, praetors, dictators, masters of horse,
and provincial governors, while in office, had *imperium*.
[2] *Adelphi*, a play of Terence.

this action had been greeted by the whole audience with repeated applause, one of the Spartans remarked : " These Athenians know what politeness is, but they won't practise it."

There are many noteworthy customs in our college of augurs, but especially in point is the one whereby each has precedence in debate according to his age, and the oldest is preferred, not only to those of higher official rank, but even to those having *imperium*.[1] What physical pleasures, then, are comparable to the distinction which influence bestows ? The men who have put these distinctions to noble use are, it seems to me, like skilful actors who have played well their parts in the drama of life to the end, and not like untrained players who have broken down in the last act.

But, the critics say, old men are morose, troubled, fretful, and hard to please ; and, if we inquire, we shall find that some of them are misers, too. However, these are faults of character, not of age. Yet moroseness and the other faults mentioned have some excuse, not a really sufficient one, but such as it may seem possible to allow, in that old men imagine themselves ignored, despised, and mocked at ; and besides, when the body is weak, the lightest blow gives pain. But nevertheless all these faults are much ameliorated by good habits and by education, as may be seen in real life, and particularly on the stage in the case of the two brothers in the play of that name.[2] What a disagreeable nature one of them has, and what an affable disposition has the other ! Indeed the case stands thus : as it is not every wine, so it is not every disposition, that grows sour with age. I approve of some

77

eam, sicut alia, modicam ; acerbitatem nullo modo ;
avaritia vero senilis quid sibi velit, non intellego.
66 Potest enim quicquam esse absurdius quam, quo
viae minus restet, eo plus viatici quaerere ?

XIX. Quarta restat causa, quae maxime angere
atque sollicitam habere nostram aetatem videtur,
appropinquatio mortis, quae certe a senectute non
potest esse longe. O miserum senem, qui mortem
contemnendam esse in tam longa aetate non viderit !
Quae aut plane neglegenda est, si omnino exstinguit
animum, aut etiam optanda, si aliquo eum deducit
ubi sit futurus aeternus. Atqui tertium certe nihil
67 inveniri potest. Quid igitur timeam, si aut non
miser post mortem, aut beatus etiam futurus sum ?
Quamquam quis est tam stultus, quamvis sit adulescens, cui sit exploratum se ad vesperum esse victurum ? Quin etiam aetas illa multo pluris quam
nostra casus mortis habet : facilius in morbos incidunt adulescentes, gravius aegrotant, tristius curan-
tur. Itaque pauci veniunt ad senectutem ; quod ni
ita accideret, melius et prudentius viveretur. Mens
enim et ratio et consilium in senibus est, qui si nulli
fuissent, nullae omnino civitates fuissent.

Sed redeo ad mortem impendentem. Quod est
istud crimen senectutis, cum id ei videatis cum
68 adulescentia esse commune ? Sensi ego in optimo

austerity in the old, but I want it, as I do everything else, in moderation. Sourness of temper I like not at all. As for avariciousness in the old, what purpose it can serve I do not understand, for can anything be more absurd in the traveller than to increase his luggage as he nears his journey's end?

XIX. It remains to consider now the fourth reason—one that seems especially calculated to render my time of life anxious and full of care—the nearness of death; for death, in truth, cannot be far away. O wretched indeed is that old man who has not learned in the course of his long life that death should be held of no account! For clearly death is negligible, if it utterly annihilates the soul, or even desirable, if it conducts the soul to some place where it is to live for ever. Surely no other alternative can be found. What, then, shall I fear, if after death I am destined to be either not unhappy or happy? And yet is there anyone so foolish, even though he is young, as to feel absolutely sure that he will be alive when evening comes? Nay, even youth, much more than old age, is subject to the accident of death; the young fall sick more easily, their sufferings are more intense, and they are cured with greater difficulty. Therefore few arrive at old age, and, but for this, life would be lived in better and wiser fashion. For it is in old men that reason and good judgement are found, and had it not been for old men no state would have existed at all.

But I return to the question of impending death. What fault is this which you charge against old age, when, as you see, it is one chargeable likewise to youth? That death is common to every age has been brought home to me by the loss of my

filio, tu in exspectatis ad amplissimam dignitatem
fratribus, Scipio, mortem omni aetati esse communem.   At sperat adulescens diu se victurum,
quod sperare idem senex non potest.   Insipienter
sperat ;   quid enim stultius quam incerta pro certis
habere, falsa pro veris ?   At senex ne quod speret
quidem habet.   At est eo meliore condicione quam
adulescens, quoniam[1] id quod ille sperat hic consecutus est : ille volt diu vivere, hic diu vixit.

69   Quamquam, o di boni, quid est in hominis natura
diu ?   Da enim supremum tempus ; exspectemus
Tartessiorum regis aetatem—fuit enim, ut scriptum
video, Arganthonius quidam Gadibus, qui octoginta
regnaverat annos, centum viginti vixerat—sed mihi
ne diuturnum quidem quicquam videtur, in quo est
aliquid extremum ; cum enim id advenit, tum illud,
quod praeteriit, effluxit ; tantum remanet, quod
virtute et recte factis consecutus sis.   Horae quidem
cedunt et dies et menses et anni, nec praeteritum
tempus umquam revertitur nec quid sequatur sciri
potest.   Quod cuique temporis ad vivendum datur,
eo debet esse contentus.

70   Neque enim histrioni, ut placeat, peragenda
fabula est, modo in quocunque fuerit actu probetur ;
neque sapientibus usque ad " plaudite " veniendum
est, breve enim tempus aetatis satis longum est ad

---

[1] quoniam *Reid* ; cum MSS. ; quod *Lambinus, Müller.*

---

[1] Herod. i. 163.
[2] Literally until (the words) " now applaud " (are spoken).
All the plays of Terence and most of those of Plautus
close with *plaudite.*

dearest son, and to you, Scipio, by the untimely
end of your two brothers, when they were giving
promise of attaining to the highest honours in the
State. But, you may say, the young man hopes
that he will live for a long time and this hope the
old man cannot have. Such a hope is not wise,
for what is more unwise than to mistake uncertainty
for certainty, falsehood for truth ? They say, also,
that the old man has nothing even to hope for.
Yet he is in better case than the young man, since
what the latter merely hopes for, the former has
already attained ; the one wishes to live long,
the other has lived long.

But, ye gods ! what is there in human nature
that is for long ? For grant the utmost limit of
life ; let us hope to reach the age of the Tartessian
king—for at Cadiz there was, as I have seen it
recorded,[1] a certain Arganthonius, who had reigned
eighty and had lived one hundred and twenty years—,
but to me nothing whatever seems " lengthy " if it
has an end ; for when that end arrives, then that
which was is gone ; naught remains but the fruit
of good and virtuous deeds. Hours and days, and
months and years, go by ; the past returns no more,
and what is to be we cannot know ; but whatever
the time given us in which to live, we should therewith be content.

The actor, for instance, to please his audience
need not appear in every act to the very end ; it is
enough if he is approved in the parts in which he
plays ; and so it is not necessary for the wise man
to stay on this mortal stage to the last fall of the
curtain.[2] For even if the allotted space of life be
short, it is long enough in which to live honourably

81

bene honesteque vivendum ; sin processerit longius,
non magis dolendum est, quam agricolae dolent
praeterita verni temporis suavitate aestatem autum-
numque venisse. Ver enim tamquam adulescentia
significat ostenditque fructus futuros ; reliqua autem
tempora demetendis fructibus et percipiendis accommodata sunt.

71 Fructus autem senectutis est, ut saepe dixi, ante
partorum bonorum memoria et copia. Omnia autem,
quae secundum naturam fiunt, sunt habenda in bonis ;
quid est autem tam secundum naturam quam senibus
emori ? Quod idem contingit adulescentibus adver-
sante et repugnante natura. Itaque adulescentes
mihi mori sic videntur, ut cum aquae multitudine
flammae vis opprimitur, senes autem sic, ut cum sua
sponte, nulla adhibita vi, consumptus ignis exstinguitur, et quasi poma ex arboribus, cruda si sunt, vix[1]
evelluntur, si matura et cocta, decidunt, sic vitam
adulescentibus vis aufert, senibus maturitas ; quae
quidem mihi tam iucunda est, ut, quo propius ad
mortem accedam, quasi terram videre videar ali-
quandoque in portum ex longa navigatione esse
venturus.

72 XX. Senectutis autem nullus est certus terminus,
recteque in ea vivitur, quoad munus offici exsequi
et tueri possit mortemque contemnere, ex quo fit ut
animosior etiam senectus sit quam adulescentia et
fortior. Hoc illud est, quod Pisistrato tyranno a

---

[1] vix *edd.* ; vi *most* MSS.

and well ; but if a longer period of years should be granted, one has no more cause to grieve than the farmers have that the pleasant springtime has passed and that summer and autumn have come. For spring typifies youth and gives promise of future fruits ; while the other seasons are designed for gathering in those fruits and storing them away.

Now the fruit of old age, as I have often said, is the memory of abundant blessings previously acquired. Moreover, whatever befalls in accordance with Nature should be accounted good ; and indeed, what is more consonant with Nature than for the old to die ? But the same fate befalls the young, though Nature in their case struggles and rebels. Therefore, when the young die I am reminded of a strong flame extinguished by a torrent ; but when old men die it is as if a fire had gone out without the use of force and of its own accord, after the fuel had been consumed ; and, just as apples when they are green are with difficulty plucked from the tree, but when ripe and mellow fall of themselves, so, with the young, death comes as a result of force, while with the old it is the result of ripeness. To me, indeed, the thought of this " ripeness " for death is so pleasant, that the nearer I approach death the more I feel like one who is in sight of land at last and is about to anchor in his home port after a long voyage.

XX. But old age has no certain term, and there is good cause for an old man living so long as he can fulfil and support his proper duties and hold death of no account. By this means old age actually becomes more spirited and more courageous than youth. This explains the answer which Solon gave to the

Solone responsum est, cum illi quaerenti qua tandem
re fretus sibi tam audaciter obsisteret respondisse
dicitur " senectute." Sed vivendi est finis optimus,
cum integra mente certisque sensibus opus ipsa
suum eadem quae coagmentavit natura dissolvit.
Ut navem, ut aedificium idem destruit facillime qui
construxit, sic hominem eadem optime quae con-
glutinavit natura dissolvit. Iam omnis conglutinatio
recens aegre, inveterata facile divellitur.

Ita fit ut illud breve vitae reliquum nec avide ap-
petendum senibus nec sine causa deserendum sit ;
73 vetatque Pythagoras iniussu imperatoris, id est dei,
de praesidio et statione vitae decedere. Solonis
quidem sapientis est elogium, quo se negat velle
suam mortem dolore amicorum et lamentis vacare.
Volt, credo, se esse carum suis. Sed haud scio an
melius Ennius :

> nemo me lacrumis decoret, neque funera fletu
> faxit.

Non censet lugendam esse mortem, quam immortalitas
consequatur.
74 Iam sensus moriendi aliquis esse potest, isque ad
exiguum tempus, praesertim seni : post mortem
quidem sensus aut optandus aut nullus est. Sed
hoc meditatum ab adulescentia debet esse, mortem

---

[1] Plato, *Phaedo* 6 ; Cic. *Somn. Scip.* 3 ; Cic. *Tusc.* i. 20.
[2] Plutarch in his comparison of Solon and Publicola
gives these lines.

tyrant Pisistratus who asked, " Pray, what do you rely upon in opposing me so boldly ? " and Solon replied, " Old age." But the most desirable end of life is that which comes while the mind is clear and the faculties are unimpaired, when Nature herself takes apart the work which she has put together. As the builder most readily destroys the ship or the house which he has built, so Nature is the agent best fitted to give dissolution to her creature, man. Now every structure when newly built is hard to pull apart, but the old and weather-beaten house comes easily down.

Hence, it follows that old men ought neither to cling too fondly to their little remnant of life, nor give it up without a cause. Pythagoras[1] bids us stand like faithful sentries and not quit our post until God, our Captain, gives the word. Solon the Wise has a couplet in which he says that he does not want his death to be free from the grief and mourning of his friends.[2] He wishes, no doubt to make out that he is dear to his friends, but I am inclined to think that Ennius has expressed it better when he says :

> I do not wish the honour of a tear,
> Or any wailing cries about my bier.

He does not think that death, which is followed by eternal life, should be a cause of grief.

Now, there may be some sensation in the process of dying, but it is a fleeting one, especially to the old ; after death the sensation is either pleasant or there is none at all. But this should be thought on from our youth up, so that we may be indifferent to death,

ut neglegamus; sine qua meditatione tranquillo animo esse nemo potest. Moriendum enim certe est, et incertum an hoc ipso die. Mortem igitur omnibus horis impendentem timens qui poterit
75 animo consistere? De qua non ita longa disputatione opus esse videtur, cum recordor[1] non L. Brutum, qui in liberanda patria est interfectus, non duos Decios, qui ad voluntariam mortem cursum equorum incitaverunt, non M. Atilium, qui ad supplicium est profectus ut fidem hosti datam conservaret, non duos Scipiones, qui iter Poenis vel corporibus suis obstruere voluerunt, non avum tuum L. Paulum, qui morte luit collegae in Cannensi ignominia temeritatem, non M. Marcellum, cuius interitum ne crudelissimus quidem hostis honore sepulturae carere passus est, sed legiones nostras, quod scripsi in Originibus, in eum locum saepe profectas alacri animo et erecto, unde se redituras numquam arbitrarentur. Quod igitur adulescentes, et ei quidem non solum indocti sed etiam rustici contemnunt, id docti senes extimescent?

76 Omnino, ut mihi quidem videtur studiorum[2] omnium satietas vitae facit satietatem. Sunt pueritiae studia certa: num igitur ea desiderant adulescentes? Sunt ineuntis adulescentiae: num ea constans iam requirit aetas, quae media dicitur? Sunt etiam eius aetatis: ne ea quidem quaeruntur in senectute. Sunt extrema quaedam studia senectutis: ergo, ut superiorum aetatum studia occidunt,

---

[1] recordor *Reid*; recorder MSS.
[2] studiorum *LPIS Müller*; rerum *ER*.

and without this thought no one can be in a tranquil state of mind. For it is certain that we must die, and, for aught we know, this very day. Therefore, since death threatens every hour, how can he who fears it have any steadfastness of soul? No very extended argument on this point seems necessary when I recall—not the conduct of Lucius Brutus, who was killed in liberating his country; nor that of the two Decii who rode full speed to a voluntary death; nor that of Marcus Atilius Regulus, who set out from home to undergo torture and keep the faith pledged to his foe; nor that of the two Scipios, who with their bodies sought to stay the Punic march; nor that, Scipio, of your grandfather Lucius Paulus who, in the shameful rout at Cannae, gave his life to atone for his colleague's folly; nor that of Marcus Marcellus, to whom not even his most pitiless foe denied the honours of a funeral—but rather when I recall, as I have noted in my *Antiquities*, how our legions have often marched with cheerful and unwavering courage into situations whence they thought they would never return. Then shall wise old men fear a thing which is despised by youths, and not only by those who are untaught, but by those also who are mere clowns?

Undoubtedly, as it seems to me at least, satiety of all pursuits causes satiety of life. Boyhood has certain pursuits: does youth yearn for them? Early youth has its pursuits: does the matured or so-called middle stage of life need them? Maturity, too, has such as are not even sought in old age, and finally, there are those suitable to old age. Therefore as the pleasures and pursuits of the earlier periods of life fall away, so also do those of old age;

87

sic occidunt etiam senectutis; quod cum evenit,
satietas vitae tempus maturum mortis affert.

77 XXI. Non enim video, cur, quid ipse sentiam de
morte, non audeam vobis dicere, quod eo cernere
mihi melius videor, quo ab ea propius absum. Ego
vestros patres, P. Scipio tuque, C. Laeli, viros claris-
simos mihique amicissimos, vivere arbitror et eam
quidem vitam, quae est sola vita nominanda. Nam
dum sumus inclusi in his compagibus corporis, munere
quodam necessitatis et gravi opere perfungimur;
est enim animus caelestis ex altissimo domicilio
depressus et quasi demersus in terram, locum divinae
naturae aeternitatique contrarium. Sed credo deos
immortalis sparsisse animos in corpora humana, ut
essent qui terras tuerentur quique caelestium
ordinem contemplantes imitarentur eum vitae modo
atque constantia. Nec me solum ratio ac disputatio
impulit ut ita crederem, sed nobilitas etiam sum-
morum philosophorum et auctoritas.

78 Audiebam Pythagoran Pythagoriosque, incolas
paene nostros, qui essent Italici philosophi quondam
nominati, numquam dubitasse quin ex universa mente
divina delibatos animos haberemus. Demonstra-
bantur mihi praeterea quae Socrates supremo vitae
die de immortalitate animorum disseruisset, is qui
esset omnium sapientissimus oraculo Apollinis iudicatus. Quid multa? Sic mihi persuasi, sic sentio,
cum tanta celeritas animorum sit, tanta memoria

---

[1] Or " fate."

and when that happens man has his fill of life and
the time is ripe for him to go.

XXI. Really I do not see why I should not
venture to tell you what I, myself, think of death;
for it seems to me that I apprehend it better as I
draw nearer to it. It is my belief, Scipio, that your
father, and yours, Laelius—both of them most
illustrious men and very dear to me—are living yet,
and living the only life deserving of the name.
For while we are shut up within these frames of
flesh we perform a sort of task imposed by necessity [1]
and endure grievous labour; for the soul is celestial,
brought down from its most exalted home and
buried, as it were, in earth, a place uncongenial
to its divine and eternal nature. But I believe that
the immortal gods implanted souls in human bodies
so as to have beings who would care for the earth
and who, while contemplating the celestial order,
would imitate it in the moderation and consistency
of their lives. Nor have I been driven to this belief
solely by the force of reason and of argument, but
also by the reputation and authority of philosophers
of the highest rank.

I used to be told that Pythagoras and his disciples,
—who were almost fellow-countrymen of ours, inasmuch as they were formerly called "Italian
philosophers,"—never doubted that our souls were
emanations of the Universal Divine Mind. Moreover, I had clearly set before me the arguments
touching the immortality of the soul, delivered on the
last day of his life by Socrates, whom the oracle of
Apollo had pronounced the wisest of men. Why
multiply words? That is my conviction, that is what
I believe—since such is the lightning-like rapidity of

89

praeteritorum futurorumque prudentia, tot artes,
tantae scientiae, tot inventa, non posse eam naturam,
quae res eas contineat, esse mortalem ; cumque
semper agitetur animus nec principium motus habeat,
quia se ipse moveat, ne finem quidem habiturum
esse motus, quia numquam se ipse sit relicturus ;
et cum simplex animi natura esset neque haberet in
se quicquam admixtum dispar sui atque dissimile,
non posse eum dividi, quod si non posset, non posse
interire ; magnoque esse argumento homines scire
pleraque ante quam nati sint, quod iam pueri, cum
artis difficilis discant, ita celeriter res innumerabilis
arripiant, ut eas non tum primum accipere videantur,
sed reminisci et recordari.   Haec Platonis fere.

79   XXII. Apud Xenophontem autem moriens Cyrus
maior haec dicit : " nolite arbitrari, o mihi carissimi
filii, me, cum a vobis discessero, nusquam aut nullum
fore. Nec enim, dum eram vobiscum, animum meum
videbatis, sed eum esse in hoc corpore ex eis rebus
quas gerebam intellegebatis. Eundem igitur esse
80 creditote, etiam si nullum videbitis. Nec vero
clarorum virorum post mortem honores permane-
rent, si nihil eorum ipsorum animi efficerent, quo
diutius memoriam sui teneremus. Mihi quidem
numquam persuaderi potuit animos dum in corporibus essent mortalibus vivere, cum excessissent ex
eis emori ; nec vero tum animum esse insipientem
cum ex insipienti corpore evasisset, sed cum omni

---

[1] *Cf.* Plato, *Phaedo* 72 E–73 B, 78–80 ; *Phaedrus* 245 **c.**
[2] Xenophon, *Cyropaedia*, viii. 7. 17–22.

the soul, such its wonderful memory of things that
are past, such its ability to forecast the future, such
its mastery of many arts, sciences, and inventions,
that its nature, which encompasses all these things,
cannot be mortal; and since the soul is always
active and has no source of motion because it is
self-moving, its motion will have no end, because
it will never leave itself; and since in its nature the
soul is of one substance and has nothing whatever
mingled with it unlike or dissimilar to itself, it
cannot be divided, and if it cannot be divided it
cannot perish. And a strong argument that men's
knowledge of numerous things antedates their
birth is the fact that mere children, in studying
difficult subjects, so quickly lay hold upon innumerable things that they seem not to be then learning
them for the first time, but to be recalling and
remembering them. This, in substance, is Plato's
teaching.[1]

XXI. Again, in Xenophon,[2] Cyrus the Elder
utters the following words as he is dying: "Think
not, my dearest sons, that, when I have left you,
I shall cease to be. For while I was with you you
did not see my soul, but you knew that it was in
this body from the deeds that I performed. Continue to believe, therefore, that it exists as before,
even though you see it not. Nor, indeed, would
the fame of illustrious men survive their death if
the souls of those very men did not cause us to retain
their memory longer. I, for my part, could never
be persuaded that souls, which lived while they were
in human bodies, perished when they left those
bodies; nor, indeed, that the soul became incapable
of thought when it had escaped from the unthinking

91

admixtione corporis liberatus purus et integer esse
coepisset, tum esse sapientem. Atque etiam, cum
hominis natura morte dissolvitur, ceterarum rerum
perspicuum est quo quaeque discedat, abeunt enim
illuc omnia, unde orta sunt ; animus autem solus nec
cum adest nec cum discessit apparet. Iam vero
videtis nihil esse morti tam simile quam somnum.
81 Atqui dormientium animi maxime declarant divini-
tatem suam ; multa enim, cum remissi et liberi sunt,
futura prospiciunt ; ex quo intellegitur quales
futuri sint, cum se plane corporis vinculis relaxa-
verint. Qua re, si haec ita sunt, sic me colitote,"
inquit, " ut deum, sin una est interiturus animus cum
corpore, vos tamen, deos verentes, qui hanc omnem
pulchritudinem tuentur et regunt, memoriam nostri
pie inviolateque servabitis." XXIII. Cyrus quidem
haec moriens ; nos, si placet, nostra videamus.

82   Nemo umquam mihi, Scipio, persuadebit aut patrem
tuum Paulum, aut duos avos Paulum et Africanum,
aut Africani patrem aut patruum, aut multos prae-
stantis viros, quos enumerare non est necesse, tanta
esse conatos quae ad posteritatis memoriam per-
tinerent, nisi animo cernerent posteritatem ad ipsos
pertinere. Anne censes, ut de me ipse aliquid more
senum glorier, me tantos labores diurnos noctur-
nosque domi militiaeque suscepturum fuisse, si isdem
finibus gloriam meam quibus vitam essem termina-

---

[1] But *cf. De divinatione*, ii. 58. 119 ff.. where Cicero refutes
and derides this theory.

corpse, but rather that, when it had been freed from every admixture of flesh and had begun to exist pure and undefiled, then only was it wise. And even when man is dissolved by death it is evident to the sight whither each bodily element departs ; for the corporeal returns to the visible constituents from which it came, but the soul alone remains unseen, both when it is present and when it departs. Again, you really see nothing resembling death so much as sleep ; and yet it is when the body sleeps that the soul most clearly manifests its divine nature ; for when it is unfettered and free it sees many things that are to come.[1] Hence we know what the soul's future state will be when it has been wholly released from the shackles of the flesh. Wherefore, if what I have said be true, cherish me as you would a god. But on the other hand, if my soul is going to perish along with my body, still you, who revere the gods as the guardians and rulers of this beautiful universe, will keep me in loving and sacred memory." XXIII. This was the view of the dying Cyrus. Let me, if you please, give my own.

No one, my dear Scipio, will ever convince me that your father Paulus, or your two grandfathers, Paulus and Africanus, or the latter's father and uncle, or many other illustrious men, unnecessary now to name, would have attempted such mighty deeds, to be remembered by posterity, if they had not known that posterity belonged to them. Or, to boast somewhat of myself after the manner of the old, do you think that I should have undertaken such heavy labours by day and by night, at home and abroad, if I had believed that the term of my earthly life would mark the limits of my fame ? Would

93

turus ? Nonne melius multo fuisset otiosam et
quietam aetatem sine ullo labore et contentione
traducere ? Sed nescio quo modo animus erigens se
posteritatem ita semper prospiciebat, quasi, cum
excessisset e vita, tum denique victurus esset. Quod
quidem ni ita se haberet ut animi immortales essent,
haud optimi cuiusque animus maxime ad immor-
talitatis gloriam niteretur. Quid quod sapientissi-
83 mus quisque aequissimo animo moritur, stultissimus
iniquissimo, nonne vobis videtur is animus, qui plus
cernat et longius, videre se ad meliora proficisci,
ille autem, cuius obtusior sit acies, non videre ?

Equidem efferor studio patres vestros quos colui
et dilexi videndi, neque vero eos solum convenire
aveo, quos ipse cognovi, sed illos etiam, de quibus
audivi et legi et ipse conscripsi ; quo quidem me
proficiscentem haud sane quid facile retraxerit, nec
tamquam Pelian recoxerit. Et si quis deus mihi
largiatur ut ex hac aetate repuerascam et in cunis
vagiam, valde recusem, nec vero velim quasi decurso
84 spatio ad carceres a calce revocari. Quid habet
enim vita commodi ? Quid non potius laboris ? Sed
habeat sane ; habet certe tamen aut satietatem
aut modum. Non libet enim mihi deplorare vitam,
quod multi et ei docti saepe fecerunt, neque me
vixisse paenitet, quoniam ita vixi, ut non frustra

---

[1] Cicero here confuses Pelias with his half-brother Aeson,
whom Medea restored to youth by cutting him up and
boiling him in a cauldron.

it not have been far better for me to spend a leisured and quiet life, free from toil and strife? But somehow, my soul was ever on the alert, looking forward to posterity, as if it realized that when it had departed from this life, then at last would it be alive. And, indeed, were it not true that the soul is immortal, it would not be the case that it is ever the souls of the best men that strive most for immortal glory. And what of the fact that the wisest men die with the greatest equanimity, the most foolish with the least? Is it not apparent to you that it is because the soul of the one, having a keener and wider vision, sees that it is setting out for a better country, while that of the other, being of duller sight, sees not its path?

Really, Scipio, I am carried away with the desire to see your father, and yours too, Laelius, both of whom I honoured and loved; and, indeed, I am eager to meet not only those whom I have known, but those also of whom I have heard and read and written. And when I shall have set out to join them, assuredly no one will easily draw me back, or boil me up again, as if I were a Pelias.[1] Nay, if some god should give me leave to return to infancy from my old age, to weep once more in my cradle, I should vehemently protest; for, truly, after I have run my race I have no wish to be recalled, as it were, from the goal to the starting-place. For what advantage has life—or, rather, what trouble does it not have? But even grant that it has great advantage, yet undoubtedly it has either satiety or an end. I do not mean to complain of life as many men, and they learned ones, have often done; nor do I regret that I have lived, since I have so lived

me natum existimem, et ex vita ita discedo tamquam ex hospitio, non tamquam e domo; commorandi enim natura divorsorium nobis, non habitandi dedit.

O praeclarum diem cum in illud divinum animorum concilium coetumque proficiscar cumque ex hac turba et colluvione discedam! Proficiscar enim non ad eos solum viros, de quibus ante dixi, verum etiam ad Catonem meum, quo nemo vir melior natus est, nemo pietate praestantior, cuius a me corpus est crematum, quod contra decuit ab illo meum, animus vero non me deserens sed respectans, in ea profecto loca discessit quo mihi ipsi cernebat esse veniendum. Quem ego meum casum fortiter ferre visus sum, non quo aequo animo ferrem, sed me ipse consolabar existimans non longinquum inter nos digressum et discessum fore.

85 His mihi rebus, Scipio, id enim te cum Laelio admirari solere dixisti, levis est senectus, nec solum non molesta, sed etiam iucunda. Quod si in hoc erro, qui animos hominum immortalis esse credam, libenter erro nec mihi hunc errorem, quo delector, dum vivo, extorqueri volo; sin mortuus, ut quidam minuti philosophi censent, nihil sentiam, non vereor ne hunc errorem meum philosophi mortui irrideant. Quod si non sumus immortales futuri, tamen exstingui homini suo tempore optabile est. Nam habet natura, ut aliarum omnium rerum, sic vivendi modum. Senectus autem aetatis est peractio tamquam fabulae,

that I think I was not born in vain, and I quit life as if it were an inn, not a home. For Nature has given us an hostelry in which to sojourn, not to abide.

O glorious day, when I shall set out to join the assembled hosts of souls divine and leave this world of strife and sin! For I shall go to meet not only the men already mentioned, but my Cato, too, than whom no better man, none more distinguished for filial duty, was ever born. His body was burned by me, whereas, on the contrary it were more fitting that mine had been burned by him; but his soul, not deserting me, but ever looking back, has surely departed for that realm where it knew that I, myself, must come. People think that I have bravely borne my loss — not that I bore it with an untroubled heart, but I found constant solace in the thought that our separation would not be long.

For these reasons, Scipio, my old age sits light upon me (for you said that this has been a cause of wonder to you and Laelius), and not only is not burdensome, but is even happy. And if I err in my belief that the souls of men are immortal, I gladly err, nor do I wish this error which gives me pleasure to be wrested from me while I live. But if when dead I am going to be without sensation (as some petty philosophers think), then I have no fear that these seers, when they are dead, will have the laugh on me! Again, if we are not going to be immortal, nevertheless, it is desirable for a man to be blotted out at his proper time. For as Nature has marked the bounds of everything else, so she has marked the bounds of life. Moreover, old age is the final scene, as it were, in life's drama, from

97

cuius defetigationem[1] fugere debemus, praesertim adiuncta satietate.

Haec habui de senectute quae dicerem, ad quam utinam veniatis, ut ea, quae ex me audistis, re experti probare possitis!

---

[1] defetigationem *IRS, Reid*; defectionem *QE, Müller*.

which we ought to escape when it grows wearisome and, certainly, when we have had our fill.

Such, my friends, are my views on old age. May you both attain it, and thus be able to prove by experience the truth of what you have heard from me.

LAELIUS DE AMICITIA

INTRODUCTION TO THE LAELIUS

1. Date of Composition

ENOUGH has been said in the introduction to the *Cato Maior* to show the amazing fecundity of Cicero's genius in the years 45 and 44 B.C., during which time this treatise was written. The date of its composition belongs within the year 44, but the month cannot be fixed with absolute certainty. It was written after the *Cato Maior* and after the completion of *Divination*, in which (*Div.* ii. 3) Cicero gives the names of his philosophic books so far written and does not mention this work. It is referred to in the second volume of *De officiis* (ii. 9. 31), which was written in November. In a letter to Atticus (*Ad Att.* xvi. 13 c) Cicero, on November 5, 44, asks when " Fannius, son of Marcus " (one of the interlocutors), was tribune. This inquiry suggests that he was then writing or revising the *Laelius* and tends to fix the date of composition in the autumn of 44 B.C.

2. Occasion of Writing the LAELIUS

It was in the year 90 B.C. that Cicero, then just sixteen, was introduced by his father to Quintus

Mucius Scaevola the augur, to receive instruction in Roman law. While he was in constant attendance on the lectures of this learned man occurred the war of the Samnites and other Italian tribes against Rome for a larger share of Roman suffrage and in the government of the Empire. This revolution was still smouldering when in 88 B.C. Publius Sulpicius, the most powerful orator of his day, became tribune of the plebs, and proposed certain reforms which resulted in the civil war between Marius and Sulla and his own break with Pompeius Strabo. It was at this exciting time that Cicero, sitting at the feet of the aged Roman lawyer Scaevola, heard him repeat, as he tells us, the discourse of Laelius on friendship. This discourse Laelius in turn had heard from his bosom friend, Scipio Africanus the Younger.

3. Time of the Dialogue and its Interlocutors

The time of the present dialogue is 129 B.C., just a few days after the mysterious death of Scipio Minor. The interlocutors are Laelius (who was also one of the interlocutors in the *Cato Maior*), and his two sons-in-law, Quintus Mucius Scaevola and Gaius Fannius.

Gaius Laelius, born in 186 B.C., was the son of a distinguished father of the same name who was the friend and companion of the elder Scipio Africanus. The younger Laelius became praetor in 145 B.C., and consul in 140, after his defeat in the previous year by Quintus Pompeius. He gained great credit as commander in the war against the Spanish chieftain, Viriathus. Next to Scipio, he

was regarded as the foremost orator of his day in eloquence and purity of style. But it was as a student and man of letters that he was chiefly distinguished. His title of " the Wise " was due to his great learning and to his knowledge of philosophy. He was a pupil of Diogenes the Stoic and later, in company with Scipio, studied under Panaetius, who made his home with Scipio. Laelius was such a master of elegant diction that the plays of his poet-friend Terence, which were so much admired for the purity of their Latinity, were by many attributed in whole or in part to him. In his culture, wisdom, evenness of temper, integrity of life, keen sense of justice, and nobility of thought and speech we find ample justification for the unstinted praise accorded him by all the writers of antiquity.

To the younger group of the Scipionic circle belong the other interlocutors of this essay, Quintus Mucius Scaevola the augur, and Gaius Fannius, son of Marcus, both sons-in-law of Laelius. Scaevola, himself a distinguished lawyer, belonged to a family of lawyers, of whom the most illustrious was his namesake and junior, the pontifex maximus. The augur was born about 157 b.c., became praetor in 121 b.c., later governor of Asia Minor, and was elected consul in 117. He lived until 88, after the overthrow of Sulpicius by Sulla. When called upon at that time to join in the decree of proscription against Marius he declared that for the sake of the few poor drops of blood in his old frame he would not consent to outlaw the man who had saved Rome and all Italy from the Gauls. He was celebrated for his wit, learning, and amiability.

Gaius Fannius Strabo, who was somewhat older than his brother-in-law, Scaevola, married the younger daughter of Laelius. He was, it is thought by Cicero (*Ad Att.* xvi. 13 c), tribune of the plebs, 142 B.C., while Publius Africanus and Lucius Mummius were censors and Lucius Caecilius Metellus and Quintus Fabius Maximus Servilianus were consuls. He was a writer of a Roman history, highly praised by Sallust for its accuracy, but criticized by Cicero in his *Brutus* as rough in style.

4. Greek Sources of the *Laelius*

The earliest known treatise in Greek on the subject of friendship is found in the *Lysis* of Plato, whose influence is strongly reflected in the eighth and ninth books of the *Nicomachean Ethics* of Aristotle. Many of the thoughts of this work are observed in Cicero's essay, but are not necessarily borrowed from Aristotle. In section 62 of the *Laelius* he draws upon Xenophon's *Memorabilia*, by taking the words there attributed to Socrates and placing them in the mouth of Scipio. According to Diogenes Laertius and Aulus Gellius, the chief Greek source of the present essay is a lost treatise on friendship in three volumes by Theophrastus. But in the main Cicero probably was not greatly indebted to Greek writers in the composition of this book. The arrangement, plan, style and illustrations are his own. Certainly no other author of ancient or modern times has discussed the subject of friendship with so much completeness and charm as Cicero discusses it in his *Laelius*.

DE AMICITIA

5. Manuscripts and Editions

There are nine MSS. on which the printed texts
of the *Laelius* are chiefly based : G (Gudianus),
at Wolfenbüttel, 10th century ; E (Erfurtensis),
once at Erfurt, now in Berlin, 12th century ; B
(Benedictoburanus), in Munich, 12th century ; S
(Salsiburgensis), in Munich, 11th century ; M
(Monacensis), in Munich ; and P (Parisinus),
formerly in Paris, now in Berlin, 9th or 10th century ;
two MSS., DV (Vindobonensis), in Vienna ; and
H (Harleianus), in the British Museum, London.
Of these Halm regards G as best and C. F. W.
Müller prefers P.

The text of the present edition, like that of *Cato
Maior*, is eclectic, following most closely, perhaps,
the edition of J. S. Reid, but with readings adopted
from Müller, Bennett and others. For a good
bibliography of the *Laelius* reference is made to
E. W. Bowen's *Laelius*.

The translator is indebted to Prof. Henry Strauss
and Dr. J. L. Hancock, of the University of
Arkansas, for a careful reading of the manuscript
and for many valuable suggestions in interpretation
and phrasing.

[In the Budé series we now have the edition and
French translation by L. Aurand, Paris, 1928.]

LAELIUS DE AMICITIA

I. Q. Mucius augur multa narrare de C. Laelio socero suo memoriter et iucunde solebat nec dubitare illum in omni sermone appellare sapientem. Ego autem a patre ita eram deductus ad Scaevolam sumpta virili toga, ut, quoad possem et liceret, a senis latere numquam discederem. Itaque multa ab eo prudenter disputata, multa etiam breviter et commode dicta memoriae mandabam, fierique studebam eius prudentia doctior. Quo mortuo me ad pontificem Scaevolam contuli, quem unum nostrae civitatis et ingenio et iustitia praestantissimum audeo dicere. Sed de hoc alias, nunc redeo ad augurem.

2 Cum saepe multa, tum memini domi in hemicyclio sedentem, ut solebat, cum et ego essem una et pauci admodum familiares, in eum sermonem illum incidere, qui tum fere multis[1] erat in ore. Memi-

---

[1] tum fere multis *MSS.*; tum forte *Müller*; *Nauck om.* multis

---

[1] If Cicero assumed the *toga virilis* when he was sixteen, as he probably did (or in the year 90 B.C.), and the augur died in 88 B.C., then Cicero attended his lectures about two years.

LAELIUS ON FRIENDSHIP

I. Quintus Mucius Scaevola, the augur, used to
relate with an accurate memory and in a pleasing
way many incidents about his father-in-law, Gaius
Laelius, and, in every mention of him, did not
hesitate to call him " the Wise." Now, I, upon
assuming the *toga virilis*,[1] had been introduced by
my father to Scaevola with the understanding that,
so far as I could and he would permit, I should
never leave the old man's side. And so it came to
pass that, in my desire to gain greater profit from
his legal skill, I made it a practice to commit to
memory many of his learned opinions and many,
too, of his brief and pointed sayings. After his
death I betook myself to the pontiff, Scaevola, who,
both in intellect and in integrity, was, I venture
to assert, quite the most distinguished man of our
State. But of him I shall speak at another time ;
now I return to the augur.

Numerous events in the latter's life often recur
to me, but the most memorable one of all occurred
at his home, as he was sitting, according to his
custom, on a semi-circular garden bench, when I
and only a few of his intimate friends were with
him, and he happened to fall upon a topic which,
just about that time, was in many people's mouths.

nisti enim profecto, Attice, et eo magis, quod P.
Sulpicio utebare multum, cum is tribunus plebis
capitali odio a Q. Pompeio, qui tum erat consul,
dissideret, quocum coniunctissime et amantissime
vixerat, quanta esset hominum vel admiratio vel
3 querella. Itaque tum Scaevola, cum in eam ipsam
mentionem incidisset, exposuit nobis sermonem
Laeli de amicitia habitum ab illo secum et cum
altero genero C. Fannio, Marci filio, paucis diebus
post mortem Africani. Eius disputationis sententias memoriae mandavi, quas hoc libro exposui
arbitratu meo ; quasi enim ipsos induxi loquentis,
ne " inquam " et " inquit " saepius interponeretur
atque ut tamquam a praesentibus coram haberi
4 sermo videretur. Cum enim saepe mecum ageres,
ut de amicitia scriberem aliquid, digna mihi res
cum omnium cognitione tum nostra familiaritate
visa est ; itaque feci non invitus ut prodessem
multis rogatu tuo. Sed ut in Catone maiore, qui
est scriptus ad te de senectute, Catonem induxi
senem disputantem, quia nulla videbatur aptior
persona quae de illa aetate loqueretur, quam eius,
qui et diutissime senex fuisset et in ipsa senectute
praeter ceteros floruisset ; sic, cum accepissemus a
patribus maxime memorabilem C. Laeli et P.
Scipionis familiaritatem fuisse, idonea mihi Laeli

You, Atticus, were much in the society of Publius Sulpicius, and on that account are the more certain to remember what great astonishment, or rather complaining, there was among the people when Sulpicius, while plebeian tribune, separated himself in deadly hatred from the then consul, Quintus Pompeius, with whom he had lived on the most intimate and affectionate terms. And so, Scaevola, having chanced to mention this very fact, thereupon proceeded to repeat to us a discussion on friendship, which Laelius had had with him and with another son-in-law, Gaius Fannius, son of Marcus, a few days after the death of Africanus. I committed the main points of that discussion to memory, and have set them out in the present book in my own way; for I have, so to speak, brought the actors themselves on the stage in order to avoid the too frequent repetition of " said I " and " said he," and to create the impression that they are present and speaking in person. For while you were pleading with me again and again to write something on friendship, the subject appealed to me as both worthy of general study, and also well fitted to our intimacy. Therefore I have not been unwilling to benefit the public at your request. But, as in my *Cato the Elder*, which was written to you on the subject of old age, I represented Cato, when an old man, as the principal speaker, because I thought no one more suitable to talk of that period of life than he who had been old a very long time and had been a favourite of fortune in old age beyond other men; so, since we had learned from our forefathers that the intimacy of Gaius Laelius and Publius Scipio was most noteworthy,

persona visa est quae de amicitia ea ipsa dissereret,
quae disputata ab eo meminisset Scaevola. Genus
autem hoc sermonum positum in hominum veterum
auctoritate et eorum illustrium plus nescio quo
pacto videtur habere gravitatis: itaque ipse mea
legens sic afficior interdum, ut Catonem, non me,
5 loqui existimem. Sed ut tum ad senem senex de
senectute, sic hoc libro ad amicum amicissimus
scripsi de amicitia. Tum est Cato locutus, quo erat
nemo fere senior temporibus illis, nemo prudentior;
nunc Laelius et sapiens, sic enim est habitus, et
amicitiae gloria excellens de amicitia loquetur. Tu
velim a me animum parumper avertas, Laelium
loqui ipsum putes. C. Fannius et Q. Mucius ad
socerum veniunt post mortem Africani; ab his
sermo oritur, respondet Laelius, cuius tota disputatio est de amicitia, quam legens te ipse[1] co-
gnosces

6 II. FANNIUS. Sunt ista, Laeli; nec enim melior
vir fuit Africano quisquam nec clarior. Sed existimare debes omnium oculos in te esse coniectos,
unum; te sapientem et appellant et existimant
Tribuebatur hoc modo M. Catoni, scimus L. Acilium
apud patres nostros appellatum esse sapientem, sed

---

[1] te ipse *PDE Lahm., Nauck*; te ipsum *GBSV Halm.*

---

[1] The death of Africanus occurred 129 B.C.
[2] Cato died in 149 B.C., hence Fannius by " recently "
means " twenty years ago." The date of Cato's imagined
discourse on old age was 150 B.C.

I concluded that Laelius was a fit person to expound the very views on friendship which Scaevola remembered that he had maintained. Besides, discourses of this kind seem in some way to acquire greater dignity when founded on the influence of men of ancient times, especially such as are renowned ; and, hence, in reading my own work on *Old Age* I am at times so affected that I imagine Cato is the speaker and not myself. But as in that book I wrote as one old man to another old man on the subject of old age, so now in this book I have written as a most affectionate friend to a friend on the subject of friendship. In the former work the speaker was Cato, whom scarcely any in his day exceeded in age and none surpassed in wisdom ; in the present treatise the speaker on friendship will be Laelius, a wise man (for he was so esteemed), and a man who was distinguished by a glorious friendship. Please put me out of your mind for a little while and believe that Laelius himself is talking. Gaius Fannius and Quintus Mucius Scaevola have come to their father-in-law's house just after the death of Africanus[1]; the conversation is begun by them and reply is made by Laelius, whose entire discourse is on friendship, and as you read it you will recognize in it a portrait of yourself.

II. Fannius. What you say is true, Laelius; for there was no better man than Africanus, and no one more illustrious. But you should realize that all men have fixed their eyes on you alone ; you it is whom they both call and believe to be wise. Recently[2] this title was given to Marcus Cato and we know that Lucius Acilius was called " the Wise " in our

uterque alio quodam modo: Acilius quia prudens
esse in iure civili putabatur, Cato quia multarum
rerum usum habebat et multa eius et in senatu et
in foro vel provisa prudenter vel acta constanter vel
responsa acute ferebantur; propterea quasi cognomen
7 iam habebat in senectute sapientis. Te autem alio
quodam modo non solum natura et moribus, verum
etiam studio et doctrina esse sapientem, nec sicut
volgus, sed ut eruditi solent appellare sapientem,
qualem in Graecia reliqua neminem—nam qui
septem appellantur, eos qui ista subtilius quaerunt
in numero sapientium non habent—Athenis unum
accepimus et eum quidem etiam Apollinis oraculo
sapientissimum iudicatum. Hanc esse in te sapientiam existimant, ut omnia tua in te posita esse ducas
humanosque casus virtute inferiores putes. Itaque
ex me quaerunt, credo ex hoc item Scaevola, quonam
pacto mortem Africani feras, eoque magis quod
proximis Nonis, cum in hortos D. Bruti auguris
commentandi causa, ut assolet, venissemus, tu non
affuisti, qui diligentissime semper illum diem et
illud munus solitus esses obire.

8 SCAEVOLA. Quaerunt quidem, C. Laeli, multum,

---

[1] The reference is to Socrates. Cicero often quotes this
oracle: *infra*, 2. 10; *ib.* 4. 13; *C.M.* 21. 78; *Acad.*
i. 4. 16.

[2] The Augurs regularly met in their college on the Nones
(*i.e.* the 7th of March, May, July, and October, the 5th of
other months).

[3] *Commentandi, i.e.* practising the augural art under the
open sky. *Cf.* Cic. *N.D.* ii. 11; *De rep.* i. 14.

fathers' time, but each of them in a somewhat different way : Acilius because of his reputation for skill in civil law ; Cato because of his manifold experience, and because of the many well-known instances wherein both in Senate and forum he displayed shrewdness of foresight, resolution of conduct, or sagacity in reply ; and as a result, by the time he had reached old age, he bore the title of " the Wise " as a sort of cognomen. But as to yourself, men are wont to call you wise in a somewhat different way, not only because of your mental endowments and natural character, but also because of your devotion to study and because of your culture, and they employ the term in your case, not as the ignorant do, but as learned men employ it. And in this sense we have understood that no one in all Greece was " wise " except one in Athens, and he,[1] I admit, was actually adjudged "most wise " by the oracle of Apollo—for the more captious critics refuse to admit those who are called " The Seven " into the category of the wise. Your wisdom, in public estimation, consists in this : you consider all your possessions to be within yourself and believe human fortune of less account than virtue. Hence the question is put to me and to Scaevola here, too, I believe, as to how you bear the death of Africanus, and the inquiry is the more insistent because, on the last Nones,[2] when we had met as usual for the practice [3] of our augural art in the country home of Decimus Brutus, you were not present, though it had been your custom always to observe that day and to discharge its duties with the most scrupulous care.

SCAEVOLA. There is indeed a great deal of ques-

ut est a Fannio dictum, sed ego id respondeo, quod
animum adverti, te dolorem quem acceperis cum
summi viri tum amicissimi morte ferre moderate;
nec potuisse non commoveri, nec fuisse id humanitatis tuae : quod autem Nonis in collegio nostro
non affuisses, valetudinem respondeo causam, non
maestitiam fuisse.

LAELIUS. Recte tu quidem, Scaevola, et vere ; nec
enim ab isto officio, quod semper usurpavi cum
valerem, abduci incommodo meo debui, nec ullo
casu arbitror hoc constanti homini posse contingere,
9 ut ulla intermissio fiat offici. Tu autem, Fanni, quod
mihi tantum tribui dicis, quantum ego nec agnosco
nec postulo, facis amice, sed, ut mihi videris, non
recte iudicas de Catone. Aut enim nemo, quod
quidem magis credo, aut, si quisquam, ille sapiens
fuit. Quo modo, ut alia omittam, mortem fili tulit !
Memineram Paulum, videram Gallum ; sed hi in
10 pueris, Cato in perfecto et spectato viro. Quam
ob rem cave Catoni anteponas ne istum quidem
ipsum, quem Apollo, ut ais, sapientissimum iudicavit ;
huius enim facta, illius dicta laudantur.

De me autem, ut iam cum utroque vestrum loquar,

---

[1] Cicero admired the stoical parent (*e.g.* Fabius, in *C.M.*
12 : Cato, here and in *C.M.* 84), but on the death of his only
daughter about eighteen months before this essay was written
Cicero's grief was unrestrained.

tioning, Gaius Laelius, just as Fannius has said, but I state in reply what I have observed : that you bear with composure the pain occasioned by the death of one who was at once a most eminent man and your very dear friend ; that you could not be unmoved thereby and that to be so was not consistent with your refined and tender nature and your culture ; but as to your not attending our college on the Nones, that, I answer, was due to ill-health and not to grief.

LAELIUS. Your reply was excellent, Scaevola, and it was correct ; for no personal inconvenience of any kind ought to have kept me from the discharge of the duty you mentioned, and which I have always performed when I was well, nor do I think it possible for any event of this nature to cause a man of strong character to neglect any duty. Now as for your saying, Fannius, that so great merit is ascribed to me—merit such as I neither admit nor claim —you are very kind ; but it seems to me that your estimate of Cato is scarcely high enough. For either no man was wise—which really I think is the better view—or, if anyone, it was he. Putting aside all other proof, consider how he bore the death of his son[1]! I remembered the case of Paulus, and I had been a constant witness of the fortitude of Gallus, but their sons died in boyhood, while Cato's son died in the prime of life when his reputation was assured. Therefore, take care not to give the precedence over Cato even to that man, whom, as you say, Apollo adjudged the wisest of men ; for the former is praised for his deeds, the latter for his words.

Now, as to myself, let me address you both at

sic habetote: III. Ego si Scipionis desiderio me moveri negem, quam id recte faciam viderint sapientes, sed certe mentiar. Moveor enim tali amico orbatus, qualis, ut arbitror, nemo umquam erit, ut confirmare possum, nemo certe fuit. Sed non egeo medicina: me ipse consolor et maxime illo solacio, quod eo errore careo, quo amicorum decessu plerique angi solent. Nihil mali accidisse Scipioni puto; mihi accidit, si quid accidit; suis autem incommodis graviter angi non amicum, sed se ipsum amantis est.

11 Cum illo vero quis neget actum esse praeclare? Nisi enim, quod ille minime putabat, immortalitatem optare vellet, quid non adeptus est, quod homini fas esset optare, qui summam spem civium, quam de eo iam puero habuerant, continuo adulescens incredibili virtute superavit; qui consulatum petivit numquam, factus consul est bis, primum ante tempus, iterum sibi suo tempore, rei publicae paene sero; qui duabus urbibus eversis inimicissimis huic imperio non modo praesentia, verum etiam futura bella delevit? Quid dicam de moribus facillimis, de pietate in matrem, liberalitate in sorores, boni-

---

[1] Scipio was elected consul the first time in 147 B.C., at the age of thirty-eight, when a candidate for the aedileship, and given command of the war against Carthage. He was elected again in 134 B.C. (though not a candidate), to conduct the siege against Numantia and to end a war which had gone on unsuccessfully for the Romans for eight years.

[2] Scipio's mother, Papiria, had been divorced by Paulus, and Scipio gave her the legacy received by him from his adoptive grandmother, Aemilia, wife of Scipio the Elder. After his mother's death he gave the same property to his sisters.

once and beg you to believe that the case stands thus:
III. If I were to assert that I am unmoved by grief at
Scipio's death, it would be for " wise " men to judge
how far I am right, yet, beyond a doubt, my assertion
would be false. For I am indeed moved by the
loss of a friend such, I believe, as I shall never have
again, and—as I can assert on positive knowledge—
a friend such as no other man ever was to me. But
I am not devoid of a remedy, and I find very great
consolation in the comforting fact that I am free
from the delusion which causes most men anguish
when their friends depart. I believe that no ill
has befallen Scipio ; it has befallen me, if it has
befallen anyone ; but great anguish for one's own
inconveniences is the mark of the man who loves
not his friend but himself.

But who would say that all has not gone wonder-
fully well with *him* ? For unless he had wished
to live for ever—a wish he was very far from enter-
taining—what was there, proper for a human being
to wish for, that he did not attain ? The exalted
expectation which his country conceived of him in
his childhood, he at a bound, through incredible
merit, more than realized in his youth. Though he
never sought the consulship, he was elected consul
twice—the first time [1] before he was of legal age,
the second time at a period seasonable for him,
but almost too late for the safety of the commonwealth. And he overthrew the two cities that
were the deadliest foes of our empire and thereby
put an end not only to existing wars, but to future
wars as well. Why need I speak of his most affable
manners, of his devotion to his mother, of his generosity to his sisters,[2] of his kindness to his relatives,

119

tate in suos, iustitia in omnis ? Nota sunt
vobis. Quam autem civitati carus fuerit, maerore
funeris indicatum est. Quid igitur hunc paucorum
annorum accessio iuvare potuisset ? Senectus enim
quamvis non sit gravis, ut memini Catonem anno
ante quam est mortuus, mecum et cum Scipione
disserere, tamen aufert eam viriditatem, in qua
etiam nunc erat Scipio.

12 Quam ob rem vita quidem talis fuit vel fortuna
vel gloria, ut nihil posset accedere ; moriendi autem
sensum celeritas abstulit. Quo de genere mortis
difficile dictu est ; quid homines suspicentur videtis :
hoc vere tamen licet dicere, P. Scipioni ex multis
diebus, quos in vita celeberrimos laetissimosque
viderit, illum diem clarissimum fuisse, cum senatu
dimisso domum reductus ad vesperum est a patribus
conscriptis, populo Romano, sociis et Latinis, pridie
quam excessit e vita, ut ex tam alto dignitatis gradu
ad superos videatur deos potius quam ad inferos
pervenisse.

13 IV. Neque enim adsentior eis, qui nuper haec
disserere coeperunt, cum corporibus simul animos
interire atque omnia morte deleri. Plus apud me
antiquorum auctoritas valet, vel nostrorum maiorum,
qui mortuis tam religiosa iura tribuerunt, quod non
fecissent, profecto, si nihil ad eos pertinere arbi-

---

[1] After a violent scene in the Senate, where he opposed
Carbo in the execution of the agrarian law, Scipio was
escorted home in the evening by admiring crowds. The
next morning he was found dead in bed. *Cf.* Appian, *Bell.
Civ.* i. 20 ; Vell. Pat. ii. 4. In other works (*De or.*
ii. 170 ; *Fam.* ix. 21. 3 ; *Qu. Fr.* ii. 3. 3) Cicero takes
the view that Carbo murdered him ; *cf.* also Cic. *De fat.*
18 ; Livy, *Epit.* 59 ; Plut. *C. Grac.* 10.

of his strict integrity to all men ? These things are well known to you both. Moreover, how dear he was to the State was indicated by the grief displayed at his funeral. How, then, could he have gained any advantage by the addition of a few more years of life ? For even though old age may not be a burden—as I remember Cato, the year before he died, maintained in a discourse with Scipio and myself—yet it does take away that freshness which Scipio kept even to the end.

Therefore, his life really was such that nothing could be added to it either by good fortune or by fame ; and, besides, the suddenness of his death took away the consciousness of dying. It is hard to speak of the nature of his death ; you both know what people suspect [1] ; yet I may say with truth that, of the many very joyous days which he saw in the course of his life—days thronged to the utmost with admiring crowds—the most brilliant was the day before he departed this life, when, after the adjournment of the Senate, he was escorted home toward evening by the Conscript Fathers, the Roman populace, and the Latin allies, so that from so lofty a station of human grandeur he seems to have passed to the gods on high rather than to the shades below.

IV. For I do not agree with those who have recently begun to argue that soul and body perish at the same time, and that all things are destroyed by death. I give greater weight to the old-time view, whether it be that of our forefathers, who paid such reverential rites to the dead, which they surely would not have done if they had believed those rites were a matter of indifference to the

121

trarentur, vel eorum qui in hac terra fuerunt magnamque Graeciam, quae nunc quidem deleta est,
tum florebat, institutis et praeceptis suis erudierunt,
vel eius, qui Apollinis oraculo sapientissimus est
iudicatus, qui[1] non tum hoc tum illud, ut in plerisque,
sed idem semper, animos hominum esse divinos
eisque, cum ex corpore excessissent, reditum in
caelum patere optimoque et iustissimo cuique expedi-
tissimum.

14   Quod idem Scipioni videbatur, qui quidem, quasi
praesagiret, perpaucis ante mortem diebus, cum
et Philus et Manilius adesset et alii plures, tuque
etiam Scaevola, mecum venisses, triduum disseruit
de re publica, cuius disputationis fuit extremum fere
de immortalitate animorum, quae se in quiete per
visum ex Africano audisse dicebat. Id si ita est,
ut optimi cuiusque animus in morte facillime evolet
tanquam e custodia vinclisque corporis, cui censemus
cursum ad deos faciliorem fuisse quam Scipioni?
Quocirca maerere hoc eius eventu vereor ne invidi
magis quam amici sit. Sin autem illa veriora, ut
idem interitus sit animorum et corporum nec ullus
sensus maneat, ut nihil boni est in morte, sic certe
nihil mali. Sensu enim amisso fit idem, quasi natus

---

    [1] qui *mss.* ; †qui *Müller* ; cui *Halm., Bait., Lahm.*

---

    [1] *i.e.* the Pythagoreans who had a school of philosophy at
Crotona in the fifth century B.C.
    [2] *i.e.* lower Italy.

dead ; or, whether it be the view of those[1] who lived in this land and by their principles and precepts brought culture to Great Greece,[2] which now, I admit, is wholly destroyed, but was then flourishing ; or, whether it be the view of him who was adjudged by the oracle of Apollo to be the wisest of men, who, though he would argue on most subjects now on one side and now on the other, yet always consistently maintained that human souls were of God ; that upon their departure from the body a return to heaven lay open to them, and that in proportion as each soul was virtuous and just would the return be easy and direct.

Scipio held this same view, for only a few days before his death, in the presence of Philus, Manilius and several others (you were there, too, Scaevola, having gone with me), he, as if with a premonition of his fate, discoursed for three days on the commonwealth, and devoted almost all of the conclusion of his discussion to the immortality of the soul, making use of arguments which he had heard, he said, from Africanus the Elder through a vision in his sleep. If the truth really is that the souls of all good men after death make the easiest escape from what may be termed the imprisonment and fetters of the flesh, whom can we think of as having had an easier journey to the gods than Scipio ? Therefore, I fear that grief at such a fate as his would be a sign more of envy than of friendship. But if, on the other hand, the truth rather is that soul and body perish at the same time, and that no sensation remains, then, it follows that, as there is nothing good in death, so, of a certainty, there is nothing evil. For if a man has lost sensation the result is

non esset omnino, quem tamen esse natum et nos gaudemus et haec civitas, dum erit, laetabitur.

15 Quam ob rem cum illo quidem, ut supra dixi, actum optime est, mecum incommodius, quem fuerat aequius, ut prius introieram, sic prius exire de vita. Sed tamen recordatione nostrae amicitiae sic fruor, ut beate vixisse videar, quia cum Scipione vixerim, quocum mihi coniuncta cura de publica re et de privata fuit, quocum et domus fuit et militia communis et, id in quo omnis vis est amicitiae, voluntatum studiorum sententiarum summa consensio. Itaque non tam ista me sapientiae, quam modo Fannius commemoravit, fama delectat, falsa praesertim, quam quod amicitiae nostrae memoriam spero sempiternam fore, idque eo mihi magis est cordi, quod ex omnibus saeculis vix tria aut quattuor nominantur paria amicorum, quo in genere sperare videor Scipionis et Laeli amicitiam notam posteritati fore.

16 FANNIUS. Istuc quidem, Laeli, ita necesse est. Sed quoniam amicitiae mentionem fecisti et sumus otiosi, pergratum mihi feceris—spero item Scaevolae —si, quem ad modum soles de ceteris rebus, cum ex te quaeruntur, sic de amicitia disputaris quid sentias, qualem existimes, quae praecepta des.

SCAEVOLA. Mihi vero erit gratum, atque id ipsum

---

¹ The three pairs are Theseus and Pirithous, Achilles and Patroclus, Orestes and Pylades; the fourth, probably in Cicero's mind (Cic. *Off.* iii. 45; *Fin.* ii. 79), was Damon and Phintias (*vulg.* Pythias).

the same as if he had never been born ; and yet
the fact that Scipio was born is a joy to us and will
cause this State to exult so long as it shall exist.

Wherefore, as I have already said, it has gone
very well with him, less so with me, for, as I was
before him in entering life, it had been more
reasonable to expect that I should have been before
him in leaving it. Still, such is my enjoyment in the
recollection of our friendship that I feel as if my
life has been happy because it was spent with
Scipio, with whom I shared my public and private
cares ; lived under the same roof at home ; served
in the same campaigns abroad, and enjoyed that
wherein lies the whole essence of friendship—the
most complete agreement in policy, in pursuits, and
in opinions. Hence, I am not so much delighted by
my reputation for wisdom which Fannius just now
called to mind, especially since it is undeserved, as
I am by the hope that the memory of our friendship will always endure ; and this thought is the
more pleasing to me because in the whole range
of history only three or four pairs[1] of friends are
mentioned ; and I venture to hope that among such
instances the friendship of Scipio and Laelius will
be known to posterity.

FANNIUS. That cannot be otherwise, Laelius.
But since you have mentioned friendship and we
are free from public business, it would be very
agreeable to me—and to Scaevola, too, I hope—
if, following your usual practice on other subjects
when questions concerning them are put to you,
you would discuss friendship and give us your
opinion as to its theory and practice.

SCAEVOLA. Indeed it will be agreeable to me, and,

CICERO

cum tecum agere conarer, Fannius antevertit. Quam
ob rem utrique nostrum gratum admodum feceris.

17   V. LAELIUS. Ego vero non gravarer, si mihi ipse
confiderem, nam et praeclara res est et sumus, ut
dixit Fannius, otiosi. Sed quis ego sum aut quae
est in me facultas ? Doctorum est ista consuetudo
eaque Graecorum, ut eis ponatur de quo disputent
quamvis subito. Magnum opus est egetque exercitatione non parva. Quam ob rem quae disputari
de amicitia possunt, ab eis censeo petatis, qui ista
profitentur ; ego vos hortari tantum possum, ut
amicitiam omnibus rebus humanis anteponatis ;
nihil est enim tam naturae aptum, tam conveniens
ad res vel secundas vel adversas.

18   Sed hoc primum sentio, nisi in bonis amicitiam
esse non posse ; neque id ad vivum reseco, ut illi,
qui haec subtilius disserunt, fortasse vere, sed ad
communem utilitatem parum ; negant enim quemquam esse virum bonum nisi sapientem. Sit ita
sane : sed eam sapientiam interpretantur, quam
adhuc mortalis nemo est consecutus. Nos autem
ea quae sunt in usu vitaque communi, non ea quae
finguntur aut optantur, spectare debemus. Numquam ego dicam C. Fabricium, M'. Curium, Ti.
Coruncanium, quos sapientis nostri maiores iudica-
bant, ad istorum normam fuisse sapientis. Qua re

---

[1] *i.e.* readiness acquired by practice in extemporaneous
discussion — an art practised by sophists and rhetoricians
and by the philosophers of the New Academy ; *cf.* Cic.
De fin. ii. 1 ; *De or.* i. 102.

[2] *Id ad vivum reseco*, lit. " cut back to the quick."

[3] *i.e.* those who profess the art of disputation ; *cf.* 17.

[4] The perfect " wise man " of the Stoics represents an
ideal, though they allowed that a few men, such as
Socrates, almost realized it.

in fact, I was about to make the same request when Fannius forestalled me. Hence your compliance will be very agreeable to us both.

V. LAELIUS. I certainly should raise no objection if I felt confidence in myself, for the subject is a noble one, and we are, as Fannius said, free from public business. But who am I ? or what skill[1] have I ? What you suggest is a task for philosophers and, what is more, for Greeks — that of discoursing on any subject however suddenly it may be proposed to them. This is a difficult thing to do and requires no little practice. Therefore, for a discussion of everything possible to be said on the subject of friendship, I advise you to apply to those who profess that art ; all that I can do is to urge you to put friendship before all things human ; for nothing is so conformable to nature and nothing so adaptable to our fortunes whether they be favourable or adverse.

This; however, I do feel first of all—that friendship cannot exist except among good men ; nor do I go into that too deeply,[2] as is done by those[3] who, in discussing this point with more than usual accuracy, and it may be correctly, but with too little view to practical results, say that no one is good unless he is wise. We may grant that ; but they understand wisdom to be a thing such as no mortal man has yet attained.[4] I, however, am bound to look at things as they are in the experience of everyday life and not as they are in fancy or in hope. Never could I say that Gaius Fabricius, Manius Curius, and Tiberius Coruncanius, whom our ancestors adjudged to be wise, were wise by such a standard as that.

sibi habeant sapientiae nomen et invidiosum et
obscurum, concedant ut viri boni fuerint. Ne id
quidem facient; negabunt id nisi sapienti posse
19 concedi. Agamus igitur pingui, ut aiunt, Minerva.
Qui ita se gerunt, ita vivunt, ut eorum probetur
fides integritas aequitas[1] liberalitas, nec sit in eis
ulla cupiditas libido audacia, sintque magna constantia, ut ei fuerunt, modo quos nominavi, hos viros
bonos, ut habiti sunt, sic etiam appellandos putemus,
quia sequantur, quantum homines possunt, naturam
optimam bene vivendi ducem.

Sic enim mihi perspicere videor, ita natos esse
nos, ut inter omnis esset societas quaedam, maior
autem, ut quisque proxime accederet. Itaque cives
potiores quam peregrini, propinqui quam alieni;
cum his enim amicitiam natura ipsa peperit, sed
ea non satis habet firmitatis. Namque hoc praestat
amicitia propinquitati, quod ex propinquitate benevolentia tolli potest, ex amicitia non potest; sublata
enim benevolentia amicitiae nomen tollitur, pro-
20 pinquitatis manet. Quanta autem vis amicitiae sit
ex hoc intellegi maxime potest, quod ex infinita
societate generis humani, quam conciliavit ipsa
natura, ita contracta res est et adducta in angustum,
ut omnis caritas aut inter duos aut inter paucos
iungeretur.

¹ aequitas *edd.*; aequalitas MSS.

---

[1] Lit. " at which everyone looks askance," as indicating
conceit or arrogance.

[2] *Propinquitas* may be applied to " neighbours " or
" fellow-citizens " as well as to " relatives."

Therefore, let the Sophists keep their unpopular[1] and unintelligible word to themselves, granting only that the men just named were good men. They will not do it though; they will say that goodness can be predicated only of the " wise " man. Let us then proceed " with our own dull wits," as the saying is. Those who so act and so live as to give proof of loyalty and uprightness, of fairness and generosity; who are free from all passion, caprice, and insolence, and have great strength of character —men like those just mentioned—such men let us consider good, as they were accounted good in life, and also entitled to be called by that term because, in as far as that is possible for man, they follow Nature, who is the best guide to good living.

For it seems clear to me that we were so created that between us all there exists a certain tie which strengthens with our proximity to each other. Therefore, fellow countrymen are preferred to foreigners and relatives[2] to strangers, for with them Nature herself engenders friendship, but it is one that is lacking in constancy. For friendship excels relationship[2] in this, that goodwill may be eliminated from relationship while from friendship it cannot; since, if you remove goodwill from friendship the very name of friendship is gone; if you remove it from relationship, the name of relationship still remains. Moreover, how great the power of friendship is may most clearly be recognized from the fact that, in comparison with the infinite ties uniting the human race and fashioned by Nature herself, this thing called friendship has been so narrowed that the bonds of affection always unite two persons only, or, at most, a few.

VI. Est enim amicitia nihil aliud[1] nisi omnium divinarum humanarumque rerum cum benevolentia et caritate consensio, qua quidem haud scio an excepta sapientia nil quicquam melius homini sit a dis immortalibus datum. Divitias alii praeponunt, bonam alii valetudinem, alii potentiam, alii honores, multi etiam voluptates. Beluarum hoc quidem extremum, illa autem superiora caduca et incerta, posita non tam in consiliis nostris quam in fortunae temeritate. Qui autem in virtute summum bonum ponunt, praeclare illi quidem, sed haec ipsa virtus amicitiam et gignit et continet, nec sine virtute amicitia esse 21 ullo pacto potest. Iam virtutem ex consuetudine vitae nostrae sermonisque nostri interpretemur nec eam, ut quidam docti, verborum magnificentia metiamur, virosque bonos eos qui habentur numeremus—Paulos Catones Gallos Scipiones Philos—his communis vita contenta est; eos autem omittamus, qui omnino nusquam reperiuntur.

22 Talis igitur inter viros amicitia tantas opportunitates habet, quantas vix queo dicere. Principio qui potest esse vita vitalis, ut ait Ennius, quae non in amici mutua benevolentia conquiescit? Quid dulcius quam habere quicum omnia audeas sic loqui ut tecum? Qui esset tantus fructus in prosperis rebus, nisi haberes qui illis aeque ac tu ipse gauderet?

---

[1] nihil aliud *Müller* ; nil unquam *Reid* ; quicquam *Halm's* MSS.

---

[1] The ideally perfect men of the Stoics.
[2] Or more literally " adaptabilities," " occasions when it can be fitly used."

VI. For friendship is nothing else than an accord in all things, human and divine, conjoined with mutual goodwill and affection, and I am inclined to think that, with the exception of wisdom, no better thing has been given to man by the immortal gods. Some prefer riches, some good health, some power, some public honours, and many even prefer sensual pleasures. This last is the highest aim of brutes; the others are fleeting and unstable things and dependent less upon human foresight than upon the fickleness of fortune. Again, there are those who place the "chief good" in virtue and that is really a noble view; but this very virtue is the parent and preserver of friendship and without virtue friendship cannot exist at all. To proceed then, let us interpret the word "virtue" by the familiar usage of our everyday life and speech, and not in pompous phrase apply to it the precise standards which certain philosophers use; and let us include in the number of good men those who are so considered—men like Paulus, Cato, Gallus, Scipio, and Philus—who satisfy the ordinary standard of life; but let us pass by such men as are nowhere to be found at all.[1]

Therefore, among men like those just mentioned, friendship offers advantages[2] almost beyond my power to describe. In the first place, how can life be what Ennius calls "the life worth living," if it does not repose on the mutual goodwill of a friend? What is sweeter than to have someone with whom you may dare discuss anything as if you were communing with yourself? How could your enjoyment in times of prosperity be so great if you did not have someone whose joy in them would be equal to your

131

Adversas vero ferre difficile esset sine eo, qui illas gravius etiam quam tu ferret. Denique ceterae res, quae expetuntur, opportunae sunt singulae rebus fere singulis — divitiae, ut utare ; opes, ut colare ; honores, ut laudere ; voluptates, ut gaudeas ; valetudo, ut dolore careas et muneribus fungare corporis ; amicitia res plurimas continet : quoquo te verteris praesto est, nullo loco excluditur, numquam intempestiva, numquam molesta est. Itaque non aqua, non igni, ut aiunt, pluribus locis utimur quam amicitia. Neque ego nunc de volgari aut de mediocri, quae tamen ipsa et delectat et prodest, sed de vera et perfecta loquor, qualis eorum, qui pauci nominantur, fuit. Nam et secundas res splendidiores facit amicitia, et adversas, partiens communicansque, leviores.

23 VII. Cumque plurimas et maximas commoditates amicitia contineat, tum illa nimirum praestat omnibus, quod bonam spem praelucet in posterum, nec debilitari animos aut cadere patitur. Verum etiam amicum qui intuetur, tamquam exemplar aliquod intuetur sui. Quocirca et absentes adsunt et egentes abundant et imbecilli valent et, quod difficilius dictu est, mortui vivunt ; tantus eos honos memoria desiderium prosequitur amicorum, ex quo illorum beata mors videtur, horum vita laudabilis. Quod si exe-

---

[1] Proverbial, that is, as representing the prime necessities of life.

[2] *Cf.* Bacon's *Friendship* : " This communicating of a man's self to his friend worketh two contrary effects ; for it redoubleth Joys and cutteth Griefs in Halves."

own ? Adversity would indeed be hard to bear, without him to whom the burden would be heavier even than to yourself. In short, all other objects of desire are each, for the most part, adapted to a single end—riches, for spending ; influence, for honour ; public office, for reputation ; pleasures, for sensual enjoyment ; and health, for freedom from pain and full use of the bodily functions ; but friendship embraces innumerable ends ; turn where you will it is ever at your side ; no barrier shuts it out ; it is never untimely and never in the way. Therefore, we do not use the proverbial [1] " fire and water " on more occasions than we use friendship. I am not now speaking of the ordinary and commonplace friendship—delightful and profitable as it is—but of that pure and faultless kind, such as was that of the few whose friendships are known to fame. For friendship adds a brighter radiance to prosperity and lessens the burden of adversity by dividing and sharing it.[2]

VII. Seeing that friendship includes very many and very great advantages, it undoubtedly excels all other things in this respect, that it projects the bright ray of hope into the future, and does not suffer the spirit to grow faint or to fall. Again, he who looks upon a true friend, looks, as it were, upon a sort of image of himself. Wherefore friends, though absent, are at hand ; though in need, yet abound ; though weak, are strong ; and—harder saying still— though dead, are yet alive ; so great is the esteem on the part of their friends, the tender recollection and the deep longing that still attends them. These things make the death of the departed seem fortunate and the life of the survivors worthy of praise.

133

meris ex rerum natura benevolentiae coniunctionem,
nec domus ulla nec urbs stare poterit, ne agri quidem
cultus permanebit. Id si minus intellegitur, quanta
vis amicitiae concordiaeque sit, ex dissensionibus
atque discordiis percipi potest. Quae enim domus
tam stabilis, quae tam firma civitas est, quae non
odiis et discidiis funditus possit everti ?

Ex quo, quantum boni sit in amicitia, iudicari
24 potest. Agrigentinum quidem doctum quendam
virum carminibus Graecis vaticinatum ferunt, quae
in rerum natura totoque mundo constarent quaeque
moverentur, ea contrahere amicitiam, dissipare dis-
cordiam. Atque hoc quidem omnes mortales et
intellegunt et re probant. Itaque, si quando aliquod
officium exstitit amici in periculis aut adeundis aut
communicandis, quis est qui id non maximis efferat
laudibus ? Qui clamores tota cavea nuper in hospitis
et amici mei M. Pacuvi nova fabula, cum ignorante
rege uter Orestes esset, Pylades Oresten se esse
diceret, ut pro illo necaretur, Orestes autem, ita
ut erat, Oresten se esse perseveraret ! Stantes
plaudebant in re ficta ; quid arbitramur in vera
facturos fuisse ? Facile indicabat ipsa natura vim
suam, cum homines, quod facere ipsi non possent,
id recte fieri in altero iudicarent.

---

[1] Empedocles, according to whom φιλότης (friendship)
and νεῖκος (strife) are perpetually at war, causing the four
elements to unite or disperse,

ἄλλοτε μὲν φιλότητι συνερχόμεν' εἰς ἓν ἅπαντα,
ἄλλοτε δ' αὖ δίχ' ἕκαστα φορεύμενα νείκεος ἔχθει.

[2] The title is uncertain, but the subject was that of
Euripides' *Iphigenia in Tauris.*

But if you should take the bond of goodwill out of the universe no house or city could stand, nor would even the tillage of the fields abide. If that statement is not clear, then you may understand how great is the power of friendship and of concord from a consideration of the results of enmity and disagreement. For what house is so strong, or what state so enduring that it cannot be utterly overthrown by animosities and division ?

From this it may be judged how great good there is in friendship. It is said, at any rate, that a certain learned man of Agrigentum [1] sang in inspired strain in Greek verse that in nature and the entire universe whatever things are at rest and whatever are in motion are united by friendship and scattered by discord. And indeed this is a statement which all men not only understand but also approve. Whenever, therefore, there comes to light some signal service in undergoing or sharing the dangers of a friend, who does not proclaim it with the loudest praise? What shouts recently rang through the entire theatre during the performance of the new play, written by my guest and friend, Marcus Pacuvius,[2] at the scene where, the king being ignorant which of the two was Orestes, Pylades, who wished to be put to death instead of his friend, declared, " I am Orestes," while Orestes continued steadfastly to assert, as was the fact, " I am Orestes ! " The people in the audience rose to their feet and cheered this incident in fiction ; what, think we, would they have done had it occurred in real life ? In this case Nature easily asserted her own power, inasmuch as men approved in another as well done that which they could not do themselves.

Hactenus mihi videor de amicitia quid sentirem potuisse dicere ; si quae praeterea sunt—credo autem esse multa—ab eis, si videbitur, qui ista disputant, quaeritote.

25 FANNIUS. Nos autem a te potius. Quamquam etiam ab istis saepe quaesivi et audivi non invitus equidem, sed aliud quoddam filum orationis tuae.

SCAEVOLA. Tum magis id diceres, Fanni, si nuper in hortis Scipionis, cum est de re publica disputatum, affuisses. Qualis tum patronus iustitiae fuit contra accuratam orationem Phili !

FANNIUS. Facile id quidem fuit iustitiam iustissimo viro defendere.

SCAEVOLA. Quid ? amicitiam nonne facile ei, qui ob eam summa fide, constantia iustitiaque servatam maximam gloriam ceperit ?

26 VIII. LAELIUS. Vim hoc quidem est afferre ; quid enim refert qua me ratione cogatis ? Cogitis certe. Studiis enim generorum, praesertim in re bona, cum difficile est tum ne aequum quidem obsistere.

Saepissime igitur mihi de amicitia cogitanti maxime illud considerandum videri solet, utrum propter imbecillitatem atque inopiam desiderata sit amicitia, ut dandis recipiendisque meritis, quod quisque minus per se ipse posset, id acciperet ab alio vicissimque redderet, an esset hoc quidem

Within the foregoing limits I have, I think, been able to state my estimate of friendship ; if there is anything more to be said—and I believe there is a great deal—inquire, if you please, of those who make a business of such discussions.

FANNIUS. But we prefer to inquire of you. I have, it is true, often questioned those men too, and indeed have not been an unwilling listener, but the thread of your discourse is of a somewhat different texture.

SCAEVOLA. You would say so with greater confidence, Fannius, if you had been present recently in Scipio's country home during the discussion on the Republic. What an advocate of justice Laelius was then against the elaborate speech of Philus !

FANNIUS. Ah ! but it was an easy thing for the most just of men to defend justice.

SCAEVOLA. Well, then, would not the defence of friendship be easy for that man who has preserved it with the utmost fidelity, constancy, and sense of justice, and thereby gained the greatest renown ?

VIII. LAELIUS. Really you are employing violence ; for what matters it what means you take of forcing me ? Forcing me you certainly are. For it is not only hard, but not even right, to withstand the earnest requests of one's sons-in-law, particularly in a good cause.

The oftener, therefore, I reflect on friendship the more it seems to me that consideration should be given to the question, whether the longing for friendship is felt on account of weakness and want, so that by the giving and receiving of favours one may get from another and in turn repay what he is unable to procure of himself; or, although this

137

proprium amicitiae, sed antiquior et pulchrior et
magis a natura ipsa profecta alia causa. Amor enim,
ex quo amicitia nominata est, princeps est ad benevolentiam coniungendam. Nam utilitates quidem
etiam ab eis percipiuntur saepe, qui simulatione
amicitiae coluntur et observantur temporis causa ;
in amicitia autem nihil fictum, nihil simulatum est
et, quidquid est, id est verum et voluntarium.
27 Quapropter a natura mihi videtur potius quam indigentia orta amicitia, applicatione magis animi cum
quodam sensu amandi, quam cogitatione quantum
illa res utilitatis esset habitura. Quod quidem quale
sit, etiam in bestiis quibusdam animadverti potest,
quae ex se natos ita amant ad quoddam tempus et
ab eis ita amantur, ut facile earum sensus appareat.
Quod in homine multo est evidentius, primum ex ea
caritate quae est inter natos et parentis, quae dirimi
nisi detestabili scelere non potest, deinde cum similis
sensus exstitit amoris, si aliquem nacti sumus, cuius
cum moribus et natura congruamus, quod in eo
quasi lumen aliquod probitatis et virtutis perspicere
28 videamur. Nihil est enim virtute amabilius, nihil
quod magis alliciat ad diligendum, quippe cum
propter virtutem et probitatem etiam eos, quos
numquam vidimus, quodam modo diligamus. Quis
est qui C. Fabrici, M'. Curi non cum caritate aliqua
138

mutual interchange is really inseparable from
friendship, whether there is not another cause,
older, more beautiful, and emanating more directly
from Nature herself. For it is love (*amor*), from
which the word " friendship " (*amicitia*) is derived,
that leads to the establishing of goodwill. For
while it is true that advantages are frequently
obtained even from those who, under a pretence of
friendship, are courted and honoured to suit the
occasion ; yet in friendship there is nothing false,
nothing pretended ; whatever there is is genuine
and comes of its own accord. Wherefore it seems to
me that friendship springs rather from nature than
from need, and from an inclination of the soul joined
with a feeling of love rather than from calculation
of how much profit the friendship is likely to afford.
What this feeling is may be perceived even in the
case of certain animals, which, up to a certain time,
so love their offspring and are so loved by them,
that their impulses are easily seen. But this is
much more evident in man ; first, from the affection
existing between children and parents, which cannot
be destroyed except by some execrable crime, and
again from that kindred impulse of love, which
arises when once we have met someone whose
habits and character are congenial with our own ;
because in him we seem to behold, as it were, a
sort of lamp of uprightness and virtue. For there
is nothing more lovable than virtue, nothing that
more allures us to affection, since on account of
their virtue and uprightness we feel a sort of affection even for those whom we have never seen.
Is there anyone who does not dwell with some
kindly affection on the memory of Gaius Fabricius

benevola memoriam usurpet, quos numquam viderit ?
Quis autem est qui Tarquinium Superbum, qui Sp.
Cassium, Sp. Maelium non oderit ? Cum duobus
ducibus de imperio in Italia est decertatum, Pyrrho
et Hannibale ; ab altero propter probitatem eius
non nimis alienos animos habemus ; alterum propter
crudelitatem semper haec civitas oderit.

29   IX. Quod si tanta vis probitatis est, ut eam vel in
eis, quos numquam vidimus, et, quod maius est, in
hoste etiam diligamus, quid mirum est, si animi hominum moveantur, cum eorum, quibuscum usu coniuncti esse possunt, virtutem et bonitatem perspicere
videantur ? Quamquam confirmatur amor et bene-
ficio accepto et studio perspecto et consuetudine
adiuncta, quibus rebus ad illum primum motum
animi et amoris adhibitis admirabilis quaedam exardescit benevolentiae magnitudo.

Quam si qui putant ab imbecillitate proficisci, ut
sit per quem adsequatur quod quisque desideret,
humilem sane relinquunt et minime generosum, ut
ita dicam, ortum amicitiae, quam ex inopia atque
indigentia natam volunt. Quod si ita esset, ut
quisque minimum esse in se arbitraretur, ita ad
amicitiam esset aptissimus ; quod longe secus est.

30 Ut enim quisque sibi plurimum confidit et ut quisque
maxime virtute et sapientia sic munitus est, ut nullo
egeat suaque omnia in se ipso posita iudicet, ita

---

[1] This was the traditional but unjust view held by the
Romans. *Cf.* Livy xxi. 4. 9: Hor. *Carm.* iii. 6. 361 ; *ib.*
iv. 4. 42 ; Juv. vii. 161.

and Manius Curius, though he never saw them? On the other hand, is there anyone who does not hate Tarquin the Proud, Spurius Cassius, or Spurius Maelius? Against two leaders we had bitter struggles for the empire of Italy—Pyrrhus and Hannibal; for the former, because of his uprightness, we have no great enmity; for the latter, because of his cruelty,[1] this State will always entertain hatred.

IX. Now if the force of integrity is so great that we love it, whether in those we have never seen, or, more wonderful still, even in an enemy, what wonder that men's souls are stirred when they think they see clearly the virtue and goodness of those with whom a close intimacy is possible? And yet love is further strengthened by the receiving of a kindly service, by the evidence of another's care for us, and by closer familiarity, and from all these, when joined to the soul's first impulse to love, there springs up, if I may say so, a marvellous glow and greatness of goodwill.

If people think that friendship springs from weakness and from a purpose to secure someone through whom we may obtain that which we lack, they assign her, if I may so express it, a lowly pedigree indeed, and an origin far from noble, and they would make her the daughter of poverty and want. If this were so, then just in proportion as any man judged his resources to be small, would he be fitted for friendship; whereas the truth is far otherwise. For to the extent that a man relies upon himself and is so fortified by virtue and wisdom that he is dependent on no one and considers all his possessions to be within himself, in that degree is

141

in amicitiis expetendis colendisque maxime excellit.
Quid enim? Africanus indigens mei? Minime
hercule! Ac ne ego quidem illius, sed ego admiratione quadam virtutis eius, ille vicissim opinione
fortasse non nulla quam de meis moribus habebat,
me dilexit; auxit benevolentiam consuetudo. Sed
quamquam utilitates multae et magnae consecutae
sunt, non sunt tamen ab earum spe causae diligendi
31 profectae. Ut enim benefici liberalesque sumus,
non ut exigamus gratiam—neque enim beneficium
faeneramur, sed natura propensi ad liberalitatem
sumus—sic amicitiam non spe mercedis adducti,
sed quod omnis eius fructus in ipso amore inest,
expetendam putamus.

32 Ab his, qui pecudum ritu ad voluptatem omnia
referunt, longe dissentiunt; nec mirum; nihil enim
altum, nihil magnificum ac divinum suspicere possunt,
qui suas omnis cogitationes abiecerunt in rem tam
humilem tamque contemptam. Quam ob rem hos
quidem ab hoc sermone removeamus, ipsi autem
intellegamus natura gigni sensum diligendi et benevolentiae caritatem facta significatione probitatis,
quam qui appetiverunt, applicant sese et propius
admovent, ut et usu eius, quem diligere coeperunt,
fruantur et moribus, sintque pares in amore et
aequales propensioresque ad bene merendum quam
ad reposcendum, atque haec inter eos sit honesta

---

[1] According to the Stoics the wise man needed nothing,
though there were many things advisable for him to have;
cf. Seneca, *Ep.* 9 ; Plato, *Lysis* 215 B.

he most conspicuous for seeking out and cherishing friendships. Now what need did Africanus have of me?[1] By Hercules! none at all. And I, assuredly, had no need of him either, but I loved him because of a certain admiration for his virtue, and he, in turn, loved me, because, it may be, of the fairly good opinion which he had of my character; and close association added to our mutual affection. Although many and great advantages did ensue from our friendship, still the beginnings of our love did not spring from the hope of gain. For as men of our class are generous and liberal, not for the purpose of demanding repayment—for we do not put our favours out at interest, but are by nature given to acts of kindness—so we believe that friendship is desirable, not because we are influenced by hope of gain, but because its entire profit is in the love itself.

From this view those men who, after the manner of cattle, judge everything by the standard of pleasure, vigorously dissent; nor is it strange; for the raising of the vision to anything lofty, noble and divine is impossible to men who have abased their every thought to a thing so lowly and so mean. Therefore let us dismiss these persons from our conversation and let us for ourselves believe that the sentiments of love and of kindly affection spring from nature, when intimation has been given of moral worth; for when men have conceived a longing for this virtue they bend towards it and move closer to it, so that, by familiar association with him whom they have begun to love, they may enjoy his character, equal him in affection, become readier to deserve than to demand his favours, and vie with

143

certatio. Sic et utilitates ex amicitia maximae
capientur, et erit eius ortus a natura quam ab imbecillitate gravior et verior. Nam si utilitas conglu-
tinaret amicitias, eadem commutata dissolveret ; sed
quia natura mutari non potest, idcirco verae amicitiae
sempiternae sunt.

Ortum quidem amicitiae videtis, nisi quid ad haec
forte vultis.

FANNIUS. Tu vero perge, Laeli ! Pro hoc enim,
qui minor est natu, meo iure respondeo.

33 SCAEVOLA. Recte tu quidem : quam ob rem
audiamus.

X. LAELIUS. Audite vero, optimi viri, ea quae
saepissime inter me et Scipionem de amicitia dissere-
bantur. Quamquam ille quidem nihil difficilius esse
dicebat quam amicitiam usque ad extremum vitae
diem permanere : nam vel ut non idem expediret
incidere saepe, vel ut de re publica non idem sen-
tiretur ; mutari etiam mores hominum saepe dicebat,
alias adversis rebus, alias aetate ingravescente.
Atque earum rerum exemplum ex similitudine
capiebat ineuntis aetatis, quod summi puerorum
amores saepe una cum praetexta toga deponerentur ;
34 sin autem ad adulescentiam perduxissent, dirimi
tamen interdum contentione vel uxoriae condicionis
vel commodi alicuius, quod idem adipisci uterque

him in a rivalry of virtue. Thus the greatest advantages will be realized from friendship, and its origin, being derived from nature rather than from weakness, will be more dignified and more consonant with truth. For on the assumption that advantage is the cement of friendships, if advantage were removed friendships would fall apart; but since nature is unchangeable, therefore real friendships are eternal.

You now have my views on the origin of friendship, unless you have something to say in reply.

Fannius. Pray go on, Laelius, and I answer for my friend here, as I have the right to do, since he is my junior.

Scaevola. Well said, Fannius. Therefore, let us hear.

X. Laelius. Then listen, most worthy gentlemen, to the points very frequently mentioned between Scipio and me in our discussions of friendship. Now he, indeed, used to say that nothing was harder than for a friendship to continue to the very end of life; for it often happened either that the friendship ceased to be mutually advantageous, or the parties to it did not entertain the same political views; and that frequently, too, the dispositions of men were changed, sometimes by adversity and sometimes by the increasing burdens of age. And then he would draw an illustration of this principle from the analogy of early life. " For," said he, " the most ardent attachments of boyhood are often laid aside with the boyish dress; but if continued to the time of manhood, they are broken off, sometimes by rivalry in courtship or sometimes by a contest for some advantage, in which both of the parties to the friendship cannot be successful at the same time.

non posset. Quod si qui longius in amicitia provecti essent, tamen saepe labefactari, si in honoris contentionem incidissent ; pestem enim nullam maiorem esse amicitiis quam in plerisque pecuniae cupiditatem, in optimis quibusque honoris certamen et gloriae, ex quo inimicitias maximas saepe inter amicissimos exstitisse.

35 Magna etiam discidia et plerumque iusta nasci, cum aliquid ab amicis quod rectum non esset postularetur, ut aut libidinis ministri aut adiutores essent ad iniuriam, quod qui recusarent, quamvis honeste id facerent, ius tamen amicitiae deserere arguerentur ab eis, quibus obsequi nollent ; illos autem, qui quidvis ab amico auderent postulare, postulatione ipsa profiteri omnia se amici causa esse facturos. Eorum querella inveterata non modo familiaritates exstingui solere, sed odia etiam gigni sempiterna. Haec ita multa quasi fata impendere amicitiis, ut omnia subterfugere non modo sapientiae, sed etiam felicitatis diceret sibi videri.

36 XI. Quam ob rem id primum videamus, si placet, quatenus amor in amicitia progredi debeat. Numne, si Coriolanus habuit amicos, ferre contra patriam arma illi cum Coriolano debuerunt ? Num Vecellinum amici regnum appetentem, num Maelium

37 debuerunt iuvare ? Tiberium quidem Gracchum

146

But should the friendship continue for a longer time, yet it is often overthrown when a struggle for office happens to arise ; for while, with the generality of men, the greatest bane of friendship is the lust for money, with the most worthy men it is the strife for preferment and glory, and from this source frequently have sprung the deadliest enmities between the dearest friends."

" Then, too, disagreements of a very serious nature, and usually justifiable, arise from a demand upon friends to do something that is wrong, as, for example, to become agents of vice or abettors in violence, and when the demand is refused, however honourable the refusal, it is nevertheless charged by those to whom the compliance was denied that the laws of friendship have been disregarded ; besides, those who dare demand anything and everything of a friend, by that very demand profess a willingness to do anything whatever for the sake of a friend. By their ceaseless recriminations not only are social intimacies usually destroyed, but also everlasting enmities are produced. So many dangers of this kind," he would say, " hover like evil fates over friendships, that it seems to me to require both wisdom and good luck to escape them all."

XI. Wherefore, let us first consider, if you please, how far love ought to go in friendship. Supposing Coriolanus to have had friends, were those friends in duty bound to bear arms with him against their country ? Or ought the friends of Vecellinus, or of Maelius, to have supported them in their attempts to gain regal power ? As to Tiberius Gracchus, when he began to stir up revolution against the

147

rem publicam vexantem a Q. Tuberone aequali-
busque amicis derelictum videbamus. At C. Blossius
Cumanus, hospes familiae vestrae, Scaevola, cum
ad me, quod aderam Laenati et Rupilio consulibus
in consilio, deprecatum venisset, hanc ut sibi ignos-
cerem causam afferebat, quod tanti Ti. Gracchum
fecisset, ut quidquid ille vellet sibi faciendum
putaret. Tum ego, " etiamne," inquam, " si te in
Capitolium faces ferre vellet ? " " Numquam voluisset
id quidem, sed, si voluisset, paruissem." Videtis,
quam nefaria vox. Et hercule ita fecit, vel plus
etiam quam dixit ; non enim paruit ille Ti. Gracchi
temeritati, sed praefuit, nec se comitem illius furoris,
sed ducem praebuit. Itaque hac amentia, quaestione nova perterritus, in Asiam profugit, ad hostis
se contulit, poenas rei publicae gravis iustasque
persolvit.

Nulla ·est igitur excusatio peccati, si amici causa
peccaveris ; nam, cum conciliatrix amicitiae virtutis
opinio fuerit, difficile est amicitiam manere, si a
38 virtute defeceris. Quod si rectum statuerimus vel
concedere amicis quidquid velint vel impetrare ab
eis quidquid velimus, perfecta quidem sapientia si
simus, nihil habeat res viti ; sed loquimur de eis
amicis qui ante oculos sunt, quos videmus[1] aut de
quibus memoriam accepimus, quos novit vita com-

---

[1] videmus *P Reid* ; vidimus *ER Müller*.

---

[1] *i.e.* in 133 B.C.
[2] Cumae did not then possess the Roman franchise.
[3] Consuls in 132 B.C. when the inquiry into the acts of
Tiberius Gracchus were made.
[4] *i.e.* by his suicide after the defeat by the Romans of
Aristonicus whom he had joined.

republic,[1] we saw him utterly deserted by Quintus Tubero and by the friends of his own age. And yet Gaius Blossius of Cumae, a protégé of your family,[2] Scaevola, came to me to plead for leniency, because I was present as adviser to the consuls, Laenas and Rupilius,[3] and offered, as a reason for my pardoning him, the fact that his esteem for Tiberius Gracchus was so great he thought it was his duty to do anything that Tiberius requested him to do. Thereupon I inquired, " Even if he requested you to set fire to the Capitol ? " " He never would have requested me to do that, of course," said he, " but if he had I should have obeyed." You see what an impious remark that was ! And, by heavens ! he did all that he said he would do, or rather even more ; for he did not follow, but he directed, the infatuation of Tiberius Gracchus, and he did not offer himself as the comrade in the latter's fury, but as the leader. And so, as a result of his madness, being in fear of the special court of inquiry, he fled into Asia, joined our enemies, and paid a heavy and righteous penalty [4] for his crimes against the Republic.

Therefore it is no justification whatever of your sin to have sinned in behalf of a friend ; for, since his belief in your virtue induced the friendship, it is hard for that friendship to remain if you have forsaken virtue. But if we should resolve that it is right, either to grant our friends whatever they wish, or to get from them whatever we wish, then, assuming that we were endowed with truly faultless wisdom, no harm would result ; but I am speaking of the friends before our eyes, of those whom we see, or of men of whom we have record, and who

munis. Ex hoc numero nobis exempla sumenda
sunt, et eorum quidem maxime, qui ad sapientiam
39 proxime accedunt. Videmus Papum Aemilium C.
Luscino familiarem fuisse (sic a patribus accepimus)
bis una consules, collegas in censura ; tum et cum
eis et inter se coniunctissimos fuisse M'. Curium, Ti.
Coruncanium memoriae proditum est. Igitur ne
suspicari quidem possumus quemquam horum ab
amico quidpiam contendisse, quod contra fidem,
contra ius iurandum, contra rem publicam esset.
Nam hoc quidem in talibus viris quid attinet dicere,
si contendisset impetraturum non fuisse, cum illi
sanctissimi viri fuerint, aeque autem nefas sit tale
aliquid et facere rogatum et rogare ? At vero Ti.
Gracchum sequebantur C. Carbo, C. Cato, et minime
tum quidem Gaius frater, nunc idem acerrimus.

40 XII. Haec igitur lex in amicitia sanciatur, ut
neque rogemus res turpis nec faciamus rogati.
Turpis enim excusatio est et minime accipienda cum
in ceteris peccatis, tum si quis contra rem publicam
se amici causa fecisse fateatur. Etenim eo loco,
Fanni et Scaevola, locati sumus, ut nos longe pro-
spicere oporteat futuros casus rei publicae. Deflexit
iam aliquantulum de spatio curriculoque consuetudo

---

[1] They were consuls together, 282 and 278 B.C. and
censors, 275 B.C.
[2] *i.e.* because they were of a different and less noble
character.

are known to everyday life. It is from men of this class our examples should be drawn, but chiefly, I grant you, from those who make the nearest approach to wisdom. We read that Aemilius Papus was an intimate friend of Gaius Luscinus (so we have received it from our forefathers), that they served together twice as consuls and were colleagues in the censorship.[1] Again the tradition is that Manius Curius and Tiberius Coruncanius were most closely associated with them and with each other. Well, then, it is impossible for us even to suspect any one of these men of importuning a friend for anything contrary to good faith or to his solemn oath, or inimical to the commonwealth. What is the need of asserting in the case of men like these, that if such a request had been made it would not have been granted, seeing that they were the purest of men, and moreover, regarded it equally impious to grant and to make such a request ? But Tiberius Gracchus did find followers in Gaius Carbo and Gaius Cato,[2] and he found a follower also in his own brother Gaius, who though not very ardent then is now intensely so.

XII. Therefore let this law be established in friendship : neither ask dishonourable things, nor do them, if asked. And dishonourable it certainly is, and not to be allowed, for anyone to plead in defence of sins in general and especially of those against the State, that he committed them for the sake of a friend. For, my dear Fannius and Scaevola, we Romans are now placed in such a situation that it is our duty to keep a sharp look-out for the troubles that may befall our State. Our political practice has already swerved far from the track and course

151

41 maiorum. Ti. Gracchus regnum occupare conatus
est, vel regnavit is quidem paucos menses. Num
quid simile populus Romanus audierat aut viderat?
Hunc etiam post mortem secuti amici et propinqui
quid in P. Scipione effecerint, sine lacrimis non queo
dicere. Nam Carbonem, quocumque modo potuimus,
propter recentem poenam Ti. Gracchi sustinuimus.
De C. Gracchi autem tribunatu quid exspectem non
libet augurari; serpit deinde res,[1] quae proclivis
ad perniciem, cum semel coepit, labitur. Videtis
in tabella iam ante quanta sit facta labes, primo
Gabinia lege, biennio autem post Cassia. Videre
iam videor populum a senatu disiunctum, multitudinis arbitrio res maximas agi. Plures enim discent
quem ad modum haec fiant, quam quem ad modum
his resistatur.

42 Quorsum haec? Quia sine sociis nemo quicquam

---

[1] serpit deinde res *mss.*; serpit clam ea res *Deiter, Bennett.*
The passage is probably corrupt, as Müller thinks.

---

[1] Seyffert and Lahmeyer say that this Scipio is probably
not Africanus the Younger, the friend of Laelius, as contended by Nauck and others, but P. Cornelius Scipio Nasica
Serapis, consul 138 B.C., *pontifex maximus*, who led the
Senators in an attack on Tiberius Gracchus when the latter
was killed in 133. Scipio Serapis fled from Rome and died
soon after in Pergamum.

marked out for us by our ancestors. Tiberius
Gracchus tried to obtain regal power—or rather, he
actually did reign for a few months. Had the Roman
people ever heard of or experienced such a thing
before? What his friends and relatives, who followed him even after his death, did in the case of
Publius Scipio [1] I cannot describe without tears.
As for Carbo, because of the short time since the
punishment of Tiberius Gracchus,[2] we have borne
with him as best we could. Now what is to be
expected when Gaius Gracchus [3] becomes tribune,
I am not inclined to prophecy; however, revolution
creeps on imperceptibly at first but once it has
acquired momentum, rushes headlong to ruin.[4] You
see how much mischief has been caused already
in the matter of the ballot, first by the Gabinian
law,[5] and two years later by the Cassian law.[6] I
seem now to see the people estranged from the
Senate and the weightiest affairs of state determined
by the caprice of the mob. For more people will
learn how to start a revolution than how to withstand it.

Why do I say these things? Because without

[2] *i.e.* on account of the recent killing of Tiberius Gracchus
and the consequent excitement of the people.

[3] Gaius Gracchus, though in 129 (the time of the
dialogue) the leader of the popular party, did not become
tribune until 123.

[4] Reid translates, " Affairs soon (*deinde*) move on, for
they glide readily down the path of ruin when once they
have taken a start."

[5] Introduced voting by ballot and so called from its
author, A. Gabinius, plebeian tribune, 139 B.C.

[6] The Cassian law extended the ballot to juries in
criminal cases; it was passed in 137 and named from its
author, L. Cassius Ravilla.

tale conatur. Praecipiendum est igitur bonis, ut, si in eius modi amicitias ignari casu aliquo inciderint, ne existiment ita se alligatos, ut ab amicis in magna aliqua re publica peccantibus non discedant; improbis autem poena statuenda est, nec vero minor eis qui secuti erunt alterum, quam eis qui ipsi fuerint impietatis duces. Quis clarior in Graecia Themistocle, quis potentior? Qui cum imperator bello Persico servitute Graeciam liberavisset propterque invidiam in exsilium expulsus esset, ingratae patriae iniuriam non tulit, quam ferre debuit: fecit idem quod viginti annis ante apud nos fecerat Coriolanus. His adiutor contra patriam inventus est nemo;

43 itaque mortem sibi uterque conscivit. Qua re talis improborum consensio non modo excusatione amicitiae tegenda non est, sed potius supplicio omni vindicanda est, ut ne quis concessum putet amicum vel bellum patriae inferentem sequi. Quod quidem, ut res ire coepit, haud scio an aliquando futurum sit; mihi autem non minori curae est, qualis res publica post mortem meam futura sit, quam qualis hodie sit.

44 XIII. Haec igitur prima lex amicitiae sanciatur, ut ab amicis honesta petamus, amicorum causa honesta faciamus, ne exspectemus quidem dum

---

[1] *e.g.* as in the friendship between Carbo and Tiberius Gracchus.

[2] " Good men," in political parlance were the members of the aristocratic party.

[3] The treason of Themistocles was in 471 B.C.; that of Coriolanus in 491. Thucydides, i. 68, says that Themistocles died a natural death at Magnesia, in Asia Minor, and Livy ii. 40 quotes Pictor as saying that Coriolanus lived to an advanced age among the Volscians; see also Cic. *Att.* ix. 10. 3; Plut. *Them.* 31.

associates [1] no one attempts any such mischiefs. It must, therefore, be enjoined upon good men [2] that if by any chance they should inadvisedly fall into friendships of this kind, they must not think themselves so bound that they cannot withdraw from friends who are sinning in some important matter of public concern; for wicked men, on the other hand, a penalty must be enacted, and assuredly it will not be lighter for the followers than for the leaders in treason. Who was more eminent in Greece than Themistocles, who more powerful? But he, after having saved Greece from slavery by his leadership in the war with Persia, and after having been banished because of his unpopularity, would not submit to the injustice of an ungrateful country, as he was in duty bound to do: he did the same thing that Coriolanus had done among our people twenty years before. Not one single supporter could be found to aid these men against their country; therefore, each took his own life.[3] Hence such alliances of wicked men not only should not be protected by a plea of friendship, but rather they should be visited with summary punishment of the severest kind, so that no one may think it permissible to follow even a friend when waging war against his country. And yet this very thing, considering the course affairs have begun to take, will probably happen at some future time; as for me, I am no less concerned for what the condition of the commonwealth will be after my death, than I am for its condition to-day.

XIII. Therefore let this be ordained as the first law of friendship: Ask of friends only what is honourable; do for friends only what is honourable and

rogemur, studium semper adsit, cunctatio absit,
consilium verum dare audeamus libere, plurimum in
amicitia amicorum bene suadentium valeat auctoritas,
eaque et adhibeatur ad monendum non modo aperte,
sed etiam acriter, si res postulabit, et adhibitae
45 pareatur. Nam quibusdam, quos audio sapientes
habitos in Graecia, placuisse opinor mirabilia quaedam—sed nihil est, quod illi non persequantur
argutiis—partim fugiendas esse nimias amicitias,
ne necesse sit unum sollicitum esse pro pluribus ;
satis superque esse sibi suarum cuique rerum ; alienis
nimis implicari molestum esse ; commodissimum
esse quam laxissimas habenas habere amicitiae, quas
vel adducas cum velis vel remittas ; caput enim esse
ad beate vivendum securitatem, qua frui non possit
animus, si tamquam parturiat unus pro pluribus.

46 Alios autem dicere aiunt multo etiam inhumanius,
quem locum breviter paulo ante perstrinxi, praesidi
adiumentique causa, non benevolentiae neque caritatis
amicitias esse expetendas ; itaque ut quisque minimum firmitatis haberet minimumque virium, ita
amicitias appetere maxime : ex eo fieri ut mulier-
culae magis amicitiarum praesidia quaerant quam
viri, et inopes quam opulenti, et calamitosi quam ei

without even waiting to be asked ; let zeal be ever present, but hesitation absent ; dare to give true advice with all frankness ; in friendship let the influence of friends who are wise counsellors be paramount, and let that influence be employed in advising, not only with frankness, but, if the occasion demands, even with sternness, and let the advice be followed when given. I say this because certain men who, I am informed, are considered sages in Greece, have approved certain views, which, in my opinion, are astonishing (but there is nothing that those men will not pursue with their subtleties). Some of these men teach that too much intimacy in friendships should be avoided, lest it be necessary for one man to be full of anxiety for many ; that each one of us has business of his own, enough and to spare ; that it is annoying to be too much involved in the affairs of other people ; that it is best to hold the reins of friendship as loosely as possible, so that we may either draw them up or slacken them at will ; for, they say, an essential of a happy life is freedom from care, and this the soul cannot enjoy if one man is, as it were, in travail for many.

Again, there are others, I am told, who, with even less of human feeling, maintain (and I briefly touched on this point just now) that friendships must be sought for the sake of the defence and aid they give and not out of goodwill and affection ; therefore, that those least endowed with firmness of character and strength of body have the greatest longing for friendship ; and consequently, that helpless women, more than men, seek its shelter, the poor more than the rich, and the unfortunate more than those who are

47 qui putentur beati. O praeclaram sapientiam!
Solem enim e mundo tollere videntur ei, qui amicitiam e vita tollunt, qua nihil a dis immortalibus melius
habemus, nihil iucundius. Quae est enim ista
securitas? Specie quidem blanda, sed reapse multis
locis repudianda. Neque enim est consentaneum
ullam honestam rem actionemve, ne sollicitus sis,
aut non suscipere aut susceptam deponere. Quod
si curam fugimus, virtus fugienda est, quae necesse
est cum aliqua cura res sibi contrarias aspernetur
atque oderit, ut bonitas malitiam, temperantia
libidinem, ignaviam fortitudo. Itaque videas rebus
iniustis iustos maxime dolere, imbellibus fortis, flagi-
tiosis modestos. Ergo hoc proprium est animi bene
constituti, et laetari bonis rebus et dolere contrariis.

48 Quam ob rem si cadit in sapientem animi dolor,
qui profecto cadit, nisi ex eius animo exstirpatam
humanitatem arbitramur, quae causa est cur amicitiam funditus tollamus e vita, ne aliquas propter
eam suscipiamus molestias? Quid enim interest
motu animi sublato, non dico inter pecudem et
hominem, sed inter hominem et truncum aut saxum
aut quidvis generis eiusdem? Neque enim sunt
isti audiendi, qui virtutem duram et quasi ferream
esse quandam volunt; quae quidem est cum multis
in rebus tum in amicitia tenera atque tractabilis,
ut et bonis amici quasi diffundatur et incommodis

---

[1] *i.e.* the Stoics.

accounted fortunate. O noble philosophy! Why, they seem to take the sun out of the universe when they deprive life of friendship, than which we have from the immortal gods no better, no more delightful boon. For of what value is their vaunted " freedom from care " ? In appearance it is indeed an alluring thing, but in reality often to be shunned. For it is inconsistent not to undertake any honourable business or course of conduct, or to lay it aside when undertaken, in order to avoid anxiety. Nay, if we continually flee from trouble, we must also flee from Virtue, who necessarily meets with some trouble in rejecting and loathing things contrary to herself, as when kindness rejects ill-will, temperance lust, and bravery cowardice. And so you may see that it is the just who are most pained at injustice, the brave at cowardice, the self-restrained at profligacy. It is, therefore, characteristic of the well-ordered mind both to rejoice at good deeds and to be pained at the reverse.

Wherefore, if distress of mind befalls a wise man (as it certainly does unless we assume that human sympathy has been rooted out of his heart), why should we remove friendship entirely from our lives in order that we may suffer no worries on its account ? For when the soul is deprived of emotion, what difference is there—I do not say between man and the beasts of the field, but between man and a stock or a stone, or any such thing ? Nor are we to listen to those men [1] who maintain that virtue is hard and unyielding and is, as it were, something made of iron; whereas, in many relations of life, and especially in friendship, it is so pliable and elastic that it expands, so to speak, with a friend's

contrahatur. Quam ob rem angor iste, qui pro
amico saepe capiendus est, non tantum valet, ut
tollat e vita amicitiam, non plus quam ut virtutes,
quia non nullas curas et molestias afferunt, repu-
dientur.

XIV. Cum autem contrahat amicitiam, ut supra
dixi, si qua[1] significatio virtutis eluceat, ad quam se
similis animus applicet et adiungat, id cum contigit,
49 amor exoriatur necesse est. Quid enim tam absurdum quam delectari multis inanibus rebus, ut honore,
ut gloria, ut aedificio, ut vestitu cultuque corporis,
animante virtute praedito, eo qui vel amare vel, ut
ita dicam, redamare possit, non admodum delectari ? Nihil est enim remuneratione benevolentiae,
nihil vicissitudine studiorum officiorumque iucundius.
50 Quid ? si illud etiam addimus, quod recte addi potest,
nihil esse quod ad se rem ullam tam illiciat et tam
trahat quam ad amicitiam similitudo, concedetur
profecto verum esse, ut bonos boni diligant ascis-
cantque sibi quasi propinquitate coniunctos atque
natura. Nihil est enim appetentius similium sui nec
rapacius quam natura. Quam ob rem hoc quidem,
Fanni et Scaevola, constet, ut opinor, bonis inter
bonos quasi necessariam benevolentiam, qui est
amicitiae fons a natura constitutus. Sed eadem
bonitas etiam ad multitudinem pertinet. Non enim
est inhumana virtus neque immunis neque superba,
quae etiam populos universos tueri eisque optime

---

[1] si qua *M* ; si quasi *Reid* ; sic quasi *GBS* ; si qua quasi *D.*

---

[1] Cicero coins the word *redamare* from the Greek ἀντιφιλεῖν,
but uses it nowhere else.

prosperity and contracts with his adversity. Wherefore, that mental anguish of which I spoke and which often must be felt on a friend's account, has no more power to banish friendship from life than it has to cause us to reject virtue because virtue entails certain cares and annoyances.

XIV. But, since, as I said before, virtue knits friendship together, if there should be some exhibition of shining virtue to which a kindred spirit may attach and adjust itself, then, when that happens, love must needs spring forth. For is there anything so absurd as to delight in many inanimate things, like public office, fame, and stately buildings, or dress and personal adornment, and to take little or no delight in a sentient being endowed with virtue and capable of loving, and—if I may so term it—of loving back[1]? For nothing gives more pleasure than the return of goodwill and the interchange of zealous service. And what if I also add, as I may fairly do, that nothing so allures and attracts anything to itself as likeness does to friendship? Then it surely will be granted as a fact that good men love and join to themselves other good men, in a union which is almost that of relationship and nature. For there is nothing more eager or more greedy than nature for what is like itself. Wherefore, because of this very fact, I think it should be evident, Fannius and Scaevola, that the good have for the good, as if from necessity, a kindly feeling which nature has made the fountain of friendship. But this same goodness belongs also to the generality of men. For virtue is not unfeeling, unwilling to serve, or proudly exclusive, but it is her wont to protect even whole nations and to plan the best measures for their welfare, which she

consulere soleat, quod non faceret profecto, si e
caritate volgi abhorreret.

51 Atque etiam mihi quidem videntur, qui utilitatis
causa fingunt amicitias, amabilissimum nodum
amicitiae tollere. Non enim tam utilitas parta per
amicum quam amici amor ipse delectat, tumque
illud fit, quod ab amico est profectum, iucundum,
si cum studio est profectum. Tantumque abest ut
amicitiae propter indigentiam colantur, ut ei, qui
opibus et copiis maximeque virtute, in qua plurimum
est praesidi, minime alterius indigeant, liberalis
simi sint et beneficentissimi. Atque haud sciam an
ne opus sit quidem nihil umquam omnino deesse
amicis. Ubi enim studia nostra viguissent, si numquam consilio, numquam opera nostra nec domi nec
militiae Scipio eguisset? Non igitur utilitatem
amicitia, sed utilitas amicitiam secuta est.

52 XV. Non ergo erunt homines deliciis diffluentes
audiendi, si quando de amicitia, quam nec usu nec
ratione habent cognitam, disputabunt. Nam quis
est, pro deorum fidem atque hominum! qui velit,
ut neque diligat quemquam nec ipse ab ullo diligatur,
circumfluere omnibus copiis atque in omnium rerum
abundantia vivere? Haec enim est tyrannorum
vita, nimirum in qua nulla fides, nulla caritas, nulla

---

[1] *i.e.* those referred to in §46 *ad init.*, the Cyrenaics
followers of Aristippus of Cyrene.

[2] But *cf.* § 30 : *Quid enim ? Africanus indigens mei ?*

[3] *i.e.* Epicureans and Cyrenaics, referred to in § 46

certainly would not do if she disdained the affection of the common mass.

And again, it seems to me at any rate, that those who [1] falsely assume expediency to be the basis of friendship, take from friendship's chain its loveliest link. For it is not so much the material gain procured through a friend, as it is his love, and his love alone, that gives us delight; and that advantage which we derive from him becomes a pleasure only when his service is inspired by an ardent zeal. And it is far from being true that friendship is cultivated because of need; rather, is it cultivated by those who are most abundantly blessed with wealth and power and especially with virtue, which is man's best defence; by those least in need of another's help; and by those most generous and most given to acts of kindness. Indeed, I should be inclined to think that it is not well for friends never to need anything at all. Wherein, for example, would my zeal have displayed itself if Scipio had never been in need of my advice or assistance either at home or abroad? [2] It is not the case, therefore, that friendship attends upon advantage, but, on the contrary, that advantage attends upon friendship.

XV. It will be our duty, then, not to listen to those besotted men of pleasure [3] when they argue about friendship, of which they understand neither the practice nor the theory. For what person is there, in the name of gods and men! who would wish to be surrounded by unlimited wealth and to abound in every material blessing, on condition that he love no one and that no one love him? Such indeed is the life of tyrants—a life, I mean, in which there can be no faith, no affection, no trust in the

stabilis benevolentiae potest esse fiducia, omnia
semper suspecta atque sollicita, nullus locus amicitiae.
53 Quis enim aut eum diligat, quem metuat, aut eum,
a quo se metui putet ? Coluntur tamen simulatione
dumtaxat ad tempus. Quod si forte, ut fit plerumque, ceciderint, tum intellegitur quam fuerint inopes amicorum. Quod Tarquinium dixisse ferunt
exulantem, tum se intellexisse, quos fidos amicos
habuisset, quos infidos, cum iam neutris gratiam
referre posset.

54 Quamquam miror, illa superbia et importunitate, si
quemquam amicum habere potuit. Atque ut huius,
quem dixi, mores veros amicos parare non potuerunt,
sic multorum opes praepotentium excludunt amicitias
fidelis. Non enim solum ipsa fortuna caeca est, sed
eos etiam plerumque efficit caecos, quos complexa
est ; itaque efferuntur fere fastidio et contumacia,
nec quicquam insipiente fortunato intolerabilius fieri
potest. Atque hoc quidem videre licet, eos, qui
antea commodis fuerint moribus, imperio potestate
prosperis rebus immutari, sperni ab eis veteres ami-
55 citias, indulgeri novis. Quid autem stultius quam,
cum plurimum copiis facultatibus opibus possint,
cetera parare, quae parantur pecunia, equos famulos
vestem egregiam vasa pretiosa, amicos non parare,
optimam et pulcherrimam vitae, ut ita dicam, supel-
lectilem ? Etenim cetera cum parant, cui parent

continuance of goodwill; where every act arouses
suspicion and anxiety and where friendship has no
place. For can anyone love either the man whom
he fears, or the man by whom he believes himself
to be feared? Yet tyrants are courted under a
pretence of affection, but only for a season. For
when by chance they have fallen from power, as
they generally do, then is it known how poor they
were in friends. And this is illustrated by the
remark said to have been made by Tarquin as he
was going into exile: " I have learned what friends
of mine are true and what are false, now that I am
no longer able to reward or punish either."

And yet, such was the haughtiness and perversity
of the man that I wonder if he could have had
anyone as a friend. Now just as the character of
Tarquin could not procure him true friends, so, with
many, their power, if it be very great, is a bar to
faithful friendships. For not only is Fortune blind
herself, but as a rule she even blinds those whom
she has embraced; and thus they are generally
transported beyond themselves by wanton pride
and obstinacy—nor can anything in the world be
more insufferable than one of Fortune's fools.
Indeed we may observe that men, formerly affable
in their manners, become changed by military rank,
by power, and by prosperity, spurn their old-time
friends and revel in the new. But what is more
foolish, when men are in the plenitude of resources,
opportunities, and wealth, than to procure the other
things which money provides—horses, slaves, splendid
raiment, and costly plate—and not procure friends,
who are, if I may say so, life's best and fairest
furniture? And really while they are procuring

nesciunt nec cuius causa laborent; eius enim est
istorum quidque qui vicit viribus; amicitiarum sua
cuique permanet stabilis et certa possessio, ut etiam
si illa maneant, quae sunt quasi dona fortunae, tamen
vita inculta et deserta ab amicis non possit esse
iucunda. Sed haec hactenus.

56 XVI. Constituendi autem sunt, qui sint in amicitia
fines et quasi termini diligendi. De quibis tris video
sententias ferri, quarum nullam probo : unam, ut
eodem modo erga amicum affecti simus quo erga
nosmet ipsos ; alteram, ut nostra in amicos benevolentia illorum erga nos benevolentiae pariter
aequaliterque respondeat ; tertiam, ut, quanti
57 quisque se ipse facit, tanti fiat ab amicis. Harum
trium sententiarum nulli prorsus assentior. Nec
enim illa prima vera est, ut, quem ad modum in se
quisque, sic in amicum sit animatus. Quam multa
enim, quae nostra causa numquam faceremus,
facimus causa amicorum ! Precari ab indigno, sup-
plicare, tum acerbius in aliquem invehi insectarique
vehementius, quae in nostris rebus non satis honeste,
in amicorum fiunt honestissime ; multaeque res
sunt, in quibus de suis commodis viri boni multa
detrahunt detrahique patiuntur, ut eis amici potius
quam ipsi fruantur.

58 Altera sententia est quae definit amicitiam pari-

those material things, they know not for whom they do it, nor for whose benefit they toil; for such things are the prey of the strongest; but to every man the tenure of his friendships ever remains settled and sure, so that even if there should be a continuance of those things which are, so to speak, the gratuities of fortune, yet life unadorned and unattended by friends could not be pleasant. But enough on this point.

XVI. We now have to determine in our discussion of friendship what are the limits and, so to speak, the boundary lines of affection. On this point I observe that three views are usually advanced, none of which I approve: first, "That we should have the same feeling for our friends that we have for ourselves"; second, "That our goodwill towards our friends should correspond in all respects to their goodwill towards us," and third, "That whatever value a man places upon himself, the same value should be placed upon him by his friends." I do not agree at all with any of these views. Certainly the first one is not true which holds that "as a man feels towards himself, so should he feel towards his friend." For how many things we do for our friends that we never would do for ourselves! At one time we beg and entreat an unworthy man, and again we assail another too sharply or too loudly rail upon him—things not quite creditable in our own affairs, but exceedingly so in behalf of our friends; and there are numerous occasions when good men forgo, or permit themselves to be deprived of, many conveniences in order that their friends rather than themselves may enjoy them.

The second view limits friendship to an equal

bus officiis ac voluntatibus. Hoc quidem est nimis exigue et exiliter ad calculos vocare amicitiam, ut par sit ratio acceptorum et datorum. Divitior mihi et affluentior videtur esse vera amicitia nec observare restricte ne plus reddat quam acceperit : neque enim verendum est ne quid excidat aut ne quid in terram defluat aut ne plus aequo quid in amicitiam congeratur.

59 Tertius vero ille finis deterrimus, ut, quanti quisque se ipse faciat, tanti fiat ab amicis. Saepe enim in quibusdam aut animus abiectior est aut spes amplificandae fortunae fractior. Non est igitur amici talem esse in eum, qualis ille in se est, sed potius eniti et efficere ut amici iacentem animum excitet inducatque spem cogitationemque meliorem. Alius igitur finis verae amicitiae constituendus est, si prius, quid maxime reprehendere Scipio solitus sit, dixero. Negabat ullam vocem inimiciorem amicitiae potuisse reperiri quam eius qui dixisset ita amare oportere ut si aliquando esset osurus ; nec vero se adduci posse ut hoc, quem ad modum putaretur, a Biante esse dictum crederet, qui sapiens habitus esset unus e septem ; impuri cuiusdam aut ambitiosi aut omnia ad suam potentiam revocantis

---

[1] Aristotle, *Rhet.* ii. 13 κατὰ τὴν Βίαντος ὑποθήκην καὶ φιλοῦσιν ὡς μισήσοντες καὶ μισοῦσιν ὡς φιλήσοντες.

interchange of services and feelings. It surely is calling friendship to a very close and petty accounting to require it to keep an exact balance of credits and debits. I think true friendship is richer and more abundant than that and does not narrowly scan the reckoning lest it pay out more than it has received ; and there need be no fear that some bit of kindness will be lost, that it will overflow the measure and spill upon the ground, or that more than is due will be poured into friendship's bin.

But worst of all is the third limitation, which is that " whatever value a man places upon himself, the same value should be placed upon him by his friends." For often in some men either the spirit is too dejected, or the hope of bettering their fortune is too faint. Therefore, it is not the province of a friend, in such a case, to have the same estimate of another that the other has of himself, but rather it is his duty to strive with all his might to arouse his friend's prostrate soul and lead it to a livelier hope and into a better train of thought. Hence some other limitation of true friendship must be fixed, after I have first stated a view which Scipio used to condemn in the strongest terms. He often said that no utterance could be found more at war with friendship than that of the man who had made this remark : " We should love as if at some time we were going to hate." And Scipio really could not, he said, be induced to adopt the commonly accepted belief that this expression was made by Bias,[1] who was counted one of the Seven Sages ; but he thought that it was the speech of some abandoned wretch, or scheming politician, or of someone who regarded everything as an instru-

esse sententiam. Quonam enim modo quisquam
amicus esse poterit ei, cui se putabit inimicum esse
posse ? Quin etiam necesse erit cupere et optare
ut quam saepissime peccet amicus, quo pluris det
sibi tamquam ansas ad reprehendendum : rursum
autem recte factis commodisque amicorum necesse
60 erit angi dolere invidere. Qua re hoc quidem prae-
ceptum, cuiuscumque est, ad tollendam amicitiam
valet : illud potius praecipiendum fuit, ut eam
diligentiam adhiberemus in amicitiis comparandis,
ut ne quando amare inciperemus eum, quem aliquando odisse possemus. Quin etiam si minus
felices in deligendo fuissemus, ferendum id Scipio
potius quam inimicitiarum tempus cogitandum
putabat.
61 XVII. His igitur finibus utendum arbitror, ut,
cum emendati mores amicorum sint, tum sit inter eos
omnium rerum consiliorum voluntatum sine ulla
exceptione communitas, ut etiam si qua fortuna
acciderit ut minus iustae amicorum voluntates
adiuvandae sint, in quibus eorum aut caput agatur
aut fama, declinandum de via sit, modo ne summa
turpitudo sequatur ; est enim quatenus amicitiae
dari venia possit. Nec vero neglegenda est fama,
nec mediocre telum ad res gerendas existimare
oportet benevolentiam civium, quam blanditiis et
assentando colligere turpe est ; virtus, quam sequitur
caritas, minime repudianda est.

---

[1] This is apparently at variance with § 40 *turpis enim
excusatio est*, etc.

ment to serve his own selfish ends. For how will it be possible for anyone to be a friend to a man who, he believes, may be his foe ? Nay, in such a case it will be necessary also for him to desire and pray that his friend may sin as often as possible and thereby give him, as it were, the more handles to lay hold of ; and, again, he will be bound to feel grief, pain and envy at the good deeds and good fortune of his friends. Wherefore this maxim, whoever its author, really has the effect of destroying friendship : rather ought we to have been enjoined to exercise such care in forming friendships that we should never begin to love anyone whom we might sometime hate. Indeed, Scipio thought that, even if we had been unfortunate in our choice, we should endure it rather than plan an opportunity for a breach.

XVII. Therefore, these are the limits which I think ought to be observed, namely : when the characters of friends are blameless, then there should be between them complete harmony of opinions and inclinations in everything without any exception ; and, even if by some chance the wishes of a friend are not altogether honourable and require to be forwarded in matters which involve his life or reputation, we should turn aside from the straight path, provided, however, utter disgrace does not follow ;[1] for there are limits to the indulgence which can be allowed to friendship. Nor indeed ought a man either to disregard his reputation, or to consider the goodwill of his countrymen a poor weapon in the battle of life, though to hunt after it with fawning and flattery is disgraceful ; as to virtue we must by no means abjure it, for it is attended by regard.

62 Sed—saepe enim redeo ad Scipionem, cuius omnis sermo erat de amicitia—querebatur quod omnibus in rebus homines diligentiores essent; capras et ovis quot quisque haberet dicere posse, amicos quot haberet non posse dicere; et in illis quidem parandis adhibere curam, in amicis eligendis neglegentis esse nec habere quasi signa quaedam et notas, quibus eos, qui ad amicitiam essent idonei, iudicarent. Sunt igitur firmi et stabiles et constantes eligendi, cuius generis est magna penuria; et iudicare difficile est sane nisi expertum, experiendum autem est in ipsa amicitia: ita praecurrit amicitia iudicium

63 tollitque experiendi potestatem. Est igitur prudentis sustinere ut cursum, sic impetum benevolentiae, quo utamur, quasi equis temptatis, sic amicitia, aliqua parte periclitatis moribus amicorum. Quidam saepe in parva pecunia perspiciuntur quam sint leves; quidam autem, quos parva movere non potuit, cognoscuntur in magna. Sin vero erunt aliqui reperti qui pecuniam praeferre amicitiae sordidum existiment, ubi eos inveniemus, qui honores magistratus imperia potestates opes amicitiae non anteponant, ut, cum ex altera parte proposita haec sint, ex altera ius amicitiae, non multo illa malint? Imbecilla enim est natura ad contemnendam potentiam, quam etiam si neglecta amicitia consecuti sint, obscuratum

---

[1] *Cf.* Xen. *Mem.* ii. 4. 4; *ib.* ii. 4. 1.

But Scipio—and I often recur to him, my sole authority for a discourse on friendship—Scipio used to complain that men were more painstaking in all other things than in friendship ; that everybody could tell how many goats and sheep he had,[1] but was unable to tell the number of his friends ; and that men took pains in getting the former, but were careless in choosing the latter, and had no certain signs, or marks, so to speak, by which to determine their fitness for friendship. We ought, therefore, to choose men who are firm, steadfast and constant, a class of which there is a great dearth ; and at the same time it is very hard to come to a decision without a trial, while such trial can only be made in actual friendship : thus friendship outruns the judgement and takes away the opportunity of a trial. Hence it is the part of wisdom to check the headlong rush of goodwill as we would that of a chariot, and thereby so manage friendship that we may in some degree put the dispositions of friends, as we do those of horses, to a preliminary test. Some men often give proof in a petty money transaction how unstable they are ; while others, who could not have been influenced by a trivial sum, are discovered in one that is large. But if any shall be found who think it base to prefer money to friendship, where shall we find those who do not put office, civil and military rank, high place and power, above friendship, so that when the former advantages are placed before them on one side and the latter on the other they will not much prefer the former ? For feeble is the struggle of human nature against power, and when men have attained it even by the disregard of friendship they imagine the sin will be forgotten because

iri arbitrantur, quia non sine magna causa sit neglecta
64 amicitia. Itaque verae amicitiae difficillime reperiuntur in eis, qui in honoribus reque publica versantur.
Ubi enim istum invenias, qui honorem amici ante-
ponat suo ? Quid ? haec ut omittam, quam graves,
quam difficiles plerisque videntur calamitatum socie-
tates, ad quas non est facile inventu qui descendant.
Quamquam Ennius recte :

> amicus certus in re incerta cernitur ;

tamen haec duo levitatis et infirmitatis plerosque
convincunt, aut si in bonis rebus contemnunt aut in
malis deserunt. Qui igitur utraque in re gravem
constantem stabilem se in amicitia praestiterit, hunc
ex maxime raro genere hominum iudicare debemus
et paene divino.

65   XVIII. Firmamentum autem stabilitatis constan-
tiaeque est eius quam[1] in amicitia quaerimus
fides est ; nihil est enim stabile, quod infidum est.
Simplicem praeterea et communem et consentien-
tem, id est, qui rebus isdem moveatur, elegi par est ;
quae omnia pertinent ad fidelitatem. Neque enim
fidum potest esse multiplex ingenium et tortuosum,
neque vero, qui non isdem rebus movetur naturaque

[1] quam MSS., quem Reid.

---

[1] Cf. De nat. deor. ii. 54. 136 alvus multiplex et tortuosa.
174

friendship was not disregarded without a weighty
cause. Therefore, true friendships are very hard
to find among those whose time is spent in office
or in business of a public kind. For where can you
find a man so high-minded as to prefer his friend's
advancement to his own ? And, passing by material
considerations, pray consider this : how grievous
and how hard to most persons does association in
another's misfortunes appear ! Nor is it easy to
find men who will go down to calamity's depths
for a friend. Ennius, however, is right when he
says :

When Fortune's fickle the faithful friend is found ;

yet it is on these two charges that most men are
convicted of fickleness : they either hold a friend
of little value when their own affairs are prosperous,
or they abandon him when his are adverse. Whoever, therefore, in either of these contingencies, has
shown himself staunch, immovable, and firm in
friendship ought to be considered to belong to that
class of men which is exceedingly rare—aye, almost
divine.

XVIII. Now the support and stay of that unswerving
constancy, which we look for in friendship, is loyalty ;
for nothing is constant that is disloyal. Moreover,
the right course is to choose for a friend one who
is frank, sociable, and sympathetic—that is, one
who is likely to be influenced by the same motives
as yourself—since all these qualities conduce to
loyalty ; for it is impossible for a man to be loyal
whose nature is full of twists and twinings[1] ; and,
indeed, one who is untouched by the same influences as yourself and is naturally unsympathetic

consentit, aut fidus aut stabilis potest esse. Addendum eodem est, ut ne criminibus aut inferendis delectetur aut credat oblatis, quae pertinent omnia ad eam, quam iam dudum tracto, constantiam. Ita fit verum illud, quod initio dixi, amicitiam nisi inter bonos esse non posse.

Est enim boni viri, quem eundem sapientem licet dicere, haec duo tenere in amicitia : primum, ne quid fictum sit neve simulatum ; aperte enim vel odisse magis ingenui est quam fronte occultare sententiam ; deinde non solum ab aliquo allatas criminationes repellere, sed ne ipsum quidem esse suspiciosum, semper aliquid existimantem ab amico 66 esse violatum. Accedat huc suavitas quaedam oportet sermonum atque morum, haudquaquam mediocre condimentum amicitiae. Tristitia autem et in omni re severitas habet illa quidem gravitatem, sed amicitia remissior esse debet et liberior et dulcior et ad omnem comitatem facilitatemque proclivior.

67 XIX. Exsistit autem hoc loco quaedam quaestio subdifficilis, num quando amici novi, digni amicitia, veteribus sint anteponendi, ut equis vetulis teneros anteponere solemus. Indigna homine dubitatio ; non enim debent esse amicitiarum, sicut aliarum rerum, satietates ; veterrima quaeque, ut ea vina quae vetustatem ferunt, esse debent suavissima, verumque illud est, quod dicitur, multos modios salis simul edendos esse, ut amicitiae munus expletum

---

[1] *Supra*, § 18.

cannot be either loyal or steadfast. To this observation should be added a requirement tending to produce that steadfastness, which I have been discussing for some time: a friend must neither take pleasure in bringing charges against you nor believe them when made by others. And so, the truth of what I said in the beginning is established: " Friendship cannot exist except among good men."[1]

For it is characteristic of the good man, whom I may also call the wise man, to maintain these two rules in friendship: first, let there be no feigning or hypocrisy; for it is more befitting a candid man to hate openly than to mask his real thoughts with a lying face; secondly, let him not only reject charges preferred by another, but also let him avoid even being suspicious and ever believing that his friend has done something wrong. To this should be added a certain affability of speech and manner, which gives no mean flavour to friendship. While unvarying seriousness and gravity are indeed impressive, yet friendship ought to be more unrestrained, genial, and agreeable, and more inclined to be wholly courteous and urbane.

XIX. But at this point there arises a certain question of some little difficulty: Are new friends who are worthy of friendship, at any time to be preferred to old friends, as we are wont to prefer young horses to old ones? The doubt is unworthy of a human being, for there should be no surfeit of friendships as there is of other things; and, as in the case of wines that improve with age, the oldest friendships ought to be the most delightful; moreover, the well-known adage is true: " Men must eat many a peck of salt together before the claims of

68 sit. Novitates autem, si spem afferunt, ut tamquam
in herbis non fallacibus fructus appareat, non sunt
illae quidem repudiandae, vetustas tamen suo loco
conservanda ; maxima est enim vis vetustatis et
consuetudinis. Quin in ipso[1] equo, cuius modo feci
mentionem, si nulla res impediat, nemo est quin eo,
quo consuevit, libentius utatur quam intractato et
novo ; nec vero in hoc, quod est animal, sed in eis
etiam, quae sunt inanima, consuetudo valet, cum
locis ipsis delectemur, montuosis etiam et silves-
tribus, in quibus diutius commorati sumus.

69 Sed maximum est in amicitia superiorem parem
esse inferiori. Saepe enim excellentiae quaedam
sunt, qualis erat Scipionis in nostro, ut ita dicam,
grege. Numquam se ille Philo, numquam Rupilio,
numquam Mummio anteposuit, numquam inferioris
ordinis amicis. Q. vero Maximum fratrem, egregium
virum omnino, sibi nequaquam parem, quod is
anteibat aetate, tamquam superiorem colebat suos-
70 que omnis per se posse esse ampliores volebat. Quod
faciendum imitandumque est omnibus, ut, si quam
praestantiam virtutis ingeni fortunae consecuti sunt,
impertiant ea suis communicentque cum proximis ;
ut, si parentibus nati sint humilibus, si propinquos
habeant imbecilliore vel animo vel fortuna, eorum
augeant opes eisque honori sint et dignitati. Ut
in fabulis, qui aliquamdiu propter ignorationem

---

[1] quin in ipso *Bennett from Cornell* MS. ; qui in ipso *P* ;
quin et in ipso *GBESV* ; *Reid has* ipso equo.

---

[1] *Cf.* Aristot. *Eth. Eudem.* vii. 2 ; *Eth. Nic.* viii. 3. 8.

friendship are fulfilled."[1] But new friendships are
not to be scorned if they offer hope of bearing fruit,
like green shoots of corn that do not disappoint us
at harvest-time; yet the old friendships must
preserve their own place, for the force of age and
habit is very great. Nay, even in the case of the
horse just now referred to, everybody, nothing
preventing, would rather use one to which he has
grown accustomed than one that is untrained and
new. And habit is strong in the case not only of
animate, but also of inanimate things, since we
delight even in places, though rugged and wild, in
which we have lived for a fairly long time.

But it is of the utmost importance in friendship
that superior and inferior should stand on an equality.
For oftentimes a certain pre-eminence does exist,
as was that of Scipio in what I may call " our set."
But he never affected any superiority over Philus, or
Rupilius, or Mummius, or over his other friends of
a lower rank. For example, his brother Quintus
Maximus, a distinguished man, no doubt, though
by no means his equal, was treated by him as a
superior, because he was older than himself. Indeed
Scipio desired that he might be the cause of enhancing
the dignity of all his friends. And this course every
man should adopt and imitate, so that if he is endowed
with any superiority in virtue, intellect, or fortune
he may impart it to his relatives and share it with
his next of kin; or if, for example, his parents are
of a lowly station and his relatives are less favoured
in mind or estate than himself, he may increase
the means of the one and be the source of honour
and influence to the other; as in legends, men who
have for a long time lived the life of menials, because

179

stirpis et generis in famulatu fuerunt, cum cogniti
sunt et aut deorum aut regum filii inventi, retinent
tamen caritatem in pastores, quos patres multos
annos esse duxerunt.   Quod est multo profecto
magis in veris patribus certisque faciendum.   Fructus
enim ingeni et virtutis omnisque praestantiae tum
maximus capitur, cum in proximum quemque con-
fertur.

71   XX. Ut igitur ei, qui sunt in amicitiae coniunc-
tionisque necessitudine superiores, exaequare se cum
inferioribus debent, sic inferiores non dolere se a
suis aut ingenio aut fortuna aut dignitate superari.
Quorum plerique aut queruntur semper aliquid aut
etiam exprobrant, eoque magis si habere se putant
quod officiose et amice et cum labore. aliquo suo
factum queant dicere. Odiosum sane genus hominum
officia exprobrantium, quae meminisse debet is,
in quem collata sunt, non commemorare qui contulit.

72 Quam ob rem, ut ei, qui superiores sunt, submittere
se debent in amicitia, sic quodam modo inferiores
extollere.   Sunt enim quidam qui molestas amicitias
faciunt cum ipsi se contemni putant — quod non
fere contingit nisi eis qui etiam contemnendos se
arbitrantur ; qui hac opinione non modo verbis, sed
73 etiam opera[1] levandi sunt. Tantum autem cuique
tribuendum, primum quantum ipse efficere possis,
deinde etiam quantum ille, quem diligas atque

---

[1] opera *Reid* ; opere MSS.

---

[1] *Cf.* Seneca, *De benef.* ii. 10. 4 *haec enim beneficii inter*
duos lex est ; alter statim oblivisci dati, alter accepti
nunquam.

their lineage and family were unknown, although discovered and found to be the sons of gods or of kings, nevertheless retain affection for the shepherds whom for many years they regarded as their parents. And surely such a feeling ought to be much stronger in the case of real and undoubted parents. For the fruit of genius, of virtue, and, indeed, of every excellence, imparts its sweetest flavour when bestowed on those who are nearest and dearest to us.

XX. As, therefore, in the intimacy existing between friends and relatives the superior should put himself on a level with his inferior, so the latter ought not to grieve that he is surpassed by the former in intellect, fortune, or position. But many of the latter kind are continually uttering some complaints or reproaches even, especially if they think that they have done anything which they can speak of as an act of duty and of friendship, involving a certain amount of toil. A very disagreeable class of people, certainly, are those who are ever obtruding their own services, which ought to be kept in mind by him for whom they were performed and should not be mentioned by him who performed them.[1] As, therefore, in friendship, those who are superior should lower themselves, so, in a measure, should they lift up their inferiors. For there are certain men who render friendships disagreeable by thinking themselves slighted—a thing which rarely happens, except in the case of persons who think that they really deserve to be slighted ; but they ought to be relieved of such an opinion not by words only but by action. Now, in the first place, you must render to each friend as much aid as you can, and, in the second place, as much as he whom you love

adiuves, sustinere. Non enim neque tu possis,
quamvis excellas, omnis tuos ad honores amplissimos
perducere, ut Scipio P. Rupilium potuit consulem
efficere, fratrem eius Lucium non potuit. Quod si
etiam possis quidvis deferre ad alterum, videndum
est tamen quid ille possit sustinere.

74 Omnino amicitiae corroboratis iam confirmatisque
et ingeniis et aetatibus iudicandae sunt; nec, si qui
ineunte aetate venandi aut pilae studiosi fuerunt,
eos habere necessarios, quos tum eodem studio prae-
ditos dilexerunt. Isto enim modo nutrices et paeda-
gogi iure vetustatis plurimum benevolentiae postu-
labunt. Qui neglegendi quidem non sunt, sed alio
quodam modo aestimandi[1]; aliter amicitiae stabiles
permanere non possunt. Disparis enim mores disparia
studia sequuntur, quorum dissimilitudo dissociat amicitias; nec ob aliam causam ullam boni improbis,
improbi bonis amici esse non possunt, nisi quod
tanta est inter eos, quanta maxima potest esse,
morum studiorumque distantia.

75 Recte etiam praecipi potest in amicitiis, ne in-
temperata quaedam benevolentia, quod persaepe fit,
impediat magnas utilitates amicorum. Nec enim,
ut ad fabulas redeam, Troiam Neoptolemus capere

---

[1] aestimandi *Mommsen's conjec. for* est *or* est. et *MSS.*

---

[1] *i.e.* only by forming friendships when we are mature
in mind and in age.

and assist has the capacity to bear. For however eminent you may be, you cannot lead all your friends through the various grades to the highest official rank, as Scipio was able to do when he made Publius Rutilius consul, though he could not accomplish this result in the case of his brother, Lucius Rutilius. But even if you could bestow upon another any honour you chose, yet you must consider what he is able to bear.

As a rule decisions about friendships should be formed after strength and stability have been reached in mind and age ; nor should men who in boyhood were devoted to hunting and games of ball, keep as their intimates those whom they loved at that period simply because they were fond of the same pursuits. For on that principle nurses and the slaves who attended us to and from school, will, by right of priority of acquaintance, claim the largest share of our goodwill. I admit that they are not to be neglected, but they are to be regarded in an entirely different way ; under no other conditions can friendship remain secure.[1] For difference of character is attended by difference of taste and it is this diversity of taste that severs friendships ; nor is there any other cause why good men cannot be friends to wicked men, or wicked men to good men, except that there is the greatest possible distance between them in character and in taste.

This rule also may properly be prescribed in friendship : Let not a sort of ungoverned goodwill (as very frequently happens) hinder your friends' advantage in important matters. For indeed, if I may go back to legends, Neoptolemus could not have taken Troy if he had been willing to listen to Lyco-

potuisset, si Lycomeden, apud quem erat educatus,
multis cum lacrimis iter suum impedientem audire
voluisset. Et saepe incidunt magnae res, ut dis-
cedendum sit ab amicis ; quas qui impedire volt,
quod desiderium non facile ferat, is et infirmus est
mollisque natura et ob eam ipsam causam in amicitia
76 parum iustus. Atque in omni re considerandum est
et quid postules ab amico et quid patiare a te
impetrari.

XXI. Est etiam quaedam calamitas in amicitiis
dimittendis non numquam necessaria—iam enim a
sapientium familiaritatibus ad volgaris amicitias
oratio nostra delabitur. Erumpunt saepe vitia
amicorum tum in ipsos amicos, tum in alienos,
quorum tamen ad amicos redundet infamia. Tales
igitur amicitiae sunt remissione usus eluendae et,
ut Catonem dicere audivi, dissuendae magis quam
discindendae, nisi quaedam admodum intolerabilis
iniuria exarserit, ut neque rectum neque honestum
sit nec fieri possit ut non statim alienatio disiunc-
tioque facienda sit.

77 Sin autem aut morum aut studiorum commutatio
quaedam, ut fieri solet, facta erit, aut in rei publicae
partibus dissensio intercesserit (loquor enim iam,

---

[1] *Cf.* § 32 *verae amicitiae sempiternae sunt.*

medes, by whom he had been reared and who endeavoured with many tears to hinder him from setting out. Often, too, important duties arise which require the temporary separation of friends ; and he who would hinder the discharge of those duties because he cannot easily bear his grief at the absence of his friends, is not only weak and effeminate, but, on that very account, is far from reasonable in his friendship. In brief, it is your duty on every occasion to consider carefully both what you will demand from a friend and what you will permit him to obtain when he makes a demand on you.

XXI. Furthermore, there is a sort of disaster in connexion with breaking off friendships—for now our discussion descends from the intimacies of the wise to friendships of the ordinary kind [1]—which is sometimes unavoidable. There are often in friends outbursts of vice which affect sometimes their actual friends, sometimes strangers, yet so that the infamy of the evil flows over on to the friends. Therefore the ties of such friendships should be sundered by a gradual relaxation of intimacy, and, as I have heard that Cato used to say, "They should be unravelled rather than rent apart," unless there has been some outbreak of utterly unbearable wrongdoing, so that the only course consistent with rectitude and honour, and indeed the only one possible, is to effect an immediate withdrawal of affection and association.

But if, on the other hand, as usually happens, a mere change of disposition and of tastes should occur, or if a difference in political views should arise (for I am talking now, as I said a moment ago,

ut paulo ante dixi, non de sapientium, sed de communibus amicitiis) cavendum erit ne non solum amicitiae depositae, sed etiam inimicitiae susceptae videantur. Nihil enim est turpius quam cum eo bellum gerere, quocum familiariter vixeris. Ab amicitia Q. Pompei meo nomine se removerat, ut scitis, Scipio ; propter dissensicnem autem, quae erat in re publica, alienatus est a collega nostro Metello ; utrumque egit graviter ac moderate[1] et

78 offensione animi non acerba. Quam ob rem primum danda opera est ne qua amicorum discidia fiant, sin tale aliquid evenerit, ut exstinctae potius amicitiae quam oppressae esse videantur. Cavendum vero ne etiam in gravis inimicitias convertant se amicitiae ex quibus iurgia maledicta contumeliae gignuntur. Quae tamen si tolerabiles erunt, ferendae sunt et hic honos veteri amicitiae tribuendus, ut is in culpa sit qui faciat, non is qui patiatur, iniuriam.

Omnino omnium horum vitiorum atque incommodorum una cautio est atque una provisio, ut ne

79 nimis cito diligere incipiant neve non dignos. Digni autem sunt amicitia, quibus in ipsis inest causa cur diligantur. Rarum genus! et quidem omnia praeclara, rara, nec quicquam difficilius quam reperire quod sit omni ex parte in suo genere perfectum. Sed plerique neque in rebus humanis quicquam bonum norunt nisi

---

[1] graviter ac moderate *Reid* ; graviter auctoritate *MSS.*

---

[1] He won his election over Laelius by pretending that he was not a candidate, thus throwing Laelius off his guard.

not of friendships existing between wise men, but of those of the ordinary kind), care must be taken lest it appear, not only that friendship has been put aside, but that open hostility has been aroused. For nothing is more discreditable than to be at war with one with whom you have lived on intimate terms. Scipio, as you both know, had severed his friendship with Quintus Pompeius on my account;[1] and, moreover, because of a disagreement in politics, was estranged from my colleague, Metellus; he acted with deliberation and moderation in each instance, and without any bitter feeling of resentment. Wherefore, in the first place, pains must be taken that, if possible, no discord should arise between friends, but in case it does, then our care should be that the friendships appear to have burned out rather than to have been stamped out. And you must indeed be on your guard lest friendships be changed into serious enmities, which are the source of disputes, abuse, and invective. Yet even these, if endurable, are to be borne, and such respect is to be paid to the old-time friendship that he may be in the wrong who committed the offence and not he who suffered it.

In short : there is but one security and one provision against these ills and annoyances, and that is, neither to enlist your love too quickly nor to fix it on unworthy men. Now they are worthy of friendship who have within their own souls the reason for their being loved. A rare class indeed ! And really everything splendid is rare, and nothing is harder to find than something which in all respects is a perfect specimen of its kind. But the majority of men recognize nothing whatever in human experi-

quod fructuosum sit, et amicos tamquam pecudes eos potissimum diligunt, ex quibus sperant se maximum 80 fructum esse capturos. Ita pulcherrima illa et maxime naturali carent amicitia per se et propter se expetita, nec ipsi sibi exemplo sunt, haec vis amicitiae et qualis et quanta sit. Ipse enim se quisque diligit, non ut aliquam a se ipse mercedem exigat caritatis suae, sed quod per se quisque sibi carus est ; quod nisi idem in amicitiam transferetur, verus amicus numquam reperietur : est enim is qui est tamquam alter idem.

81　Quod si hoc apparet in bestiis, volucribus nantibus agrestibus, cicuribus feris, primum ut se ipsae diligant—id enim pariter cum omni animante nascitur —deinde, ut requirant atque appetant ad quas se applicent eiusdem generis animantis—idque faciant cum desiderio et cum quadam similitudine amoris humani—quanto id magis in homine fit natura, qui et se ipse diligit et alterum anquirit, cuius animum ita cum suo misceat, ut efficiat paene unum ex duobus !

82　XXII. Sed plerique perverse, ne dicam impudenter, habere talem amicum volunt, quales ipsi esse non possunt, quaeque ipsi non tribuunt amicis, haec ab eis desiderant. Par est autem primum ipsum esse virum bonum, tum alterum similem sui quaerere. In talibus ea, quam iam dudum tractamus, stabilitas

ence as good unless it brings some profit and they
regard their friends as they do their cattle, valuing
most highly those which give hope of the largest
gain. Thus do they fail to attain that loveliest,
most spontaneous friendship, which is desirable
in and for itself; and they do not learn from their
own experience what the power of such friendship
is and are ignorant of its nature and extent. For
everyone loves himself, not with a view of acquiring
some profit for himself from his self-love, but because
he is dear to himself on his own account; and unless
this same feeling were transferred to friendship,
the real friend would never be found; for he is, as
it were, another self.

Now if it is evident in animals, whether of the
air, the water, or the land, and whether tame or
wild, first, that they love themselves—for this
feeling is born alike in every living creature—and,
secondly, that they require and eagerly search for
other animals of their own kind to which they may
attach themselves—and this they do with a longing in
some degree resembling human love—then how much
more, by the law of his nature, is this the case with
man who both loves himself and uses his reason to
seek out another whose soul he may so mingle with
his own as almost to make one out of two!

XXII. But most men unreasonably, not to say
shamelessly, want a friend to be such as they
cannot be themselves and require from friends what
they themselves do not bestow. But the fair thing
is, first of all, to be a good man yourself and
then to seek another like yourself. It is among
such men that this stability of friendship, of
which I have been treating for some time, may

189

amicitiae confirmari potest, cum homines benevolentia coniuncti primum cupiditatibus eis quibus ceteri
serviunt imperabunt; deinde aequitate iustitiaque
gaudebunt omniaque alter pro altero suscipiet; neque
quicquam umquam nisi honestum et rectum alter ab
altero postulabit, neque solum colent inter se ac
diligent, sed etiam verebuntur. Nam maximum
ornamentum amicitiae tollit, qui ex ea tollit vere-
83 cundiam. Itaque in eis perniciosus est error, qui
existimant libidinum peccatorumque omnium patere
in amicitia licentiam. Virtutum amicitia adiutrix
a natura data est, non vitiorum comes, ut, quoniam
solitaria non posset virtus ad ea quae summa sunt
pervenire, coniuncta et consociata cum altera per-
veniret. Quae si quos inter societas aut est aut fuit
aut futura est, eorum est habendus ad summum
naturae bonum optimus beatissimusque comitatus.
84 Haec est, inquam, societas, in qua omnia insunt,
quae putant homines expetenda—honestas gloria
tranquillitas animi atque iucunditas; ut et, cum
haec adsint, beata vita sit, et sine his esse non possit

Quod cum optimum maximumque sit, si id volumus
adipisci, virtuti opera danda est, sine qua nec amicitiam neque ullam rem expetendam consequi possumus; ea vero neglecta qui se amicos habere
arbitrantur, tum se denique errasse sentiunt, cum
85 eos gravis aliquis casus experiri cogit. Quocirca,
dicendum est enim saepius, cum iudicaris, diligere

be made secure ; and when united by ties of goodwill, they will first of all subdue those passions to
which other men are slaves ; and, next, they will
delight in what is equitable and accords with law,
and will go to all lengths for each other ; they will
not demand from each other anything unless it is
honourable and just, and they will not only cherish
and love, but they will also revere, each other. For
he who takes reverence from friendship, takes away
its brightest jewel. Therefore a fatal mistake is
made by those who think that friendship opens wide
the door to every passion and to every sin. Friendship was given to us by nature as the handmaid of
virtue, not as a comrade of vice ; because virtue
cannot attain her highest aims unattended, but only
in union and fellowship with another. Such a
partnership as this, whether it is, or was, or is yet
to be, should be considered the best and happiest
comradeship along the road to nature's highest
good. In such a partnership, I say, abide all things
that men deem worthy of pursuit—honour and fame
and delightful tranquillity of mind ; so that when
these blessings are at hand life is happy, and without
them, it cannot be happy.

Since happiness is our best and highest aim, we
must, if we would attain it, give our attention to
virtue, without which we can obtain neither friendship nor any other desirable thing ; on the other
hand, those who slight virtue and yet think that
they have friends, perceive their mistake at last
when some grievous misfortune forces them to put
their friends to the test. Therefore, I repeat the
injunction, for it should be said again and again :
you should love your friend after you have appraised

191

oportet; non, cum dilexeris, iudicare. Sed cum
multis in rebus neglegentia plectimur, tum maxime
in amicis et diligendis et colendis; praeposteris
enim utimur consiliis et acta agimus, quod vetamur
vetere proverbio. Nam, implicati ultro et citro vel
usu diuturno vel etiam officiis, repente in medio
cursu amicitias exorta aliqua offensione disrum-
pimus.

86　XXIII. Quo etiam magis vituperanda est rei
maxime necessariae tanta incuria. Una est enim
amicitia in rebus humanis, de cuius utilitate omnes
uno ore consentiunt; quamquam a multis virtus
ipsa contemnitur et venditatio quaedam atque osten-
tatio esse dicitur; multi divitias despiciunt, quos
parvo contentos tenuis victus cultusque delectat;
honores vero, quorum cupiditate quidam inflammantur, quam multi ita contemnunt, ut nihil inanius,
nihil esse levius existiment! Itemque cetera, quae
quibusdam admirabilia videntur, permulti sunt qui
pro nihilo putent. De amicitia omnes ad unum idem
sentiunt; et ei qui ad rem publicam se contulerunt,
et ei qui rerum cognitione doctrinaque delectantur,
et ei qui suum negotium gerunt otiosi; postremo
ei qui se totos tradiderunt voluptatibus, sine amicitia

---

¹ From Theophrastus, Περὶ φιλίας: τοὺς ἀλλοτρίους οὐ
φιλοῦντα δεῖ κρίνειν, ἀλλὰ κρίναντα φιλεῖν. Seneca also (*Ep.*
iii.) quotes the maxim, and describes those neglecting it as
acting *praepostere.*

him ; you should not appraise him after you have begun to love him.[1] But we are punished for our negligence in many things, and especially are we most grievously punished for our carelessness in the choice and treatment of our friends ; for we deliberate after the event, and we do what the ancient proverb forbids—we argue the case after the verdict is found. Accordingly, after we have become involved with others in a mutual affection, either by long association or by interchange of favours, some cause of offence arises and we suddenly break the bonds of friendship asunder when it has run but half its course.

XXIII. Therefore carelessness so great in regard to a relation absolutely indispensable deserves the more to be censured. For the one thing in human experience about whose advantage all men with one voice agree, is friendship ; even virtue itself is regarded with contempt by many and is said to be mere pretence and display ; many disdain riches, because they are content with little and take delight in meagre fare and plain dress ; political honours, too, for which some have a burning desire—how many so despise them that they believe nothing more empty and nothing more inane ! Likewise other things, which seem to some to be worthy of admiration, are by many thought to be of no value at all. But concerning friendship, all, to a man, think the same thing : those who have devoted themselves to public life ; those who find their joy in science and philosophy ; those who manage their own business free from public cares ; and, finally, those who are wholly given up to sensual pleasures—all believe that without friendship life is no life at all, or at

vitam esse nullam, si modo velint aliqua ex parte
87 liberaliter vivere. Serpit enim nescio quo modo per
omnium vitas amicitia nec ullam aetatis degendae
rationem patitur esse expertem sui.

Quin etiam si quis asperitate ea est et immanitate
naturae, congressus ut hominum fugiat atque oderit,
qualem fuisse Athenis Timonem nescio quem accepimus, tamen is pati non possit, ut non anquirat
aliquem, apud quem evomat virus acerbitatis suae.
Atque hoc maxime iudicaretur, si quid tale possit
contingere, ut aliquis nos deus ex hac hominum
frequentia tolleret et in solitudine uspiam collocaret
atque ibi suppeditans omnium rerum quas natura
desiderat, abundantiam et copiam, hominis omnino
aspiciendi potestatem eriperet — quis tam esset
ferreus qui eam vitam ferre posset cuique non auferret
88 fructum voluptatum omnium solitudo ? Verum ergo
illud est, quod a Tarentino Archyta, ut opinor, dici
solitum nostros senes commemorare audivi ab aliis
senibus auditum : si quis in caelum ascendisset
naturamque mundi et pulchritudinem siderum per-
spexisset, insuavem illam admirationem ei fore,
quae iucundissima fuisset, si aliquem cui narraret
habuisset. Sic natura solitarium nihil amat semperque ad aliquod tamquam adminiculum adnititur, quod
in amicissimo quoque dulcissimum est.

least they so believe if they have any desire whatever to live the life of free men. For it creeps imperceptibly, I know not how, into every life, and suffers no mode of existence to be devoid of its presence.

Nay, even if anyone were of a nature so savage and fierce as to shun and loathe the society of men —such, for example, as tradition tells us a certain Timon of Athens once was—yet even such a man could not refrain from seeking some person before whom he might pour out the venom of his embittered soul. Moreover, the view just expressed might best be appraised if such a thing as this could happen : suppose that a god should remove us from these haunts of men and put us in some solitary place, and, while providing us there in plenteous abundance with all material things for which our nature yearns, should take from us altogether the power to gaze upon our fellow men—who would be such a man of iron as to be able to endure that sort of a life ? And who is there from whom solitude would not snatch the enjoyment of every pleasure ? True, therefore, is that celebrated saying of Archytas of Tarentum, I think it was—a saying which I have heard repeated by our old men who in their turn heard it from their elders. It is to this effect : " If a man should ascend alone into heaven and behold clearly the structure of the universe and the beauty of the stars, there would be no pleasure for him in the awe-inspiring sight, which would have filled him with delight if he had had someone to whom he could describe what he had seen." Thus nature, loving nothing solitary, always strives for some sort of support, and man's best support is a very dear friend.

XXIV. Sed cum tot signis eadem natura declaret
quid velit anquirat desideret, tamen obsurdescimus
nescio quo modo nec ea, quae ab ea monemur,
audimus. Est enim varius et multiplex usus amicitiae multaeque causae suspicionum offensionumque
dantur, quas tum evitare, tum elevare, tum ferre
sapientis est. Una illa subeunda[1] est offensio ut et
utilitas in amicitia et fides retineatur; nam et
monendi amici saepe sunt et obiurgandi, et haec
89 accipienda amice, cum benevole fiunt. Sed nescio
quo modo verum est, quod in Andria familiaris
meus dicit :

> obsequium amicos, veritas odium parit.

Molesta veritas, siquidem ex ea nascitur odium, quod
est venenum amicitiae, sed obsequium multo moles-
tius, quod peccatis indulgens praecipitem amicum
ferri sinit; maxima autem culpa in eo, qui et veritatem aspernatur et in fraudem obsequio impellitur.
   Omni igitur hac in re habenda ratio et diligentia
est, primum ut monitio acerbitate, deinde ut obiur-
gatio contumelia careat. In obsequio autem, quoniam Terentiano verbo lubenter utimur, comitas adsit,
assentatio vitiorum adiutrix procul amoveatur, quae
non modo amico, sed ne libero quidem digna est ;
aliter enim cum tyranno, aliter cum amico vivitur.

   [1] subeunda *edd.* ; sublevanda MSS.

---

   [1] Terence, *Andria*, i. 1. 41 : *obsequium* is chiefly used in
a good sense, = the desire to oblige, or fall in with another's
taste ; but often, as here, it is almost " flattery."

XXIV. But though this same nature declares by so many utterances what she wishes, what she seeks, and what she ardently longs for, yet we somehow grow deaf and do not hearken to her voice. For varied and complex are the experiences of friendship, and they afford many causes for suspicion and offence, which it is wise sometimes to ignore, sometimes to make light of, and sometimes to endure. But there is one cause of offence which must be encountered in order that both the usefulness and loyalty of friendship may be preserved; for friends frequently must be not only advised, but also rebuked, and both advice and rebuke should be kindly received when given in a spirit of goodwill. But somehow it is true, as put by my intimate friend in his *Andria* :

Complaisance gets us friends, plain speaking, hate.[1]

A troublesome thing is truth, if it is indeed the source of hate, which poisons friendship; but much more troublesome is complaisance, which, by showing indulgence to the sins of a friend, allows him to be carried headlong away; but the greatest fault is in him who both scornfully rejects truth and is driven by complaisance to ruin.

Therefore, in this entire matter reason and care must be used, first, that advice be free from harshness, and second, that reproof be free from insult. But in showing complaisance—I am glad to adopt Terence's word, *obsequium*—let courtesy be at hand, and let flattery, the handmaid of vice, be far removed, as it is unworthy not only of a friend but even of a free man; for we live in one way with a tyrant and in another with a friend. Now we must despair

197

90 Cuius autem aures clausae veritati sunt, ut ab amico
verum audire nequeat, huius salus desperanda est.
Scitum est enim illud Catonis, ut multa : melius
de quibusdam acerbos inimicos mereri, quam eos
amicos, qui dulces videantur ; illos verum saepe
dicere, hos numquam. Atque illud absurdum, quod
ei, qui monentur, eam molestiam quam debent
capere non capiunt, eam capiunt qua debent vacare.
Peccasse enim se non anguntur, obiurgari moleste
ferunt ; quod contra oportebat delicto dolere, cor-
rectione gaudere.

91 XXV. Ut igitur et monere et moneri proprium
est verae amicitiae, et alterum libere facere, non
aspere, alterum patienter accipere, non repugnanter,
sic habendum est nullam in amicitiis pestem esse
maiorem quam adulationem blanditiam assenta-
tionem : quamvis enim multis nominibus est hoc
vitium notandum levium hominum atque fallacium,
ad voluptatem loquentium omnia, nihil ad veri-
92 tatem. Cum autem omnium rerum simulatio vitiosa
est, tollit enim iudicium veri idque adulterat, tum
amicitiae repugnat maxime ; delet enim veritatem,
sine qua nomen amicitiae valere non potest. Nam
cum amicitiae vis sit in eo ut unus quasi animus
fiat ex pluribus, qui id fieri poterit, si ne in uno
quidem quoque unus animus erit idemque semper,
93 sed varius commutabilis multiplex ? Quid enim

198

of the safety of the man whose ears are so closed to truth that he cannot hear what is true from a friend. For there is shrewdness in that well-known saying of Cato, as there was in much that he said : " Some men are better served by their bitter-tongued enemies than by their sweet-smiling friends ; because the former often tell the truth, the latter, never." And furthermore, it is absurd that men who are admonished do not feel vexation at what ought to vex them, but do feel it at what ought not ; for they are annoyed, not at the sin, but at the reproof ; whereas, on the contrary, they ought to grieve for the offence and rejoice at its correction.

XXV. As, therefore, it is characteristic of true friendship both to give and to receive advice and, on the one hand, to give it with all freedom of speech, but without harshness, and on the other hand, to receive it patiently, but without resentment, so nothing is to be considered a greater bane of friendship than fawning, cajolery, or flattery ; for give it as many names as you choose, it deserves to be branded as a vice peculiar to fickle and false-hearted men who say everything with a view to pleasure and nothing with a view to truth. More-over, hypocrisy is not only wicked under all circumstances, because it pollutes truth and takes away the power to discern it, but it is also especially inimical to friendship, since it utterly destroys sincerity, without which the word friendship can have no meaning. And since the effect of friendship is to make, as it were, one soul out of many, how will that be possible if not even in one man taken by himself shall there be a soul always one and the same, but fickle, changeable, and manifold ? For

potest esse tam flexibile, tam devium, quam animus eius, qui ad alterius non modo sensum ac voluntatem, sed etiam voltum atque nutum convertitur ?

negat quis, nego ; ait, aio ; postremo imperavi egomet mihi omnia assentari,

ut ait idem Terentius, sed ille in Gnathonis persona, quod amici genus adhibere omnino levitatis est. 94 Multi autem Gnathonum similes, cum sint loco fortuna fama superiores, quorum[1] est assentatio molesta, 95 cum ad vanitatem accessit auctoritas. Secerni autem blandus amicus a vero et internosci tam potest adhibita diligentia, quam omnia fucata et simulata a sinceris atque veris. Contio, quae ex imperitissimis constat, tamen iudicare solet, quid intersit inter popularem, id est assentatorem et levem civem, 96 et inter constantem et verum et gravem. Quibus blanditiis C. Papirius nuper influebat in auris contionis, cum ferret legem de tribunis plebis reficiendis ! Dissuasimus nos, sed nihil de me, de Scipione dicam libentius. Quanta illi, di immortales, fuit gravitas, quanta in oratione maiestas ! ut facile ducem populi Romani, non comitem diceres. Sed affuistis, et est in manibus oratio. Itaque lex popularis suffragiis populi repudiata est.

[1] quorum *Reid* ; horum *MSS.*

---

[1] Terent. *Eunuchus*, ii. 2. 21 (l. 250).
[2] See §§ 37 and 41. The bill referred to was proposed by him in 130 B.C., and failed to pass, but at some time after the time of this dialogue (129) was again offered and carried.
[3] *i.e.* merely one of them ; he was at the time a private citizen.

what can be as pliant and erratic as the soul of the man who changes not only to suit another's humour and desire, but even his expression and his nod?

He says "nay," and "nay" say I; he says "yea," and "yea" say I; in fine, I bade myself agree with him in everything.[1]

This was said by Terence whom I quoted before, but he says it in the character of Gnatho; and to have such a man for a friend on any terms is a mark of inconstancy. However, there are many like Gnatho, though his superiors in birth, fortune, and reputation, who become dangerous flatterers when their insincerity is supported by their position. But by the exercise of care a fawning friend may be separated and distinguished from a true friend, just as everything pretended and false may be distinguished from what is genuine and true. A public assembly, though composed of very ignorant men, can, nevertheless, usually see the difference between a demagogue—that is, a smooth-tongued, shallow citizen—and one who has stability, sincerity, and weight. With what flattering words Gaius Papirius [2] not long ago insinuated himself into the favour of the assembly, when he was trying to carry a law making the people's tribunes eligible for re-election! I spoke against it—but I will not talk of myself, it will give me more pleasure to talk about Scipio. Ye gods! What weight and majesty there was in his speech on that occasion! One would have said, without hesitation, that he was the leader of the Roman people, not their comrade.[3] But you both were present; besides, his speech is published. As a result this "people's law" was rejected by the people's votes.

Atque, ut ad me redeam, meministis Q. Maximo fratre Scipionis et L. Mancino consulibus, quam popularis lex de sacerdotiis C. Licini Crassi videbatur ; cooptatio enim collegiorum ad populi beneficium transferebatur. (Atque is primus instituit in forum versus agere cum populo.) Tamen illius vendibilem orationem religio deorum immortalium nobis defendentibus facile vincebat. Atque id actum est praetore me, quinquennio ante quam consul sum factus. Ita re magis quam summa auctoritate causa illa defensa est.

97 XXVI. Quod si in scena, id est in contione, in qua rebus fictis et adumbratis loci plurimum est, tamen verum valet, si modo id patefactum et illustratum est, quid in amicitia fieri oportet, quae tota veritate perpenditur ? In qua nisi, ut dicitur, apertum pectus videas tuumque ostendas, nihil fidum, nihil exploratum habeas, ne amare quidem aut amari, cum id quam vere fiat ignores. Quamquam ista assentatio, quamvis perniciosa sit, nocere tamen nemini potest nisi ei, qui eam recipit atque ea delectatur. Ita fit ut is assentatoribus patefaciat auris suas maxime, qui ipse sibi assentetur et se maxime ipse delectet.

98 Omnino est amans sui virtus ; optime enim se ipsa novit quamque amabilis sit intellegit : ego autem

---

¹ *i.e.* in 145 B.C.

² Plutarch, *Vit. Grac.* 5, makes C. Gracchus the author of this practice.

Again—and pardon me for referring to myself—you remember when Lucius Mancinus and Scipio's brother, Quintus Maximus, were consuls,[1] how popular apparently was the proposed law of Gaius Licinius Crassus regarding the priestly offices—for the right to co-opt to vacancies possessed by the college was being converted into patronage for the people. (By the way, Crassus was the first man to begin the practice of facing towards the forum in addressing the people.[2]) Nevertheless, through my speech in reply, reverence for the immortal gods easily prevailed over the plausible oration of Crassus. And this took place while I was praetor and five years before I was elected consul. Thus the cause was won more by its own merit than by the influence of one holding a very high official rank.

XXVI. Now, if on the stage, I mean on the platform, where there is the greatest opportunity for deception and disguise, truth yet prevails, provided it is made plain and brought into the light of day, what ought to be the case with friendship which is wholly weighed in the scales of truth? For in friendship, unless, as the saying is, you behold and show an open heart, you can have no loyalty or certainty and not even the satisfaction of loving and of being loved, since you do not know what true love is. And yet this flattery of which I spoke, however deadly it may be, can harm no one except him who receives and delights in it. It follows that the man who lends the readiest ear to flatterers is the one who is most given to self-flattery and is most satisfied with himself.

I grant that Virtue loves herself; for she best knows herself and realizes how lovable she is; but

non de virtute nunc loquor, sed de virtutis opinione.
Virtute enim ipsa non tam multi praediti esse quam
videri volunt. Hos delectat assentatio, his fictus
ad ipsorum voluntatem sermo cum adhibetur,
orationem illam vanam testimonium esse laudum
suarum putant. Nulla est igitur haec amicitia,
cum alter verum audire non volt, alter ad mentien-
dum paratus est. Nec parasitorum in comoediis
assentatio faceta nobis videretur, nisi essent milites
gloriosi.

> magnas vero agere gratias Thais mihi?

Satis erat respondere " magnas." " Ingentis," inquit
Semper auget assentator id, quod is, cuius ad volun-
99 tatem dicitur, volt esse magnum. Quam ob rem,
quamquam blanda ista vanitas apud eos valet, qui
ipsi illam adlectant et invitant, tamen etiam graviores
constantioresque admonendi sunt, ut animadvertant
ne callida assentatione capiantur.

Aperte enim adulantem nemo non videt, nisi qui
admodum est excors : callidus ille et occultus ne se
insinuet studiose cavendum est. Nec enim facillime
agnoscitur, quippe qui etiam adversando saepe
assentetur et litigare se simulans blandiatur atque
ad extremum det manus vincique se patiatur, ut
is, qui illusus sit, plus vidisse videatur. Quid autem
turpius quam illudi ? Quod ut ne accidat magis
cavendum est :

---

[1] Laelius has in mind Thraso in the *Eunuch* of Terence,
from which (ii. 1. 1) the following line is taken, and Pyrgo-
polinices, the braggart soldier in Plautus' *Miles Gloriosus*.
The disgust Laelius feels at the fawning of the parasite is
relieved by the humour of the soldier.

it is not virtue I am talking about but a reputation
for virtue. For many wish not so much to be, as
to seem to be, endowed with real virtue. Such men
delight in flattery, and when a complimentary speech
is fashioned to suit their fancy they think the empty
phrase is proof of their own merits. There is nothing,
therefore, in a friendship in which one of the parties
to it does not wish to hear the truth and the other
is ready to lie. Nor should we see any humour in
the fawning parasites in comedies if there were no
braggart soldiers.[1]

> In truth did Thais send me many thanks?

It would have been enough to answer, " Many."
" Millions of them," said the parasite. The flatterer
always magnifies that which the one for whose
gratification he speaks wishes to be large. Wherefore, although that sort of hollow flattery influences
those who court and make a bid for it, yet even
stronger and steadier men should be warned to be
on their guard lest they be taken in by flattery of
the crafty kind.

No one, to be sure, unless he is an utter fool, fails
to detect the open flatterer, but we must exercise
a watchful care against the deep and crafty one lest
he steal upon us unawares. For he is very hard to
recognize, since he often fawns even by opposing,
and flatters and cajoles by pretending to quarrel,
until at last he gives in, allowing himself to be overcome so that his dupe may appear to have seen further
into the matter than himself. And yet, is there
anything more discreditable than to be made a dupe?
If not, then we should be all the more on our guard
that it does not happen to us to have to confess :

ut me hodie ante omnis comicos stultos senes
versaris atque illusseris lautissime !

100 Haec enim etiam in fabulis stultissima persona est
improvidorum et credulorum senum.

Sed nescio quo pacto ab amicitiis perfectorum
hominum, id est sapientium—de hac dico sapientia,
quae videtur in hominem cadere posse—ad levis
amicitias defluxit oratio. Quam ob rem ad-illa
prima redeamus eaque ipsa concludamus aliquando.

XXVII. Virtus, inquam, C. Fanni, et tu, Q. Muci,
et conciliat amicitias et conservat. In ea est enim
convenientia rerum, in ea stabilitas, in ea constantia ;
quae cum se extulit et ostendit suum lumen et idem
aspexit agnovitque in alio, ad id se admovet vicissimque accipit illud, quod in altero est, ex quo
exardescit sive amor sive amicitia ; utrumque enim
dictum[1] est ab amando, Amare autem nihil est
aliud nisi eum ipsum diligere quem ames, nulla
indigentia, nulla utilitate quaesita. Quae tamen
ipsa ecflorescit ex amicitia, etiam si tu eam minus
101 secutus sis. Hac nos adulescentes benevolentia
senes illos, L. Paulum, M. Catonem, C. Gallum,
P. Nasicam, Ti. Gracchum Scipionis nostri socerum
dileximus. Haec etiam magis elucet inter aequalis,

---

[1] dictum *edd.* ; ductum *PDE.*

---

[1] Lines from the *Epiclerus* by Caecilius Statius. *Cf.* Cic.
Cato Maior § 36 *nam quos ait Caecilius . . . comicos stultos
senes.*

[2] *i.e. amor*, "love "; *amicitia*, "friendship."

To-day, of all old fools that play the comic parts,
You've wheedled me the most and made your greatest dupe.[1]

For even on the stage the silliest characters take
the parts of old men lacking in foresight and easily
deceived.

But in some unaccountable way I have drifted
away from the friendship of faultless men—that is,
men of wisdom, such wisdom I mean as is observed
to fall to the lot of man—and I have rambled on to
a discussion of friendships of the frivolous kind.
Wherefore, let me return to the topic with which I
began and finally put an end even to that.

XXVII. Virtue, my dear Gaius Fannius, and you,
my dear Quintus Mucius, Virtue, I say, both creates
the bond of friendship and preserves it. For in
Virtue is complete harmony, in her is permanence,
in her is fidelity; and when she has raised her
head and shown her own light and has seen
and recognized the same light in another, she
moves towards it and in turn receives its beams;
as a result love or friendship leaps into flame; for
both words are derived from a word meaning " to
love." [2] But love is nothing other than the great
esteem and affection felt for him who inspires
that sentiment, and it is not sought because
of material need or for the sake of material
gain. Nevertheless even this blossoms forth from
friendship, although *you* did not make it your aim.
Because of this friendly impulse, I, as a young
man, became attached to those old men, Lucius
Paulus, Marcus Cato, Gaius Gallus, Publius Nasica,
and Tiberius Gracchus, father-in-law of my dear
Scipio. And while that feeling is stronger between
men of the same age, as between Scipio, Lucius

ut inter me et Scipionem, L. Furium, P. Rupilium, Sp. Mummium; vicissim autem senes in adulescentium caritate acquiescimus, ut in vestra, ut in Q. Tuberonis; equidem etiam admodum adulescentis P. Rutili, A. Vergini familiaritate delector. Quoniamque ita ratio comparata est vitae naturaeque nostrae, ut alia aetas oriatur, maxime quidem optandum est ut cum aequalibus possis, quibuscum tamquam e carceribus emissus sis, cum isdem ad calcem, ut dicitur, pervenire.

102 Sed quoniam res humanae fragiles caducaeque sunt, semper aliqui anquirendi sunt quos diligamus et a quibus diligamur; caritate enim benevolentiaque sublata omnis est e vita sublata iucunditas. Mihi quidem Scipio, quamquam est subito ereptus, vivit tamen semperque vivet; virtutem enim amavi illius viri, quae exstincta non est. Nec mihi soli versatur ante oculos, qui illam semper in manibus habui, sed etiam posteris erit clara et insignis. Nemo umquam animo aut spe maiora suscipiet qui sibi non illius memoriam atque imaginem proponendam putet.

103 Equidem ex omnibus rebus, quas mihi aut fortuna aut natura tribuit, nihil habeo quod cum amicitia Scipionis possim comparare. In hac mihi de re publica consensus; in hac rerum privatarum consilium, in eadem requies plena oblectationis fuit. Numquam illum ne minima quidem re offendi, quod quidem senserim, nihil audivi ex eo ipse quod nollem;

Furius, Publius Rupilius, Spurius Mummius, and myself; yet, in turn, now that I am old, I find pleasure in the affection of young men, like yourselves and Quintus Tubero; and I find delight also in social intercourse with still younger men like Publius Rutilius and Aulus Verginius. And since it is the law of human life and of human nature that a new generation is ever coming forth, it is really most desirable, when you can, to reach the goal, so to speak, with men of your own age—those with whom you began the race of life.

But inasmuch as things human are frail and fleeting, we must be ever on the search for some persons whom we shall love and who will love us in return; for if goodwill and affection are taken away, every joy is taken from life. For me, indeed, though he was suddenly snatched away, Scipio still lives and will always live; for it was his virtue that caused my love and that is not dead. Nor is it only in my sight and for me, who had it constantly within my reach, that his virtue lives; it will even shed its light and splendour on men unborn. No one will ever undertake with courage and hope the larger tasks of life without thinking that he must continually keep before him the memory and example of that illustrious man.

For my part, of all the blessings that fortune or nature has bestowed on me, there is none which I can compare with Scipio's friendship. In it I found agreement on public questions; in it, counsel in private business, and in it, too, a leisure of unalloyed delight. And, so far as I was aware, I never offended him in even the most trivial point; nor did I ever hear a word from him that I could wish

una domus erat, idem victus isque communis, neque
solum militia, sed etiam peregrinationes rusticationes-
104 que communes. Nam quid ego de studiis dicam
cognoscendi semper aliquid atque discendi, in quibus
remoti ab oculis populi omne otiosum tempus con-
trivimus ? Quarum rerum recordatio et memoria
si una cum illo occidisset, desiderium coniunctis-
simi atque amantissimi viri ferre nullo modo possem.
Sed nec illa exstincta sunt alunturque potius et
augentur cogitatione et memoria mea, et, si illis
plane orbatus essem, magnum tamen affert mihi
aetas ipsa solacium ; diutius enim iam in hoc desiderio esse non possum ; omnia autem brevia tolera-
bilia esse debent, etiam si magna sunt.

Haec habui de amicitia quae dicerem ; vos autem
hortor ut ita virtutem locetis (sine qua amicitia esse
non potest) ut ea excepta nihil amicitia praestabilius
putetis.

unsaid; there was one home for us both; we had the same fare and shared it in common, and we were together not only in our military campaigns, but also in our foreign tours and on our vacations in the country. Why need I speak of our constant devotion to investigation and to learning in which, remote from the gaze of men, we spent all our leisure time? If my recollection and memory of these things had died with him, I could not now by any means endure the loss of a man so very near and dear to me. But those experiences with him are not dead; rather they are nourished and made more vivid by my reflection and memory; and even if I were utterly deprived of the power to recall them, yet my age would of itself afford me great relief; for I cannot have much longer time to bear this bereavement; besides, every trial, which is of brief duration, ought to be endurable, even if it be severe.

This is all that I had to say about friendship; but I exhort you both so to esteem virtue (without which friendship cannot exist), that, excepting virtue, you will think nothing more excellent than friendship.

DE DIVINATIONE

INTRODUCTION TO THE
DE DIVINATIONE

1. DATE OF COMPOSITION

THIS treatise was intended by Cicero to supple-
ment his earlier work, *De natura deorum*, which was
finished probably in August 45 B.C. The greater
part of the first book of the *De divinatione* was
written (in part at least) before the assassination
of Caesar, but the work was not completed and
published until after that event.[1]

2. THE INTERLOCUTORS

The dialogue is represented as taking place
between Cicero and his only brother Quintus, at
Cicero's country home at Tusculum, about ten miles
from Rome.

[1] René Durand in " La Date du *De divinatione*," *Mélanges
Boissier*, takes the view (now generally accepted) that this
work was wholly written (except for some interpolations and
changes) prior to Caesar's death, and after that event
revised and published. The translator, after a careful study
of all the evidence bearing on the question, is unable to
accept M. Durand's view, and feels convinced that the latter
part of Book I. and all of Book II. were written after
March 15, 44 B.C.

DE DIVINATIONE

Quintus Cicero was born about 102 B.C.; received instruction in the best schools at Rome and in Greece; was aedile in 65; praetor in 62; governor of Asia from March 61 to April 58; and served as *legatus* under Pompey in Sardinia in 56, under Caesar in Gaul in 54 and 53, and under Marcus, his brother, in Cilicia, from July 51 to July 50. In the Civil War he first joined Pompey, but, after the latter's defeat, offered his services to Caesar. Quintus was fond of reading and study and devoted much of his leisure to writing. During his stay in Gaul he wrote four tragedies, which are lost. The authorship of the *Commentariolum Petitionis* is generally conceded to him. He (like his brother) died in December 43, in the proscription of the Second Triumvirate.

3. Plan and Sources of the Dialogue

In this treatise, as in his other philosophic works, Cicero draws his arguments chiefly from Greek sources, but develops them in his own inimitable way and illustrates them with examples from his varied experiences and from his vast stores of learning. As an adherent of the New Academy he was free to question the views of the other philosophic schools, to compare argument with argument, and to adopt that theory which seemed to him most consistent with reason. After a thorough and impartial study of all the extant literature on the subject, from the time of Xenophanes of Colophon, a philosopher of the Eleatic school of the sixth century B.C., to that of Cratippus of his own day, and including the teachings of the Pyth-

agoreans, the Socratics, the Peripatetics, the Epicureans and the Stoics, he became convinced that the commonly accepted belief in divination was a superstition which " should be torn up by the roots." He was himself an augur, and in his book *On the Republic* had written in favour of maintenance of the rites of augury and of auspices. But these practices were engrafted on the Roman constitution and he advocated their observance because of his belief in obedience to law and because, as a member of the aristocratic party, he thought augury and auspices the best means of controlling the excesses of democracy.

4. The Argument in favour of Divination

In treating the subject he proceeded, not as a special pleader, but in a truly philosophic spirit. As the chief apologists for divination he selected the Stoics, who defended it with great force and plausibility, accepted it as a part of their philosophic system, and sought to bring the world into conformity with their views. They endeavoured to unite religion with philosophy to prove that the nature of the gods is adapted to reveal the divine will through divine prophecy. The belief in a superintending care of the gods seemed to them to imply a means of communication between God and man, whereby the latter might know the divine will in advance and obey it. This means they called *Divination*, the *vis divinandi* of the Romans, the μαντική of the Greeks.

The arguments in the first book in favour of divination are based chiefly on the writings of

216

DE DIVINATIONE

Posidonius the Stoic. While many of the arguments in the second book go back to Carneades, the founder of the New Academy, the immediate source of the material is not Carneades himself (for he left no writings) but one of his disciples, probably Clitomachus, who was his successor in the New Academy and expounded his doctrines. The discussion of the Chaldean *monstra* in the second book, from sections 87 to 97, is derived from the Stoic Panaetius. The entire discussion is divided into two main parts. In the first Quintus, taking the affirmative side, sets out the reasons for his belief in divination, and in the second Marcus proceeds to overwhelm his adversary with merciless logic and, with a rare display of abounding humour and sarcasm, laughs him out of court.

Quintus defines divination as " the foreknowledge and foretelling of events that happen by chance." He divides it into two classes : the first, Artificial, which depends partly on conjecture and partly on long-continued observation, and includes astrology, auspices, augury, divining by portents, prodigies, thunder, lightning, and other natural phenomena ; the second, Natural, embraces divination by means of dreams and prophecies, made by persons inspired, as seers and prophets like Calchas, Cassandra, and others, and by those in a state of ecstasy or rapture, like the Pythian priestess of Apollo, whose prophetic powers were induced by exhalations from the earth. In defence of these various kinds of divination he urged the fact of their acceptance from the earliest times by every nation, and by the greatest philosophers including Pythagoras, Socrates, and Plato. He was not troubled by his inability to explain the

217

causes of divination. Those who denied the
existence of what they could not explain and were
not convinced by results and by the evidence of
their own senses, for the same reason should deny
the power of the magnet to attract iron, or the
efficacy of drugs to effect certain cures. Divination,
he urges, was established by many infallible proofs :
by augury, the city of Rome had been founded and
the kingdom given to Romulus ; by the flight of
an eagle, King Deiotarus had been warned to dis-
continue a journey and thereby was saved from
certain death ; the entrails foretold Caesar's ap-
proaching fate ; in a dream the Rhodian sailor had
a vision of Pompey's defeat at Pharsalus. He also
does not disdain the *argumentum ad hominem*, but
quotes freely from his brother's poetry to show that
he, too, accepts divination.[1]

Following the method of Posidonius, Quintus
sought to bring divination into conformity with the
principles of philosophy in three ways ; by tracing
its source to God, to nature, and to fate. The
reasoning for its origin from God was borrowed
from Cratippus. The human soul is an emanation
from the Divine Soul which pervades and governs
all things. Between the Divine Soul and the
human soul, both of which are divine and eternal,
there is a sympathy and a connexion which permit
of communication from one to the other. The human
soul when divorced from bodily influences, as in
sleep and in ecstasy, is most responsive to the
divine will and most endowed with divine foresight.

In discussing the origin of divination from the

[1] The artifice by which Cicero thus quotes himself is
delightfully characteristic.

second source, Quintus defines Fate or εἱμαρμένη as " the orderly succession of causes wherein cause is linked to cause and every cause has its effect." Therefore nothing has happened which was not bound to happen and nothing will happen which will not find its efficient cause in nature. He who knows the links that join cause to cause, knows all the results of causes and can foretell every coming event. While such omniscience is possible only to God, yet since every cause has its sign and there are men who can often read those signs, in the lapse of time a science has been evolved from the recording of signs and the noting of the connexion between them and their results.

The argument from nature is based on the phenomena of dreams and ecstasy. The power of the soul is much enhanced when divorced from bodily sensation. Then it sees things which are invisible to it when shackled by the flesh. During frenzy or inspiration or ecstasy nature seems most to impel the human soul to prophecy.

To the objection that the forecasts of augurs, seers, soothsayers and other diviners are often erroneous, Quintus replies that the same point may be urged against experts in other arts and callings, as, for example, physicians, mariners, and statesmen.

In closing Quintus makes a qualification or partial retractation by stating that he does not countenance fortune-tellers, necromancers, snake-charmers, astrologers, or interpreters of dreams who are not true diviners.

5. The Argument against Divination

Marcus, in reply, first directs his attack against divination in general and adopts the reasoning of Carneades. "Divination," he says, "has no application to things perceived by the senses, which are sufficient of themselves and require no aid from divination. Nor is there any place for it in matters within the domain of science and of art. Likewise divination has no place in resolving questions in philosophy, in dialectic or in politics. And since it is of no use in any of these cases there is no use for it anywhere." Next, he takes the Stoic definition of divination as "the foreknowledge and foretelling of things that happen by chance," and shows that since such things may or may not happen, or may happen in one way or another, they cannot be foreseen by any amount of reason or skill. But if it can be known in advance that an event is going to happen, then that event is certain and not subject to chance and, by the definition, is removed from the scope of divination.

Furthermore, even if it was possible to know the future the disadvantages would far outweigh the gain. Cicero then takes up separately the various modes of divination under their proper divisions of Artificial and Natural and shows how utterly unreasonable they are and heaps his ridicule upon them.

6. Manuscripts, Editions, and Translations

The best mss. of the *De divinatione* are : V. Vindob., 10th century, and three Leyden mss., A, B, and H, Leid., 12th century.

The text of this edition is based chiefly on that of

DE DIVINATIONE

John Davies, Cambridge, 1730, but emended in many places by readings adopted from the editions of George A. Moser, Frankfort-on-the-Main, 1828, Aug. Geise, Leipsig, 1829, and C. F. W. Müller, Leipzig, 1910. Many changes have also been made in Davies' spelling, punctuation and paragraphing.

[In the Teubner series, see the edition by O. Plasberg and W. Ax, Stuttgart, 1969 (1938).]

I have consulted the following translations : C. D. Yonge, London, Bohn's series, 1848, in English ; D. Goldbéry, Paris, Garnier Frères, in French ; Ralph Kühner, Berlin, Langenscheidt, in German.

Among books that may be mentioned as useful in the study of *De divinatione* are the following :

C. Wachsmuth, *Die Ansichten der Stoiker über Mantik und Dämonen.*

Th. Schiche, *De fontibus librorum Ciceronis quae sunt de divinatione.*

C. Hartfelder, *Die Quellen von Cicero's De divinatione.*

A. Schmekel, *Die Philosophie der Mittleren Stoa.*

F. Malchin, *De auctoribus quibusdam qui Posidonii libros meteorologicos adhibuerunt.*

The best edition of the *De divinatione* is that of Prof. Pease, University of Illinois Press, 1923.

A. Bouché-Leclercq, *Histoire de la divination.*

J. Wight Duff, *Literary History of Rome.*

I am indebted to Dr. Gordon J. Laing of the University of Chicago for a critical reading of this translation and for many helpful suggestions.

Wm. Armistead Falconer.

Fort Smith, Arkansas

DE DIVINATIONE

LIBER PRIMUS

I. Vetus opinio est iam usque ab heroicis ducta
temporibus, eaque et populi Romani et omnium
gentium firmata consensu, versari quandam inter
homines divinationem, quam Graeci μαντικήν appellant, id est praesensionem et scientiam rerum
futurarum. Magnifica quaedam res et salutaris, si
modo est ulla, quaque proxime ad deorum vim natura
mortalis possit accedere. Itaque ut alia nos melius
multa quam Graeci, sic huic praestantissimae rei
nomen nostri a divis, Graeci, ut Plato interpretatur,
a furore duxerunt.

2   Gentem quidem nullam video neque tam humanam
atque doctam neque tam immanem atque barbaram,
quae non significari futura et a quibusdam intellegi
praedicique posse censeat. Principio Assyrii, ut
ab ultimis auctoritatem repetam, propter planitiem
magnitudinemque regionum, quas incolebant, cum
caelum ex omni parte patens atque apertum intue-

DIVINATION

BOOK I

I. THERE is an ancient belief, handed down to us even from mythical times and firmly established by the general agreement of the Roman people and of all nations, that divination of some kind exists among men ; this the Greeks call μαντική—that is, the foresight and knowledge of future events. A really splendid and helpful thing it is—if only such a faculty exists—since by its means men may approach very near to the power of gods. And, just as we Romans have done many other things better than the Greeks, so have we excelled them in giving to this most extraordinary gift a name, which we have derived from *divi*, a word meaning " gods," whereas, according to Plato's interpretation, they have derived it from *furor*, a word meaning " frenzy." [1]

Now I am aware of no people, however refined and learned or however savage and ignorant, which does not think that signs are given of future events, and that certain persons can recognize those signs and foretell events before they occur. First of all— to seek authority from the most distant sources—the Assyrians, on account of the vast plains inhabited by them, and because of the open and unobstructed view of the heavens presented to them on every

rentur, traiectiones motusque stellarum observita-
verunt, quibus notatis, quid cuique significaretur
memoriae prodiderunt. Qua in natione Chaldaei,
non ex artis sed ex gentis vocabulo nominati,
diuturna observatione siderum scientiam putantur
effecisse, ut praedici posset quid cuique eventurum
et quo quisque fato natus esset.

Eandem artem etiam Aegyptii longinquitate temporum innumerabilibus paene saeculis consecuti
putantur. Cilicum autem et Pisidarum gens et his
finitima Pamphylia, quibus nationibus praefuimus
ipsi, volatibus avium cantibusque certissimis signis
3 declarari res futuras putant. Quam vero Graecia
coloniam misit in Aeoliam, Ioniam, Asiam, Siciliam,
Italiam sine Pythio aut Dodonaeo aut Hammonis
oraculo ? aut quod bellum susceptum ab ea sine
consilio deorum est ?

II. Nec unum genus est divinationis publice pri-
vatimque celebratum. Nam, ut omittam ceteros
populos, noster quam multa genera complexus est !
Principio huius urbis parens Romulus non solum
auspicato urbem condidisse, sed ipse etiam optimus
augur fuisse traditur. Deinde auguribus et reliqui
reges usi, et exactis regibus, nihil publice sine
auspiciis nec domi nec militiae gerebatur. Cumque

---

[1] Cicero adds this because *Chaldaei* had come to be used
="astrologers." They were the ruling class among the
Babylonians.

side, took observations of the paths and movements of the stars, and, having made note of them, transmitted to posterity what significance they had for each person. And in that same nation the Chaldeans—a name which they derived not from their art but their race [1]—have, it is thought, by means of long-continued observation of the constellations, perfected a science which enables them to foretell what any man's lot will be and for what fate he was born.

The same art is believed to have been acquired also by the Egyptians through a remote past extending over almost countless ages. Moreover, the Cilicians, Pisidians, and their neighbours, the Pamphylians—nations which I once governed—think that the future is declared by the songs and flights of birds, which they regard as most infallible signs. And, indeed, what colony did Greece ever send into Aeolia, Ionia, Asia, Sicily, or Italy without consulting the Pythian or Dodonian oracle, or that of Jupiter Hammon? Or what war did she ever undertake without first seeking the counsel of the gods?

II. Nor is it only one single mode of divination that has been employed in public and in private. For, to say nothing of other nations, how many our own people have embraced! In the first place, according to tradition, Romulus, the father of this City, not only founded it in obedience to the auspices, but was himself a most skilful augur. Next, the other Roman kings employed augurs; and, again, after the expulsion of the kings, no public business was ever transacted at home or abroad without first taking the auspices. Furthermore, since our fore-

magna vis videretur esse et impetriendis[1] consulen-
disque rebus et monstris interpretandis ac procu-
randis in haruspicum disciplina, omnem hanc ex
Etruria scientiam adhibebant, ne genus esset ullum
divinationis, quod neglectum ab eis videretur.

4   Et cum duobus modis animi sine ratione et scientia
motu ipsi suo soluto et libero incitarentur, uno furente,
altero somniante, furoris divinationem Sibyllinis
maxime versibus contineri arbitrati eorum decem
interpretes delectos e civitate esse voluerunt. Ex
quo genere saepe hariolorum etiam et vatum furi-
bundas praedictiones, ut Octaviano bello Cornelii
Culleoli, audiendas putaverunt. Nec vero somnia
graviora, si quae ad rem publicam pertinere visa sunt,
a summo consilio neglecta sunt. Quin etiam memoria nostra templum Iunonis Sospitae L. Iulius, qui
cum P. Rutilio consul fuit, de senatus sententia
refecit ex Caeciliae, Baliarici filiae, somnio.

5   III. Atque haec, ut ego arbitror, veteres rerum
magis eventis moniti quam ratione docti probaverunt.
Philosophorum vero exquisita quaedam argumenta,
cur esset vera divinatio, collecta sunt. E quibus,
ut de antiquissimis loquar, Colophonius Xenophanes

---

[1] impetriendis *Manutius*; impetrandis MSS.

---

[1] The *haruspex* divines by the inspection of entrails.
[2] From the gods.
[3] This number was changed to fifteen in the time of Sulla.
[4] The Octavian War occurred in 87 B.C., between Octavius
and Sulla on the one side and Cinna and Marius on the other.
[5] This was in 105 B.C. when Cicero was one year old.
[6] Q. Caecilius Metellus Balearicus, consul 123 B.C.
[7] Cicero approved of the practice of divination, especially
of augury, from reasons of political expediency, not because
he thought it had any prophetic value; *cf.* ii. 33. 70.

fathers believed that the soothsayers'[1] art had great efficacy in seeking for omens and advice,[2] as well as in cases where prodigies were to be interpreted and their effects averted, they gradually introduced that art in its entirety from Etruria, lest it should appear that any kind of divination had been disregarded by them.

And since they thought that the human mind, when in an irrational and unconscious state, and moving by its own free and untrammelled impulse, was inspired in two ways, the one by frenzy and the other by dreams, and since they believed that the divination of frenzy was contained chiefly in the Sibylline verses, they decreed that ten [3] men should be chosen from the State to interpret those verses. In this same category also were the frenzied prophecies of soothsayers and seers, which our ancestors frequently thought worthy of belief—like the prophecies of Cornelius Culleolus, during the Octavian War.[4] Nor, indeed, were the more significant dreams, if they seemed to concern the administration of public affairs, disregarded by our Supreme Council. Why, even within my own memory, Lucius Julius, who was consul with Publius Rutilius, by a vote of the Senate rebuilt the temple of Juno, the Saviour,[5] in accordance with a dream of Caecilia, daughter of Balearicus.[6]

III. Now my opinion is that, in sanctioning such usages, the ancients were influenced more by actual results than convinced by reason.[7] However certain very subtle arguments to prove the trustworthiness of divination have been gathered by philosophers. Of these—to mention the most ancient—Xenophanes of Colophon, while asserting

unus, qui deos esse diceret, divinationem funditus
sustulit ; reliqui vero omnes praeter Epicurum balbu-
tientem de natura deorum divinationem probaverunt,
sed non uno modo. Nam cum Socrates omnesque
Socratici Zenoque et ei qui ab eo essent profecti
manerent in antiquorum philosophorum sententia
vetere Academia et Peripateticis consentientibus ;
cumque huic rei magnam auctoritatem Pythagoras
iam ante tribuisset, qui etiam ipse augur vellet esse,
plurimisque locis gravis auctor Democritus praesensionem rerum futurarum comprobaret, Dicaearchus
Peripateticus cetera divinationis genera sustulit,
somniorum et furoris reliquit ; Cratippus quoque
familiaris noster, quem ego parem summis Peripateticis iudico, eisdem rebus fidem tribuit, reliqua
divinationis genera reiecit.

6   Sed cum Stoici omnia fere illa defenderent, quod
et Zeno in suis commentariis quasi semina quaedam
sparsisset et ea Cleanthes paulo uberiora fecisset,
accessit acerrimo vir ingenio, Chrysippus, qui totam
de divinatione duobus libris explicavit sententiam,
uno praeterea de oraculis, uno de somniis ; quem
subsequens unum librum Babylonius Diogenes edidit,
eius auditor, duo Antipater, quinque noster Posidonius. Sed a Stoicis vel princeps eius disciplinae,
Posidonii doctor, discipulus Antipatri, degeneravit
Panaetius ; nec tamen ausus est negare vim esse
divinandi, sed dubitare se dixit. Quod illi in aliqua

the existence of gods, was the only one who repudiated divination in its entirety; but all the others, with the exception of Epicurus, who babbled about the nature of the gods, approved of divination, though not in the same degree. For example, Socrates and all of the Socratic School, and Zeno and his followers, continued in the faith of the ancient philosophers and in agreement with the Old Academy and with the Peripatetics. Their predecessor, Pythagoras, who even wished to be considered an augur himself, gave the weight of his great name to the same practice; and that eminent author, Democritus, in many passages, strongly affirmed his belief in a presentiment of things to come. Moreover, Dicaearchus, the Peripatetic, though he accepted divination by dreams and frenzy, cast away all other kinds; and my intimate friend, Cratippus, whom I consider the peer of the greatest of the Peripatetics, also gave credence to the same kinds of divination but rejected the rest.

The Stoics, on the other hand (for Zeno in his writings had, as it were, scattered certain seed which Cleanthes had fertilized somewhat), defended nearly every sort of divination. Then came Chrysippus, a man of the keenest intellect, who exhaustively discussed the whole theory of divination in two books, and, besides, wrote one book on oracles and another on dreams. And following him, his pupil, Diogenes of Babylon, published one book, Antipater two, and my friend, Posidonius, five. But Panaetius, the teacher of Posidonius, a pupil, too, of Antipater, and, even a pillar of the Stoic school, wandered off from the Stoics, and, though he dared not say that there was no efficacy in divination, yet he did say that he

re invitissimis Stoicis Stoico facere licuit, id nos ut in
reliquis rebus faciamus, a Stoicis non concedetur,
praesertim cum id, de quo Panaetio non liquet,
reliquis eiusdem disciplinae solis luce videatur clarius ?
7 Sed haec quidem laus Academiae praestantissimi philosophi iudicio et testimonio comprobata est.

IV. Etenim nobismet ipsis quaerentibus quid sit
de divinatione iudicandum, quod a Carneade multa
acute et copiose contra Stoicos disputata sint,
verentibusque ne temere vel falsae rei vel non satis
cognitae assentiamur, faciendum videtur ut diligenter
etiam atque etiam argumenta cum argumentis com-
paremus, ut fecimus in eis tribus libris quos de natura
deorum scripsimus. Nam cum omnibus in rebus
temeritas in assentiendo errorque turpis est, tum in
eo loco maxime in quo iudicandum est quantum
auspiciis rebusque divinis religionique tribuamus;
est enim periculum, ne aut neglectis iis impia
fraude aut susceptis anili superstitione obligemur.

8 V. Quibus de rebus et alias saepe et paulo accuratius
nuper, cum essem cum Q. fratre in Tusculano, disputatum est. Nam cum ambulandi causa in Lyceum
venissemus (id enim superiori gymnasio nomen est),

---

[1] *i.e.* Panaetius.
[2] Cicero had two gymnasia at Tusculum : the Lyceum,
so called from the place in which Aristotle taught at Athens,
the other, the Academia, named from the place where
Plato lectured. *Cf.* Cic. *Tusc.* ii. 3.

was in doubt. Then, since the Stoics—much against their will I grant you—permitted this famous Stoic to doubt on one point will they not grant to us Academicians the right to do the same on all other points, especially since that about which Panaetius is not clear is clearer than the light of day to the other members of the Stoic school ? At any rate, this praiseworthy tendency of the Academy to doubt has been approved by the solemn judgement of a most eminent philosopher.[1]

IV. Accordingly, since I, too, am in doubt as to the proper judgement to be rendered in regard to divination because of the many pointed and exhaustive arguments urged by Carneades against the Stoic view, and since I am afraid of giving a too hasty assent to a proposition which may turn out either false or insufficiently established, I have determined carefully and persistently to compare argument with argument just as I did in my three books *On the Nature of the Gods*. For a hasty acceptance of an erroneous opinion is discreditable in any case, and especially so in an inquiry as to how much weight should be given to auspices, to sacred rites, and to religious observances ; for we run the risk of committing a crime against the gods if we disregard them, or of becoming involved in old women's superstition if we approve them.

V. This subject has been discussed by me frequently on other occasions, but with somewhat more than ordinary care when my brother Quintus and I were together recently at my Tusculan villa. For the sake of a stroll we had gone to the Lyceum,[2] which is the name of my upper gymnasium, when Quintus remarked :

"Perlegi," inquit, "tuum paulo ante tertium *de Natura Deorum,* in quo disputatio Cottae, quamquam labefactavit sententiam meam, non funditus tamen sustulit."

"Optime vero," inquam; "etenim ipse Cotta sic disputat ut Stoicorum magis argumenta confutet quam hominum deleat religionem."

Tum Quintus: "Dicitur quidem istuc," inquit, "a Cotta, et vero saepius, credo, ne communia iura migrare videatur; sed studio contra Stoicos dis-9 serendi deos mihi videtur funditus tollere. Eius rationi non sane desidero quid respondeam; satis enim defensa religio est in secundo libro a Lucilio, cuius disputatio tibi ipsi, ut in extremo tertio scribis, ad veritatem est visa propensior. Sed, quod praetermissum est in illis libris (credo, quia commodius arbitratus es separatim id quaeri deque eo disseri), id est de divinatione, quae est earum rerum, quae fortuitae putantur, praedictio atque praesensio. Id, si placet, videamus quam habeat vim et quale sit. Ego enim sic existimo, si sint ea genera divinandi vera, de quibus accepimus quaeque colimus, esse deos, vicissimque, si di sint, esse qui divinent.

10 VI. "Arcem tu quidem Stoicorum," inquam, "Quinte, defendis, siquidem ista sic reciprocantur, ut et, si divinatio sit, di sint et, si di sint, sit divinatio.

---

[1] Gaius Aurelius Cotta, consul 75 B.C., an eminent orator, and Q. Lucilius Balbus were two of the disputants in *The Nature of the Gods,* the former as an Academician and the latter as a Stoic.

[2] *Cf.* Cic. *N.D.* iii. 40. 95 "haec cum essent dicta, ita discessimus, ut Velleio Cottae disputatio verior, mihi Balbi ad veritatis similitudinem videretur esse propensior."

[3] This question, however, is briefly discussed in *De nat. d.* ii. 3-5.

"I have just finished a careful reading of the third book of your treatise, *On the Nature of the Gods*, containing Cotta's discussion, which, though it has shaken my views of religion, has not overthrown them entirely."

"Very good," said I; "for Cotta's argument is intended rather to refute the arguments of the Stoics than to destroy man's faith in religion."

Quintus then replied: "Cotta[1] says the very same thing, and says it repeatedly, in order, as I think, not to appear to violate the commonly accepted canons of belief; yet it seems to me that, in his zeal to confute the Stoics, he utterly demolishes the gods. However, I am really at no loss for a reply to his reasoning; for in the second book Lucilius has made an adequate defence of religion and his argument, as you yourself state at the end of the third book,[2] seemed to you nearer to the truth than Cotta's. But there is a question[3] which you passed over in those books because, no doubt, you thought it more expedient to inquire into it in a separate discussion: I refer to divination, which is the foreseeing and foretelling of events considered as happening by chance. Now let us see, if you will, what efficacy it has and what its nature is. My own opinion is that, if the kinds of divination which we have inherited from our forefathers and now practise are trustworthy, then there are gods and, conversely, if there are gods then there are men who have the power of divination."

VI. "Why, my dear Quintus," said I, "you are defending the very citadel of the Stoics in asserting the interdependence of these two propositions: 'if there is divination there are gods,' and, 'if there are

Quorum neutrum tam facile quam tu arbitraris
conceditur. Nam et natura significari futura sine
deo possunt, et ut sint di potest fieri ut nulla ab
eis divinatio generi humano tributa sit."

Atque ille : " Mihi vero," inquit, " satis est argu-
menti et esse deos et eos consulere rebus humanis,
quod esse clara et perspicua divinationis genera
iudico. De quibus quid ipse sentiam, si placet,
exponam, ita tamen, si vacas animo neque habes
aliquid, quod huic sermoni praevertendum putes."

11 " Ego vero," inquam, " philosophiae, Quinte,
semper vaco ; hoc autem tempore, cum sit nihil
aliud quod libenter agere possim, multo magis aveo
audire de divinatione quid sentias."

" Nihil," inquit, " equidem novi, nec quod praeter
ceteros ipse sentiam ; nam cum antiquissimam sententiam, tum omnium populorum et gentium consensu comprobatam sequor. Duo sunt enim divinandi genera, quorum alterum artis est, alterum
12 naturae. Quae est autem gens aut quae civitas quae
non aut extispicum[1] aut monstra aut fulgora inter-
pretantium, aut augurum, aut astrologorum, aut
sortium (ea enim fere artis sunt), aut somniorum aut
vaticinationum (haec enim duo naturalia putantur),
praedictione moveatur ? Quarum quidem rerum
eventa magis arbitror quam causas quaeri oportere.

---

[1] extispicum *edd.* ; extis pecudum *MSS.*

---

[1] *Cf.* Cic. *N.D.* ii. 12.
[2] Cicero here refers to the deplorable condition of Roman
politics and his exclusion from the courts and from any
leading part in the government.
[3] *Vaticinatio* is employed here and elsewhere in this

gods there is divination.'[1]   But neither is granted
as readily as you think.   For it is possible that nature
gives signs of future events without the intervention of
a god, and it may be that there are gods without their
having conferred any power of divination upon men."

To this he replied : " I, at any rate, find sufficient
proof to satisfy me of the existence of gods and of
their concern in human affairs in my conviction that
there are some kinds of divination which are clear
and manifest.   With your permission I will set forth
my views on this subject, provided you are at leisure
and have nothing else which you think should be
preferred to such a discussion."

" Really, my dear Quintus," said I, " I always
have time for philosophy.   Moreover, since there is
nothing else at this time that I can do with pleasure,[2]
I am all the more eager to hear what you think
about divination."

" There is, I assure you," said he, " nothing new
or original in my views ; for those which I adopt
are not only very old, but they are endorsed by the
consent of all peoples and nations.   There are two
kinds of divination : the first is dependent on art,
the other on nature.   Now—to mention those almost
entirely dependent on art—what nation or what
state disregards the prophecies of soothsayers, or
of interpreters of prodigies and lightnings, or of
augurs, or of astrologers, or of oracles, or—to mention
the two kinds which are classed as natural means of
divination—the forewarnings of dreams, or of frenzy ?[3]
Of these methods of divining it behoves us, I think,
to examine the results rather than the causes.   For

work to mean the prophecies of those in a frenzy or under
the influence of great mental excitement.

Est enim vis et natura quaedam, quae tum observatis longo tempore significationibus, tum aliquo instinctu inflatuque divino futura praenuntiat.

VII. " Quare omittat urguere Carneades, quod faciebat etiam Panaetius requirens, Iuppiterne corni-cem a laeva, corvum ab dextera, canere iussisset. Observata sunt haec tempore immenso et eventis[1] animadversa et notata. Nihil est autem quod non longinquitas temporum excipiente memoria pro-dendisque monumentis efficere atque assequi possit.

13 Mirari licet quae sint animadversa a medicis herba-rum genera, quae radicum ad morsus bestiarum, ad oculorum morbos, ad vulnera, quorum vim atque naturam ratio numquam explicavit, utilitate et ars est et inventor probatus.

" Age ea, quae quamquam ex alio genere sunt, tamen divinationi sunt similiora, videamus :

> atque etiam ventos praemonstrat saepe futuros
> inflatum mare, cum subito penitusque tumescit,
> saxaque cana salis niveo spumata liquore
> tristificas certant Neptuno reddere voces,
> aut densus stridor cum celso e vertice montis
> ortus adaugescit scopulorum saepe repulsus.[2]

VIII. " Atque his rerum praesensionibus Prognos-tica tua referta sunt. Quis igitur elicere causas praesensionum potest ? Etsi video Boëthum Stoicum esse conatum, qui hactenus aliquid egit, ut earum rationem rerum explicaret, quae in mari caelove

---

[1] et eventis *Müller* ; et in significatione eventus *MSS.*

[2] saepe repulsus *MSS.*, *Müller* ; saepe repulsu *Dav.*, *Giese*, *who take* saepe *as adverb* = " with oft repulse from the rocks."

---

[1] The following verses and those in §§ 14, 15 are from Cicero's translation of the *Diosemeia* of Aratus.

there is a certain natural power, which now, through long-continued observation of signs and now, through some divine excitement and inspiration, makes prophetic announcement of the future.

VII. " Therefore let Carneades cease to press the question, which Panaetius also used to urge, whether Jove had ordered the crow to croak on the left side and the raven on the right. Such signs as these have been observed for an unlimited time, and the results have been checked and recorded. Moreover, there is nothing which length of time cannot accomplish and attain when aided by memory to receive and records to preserve. We may wonder at the variety of herbs that have been observed by physicians, of roots that are good for the bites of wild beasts, for eye affections, and for wounds, and though reason has never explained their force and nature, yet through their usefulness they have won approval for the medical art and for their discoverer.

" But come, let us consider instances, which although outside the category of divination, yet resemble it very closely : [1]

> The heaving sea oft warns of coming storms,
> When suddenly its depths begin to swell ;
> And hoary rocks, o'erspread with snowy brine,
> To the sea, in boding tones, attempt reply ;
> Or when from lofty mountain-peak upsprings
> A shrilly whistling wind, which stronger grows
> With each repulse by hedge of circling cliffs.

VIII. " Your book, *Prognostics*, is full of such warning signs, but who can fathom their causes ? And yet I see that the Stoic Boëthus has attempted to do so and has succeeded to the extent of explaining

14 fierent. Illa vero cur eveniant, quis probabiliter dixerit ?

> rava fulix itidem[1] fugiens e gurgite ponti
> nuntiat horribilis clamans instare procellas
> haud modicos tremulo fundens e gutture cantus.
> saepe etiam pertriste canit de pectore carmen
> et matutinis acredula vocibus instat,
> vocibus instat et assiduas iacit ore querellas,
> cum primum gelidos rores aurora remittit.
> fuscaque non numquam cursans per litora cornix
> demersit caput et fluctum cervice recepit.

15 IX. " Videmus haec signa numquam fere mentientia nec tamen cur ita fiat videmus.

> vos quoque signa videtis, aquai dulcis alumnae,
> cum clamore paratis inanis fundere voces
> absurdoque sono fontis et stagna cietis.

Quis est qui ranunculos hoc videre suspicari possit ? Sed inest in ranunculis vis et natura quaedam significans aliquid per se ipsa satis certa, cognitioni autem hominum obscurior.

> mollipedesque boves spectantes lumina caeli
> naribus umiferum duxere ex aëre sucum.

Non quaero cur, quoniam quid eveniat intellego.

---

[1] rava fulix itidem *Lambin.* ; rava fluxit itidem MSS., *Cana.*, *Müller.*

---

[1] *Fulix* is really " coot " ; but Aratus, *Dios.* 181 has ἐρωδιός, *ardea*, heron.

[2] *Acredula* (Cicero's translation of ὀλολυγών of Aratus, 216) is used nowhere else in Latin except in this passage and its meaning is uncertain. The rendering " nightingale " accords with the sense, whereas " owl," the translation of Meyer, Hottinger, and Kühner, does not. Others understand it to mean " tree-frog," " dove," etc.

[3] For frogs as weather-prophets *cf.* Arat. 214 ; Pliny *H.N.* xviii. 87 ; Virg. *Georg.* i. 378.

the phenomena of sea and sky. But who can give a satisfactory reason why the following things occur ?

Blue-grey herons,[1] in fleeing the raging abyss of the ocean,
Utter their warnings, discordant and wild, from tremulous gullets,
Shrilly proclaiming that storms are impending and laden with terrors.
Often at dawn, when Aurora releases the frost in the dewdrops,
Does the nightingale [2] pour from its breast predictions of evil ;
Then does it threaten and hurl from its throat its incessant complaining.
Often the dark-hued crow, while restlessly roaming the seashore,
Plunges its crest in the flood, as its neck encounters the billows.

IX. " Hardly ever do we see such signs deceive us and yet we do not see why it is so.

Ye, too, distinguish the signs, ye dwellers in waters delightful,
When, with a clamour, you utter your cries that are empty of meaning,
Stirring the fountains and ponds with absurd and ridiculous croaking.[3]

Who could suppose that frogs had this foresight ? And yet they do have by nature some faculty of premonition, clear enough of itself, but too dark for human comprehension.

Slow, clumsy oxen, their glances upturned to the light of the heavens,
Sniff at the air with their nostrils and know it is freighted with moisture.

I do not ask why, since I know what happens.

Iam vero semper viridis semperque gravata
lentiscus triplici solita grandescere fetu
ter fruges fundens tria tempora monstrat arandi.

16 Nec hoc quidem quaero, cur haec arbor una ter
floreat aut cur arandi maturitatem ad signum floris
accommodet ; hoc sum contentus, quod, etiamsi,
cur quidque fiat, ignorem, quid fiat, intellego. Pro
omni igitur divinatione idem, quod pro rebus eis,
quas commemoravi, respondebo.

X. " Quid scammoneae radix ad purgandum, quid
aristolochia ad morsus serpentium possit—quae nomen
ex inventore repperit, rem ipsam inventor ex somnio—
video, quod satis est ; cur possit, nescio. Sic ventorum et imbrium signa, quae dixi, rationem quam
habeant, non satis perspicio ; vim et eventum
agnosco, scio, approbo. Similiter, quid fissum in
extis, quid fibra valeat, accipio ; quae causa sit,
nescio. Atque horum quidem plena vita est ; extis
enim omnes fere utuntur.[1] Quid ? de fulgurum vi
dubitare num possumus ? Nonne cum multa alia
mirabilia, tum illud in primis ? Cum Summanus in
fastigio Iovis optimi maximi, qui tum erat fictilis, e
caelo ictus esset nec usquam eius simulacri caput
inveniretur, haruspices in Tiberim id depulsum esse

[1] utuntur *Müller* ; utimur *Dav.*

---

[1] *Convolvulus scammonia.*
[2] Birthwort, *Aristolochia rotunda.*

Now 'tis a fact that the evergreen mastic, e'er burdened
    with leafage,
Thrice is expanding and budding and thrice producing its
    berries ;
Triple its signs for the purpose of showing three seasons for
    ploughing.

Nor do I ever inquire why this tree alone blooms
three times, or why it makes the appearance of its
blossoms accord with the proper time for ploughing.
I am content with my knowledge that it does,
although I may not know why. Therefore, as
regards all kinds of divination I will give the same
answer that I gave in the cases just mentioned.

X. " I see the purgative effect of the scammony
root [1] and I see an antidote for snake-bite in the
aristolochia plant [2]—which, by the way, derives its
name from its discoverer who learned of it in a dream
—I see their power and that is enough ; why they
have it I do not know. Thus as to the cause of those
premonitory signs of winds and rains already mentioned I am not quite clear, but their force and effect
I recognize, understand, and vouch for. Likewise as
to the cleft or thread in the entrails : I accept their
meaning ; I do not know their cause. And life is
full of individuals in just the same situation that I
am in, for nearly everybody employs entrails in
divining. Again : is it possible for us to doubt the
prophetic value of lightning ? Have we not many
instances of its marvels ? and is not the following
one especially remarkable ? When the statue of
Summanus which stood on the top of the temple of
Jupiter Optimus Maximus—his statue was then made
of clay—was struck by a thunderbolt and its head
could not be found anywhere, the soothsayers
declared that it had been hurled into the Tiber ;

dixerunt; idque inventum est eo loco qui est ab haruspicibus demonstratus.

17 XI. "Sed quo potius utar aut auctore aut teste quam te? cuius edidici etiam versus, et lubenter quidem, quos in secundo de *Consulatu* Urania Musa pronuntiat :

> principio aetherio flammatus Iuppiter igni
> vertitur et totum conlustrat lumine mundum,
> menteque divina caelum terrasque petessit,
> quae penitus sensus hominum vitasque retentat
> aetheris aeterni saepta atque inclusa cavernis.

> Et, si stellarum motus cursusque vagantis
> nosse velis, quae sint signorum in sede locatae
> (quae verbo et falsis Graiorum vocibus errant,
> re vera certo lapsu spatioque feruntur),
> omnia iam cernes divina mente notata.

18 > Nam primum astrorum volucris te consule motus
> concursusque gravis stellarum ardore micantis
> tu quoque, cum tumulos Albano in monte nivalis
> lustrasti et laeto mactasti lacte Latinas,
> vidisti et claro tremulos ardore cometas,
> multaque misceri nocturna strage putasti,
> quod ferme dirum in tempus cecidere Latinae,

---

[1] For *cometa = aurora septentrionalis* cf. Sen. *Q.N.* vii. 6.
[2] The *feriae Latinae*, in honour of the Latin League, were celebrated by the consuls immediately upon assuming office, in the presence of all the magistrates, in part on the Alban Mount and in part on the Capitol, and lasted four days.

and it was discovered in the very spot which they had pointed out.

XI. " But what authority or what witness can I better employ than yourself? I have even learned by heart and with great pleasure the following lines uttered by the Muse, Urania, in the second book of your poem entitled, *My Consulship* :

First of all, Jupiter, glowing with fire from regions celestial,
Turns, and the whole of creation is filled with the light of
    his glory ;
And, though the vaults of aether eternal begird and con-
    fine him,
Yet he, with spirit divine, ever searching the earth and
    the heavens,
Sounds to their innermost depths the thoughts and the
    actions of mortals.

When one has learned the motions and variant paths of
    the planets,
Stars that abide in the seat of the signs, in the Zodiac's
    girdle,
(Spoken of falsely as vagrants or rovers in Greek nomen-
    clature,
Whereas in truth their distance is fixed and their speed is
    determined,)
Then will he know that *all* are controlled by an Infinite
    Wisdom.

You, being consul, at once did observe the swift constellations,
Noting the glare of luminous stars in direful conjunction ;
Then you beheld the tremulous sheen of the Northern
    aurora,[1]
When, on ascending the mountainous heights of snowy
    Albanus,
You offered joyful libations of milk at the Feast of the
    Latins[2] ;
Ominous surely the time wherein fell that Feast of the
    Latins :
Many a warning was given, it seemed, of slaughter noc-
    turnal ;

eum claram speciem concreto lumine luna
abdidit et subito stellanti nocte perempta est.
quid vero Phoebi fax, tristis nuntia belli,
quae magnum ad columen flammato ardore volabat,
praecipitis caeli partis obitusque petessens ?
aut cum terribili perculsus fulmine civis
luce serenanti vitalia lumina liquit ?
aut cum se gravido tremefecit corpore tellus ?
iam vero variae nocturno tempore visae
terribiles formae bellum motusque monebant,
multaque per terras vates oracla furenti
pectore fundebant tristis minitantia casus,

19   atque ea, quae lapsu tandem cecidere vetusto,
haec fore perpetuis signis clarisque frequentans
ipse deum genitor caelo terrisque canebat.

XII.   Nunc ea, Torquato quae quondam et consule Cotta
Lydius ediderat Tyrrhenae gentis haruspex,
omnia fixa tuus glomerans determinat annus.
nam pater altitonans stellanti nixus Olympo
ipse suos quondam tumulos ac templa petivit
et Capitolinis iniecit sedibus ignis.
tum species ex aere vetus venerataque[1] Nattae
concidit, elapsaeque vetusto numine leges,
et divom simulacra peremit fulminis ardor.

> [1] venerataque *Müller* ; generataque MSS., *Dav.*

---

[1] *Concreto lumine, i.e. quum iunctis cornibus pleno orbe
luceret,* Hott.

[2] *Phoebi fax=bolida,* an arrow-shaped torch.

[3] They were consuls 65 B.C., two years before Cicero ;
cf. Cic. *Cat.* iii. 8. 19.

[4] The Etruscans were thought to have come originally
from Lydia.

Then, of a sudden, the moon at her full[1] was blotted
 from heaven—
Hidden her features resplendent, though night was be-
 jewelled with planets ;
Then did that dolorous herald of War, the torch of Apollo,[2]
Mount all aflame to the dome of the sky, to the zenith of
 heaven,
Seeking a place on the westerly slopes, where the sun has
 its setting ;
Then did a Roman depart from these radiant abodes of the
 living,
Stricken by terrible lightning from heavens serene and
 unclouded.
Then through the fruit-laden body of earth ran the shock
 of an earthquake ;
Spectres at night were observed, appalling and changeful
 of figure,
Giving their warning that war was at hand, and internal
 commotion ;
Over all lands there outpoured, from the frenzied bosoms
 of prophets,
Dreadful predictions, gloomy forecasts of impending disaster.
And the misfortunes which happened at last and were
 long in their passing—
These were foretold by the Father of Gods, in earth and
 in heaven,
Through unmistakable signs that he gave and often
 repeated.

II.   Now, of those prophecies made when Torquatus and
 Cotta[3] were consuls,—
Made by a Lydian diviner,[4] by one of Etruscan extraction—
All, in the round of your crowded twelve months, were
 brought to fulfilment.
For high-thundering Jove, as he stood on starry Olympus,
Hurled forth his blows at the temples and monuments raised
 in his honour,
And on the Capitol's site he unloosed the bolts of his
 lightning.
Then fell the brazen image of Natta, ancient and honoured :
Vanished the tablets of laws long ago divinely enacted ;
Wholly destroyed were the statues of gods by the heat of
 the lightning.

CICERO

20   Hic silvestris erat Romani nominis altrix,
Martia, quae parvos Mavortis semine natos
uberibus gravidis vitali rore rigabat;
quae tum cum pueris flammato fulminis ictu
concidit atque avolsa pedum vestigia liquit.

      Tum quis non artis scripta ac monumenta volutans
voces tristificas chartis promebat Etruscis?
omnes civili generosa stirpe profectam
vitare ingentem cladem pestemque monebant,
vel legum exitium constanti voce ferebant,
templa deumque adeo flammis urbemque iubebant
eripere et stragem horribilem caedemque vereri;
atque haec fixa gravi fato ac fundata teneri,
ni prius[1] excelsum ad columen formata decore
sancta Iovis species claros spectaret in ortus;
tum fore ut occultos populus sanctusque senatus
cernere conatus posset, si solis ad ortum
conversa inde patrum sedes populique videret.

21   Haec tardata diu species multumque morata,
consule te, tandem celsa est in sede locata,
atque una fixi ac signati temporis hora
Iuppiter excelsa clarabat sceptra columna,
et[2] clades patriae flamma ferroque parata
vocibus Allobrogum patribus populoque patebat.

      [1] prius *Giese*; post *Dav.*
      [2] et *Giese*; at *Dav.*

      [1] *Cf.* Cic. *Cat.* i. 1; *ib.* iii. 8.

246

Here was the Martian beast, the nurse of Roman dominion.
Suckling with life-giving dew, that issued from udders
distended,
Children divinely begotten, who sprang from the loins
of the War God;
Stricken by lightning she toppled to earth, bearing with
her children;
Torn from her station, she left the prints of her feet in
descending.

Then what diviner, in turning the records and tomes of the
augurs,
Failed to relate the mournful forecasts the Etruscans had
written?
Seers all advised to beware the monstrous destruction and
slaughter,
Plotted by Romans who traced their descent from a noble
ancestry;
Or they proclaimed the law's overthrow with voices
insistent,
Bidding us rescue the city from flames, and the deities'
temples;
Fearful they bade us become of horrible chaos and carnage;
These, by a rigorous Fate, would be certainly fixed and
determined,
Were not a sacred statue of Jove, one comely of figure,
High on a column erected beforehand, with eyes to the
eastward;
Then would the people and venerable senate be able to fathom
Hidden designs, when that statue—its face to the sun at
its rising—
Should behold from its station the seats of the people and
Senate.

Long was the statue delayed and much was it hindered in
making.
Finally, you being consul, it stood in its lofty position.
Just at the moment of time, which the gods had set and
predicted,
When on column exalted the sceptre of Jove was illumined,
Did Allobrogian voices proclaim to Senate and people
What destruction by dagger and torch was prepared for
our country.[1]

XIII. Rite igitur veteres, quorum monumenta tenetis,
       qui populos urbisque modo ac virtute regebant,
       rite etiam vestri, quorum pietasque fidesque
       praestitit et longe vicit sapientia cunctos,
       praecipue coluere vigenti numine divos.

       Haec adeo penitus cura videre sagaci,
       otia qui studiis laeti tenuere decoris,
22   inque Academia umbrifera nitidoque Lyceo
       fuderunt claras fecundi pectoris artis.
       e quibus ereptum primo iam a flore iuventae
       te patria in media virtutum mole locavit.
       tu tamen anxiferas curas requiete relaxas,
       quod patriae vacat, id studiis nobisque sacrasti.

" Tu igitur animum poteris inducere contra ea,
quae a me disputantur de divinatione, dicere, qui
et gesseris ea, quae gessisti, et ea, quae pronuntiavi,
accuratissime scripseris ?

23   " Quid ? quaeris, Carneades, cur haec ita fiant
aut qua arte perspici possint ? Nescire me fateor,
evenire autem te ipsum dico videre. ' Casu,' inquis.
Itane vero ? quicquam potest casu esse factum, quod
omnes habet in se numeros veritatis ? Quattuor tali
iacti casu Venerium efficiunt ; num etiam centum

---

¹ Plato lectured in the Academy, and Aristotle in the
Lyceum.
² The Venus throw occurred when each of the four dice
fell with a different number on its upper face.

I.　Rightly, therefore, the ancients whose monuments you
  have in keeping,
Romans whose rule over peoples and cities was just and
  courageous,
Rightly your kindred, foremost in honour and pious
  devotion,
Far surpassing the rest of their fellows in shrewdness and
  wisdom,
Held it a duty supreme to honour the Infinite Godhead.

Such were the truths they beheld who painfully searching
  for wisdom
Gladly devoted their leisure to study of all that was noble,
Who, in Academy's shade and Lyceum's[1] dazzling efful-
  gence,
Uttered the brilliant reflections of minds abounding in
  culture.
Torn from these studies, in youth's early dawn, your
  country recalled you,
Giving you place in the thick of the struggle for public
  preferment ;
Yet, in seeking surcease from the worries and cares that
  oppress you,
Time, that the State leaves free, you devote to us and to
  learning.

 " In view, therefore, of your acts, and in view
too of your own verses which I have quoted and which
were composed with the utmost care, could *you* be
persuaded to controvert the position which I maintain in regard to divination ?
 " But what ?　You ask, Carneades, do you, why
these things so happen, or by what rules they may
be understood ?　I confess that I do not know,
but that they do so fall out I assert that you yourself see.　' Mere accidents,' you say.　Now, really,
is that so ?　Can anything be an ' accident ' which
bears upon itself every mark of truth ?　Four dice
are cast and a Venus throw [2] results—that is chance ;

Venerios. si quadringentos talos ieceris, casu futuros
putas ? Aspersa temere pigmenta in tabula oris
liniamenta efficere possunt ; num etiam Veneris Coae
pulchritudinem effici posse aspersione fortuita putas ?
Sus rostro si humi A litteram impresserit, num
propterea suspicari poteris Andromacham Ennii ab
ea posse describi ? Fingebat Carneades in Chiorum
lapicidinis saxo diffisso caput extitisse Panisci ; credo,
aliquam non dissimilem figuram, sed certe non talem
ut eam factam a Scopa diceres. Sic enim se profecto
res habet, ut numquam perfecte veritatem casus
imitetur.

24   XIV. " ' At non numquam ea, quae praedicta sunt
minus eveniunt.' Quae tandem id ars non habet ?
earum dico artium, quae coniectura continentur et
sunt opinabiles. An medicina ars non putanda est ?
quam tamen multa fallunt. Quid ? gubernatores
nonne falluntur ? An Achivorum exercitus et tot
navium rectores non ita profecti sunt ab Ilio, ut
' profectione laeti piscium lasciviam intuerentur,' ut
ait Pacuvius, ' nec tuendi satietas capere posset ? '

interea prope iam óccidente sóle inhorrescít mare,
ténebrae conduplicántur noctisque ét nimbum occaecát
    nigror.

---

[1] This was a painting by Apelles and one of the greatest
of antiquity.   Later it was brought to Rome by Augustus.
[2] In his *Dulorestes*.

but do you think it would be chance, too, if in one hundred casts you made one hundred Venus throws ? It is possible for paints flung at random on a canvas to form the outlines of a face ; but do you imagine that an accidental scattering of pigments could produce the beautiful portrait of Venus of Cos [1] ? Suppose that a hog should form the letter ' A ' on the ground with its snout ; is that a reason for believing that it could write out Ennius's poem *The Andromache* ?

" Carneades used to have a story that once in the Chian quarries when a stone was split open there appeared the head of the infant god Pan ; I grant that the figure may have borne some resemblance to the god, but assuredly the resemblance was not such that you could ascribe the work to a Scopas. For it is undeniably true that no perfect imitation of a thing was ever made by chance.

XIV. " ' But,' it is objected, ' sometimes predictions are made which do not come true.' And pray what art—and by art I mean the kind that is dependent on conjecture and deduction—what art, I say, does not have the same fault ? Surely the practice of medicine is an art, yet how many mistakes it makes ! And pilots—do they not make mistakes at times ? For example, when the armies of the Greeks and the captains of their mighty fleet set sail from Troy, they, as Pacuvius says,[2]

Glad at leaving Troy behind them, gazed upon the fish at play,
Nor could get their fill of gazing—thus they whiled the time away.
Meantime, as the sun was setting, high uprose the angry main :
Thick and thicker fell the shadows ; night grew black with blinding rain.

Num igitur tot clarissimorum ducum regumque
naufragium sustulit artem gubernandi ? aut num
imperatorum scientia nihil est, quia summus imperator nuper fugit amisso exercitu ? aut num
propterea nulla est rei publicae gerendae ratio atque
prudentia, quia multa Cn. Pompeium, quaedam M.
Catonem, non nulla etiam te ipsum fefellerunt ?
Similis est haruspicum responsio omnisque opinabilis
divinatio ; coniectura enim nititur, ultra quam pro-
25 gredi non potest. Ea fallit fortasse non numquam,
sed tamen ad veritatem saepissime derigit ; est
enim ab omni aeternitate repetita, in qua cum paene
innumerabiliter res eodem modo evenirent isdem
signis antegressis, ars est effecta eadem saepe
animadvertendo ac notando.

XV. " Auspicia vero vestra quam constant ! quae
quidem nunc a Romanis auguribus ignorantur (bona
hoc tua venia dixerim), a Cilicibus, Pamphyliis,
26 Pisidis, Lyciis tenentur. Nam quid ego hospitem
nostrum, clarissimum atque optimum virum, Deiotarum regem, commemorem, qui nihil umquam
nisi auspicato gerit ? Qui cum ex itinere quodam
proposito et constituto revertisset aquilae admonitus
volatu, conclave illud, ubi erat mansurus, si ire
27 perrexisset, proxima nocte corruit. Itaque, ut ex

---

[1] Referring to Pompey's defeat by Caesar at Pharsalus,
48 B.C.
[2] Cicero was elected to the college and became a colleague
of Pompey and Hortensius in 53 B.C. Quintus proceeds
now to contrast the state of augury in 53-63 B.C. with that
of the time of the dialogue, 44.

Then, did the fact that so many illustrious captains and kings suffered shipwreck deprive navigation of its right to be called an art ? And is military science of no effect because a general of the highest renown recently lost his army and took to flight ?[1] Again, is statecraft devoid of method or skill because political mistakes were made many times by Gnaeus Pompey, occasionally by Marcus Cato, and once or twice even by yourself ? So it is with the responses of soothsayers, and, indeed, with every sort of divination whose deductions are merely probable ; for divination of that kind depends on inference and beyond inference it cannot go. It sometimes misleads perhaps, but none the less in most cases it guides us to the truth. For this same conjectural divination is the product of boundless eternity and within that period it has grown into an art through the repeated observation and recording of almost countless instances in which the same results have been preceded by the same signs.

XV. " Indeed how trustworthy were the auspices taken when you were augur ! [2] At the present time—pray pardon me for saying so—Roman augurs neglect auspices, although the Cilicians, Pamphylians, Pisidians, and Lycians hold them in high esteem. I need not remind you of that most famous and worthy man, our guest-friend, King Deiotarus, who never undertook any enterprise without first taking the auspices. On one occasion after he had set out on a journey for which he had made careful plans beforehand, he returned home because of the warning given him by the flight of an eagle. The room in which he would have been staying, had he continued on his road, collapsed the very next

ipso audiebam, persaepe revertit ex itinere, cum iam progressus esset multorum dierum viam. Cuius quidem hoc praeclarissimum est, quod, posteaquam a Caesare tetrarchia et regno pecuniaque multatus est, negat se tamen eorum auspiciorum, quae sibi ad Pompeium proficiscenti secunda evenerint, paenitere ; senatus enim auctoritatem et populi Romani libertatem atque imperii dignitatem suis armis esse defensam, sibique eas aves, quibus auctoribus officium et fidem secutus esset, bene consuluisse ; antiquiorem enim sibi fuisse possessionibus suis gloriam. Ille mihi videtur igitur vere augurari.

" Nam nostri quidem magistratus auspiciis utuntur coactis ; necesse est enim offa obiecta cadere frustum 28 ex pulli ore cum pascitur. Quod autem scriptum habetis hinc tripudium fieri, si ex ea quid in solum ceciderit, hoc quoque, quod dixi, coactum tripudium solistimum dicitis. Itaque multa auguria, multa auspicia, quod Cato ille sapiens queritur, neglegentia collegi amissa plane et deserta sunt.

XVI. " Nihil fere quondam maioris rei nisi auspicato ne privatim quidem gerebatur, quod etiam nunc nuptiarum auspices declarant, qui, re omissa, nomen

---

[1] Deiotarus was tetrarch of Gallograecia and king of Lesser Armenia ; *cf.* ii. 37. 78 ; *Bell. Alex.* 67.

[2] In such cases the chickens were so fed that the sign desired must be given ; *cf.* ii. chaps. 34 and 35.

[3] When the chickens ate so eagerly that some of the food fell to ground and struck it—that was a good omen. See ii. chaps. 34 and 35 where *terripudium* is explained as =*terripavium* (from *terra* and *pavire*) and *solistimum* has apparently almost the same meaning. Quintus seems to complain that this was not a true method of divination, as the result was inevitable.

night. This is why, as he told me himself, he had
time and again abandoned a journey even though
he might have been travelling for many days. By
the way, that was a very noble utterance of his
which he made after Caesar had deprived him of his
tetrarchy and kingdom,[1] and had forced him to pay
an indemnity too. ' Notwithstanding what has
happened,' said he, ' I do not regret that the auspices
favoured my joining Pompey. By so doing I enlisted
my military power in defence of senatorial authority,
Roman liberty, and the supremacy of the empire.
The birds, at whose instance I followed the course
of duty and of honour, counselled well, for I value
my good name more than riches.' His conception
of augury, it seems to me, is the correct one.

" For with us magistrates make use of auspices,
but they are ' forced auspices,'[2] since the sacred
chickens in eating the dough pellets thrown must
let some fall from their beaks. But, according to
the writings of you augurs, a *tripudium* results if
any of the food should fall to the ground, and what
I spoke of as a ' forced augury ' your fraternity
calls a *tripudium solistimum*.[3] And so through the
indifference of the college, as Cato the Wise laments,
many auguries and auspices have been entirely
abandoned and lost.

XVI. " In ancient times scarcely any matter out
of the ordinary was undertaken, even in private life,
without first consulting the auspices, clear proof
of which is given even at the present time by our
custom of having ' nuptial auspices,'[4] though they
have lost their former religious significance and only

[4] *Cf.* Val. Max. ii. 1 ; Juv. *Sat.* x. 336 ; Suet. *Claud.*
ch. 26.

tantum tenent. Nam ut nunc extis (quamquam id
ipsum aliquanto minus quam olim), sic tum avibus
magnae res impetriri solebant. Itaque, sinistra dum
non exquirimus, in dira et in vitiosa incurrimus.
29 Ut P. Claudius, Appii Caeci filius, eiusque collega
L. Iunius classis maximas perdiderunt, cum vitio
navigassent. Quod eodem modo evenit Agamem-
noni ; qui, cum Achivi coepissent

> inter se strépere aperteque ártem obterere extíspicum,
> sólvere imperát secundo rúmore adversáque avi.

" Sed quid vetera ?   M. Crasso quid acciderit,
videmus, dirarum obnuntiatione neglecta.   In quo
Appius, collega tuus, bonus augur, ut ex te audire
soleo, non satis scienter virum bonum et civem
egregium censor C. Ateium notavit, quod ementitum
auspicia subscriberet.   Esto ; fuerit hoc censoris, si
iudicabat ementitum ; at illud minime auguris, quod
adscripsit ob eam causam populum Romanum calamitatem maximam cepisse.   Si enim ea causa calamitatis fuit, non est in eo culpa, qui obnuntiavit, sed
in eo, qui non paruit.   Veram enim fuisse obnuntia-

---

[1] In the first Punic War 249 B.C.; *cf.* Cic. *De nat. d.* ii.
3. 7 ; Polyb. i. 54.
[2] Probably from the *Dulorestes* of Pacuvius.
[3] Triumvir with Caesar and Pompey, killed in the Par-
thian War, 53 B.C.   See ii. 84.

preserve the name. For just as to-day on important occasions we make use of entrails in divining—though even they are employed to a less extent than formerly—so in the past resort was usually had to divination by means of birds. And thus it is that by failing to seek out the unpropitious signs we run into awful disasters. For example, Publius Claudius, son of Appius Caecus,[1] and his colleague Lucius Junius, lost very large fleets by going to sea when the auguries were adverse. The same fate befell Agamemnon ; for, after the Greeks had begun to

Raise aloft their frequent clamours, showing scorn of augur's art,
Noise prevailed and not the omen : he then bade the ships depart.[2]

" But why cite such ancient instances ? We see what happened to Marcus Crassus [3] when he ignored the announcement of unfavourable omens. It was on the charge of having on this occasion falsified the auspices that Gaius Ateius, an honourable man and a distinguished citizen, was, on insufficient evidence, stigmatized by the then censor Appius, who was your associate in the augural college, and an able one too, as I have often heard you say. I grant you that in pursuing the course he did Appius was within his rights as a censor, if, in his judgement, Ateius had announced a fraudulent augury. But he showed no capacity whatever as an augur in holding Ateius responsible for that awful disaster which befell the Roman people. Had this been the cause then the fault would not have been in Ateius, who made the announcement that the augury was unfavourable, but in Crassus, who disobeyed it ; for the issue proved that the announce-

257

tionem, ut ait idem augur et censor, exitus approbavit;
quae si falsa fuisset, nullam afferre potuisset causam
calamitatis. Etenim dirae, sicut cetera auspicia, ut
omina, ut signa, non causas afferunt, cur quid eveniat,
30 sed nuntiant eventura, nisi provideris. Non igitur
obnuntiatio Atei causam finxit calamitatis, sed signo
obiecto monuit Crassum, quid eventurum esset, nisi
cavisset. Ita aut illa obnuntiatio nihil valuit, aut si,
ut Appius iudicat, valuit, id valuit ut peccatum
haereat non in eo qui monuerit, sed in eo qui non
obtemperarit.

XVII. " Quid ? lituus iste vester quod clarissimum
est insigne auguratus, unde vobis est traditus ?
Nempe eo Romulus regiones direxit¹ tum cum urbem
condidit. Qui quidem Romuli lituus, id est incurvum
et leviter a summo inflexum bacillum, quod ab eius
litui quo canitur similitudine nomen invenit, cum
situs esset in curia Saliorum, quae est in Palatio,
31 eaque deflagravisset, inventus est integer.² Quid ?
multis annis post Romulum Prisco regnante Tarquinio
quis veterum scriptorum non loquitur, quae sit ab
Atto Navio per lituum regionum facta discriptio ?
Qui cum propter paupertatem sues puer pasceret,
una ex iis amissa vovisse dicitur, si recuperasset,

---

¹ i.e. marked out with his staff a certain quarter (templum)
where he would take his augury. In Livy i. 6 Romulus
takes the Palatine as his templum, Remus the Aventine ;
but usually templum=a quarter in the sky.
² This temple was burned 390 B.C. by the Gauls when they
sacked the city, and everything in the temple, except this
staff, was burned. Cf. Val. Max. i. 1 ; Livy v. 41 ; Plut.
Camil. 32.

ment was true, as this same augur and censor admits.
But even if the augury had been false it could not
have been the cause of the disaster ; for unfavourable auguries—and the same may be said of auspices,
omens, and all other signs—are not the causes of
what follows : they merely foretell what will occur
unless precautions are taken. Therefore Ateius, by
his announcement, did not create the cause of the
disaster ; but having observed the sign he simply
advised Crassus what the result would be if the
warning was ignored. It follows, then, that the
announcement by Ateius of the unfavourable
augury had no effect ; or if it did, as Appius thinks,
then the sin is not in him who gave the warning,
but in him who disregarded it.

XVII. " And whence, pray, did you augurs derive
that staff, which is the most conspicuous mark of
your priestly office ? It is the very one, indeed,
with which Romulus marked out[1] the quarter for
taking observations when he founded the city.
Now this staff is a crooked wand, slightly curved at
the top, and, because of its resemblance to a trumpet,
derives its name from the Latin word meaning
' the trumpet with which the battle-charge is sounded.'
It was placed in the temple of the Salii on the
Palatine hill and, though the temple was burned,
the staff was found uninjured.[2] What ancient
chronicler fails to mention the fact that in the reign
of Tarquinius Priscus, long after the time of Romulus,
a quartering of the heavens was made with this
staff by Attus Navius ? Because of poverty Attus
was a swineherd in his youth. As the story goes, he,
having lost one of his hogs, made a vow that if he
recovered it he would make an offering to the god

uvam se deo daturum, quae maxima esset in vinea ;
itaque sue inventa ad meridiem spectans in vinea
media dicitur constitisse, cumque in quattuor partis
vineam divisisset trisque partis aves abdixissent,
quarta parte, quae erat reliqua, in regiones dis-
tributa, mirabili magnitudine uvam, ut scriptum
videmus, invenit.

"Qua re celebrata cum vicini omnes ad eum de
rebus suis referrent, erat in magno nomine et gloria.
32 Ex quo factum est, ut eum ad se rex Priscus arcesseret.
Cuius cum temptaret scientiam auguratus, dixit ei
cogitare se quiddam ; id possetne fieri consuluit.
Ille, augurio acto, posse respondit. Tarquinius autem
dixit se cogitasse cotem novacula posse praecidi.
Tum Attum iussisse experiri. Ita cotem in comitium
allatam, inspectante et rege et populo, novacula
esse discissam. Ex eo evenit ut et Tarquinius
augure Atto Navio uteretur et populus de suis rebus
33 ad eum referret. Cotem autem illam et novaculam
defossam in comitio supraque impositum puteal
accepimus.

"Negemus omnia, comburamus annales, ficta haec
esse dicamus, quidvis denique potius quam deos res
humanas curare fateamur. Quid ? quod scriptum
apud te est de Ti. Graccho, nonne et augurum et
haruspicum comprobat disciplinam ? qui cum taber-

---

[1] *Cf.* Cic. *De nat. d.* ii. 4.

of the largest bunch of grapes in his vineyard
Accordingly, after he had found the hog, he took
his stand, we are told, in the middle of the vineyard,
with his face to the south and divided the vineyard
into four parts. When the birds had shown three
of these parts to be unfavourable, he subdivided the
fourth and last part and then found, as we see it
recorded, a bunch of grapes of marvellous size.

"This occurrence having been noised abroad, all
his neighbours began to consult him about their
own affairs and thus greatly enhanced his name
and fame. The consequence was that King Priscus
summoned him to his presence. The king, wishing
to make trial of his skill as an augur, said to him :
' I am thinking of something ; tell me whether
it can be done or not.' Attus, having taken the
auspices, replied that it could be done. Thereupon Tarquin said that what he had been thinking
of was the possibility of cutting a whetstone in two
with a razor, and ordered the trial to be made. So
the stone was brought into the comitium, and, while
the king and his people looked on, it was cut in two
with a razor. The result was that Tarquin employed
him as his augur, and the people consulted him about
their private concerns. Moreover, according to
tradition, the whetstone and razor were buried in
the comitium and a stone curbing placed over them.

" Let us declare this story wholly false ; let us
burn the chronicles that contain it ; let us call it a
myth and admit almost anything you please rather
than the fact that the gods have any concern in
human affairs. But look at this : does not the story
about Tiberius Gracchus found in your own writings[1]
acknowledge that augury and soothsaying are arts ?

naculum vitio cepisset imprudens, quod inauspicatc pomoerium transgressus esset, comitia consulibus rogandis habuit. Nota res est et a te ipso mandata monumentis. Sed et ipse augur Ti. Gracchus auspiciorum auctoritatem confessione errati sui comprobavit; et haruspicum disciplinae magna accessit auctoritas, qui recentibus comitiis in senatum introducti negaverunt iustum comitiorum rogatorem fuisse.

34   XVIII. " Eis igitur assentior, qui duo genera divinationum esse dixerunt, unum, quod particeps esset artis, alterum, quod arte careret. Est enim ars in eis qui novas res coniectura persequuntur, veteres observatione didicerunt. Carent autem arte ei qui, non ratione aut coniectura observatis ac notatis signis, sed concitatione quadam animi aut soluto liberoque motu, futura praesentiunt, quod et somniantibus saepe contingit et non numquam vaticinantibus per furorem, ut Bacis Boeotius, ut Epimenides Cres, ut Sibylla Erythraea. Cuius generis oracula etiam habenda sunt, non ea, quae aequatis sortibus ducuntur, sed illa, quae instinctu divino afflatuque funduntur; etsi ipsa sors contemnenda non est, si auctoritatem habet vetustatis, ut eae sunt sortes, quas e terra editas accepimus; quae

---

¹ The *tabernaculum* was the tent placed in the centre of the station on which the augur made his observation. The *pomerium* was the sacred boundary of the city, and in it the *tabernaculum* was placed. If the celebrant crossed the *pomerium* before completing the auspices he must choose a new station and take the auspices again.

² An alternative translation is : " He having made a technical error in placing his *tabernaculum*, without realizing what he had done—he crossed the *pomerium* before completing the auspices—held the consular election."

He, having placed his *tabernaculum*,[1] unwittingly violated augural law by crossing the *pomerium* before completing the auspices ; nevertheless he held the consular election.[2] The fact is well known to you since you have recorded it. Besides, Tiberius Gracchus, who was himself an augur, confirmed the authority of auspices by confessing his error ; and the soothsayers, too, greatly enhanced the reputation of their calling, when brought into the Senate immediately after the election, by declaring that the election supervisor had acted without authority.

XVIII. " I agree, therefore, with those who have said that there are two kinds of divination : one, which is allied with art ; the other, which is devoid of art. Those diviners employ art, who, having learned the known by observation, seek the unknown by deduction. On the other hand those do without art who, unaided by reason or deduction or by signs which have been observed and recorded, forecast the future while under the influence of mental excitement, or of some free and unrestrained emotion. This condition often occurs to men while dreaming and sometimes to persons who prophesy while in a frenzy—like Bacis of Boeotia, Epimenides of Crete and the Sibyl of Erythraea.[3] In this latter class must be placed oracles—not oracles given by means of ' equalized lots '[4]—but those uttered under the impulse of divine inspiration ; although divination by lot is not in itself to be despised, if it has the sanction of antiquity, as in the case of those lots which, according to tradition, sprang out of the

---

[3] This Sibyl was Herophile, who finally went to Cumae.
[4] What is meant by *aequatis sortibus* is not known.

tamen ductae ut in rem apte cadant, fieri credo
posse divinitus. Quorum omnium interpretes, ut
grammatici poetarum, proxime ad eorum, quos interpretantur, divinationem videntur accedere.

35   " Quae est igitur ista calliditas res vetustate
robustas calumniando velle pervertere ? Non reperio
causam. Latet fortasse obscuritate involuta naturae ;
non enim me deus ista scire, sed his tantum modo
uti voluit. Utar igitur nec adducar aut in extis
totam Etruriam delirare aut eandem gentem in
fulguribus errare aut fallaciter portenta interpretari,
cum terrae saepe fremitus, saepe mugitus, saepe
motus multa nostrae rei publicae, multa ceteris
36 civitatibus gravia et vera praedixerint. Quid ? qui
irridetur, partus hic mulae nonne, quia fetus extitit
in sterilitate naturae, praedictus est ab haruspicibus
incredibilis partus malorum ?

" Quid ? Ti. Gracchus P. F., qui bis consul et
censor fuit, idemque et summus augur et vir sapiens
civisque praestans, nonne, ut C. Gracchus, filius eius,
scriptum reliquit, duobus anguibus domi comprehensis haruspices convocavit ? qui cum respondis-

---

¹ These were small oak tablets which were in the temple
of Fortuna at Praeneste (ii. 41. 86), and had words engraved
on them.
² *Cf.* Plato, *Ion* 533 *seq.* where the rhapsodist Ion claims
a θεία δύναμις in interpreting Homer.
³ For another instance see Herod. iii. 151-153.

earth[1]; for in spite of everything, I am inclined to think that they may, under the power of God, be so drawn as to give an appropriate response. Men capable of correctly interpreting all these signs of the future seem to approach very near to the divine spirit of the gods whose wills they interpret, just as scholars[2] do when they interpret the poets.

" What sort of cleverness is it, then, that would attempt by sophistry to overthrow facts that antiquity has established ? I fail—you tell me—to discover their cause. That, perhaps, is one of Nature's hidden secrets. God has not willed me to know the cause, but only that I should use the means which he has given. Therefore, I will use them and I will not allow myself to be persuaded that the whole Etruscan nation has gone stark mad on the subject of entrails, or that these same people are in error about lightnings, or that they are false interpreters of portents ; for many a time the rumblings and roarings and quakings of the earth have given to our republic and to other states certain forewarnings of subsequent disaster. Why, then, when here recently a mule (which is an animal ordinarily sterile by nature) brought forth a foal,[3] need anyone have scoffed because the soothsayers from that occurrence prophesied a progeny of countless evils to the state ?

" What, pray, do you say of that well-known incident of Tiberius Gracchus, the son of Publius ? He was censor and consul twice ; besides that he was a most competent augur, a wise man and a pre-eminent citizen. Yet he, according to the account left us by his son Gaius, having caught two snakes in his home, called in the soothsayers to consult

sent, si marem emisisset, uxori brevi tempore esse
moriendum, si feminam, ipsi ; aequius esse censuit
se maturam oppetere mortem quam P. Africani
filiam adulescentem ; feminam emisit, ipse paucis
post diebus est mortuus. XIX. Irrideamus haruspices, vanos, futiles esse dicamus, quorumque disciplinam et sapientissimus vir et eventus ac res comprobavit, contemnamus ; contemnamus etiam Babylonios, et eos, qui e Caucaso caeli signa servantes
numeris[1] stellarum cursus persequuntur. Condem-
nemus, inquam, hos aut stultitiae aut vanitatis aut
impudentiae, qui quadringenta septuaginta milia
annorum, ut ipsi dicunt, monumentis comprehensa
continent, et mentiri iudicemus, nec saeculorum
reliquorum iudicium quod de ipsis futurum sit
37 pertimescere.   Age, barbari vani atque fallaces ;
num etiam Graiorum historia mentita est ?

" Quae Croeso Pythius Apollo, ut de naturali
divinatione dicam, quae Atheniensibus, quae Lacedaemoniis, quae Tegeatis, quae Argivis, quae Co-
rinthiis responderit, quis ignorat ? Collegit innumerabilia oracula Chrysippus nec ullum sine locuplete
auctore atque teste ; quae, quia nota tibi sunt,
relinquo ; defendo unum hoc : Numquam illud
oraculum Delphis tam celebre et tam clarum fuisset
neque tantis donis refertum omnium populorum
atque regum, nisi omnis aetas oraculorum illorum

---

[1] numeris et modis *Müller* ; numeris et motibus *Dav.*

---

[1] *Cf.* Diodorus Sic. *Bibl.* ii. p. 118 (473,000) ; Lac
tantius, *Div. Inst.* vii. ch. 14.   But see Pliny, *H.N.* vii. 56.

them. They advised him that if he let the male
snake go his wife must die in a short time ; and if
he released the female snake his own death must
soon occur. Thinking it more fitting that a speedy
death should overtake him rather than his young
wife, who was the daughter of Publius Africanus,
he released the female snake and died within a
few days. XIX. Let us laugh at the soothsayers,
brand them as frauds and impostors and scorn their
calling, even though a very wise man, Tiberius
Gracchus, and the results and circumstances of
his death have given proof of its trustworthiness ;
let us scorn the Babylonians, too, and those astrologers who, from the top of Mount Caucasus, observe
the celestial signs and with the aid of mathematics
follow the courses of the stars ; let us, I say, convict
of folly, falsehood, and shamelessness the men whose
records, as they themselves assert, cover a period
of four hundred and seventy thousand years ;[1]
and let us pronounce them liars, utterly indifferent
to the opinion of succeeding generations. Come,
let us admit that the barbarians are all base de-
ceivers, but are the Greek historians liars too ?

" Speaking now of natural divination, everybody
knows the oracular responses which the Pythian
Apollo gave to Croesus, to the Athenians, Spartans,
Tegeans, Argives, and Corinthians. Chrysippus has
collected a vast number of these responses, attested
in every instance by abundant proof. But I pass
them by as you know them well. I will urge only
this much, however, in defence : the oracle at
Delphi never would have been so much frequented,
so famous, and so crowded with offerings from peoples
and kings of every land, if all ages had not tested

veritatem esset experta. Idem iam diu non facit.
38 Ut igitur nunc minore gloria est, quia minus oraculorum veritas excellit, sic tum nisi summa veritate in
tanta gloria non fuisset. Potest autem vis illa terrae
quae mentem Pythiae divino afflatu concitabat
evanuisse vetustate, ut quosdam evanuisse et
exaruisse amnes aut in alium cursum contortos et
deflexos videmus. Sed ut vis acciderit, magna enim
quaestio est, modo maneat id quod negari non potest,
nisi omnem historiam perverterimus, multis saeclis
verax fuisse id oraculum.

39 XX. " Sed omittamus oracula ; veniamus ad
somnia. De quibus disputans Chrysippus, multis et
minutis somniis colligendis, facit idem quod Antipater ea conquirens, quae Antiphontis interpretatione explicata declarant illa quidem acumen
interpretis, sed exemplis grandioribus decuit uti.
Dionysii mater, eius qui Syracosiorum tyrannus fuit,
ut scriptum apud Philistum est, et doctum hominem
et diligentem et aequalem temporum illorum, cum
praegnans hunc ipsum Dionysium alvo contineret,
somniavit se peperisse Satyriscum. Huic interpretes
portentorum, qui Galeotae tum in Sicilia nomina-

the truth of its prophecies. For a long time now that has not been the case. Therefore, as at present its glory has waned because it is no longer noted for the truth of its prophecies, so formerly it would not have enjoyed so exalted a reputation if it had not been trustworthy in the highest degree. Possibly, too, those subterranean exhalations which used to kindle the soul of the Pythian priestess with divine inspiration have gradually vanished in the long lapse of time ; just as within our own knowledge some rivers have dried up and disappeared, while others, by winding and twisting, have changed their course into other channels. But explain the decadence of the oracle as you wish, since it offers a wide field for discussion, provided you grant what cannot be denied without distorting the entire record of history, that the oracle at Delphi made true prophecies for many hundreds of years.

XX. " But let us leave oracles and come to dreams. In his treatise on this subject Chrysippus, just as Antipater does, has assembled a mass of trivial dreams which he explains according to Antiphon's rules of interpretation. The work, I admit, displays the acumen of its author, but it would have been better if he had cited illustrations of a more serious type. Now, Philistus, who was a learned and painstaking man and a contemporary of the times of which he writes, gives us the following story of the mother of Dionysius, the tyrant of Syracuse : while she was with child and was carrying this same Dionysius in her womb, she dreamed that she had been delivered of an infant satyr. When she referred this dream to the interpreters of portents, who in Sicily were called ' Galeotae,' they

bantur, responderunt, ut ait Philistus, eum, quem
illa peperisset, clarissimum Graeciae diuturna cum
fortuna fore.

40 " Num te ad fabulas revoco vel nostrorum vel
Graecorum poëtarum ? Narrat enim et apud
Ennium Vestalis illa :

> excita cum tremulis anus attulit artubu' lumen,
> talia tum memorat lacrimans exterrita somno :
> ' Eurydica prognata, pater quam noster amavit,
> vires vitaque corpu' meum nunc deserit omne.
> nam me visus homo pulcher per amoena salicta
> et ripas raptare locosque novos ; ita sola
> postilla, germana soror, errare videbar
> tardaque vestigare et quaerere te neque posse
> corde capessere ; semita nulla pedem stabilibat.

41
> exin compellare pater me voce videtur
> his verbis : " O gnata, tibi sunt ante gerendae
> aerumnae, post ex fluvio fortuna resistet."
> haec effatu' pater, germana, repente recessit
> nec sese dedit in conspectum corde cupitus,
> quamquam multa manus ad caeli caerula templa
> tendebam lacrumans et blanda voce vocabam.
> vix aegro tum corde meo me somnus reliquit.'

42 XXI. " Haec, etiamsi ficta sunt a poëta, non absunt
tamen a consuetudine somniorum. Sit sane etiam
illud commenticium, quo Priamus est conturbatus, quia

> máter gravida párere se ardentém facem
> visá est in somnis Hécuba ; quo factó pater
> rex ípse Priamus sómnio mentís metu
> percúlsus curis súmptus suspirántibus
> exsácrificabat hóstiis balántibus.
> tum cóniecturam póstulat pacém petens,

---

[1] From his *Annales*. The Vestal was Rhea Silvia, or
Ilia, the daughter of Numitor, and mother by Mars of
Romulus and Remus.

[2] The god Mars is referred to. *Cf.* Ovid, *Fast.* iii. 13.

[3] The author of this quotation is not known.

270

replied, so Philistus relates, that she would bring
forth a son who would be very eminent in Greece
and would enjoy a long and prosperous career.

" May I not recall to your memory some stories
to be found in the works of Roman and of Greek
poets ? For example, the following dream of the
Vestal Virgin [1] is from Ennius :

> The vestal from her sleep in fright awoke
> And to the startled maid, whose trembling hands
> A lamp did bear, thus spoke in tearful tones :
> ' O daughter of Eurydice, thou whom
> Our father loved, from my whole frame departs
> The vital force. For in my dreams I saw
> A man [2] of beauteous form, who bore me off
> Through willows sweet, along the fountain's brink,
> To places strange. And then, my sister dear,
> Alone, with halting step and longing heart,
> I seemed to wander, seeking thee in vain ;
> There was no path to make my footing sure.
> And then I thought my father spoke these words :
> " Great sorrows, daughter, thou must first endure
> Until thy fortune from the Tiber rise."
> When this was said he suddenly withdrew ;
> Nor did his cherished vision come again,
> Though oft I raised my hand to heaven's dome
> And called aloud in tearful, pleading voice.
> Then sleep departing left me sick at heart.'

XXI. " This dream, I admit, is the fiction of a
poet's brain, yet it is not contrary to our experience
with real dreams. It may well be that the following
story of the dream which greatly disturbed Priam's
peace of mind is fiction too : [3]

> When mother Hecuba was great with child,
> She dreamed that she brought forth a flaming torch.
> Alarmed at this, with sighing cares possessed,
> The king and father, Priam, to the gods
> Did make a sacrifice of bleating lambs.
> He, seeking peace and answer to the dream,

ut se édoceret, óbsecrans Apóllinem,
quo sése vertant tántae sortes sómnium.
ibi éx oraclo vóce divina édidit
Apóllo, puerum, prímus Priamo quí foret
postílla natus, témperaret tóllere ;
eum ésse exitium Tróiae, pestem Pérgamo.

43 Sint haec, ut dixi, somnia fabularum, hisque adiunga-
tur etiam Aeneae somnium, quod in nostri Fabi
Pictoris Graecis annalibus eius modi est, ut omnia.
quae ab Aenea gesta sunt quaeque illi acciderunt,
ea fuerint, quae ei secundum quietem visa sunt.

XXII. " Sed propiora videamus. Cuiusnam modi
est Superbi Tarquini somnium, de quo in Bruto Acci
loquitur ipse ?

44   quom iám quieti córpus nocturno ímpetu
dedí sopore plácans artus lánguidos,
visúst in somnis pástor ad me appéllere
pecús lanigerum exímia puchritúdine ;
duós consanguineos árietes inde éligi
praeclárioremque álterum immoláre me ;
deinde eíus germanum córnibus conítier,
in me árietare, eoque íctu me ad casúm dari ;
exín prostratum térra, graviter saúcium,
resupínum in caelo cóntueri máximum ac
miríficum facinus : déxtrorsum orbem flámmeum
radiátum solis líquier cursú novo.

45 Eius igitur somnii a coniectoribus quae sit interpretatio facta, videamus :

réx. quae in vita usúrpant homines, cógitant, curánt,
     vident,
quaéque aiunt vigilántes agitantque, éa si cui in somno
     áccidunt,
mínus mirum est; séd in re tanta haud temere visa se
     ófferunt.
próin vide ne, quém tu esse hebetem députes aeque ác
     pecus,
is sapientiá munitum péctus egregié gerat
téque regno expéllat. nam id quod dé sole ostentúm est tibi,
272

Implored Apollo's aid to understand
What great events the vision did foretell.
Apollo's oracle, with voice divine,
Then gave this explanation of the dream :
" Thy next-born son forbear to rear, for he
Will be the death of Pergamos and Troy."

Grant, I repeat, that these dreams are myths and
in the same category put Aeneas's dream, related
in the Greek annals of our countryman, Fabius
Pictor. According to Pictor everything that Aeneas
did or suffered turned out just as it had been predicted to him in a dream.

XXII. "But let us look at examples nearer our own
times. Would you dare call that famous dream of
Tarquin the Proud a myth ? He describes it himself
in the following lines from the *Brutus* of Accius :

At night's approach I sought my quiet couch
To soothe my weary limbs with restful sleep.
Then in my dreams a shepherd near me drove
A fleecy herd whose beauty was extreme.
I chose two brother rams from out the flock
And sacrificed the comelier of the twain.
And then, with lowered horns, the other ram
Attacked and bore me headlong to the ground.
While there I lay outstretched and wounded sore,
The sky a wondrous miracle disclosed :
The blazing star of day reversed its course
And glided to the right by pathway new.

Now observe how the diviners interpreted this dream :

It is not strange, O king, that dreams reflect
The day's desires and thoughts, its sights and deeds,
And everything we say or do awake.
But in so grave a dream as yours we see
A message clearly sent, and thus it warns :
Beware of him you deem bereft of wit
And rate no higher than a stupid ram,
Lest he, with wisdom armed, should rise to fame
And drive you from your throne. The sun's changed course

273

pópulo commutátionem rérum portendít fore
pérpropinquam.   haec béne verruncent pópulo.   nam quod
  ad dexteram
cépit cursum ab laéva signum praépotens, pulchérrime
aúguratum est rém Romanam públjcam summám fore.

46   XXIII. " Age nunc ad externa redeamus.   Matrem
Phalaridis scribit Ponticus Heraclides, doctus vir,
auditor et discipulus Platonis, visam esse videre in
somnis simulacra deorum, quae ipsa domi consecra-
visset ; ex eis Mercurium e patera, quam dextera
manu teneret, sanguinem visum esse fundere ; qui
cum terram attigisset, refervescere videretur sic, ut
tota domus sanguine redundaret.   Quod matris
somnium inmanis fili crudelitas comprobavit.

" Quid ego, quae magi Cyro illi principi interpretati
sint, ex Dinonis Persicis proferam ?   Nam cum dormienti ei sol ad pedes visus esset, ter eum scribit
frustra appetivisse manibus, cum se convolvens sol
elaberetur et abiret ; ei magos dixisse, quod genus
sapientium et doctorum habebatur in Persis, ex
triplici appetitione solis triginta annos Cyrum
regnaturum esse portendi.   Quod ita contigit ; nam
ad septuagesimum pervenit, cum quadraginta natus
annos regnare coepisset.

47   " Est profecto quiddam etiam in barbaris gentibus
praesentiens atque divinans, siquidem ad mortem
proficiscens Callanus Indus, cum inscenderet in
rogum ardentem, ' O praeclarum discessum,' inquit,

---

[1] This is the length of his reign as usually given, but some
give it as thirty-one years. *Cf.* Herod. i. 214 ; Sulpic. Sev.
H.S. ii. 9.

Unto the state portends immediate change.
And may that prove benignant to the state ;
For since the almighty orb from left to right
Revolved, it was the best of auguries
That Rome would be supreme o'er all the earth.

XXIII. " But come now and let us return to
foreign instances. Heraclides Ponticus, a man of
learning, and both a pupil and a disciple of Plato's,
relates a dream of the mother of Phalaris. She
fell asleep and dreamed that, while looking at the
consecrated images of the gods set up in her house,
she saw the statue of Mercury pouring blood from
a bowl which it held in its right hand and that the
blood, as it touched the ground, welled up and
completely filled the house. The truth of the dream
was subsequently established by the inhuman cruelty
of her son.

" Why need I bring forth from Dinon's Persian
annals the dreams of that famous prince, Cyrus,
and their interpretations by the magi ? But take
this instance : Once upon a time Cyrus dreamed
that the sun was at his feet. Three times, so Dinon
writes, he vainly tried to grasp it and each time it
turned away, escaped him, and finally disappeared.
He was told by the magi, who are classed as wise and
learned men among the Persians, that his grasping
for the sun three times portended that he would reign
for thirty years.[1] And thus it happened ; for he lived
to his seventieth year, having begun to reign at forty.

" It certainly must be true that even barbarians
have some power of foreknowledge and of prophecy,
if the following story of Callanus of India be true :
As he was about to die and was ascending his
funeral pyre, he said : ' What a glorious death !

' e vita, cum, ut Herculi contigit, mortali corpore
cremato in lucem animus excesserit ! ' Cumque
Alexander eum rogaret, si quid vellet, ut diceret,
' Optime,' inquit ; ' propediem te videbo.' Quod ita
contigit ; nam Babylone paucis post diebus Alexander est mortuus. Discedo parumper a somniis, ad
quae mox revertar. Qua nocte templum Ephesiae
Dianae deflagravit, eadem constat ex Olympiade
natum esse Alexandrum, atque, ubi lucere coepisset,
clamitasse magos pestem ac perniciem Asiae proxima
nocte natam. Haec de Indis et magis.

48 XXIV. " Redeamus ad somnia. Hannibalem
Coelius scribit, cum columnam auream, quae esset
in fano Iunonis Laciniae, auferre vellet dubitaretque,
utrum ea solida esset an extrinsecus inaurata, per-
terebravisse ; cumque solidam invenisset, statuisse
tollere ; ei secundum quietem visam esse Iunonem
praedicere, ne id faceret, minarique, si fecisset, se
curaturam, ut eum quoque oculum, quo bene videret,
amitteret. Idque ab homine acuto non esse neglectum ; itaque ex eo auro quod exterebratum esset
buculam curasse faciendam et eam in summa columna
49 collocavisse. Hoc item in Sileni, quem Coelius
sequitur, Graeca historia est (is autem diligentissime
res Hannibalis persecutus est) : Hannibalem, cum
cepisset Saguntum, visum esse in somnis a Iove in
deorum concilium vocari ; quo cum venisset, Iovem
imperavisse, ut Italiae bellum inferret, ducemque ei
unum e concilio datum, quo illum utentem cum
exercitu progredi coepisse ; tum ei ducem illum

The fate of Hercules is mine. For when this mortal frame is burned the soul will find the light.' When Alexander directed him to speak if he wished to say anything to him, he answered : ' Thank you, nothing, except that I shall see you very soon.' So it turned out, for Alexander died in Babylon a few days later. I am getting slightly away from dreams, but I shall return to them in a moment. Everybody knows that on the same night in which Olympias was delivered of Alexander the temple of Diana at Ephesus was burned, and that the magi began to cry out as the day was breaking : ' Asia's deadly curse was born last night.' But enough of Indians and magi.

XXIV. " Let us go back to dreams. Coelius writes that Hannibal wished to carry off a golden column from Juno's temple at Lacinium, but since he was in doubt whether it was solid or plated, he bored into it. Finding it solid he decided to take it away. But at night Juno came to him in a vision and warned him not to do so, threatening that if he did she would cause the loss of his good eye. That clever man did not neglect the warning. Moreover out of the gold filings he ordered an image of a calf to be made and placed on top of the column. Another story of Hannibal is found in the history written in Greek by Silenus, whom Coelius follows, and who, by the way, was a very painstaking student of Hannibal's career. After his capture of Saguntum Hannibal dreamed that Jupiter summoned him to a council of the gods. When he arrived Jupiter ordered him to carry the war into Italy, and gave him one of the divine council as a guide whom he employed when he began the march with his army.

praecepisse, ne respiceret ; illum autem id diutius
facere non potuisse elatumque cupiditate respexisse ;
tum visam beluam vastam et immanem circumplica-
tam serpentibus quacumque incederet omnia arbusta,
virgulta, tecta pervertere ; et eum admiratum
quaesisse de deo quodnam illud esset tale monstrum,
et deum respondisse vastitatem esse Italiae prae-
cepisseque, ut pergeret protinus, quid retro atque a
tergo fieret ne laboraret.

50   " Apud Agathoclem scriptum in historia est Hamil-
carem Karthaginiensem, cum oppugnaret Syracusas,
visum esse audire vocem, se postridie cenaturum
Syracusis ; cum autem is dies illuxisset, magnam
seditionem in castris eius inter Poenos et Siculos
milites esse factam ; quod cum sensissent Syra-
cusani, inproviso eos in castra irrupisse, Hamilcarem-
que ab eis vivum esse sublatum. Ita res somnium
comprobavit.

    " Plena exemplorum est historia, tum referta vita
51 communis. At vero P. Decius ille Q. F., qui primus
e Deciis consul fuit, cum esset tribunus militum,
M. Valerio A. Cornelio consulibus, a Samnitibusque
premeretur noster exercitus, cum pericula proeliorum
iniret audacius monereturque, ut cautior esset, dixit,
quod extat in annalibus, sibi in somnis visum esse,
cum in mediis hostibus versaretur, occidere cum maxima gloria. Et tum quidem incolumis exercitum
obsidione liberavit ; post triennium autem, cum

---

[1] 343 B.C.

This guide cautioned Hannibal not to look back
But, carried away by curiosity, he could refrain
no longer and looked back. Then he saw a horrible
beast of enormous size, enveloped with snakes, and
wherever it went it overthrew every tree and shrub
and every house. In his amazement Hannibal
asked what the monster was. The god replied
that it was the desolation of Italy and ordered him
to press right on and not to worry about what
happened behind him and in the rear.

" We read in a history by Agathocles that Hamilcar, the Carthaginian, during his siege of Syracuse
heard a voice in his sleep telling him that he would
dine the next day in Syracuse. At daybreak the
following day a serious conflict broke out in his
camp between the troops of the Carthaginians and
their allies, the Siculi. When the Syracusans saw
this they made a sudden assault on the camp and
carried Hamilcar off alive. Thus the event verified
the dream.

" History is full of such instances, and so is everyday life. And yet let me cite another : the famous
Publius Decius, son of Quintus, and the first of
that family to become consul, was military tribune
in the consulship[1] of Marcus Valerius and Aulus
Cornelius while our army was being hard pressed
by the Samnites. When, because of his rushing
too boldly into the dangers of battle, he was
advised to be more cautious, he replied, according
to the annals, 'I dreamed that by dying in the
midst of the enemy I should win immortal fame.'
And though he was unharmed at that time and
extricated the army from its difficulties, yet
three years later, when consul, he devoted himself

279

consul esset, devovit se et in aciem Latinorum
irrupit armatus. Quo eius facto superati sunt et
deleti Latini; cuius mors ita gloriosa fuit, ut eandem
52 concupisceret filius. Sed veniamus nunc, si placet,
ad somnia philosophorum.

XXV. "Est apud Platonem Socrates, cum esset in
custodia publica, dicens Critoni, suo familiari, sibi
post tertium diem esse moriendum; vidisse enim se
in somnis pulchritudine eximia feminam, quae se
nomine appellans, diceret Homericum quendam
eius modi versum:

> tertia te Phthiae tempestas laeta locabit.

Quod, ut est dictum, sic scribitur contigisse. Xenophon Socraticus (qui vir et quantus!) in ea militia,
qua cum Cyro minore perfunctus est, sua scribit
somnia, quorum eventus mirabiles exstiterunt.
53 Mentiri Xenophontem an delirare dicemus?

" Quid? singulari vir ingenio Aristoteles et paene
divino ipsene errat an alios vult errare, cum scribit
Eudemum Cyprium, familiarem suum, iter in Mace-
doniam facientem Pheras venisse, quae erat urbs in
Thessalia tum admodum nobilis, ab Alexandro autem
tyranno crudeli dominatu tenebatur; in eo igitur
oppido ita graviter aegrum Eudemum fuisse, ut
omnes medici diffiderent; ei visum in quiete egregia
facie iuvenem dicere fore ut perbrevi convalesceret,

---

[1] For the ceremony of devotion see Livy viii. 9.
[2] *Iliad* ix. 363, where Achilles says ἤματί κεν τριτάτῳ
Φθίην ἐρίβωλον ἱκοίμην. Phthia, in Thessaly, was his home,
and to Socrates death was a " return home "; *cf.* § 54
at end. To Socrates Phthia implied his heavenly home.
[3] Xen. *Anab.* iii. 1. 11; iv. 3. 8.

to death [1] and rushed full-armed against the battle-line of the Latins. By this act of his the Latins were overcome and destroyed; and so glorious was his death that his son sought the same fate. But let us come now, if you please, to the dreams of philosophers.

XXV. "We read in Plato that Socrates, while in prison, said in a conversation with his friend Crito: 'I am to die in three days; for in a dream I saw a woman of rare beauty, who called me by name and quoted this verse from Homer: [2]

'Gladly on Phthia's shore the third day's dawn shall behold thee.'

And history informs us that his death occurred as he had foretold. That disciple of Socrates, Xenophon—and what a man he was !—records[3] the dreams he had during his campaign with Cyrus the Younger, and their remarkable fulfilment. Shall we say that Xenophon is either a liar or a madman ?

"And Aristotle, who was endowed with a matchless and almost godlike intellect,—is he in error, or is he trying to lead others into error in the following account of his friend, Eudemus [4] the Cyprian ? Eudemus, while on his way to Macedonia, reached Pherae, then a very famous city of Thessaly, but groaning under the cruel sway of the tyrant, Alexander.[5] There he became so violently ill that the physicians despaired of his recovery. While sick he had a dream in which a youth of striking beauty told him that he would speedily get well; that the

[4] His work *Eudemos*, or Περὶ ψυχῆς, is lost. *Cf.* Plut. *Dion*, 22.
[5] He was killed by his brothers-in-law about 350 B.C. *Cf.* Xen. *Hellen.* vi. 4. 35.

paucisque diebus interiturum Alexandrum tyrannum,
ipsum autem Eudemum quinquennio post domum
esse rediturum. Atque ita quidem prima statim
scribit Aristoteles consecuta, et convaluisse Eudemum,
et ab uxoris fratribus interfectum tyrannum ; quinto
autem anno exeunte, cum esset spes ex illo somnio in
Cyprum illum ex Sicilia esse rediturum, proeliantem
eum ad Syracusas occidisse ; ex quo ita illud somnium esse interpretatum, ut, cum animus Eudemi e
corpore excesserit, tum domum revertisse videatur.

54 " Adiungamus philosophis doctissimum hominem,
poëtam quidem divinum, Sophoclem ; qui, cum ex
aede Herculis patera aurea gravis subrepta esset,
in somnis vidit ipsum deum dicentem, qui id fecisset.
Quod semel ille iterumque neglexit. Ubi idem
saepius, ascendit in Areopagum, detulit rem ;
Areopagitae conprehendi iubent eum, qui a Sophocle
erat nominatus ; is, quaestione adhibita, confessus
est pateramque rettulit. Quo facto fanum illud
Indicis Herculis nominatum est.

55 XXVI. " Sed quid ego Graecorum ? nescio quo
modo me magis nostra delectant. Omnes hoc
historici, Fabii, Gellii, sed proxime Coelius : Cum
bello Latino ludi votivi maximi primum fierent,
civitas ad arma repente est excitata, itaque ludis
intermissis instaurativi constituti sunt. Qui ante

despot Alexander would die in a few days, and that he himself would return home five years later. And so, indeed, the first two prophecies, as Aristotle writes, were immediately fulfilled by the recovery of Eudemus and by the death of the tyrant at the hands of his wife's brothers. But at the end of five years, when, in reliance upon the dream, he hoped to return to Cyprus from Sicily, he was killed in battle before Syracuse. Accordingly the dream was interpreted to mean that when his soul left the body it then had returned home.

" To the testimony of philosophers let us add that of a most learned man and truly divine poet, Sophocles. A heavy gold dish having been stolen from the temple of Hercules, the god himself appeared to Sophocles in a dream and told who had committed the theft. But Sophocles ignored the dream a first and second time. When it came again and again, he went up to the Areopagus and laid the matter before the judges who ordered the man named by Sophocles to be arrested. The defendant after examination confessed his crime and brought back the dish. This is the reason why that temple is called ' the temple of Hercules the Informer.'

XXVI. " But why am I dwelling on illustrations from Greek sources when—though I can't explain it —those from our own history please me more ? Now here is a dream which is mentioned by all our historians, by the Fabii and the Gellii and, most recently, by Coelius : During the Latin War when the Great Votive Games were being celebrated for the first time the city was suddenly called to arms and the games were interrupted. Later it was determined to repeat them, but before they began,

quam fierent, cumque iam populus consedisset, servus
per circum cum virgis caederetur furcam ferens ductus
est. Exin cuidam rustico Romano dormienti visus est
venire, qui diceret praesulem sibi non placuisse ludis,
idque ab eodem iussum esse eum senatui nuntiare ;
illum non esse ausum. Iterum esse idem iussum et
monitum, ne vim suam experiri vellet ; ne tum
quidem esse ausum. Exin filium eius esse mortuum,
eandem in somnis admonitionem fuisse tertiam. Tum
illum etiam debilem factum rem ad amicos detulisse,
quorum de sententia lecticula in curiam esse delatum,
cumque senatui somnium enarravisset, pedibus suis
salvum domum revertisse. Itaque somnio compro-
bato a senatu ludos illos iterum instauratos memoriae
56 proditum est. C. vero Gracchus multis dixit, ut
scriptum apud eundem Coelium est, sibi in somnis
quaesturam petenti Ti. fratrem visum esse dicere,
quam vellet cunctaretur, tamen eodem sibi leto, quo
ipse interisset, esse pereundum. Hoc, ante quam
tribunus plebi C. Gracchus factus esset, et se audisse
scribit Coelius et dixisse illum[1] multis. Quo somnio
quid inveniri potest certius ?

XXVII. " Quid ? illa duo somnia, quae creberrime
commemorantur a Stoicis, quis tandem potest contemnere ? unum de Simonide : Qui cum ignotum
quendam proiectum mortuum vidisset eumque
humavisset haberetque in animo navem conscendere,

[1] illum *Orelli* ; *Dav. om.*

---

[1] *i.e.* the slave just referred to. The games were opened
by beating him round the arena. The name of the rustic
was Tib. Atinius, Livy ii. 36 ; Val. Max. i. 7. 4.

and while the people were taking their seats, a slave bearing a yoke was led about the circus and beaten with rods. After that a Roman rustic had a dream in which someone appeared to him and said that he disapproved of the leader [1] of the games and ordered this statement to be reported to the Senate. But the rustic dared not do as he was bid. The order was repeated by the spectre with a warning not to put his power to the test. Not even then did the rustic dare obey. After that his son died and the same vision was repeated the third time. Thereupon he became ill and told his friends of his dream. On their advice he was carried to the Senate-house on a litter and, having related his dream to the Senate, his health was restored and he walked home unaided. And so, the tradition is, the Senate gave credence to the dream and had the games repeated.

" According to this same Coelius, Gaius Gracchus told many persons that his brother Tiberius came to him in a dream when he was a candidate for the quaestorship and said : ' However much you may try to defer your fate, nevertheless you must die the same death that I did.' This happened before Gaius was tribune of the people, and Coelius writes that he himself heard it from Gaius who had repeated it to many others. Can you find anything better authenticated than this dream ?

XXVII. " And who, pray, can make light of the two following dreams which are so often recounted by Stoic writers ? The first one is about Simonides, who once saw the dead body of some unknown man lying exposed and buried it. Later, when he had it in mind to go on board a ship he was warned

moneri visus est, ne id faceret, ab eo, quem sepultura affecerat ; si navigasset, eum naufragio esse periturum ; itaque Simonidem redisse, perisse ceteros, qui tum navigassent.

57 " Alterum ita traditum clarum admodum somnium : Cum duo quidam Arcades familiares iter una facerent et Megaram venissent, alterum ad cauponem devertisse, ad hospitem alterum. Qui ut cenati quiescerent, concubia nocte visum esse in somnis ei, qui erat in hospitio, illum alterum orare, ut subveniret, quod sibi a caupone interitus pararetur ; eum primo perterritum somnio surrexisse ; dein cum se collegisset idque visum pro nihilo habendum esse duxisset, recubuisse ; tum ei dormienti eundem illum visum esse rogare, ut, quoniam sibi vivo non subvenisset, mortem suam ne inultam esse pateretur ; se interfectum in plaustrum a caupone esse coniectum et supra stercus iniectum ; petere, ut mane ad portam adesset, prius quam plaustrum ex oppido exiret. Hoc vero eum somnio commotum mane bubulco praesto ad portam fuisse, quaesisse ex eo, quid esset in plaustro ; illum perterritum fugisse, mortuum erutum esse, cauponem re patefacta poenas dedisse. XXVIII. Quid hoc somnio dici potest divinius ?

58 " Sed quid aut plura aut vetera quaerimus ? Saepe tibi meum narravi, saepe ex te audivi tuum somnium :

in a vision by the person to whom he had given burial not to do so and that if he did he would perish in a shipwreck. Therefore he turned back and all the others who sailed were lost.

" The second dream is very well known and is to this effect : Two friends from Arcadia who were taking a journey together came to Megara, and one traveller put up at an inn and the second went to the home of a friend. After they had eaten supper and retired, the second traveller, in the dead of the night, dreamed that his companion was imploring him to come to his aid, as the innkeeper was planning to kill him. Greatly frightened at first by the dream he arose, and later, regaining his composure, decided that there was nothing to worry about and went back to bed. When he had gone to sleep the same person appeared to him and said : ' Since you would not help me when I was alive, I beg that you will not allow my dead body to remain unburied. I have been killed by the innkeeper, who has thrown my body into a cart and covered it with dung. I pray you to be at the city gate in the morning before the cart leaves the town.' Thoroughly convinced by the second dream he met the cart-driver at the gate in the morning, and, when he asked what he had in the cart, the driver fled in terror. The Arcadian then removed his friend's dead body from the cart, made complaint of the crime to the authorities, and the innkeeper was punished. XXVIII. What stronger proof of a divinely inspired dream than this can be given ?

" But why go on seeking illustrations from ancient history ? I had a dream which I have often related to you, and you one which you have

me, cum Asiae proconsul praeessem, vidisse in quiete,
cum tu equo advectus ad quandam magni fluminis
ripam provectus subito atque delapsus in flumen
nusquam apparuisses, me contremuisse timore perterritum ; tum te repente laetum exstitisse eodemque
equo adversam ascendisse ripam, nosque inter nos
esse complexos.   Facilis coniectura huius somnii,
mihique a peritis in Asia praedictum est fore eos
eventus rerum, qui acciderunt.

59   " Venio nunc ad tuum.   Audivi equidem ex te
ipso, sed mihi saepius noster Sallustius narravit, cum
in illa fuga nobis gloriosa, patriae calamitosa, in villa
quadam campi Atinatis maneres magnamque partem
noctis vigilasses, ad lucem denique arcte et graviter
dormire te coepisse. Itaque, quamquam iter instaret,
se tamen silentium fieri iussisse neque esse passum
te excitari ;   cum autem experrectus esses hora
secunda fere, te sibi somnium narravisse : visum
tibi esse, cum in locis solis maestus errares, C.
Marium cum fascibus laureatis quaerere ex te, quid
tristis esses, cumque tu te patria vi pulsum esse
dixisses, prehendisse eum dextram tuam et bono
animo te iussisse esse lictorique proximo tradidisse,
ut te in monumentum suum deduceret, et dixisse in
eo tibi salutem fore. Tum et se exclamasse Sallustius

---

[1] In 61 B.C. ; *cf. Ad Att.* i. 15 *Asiae Quinto obtigisse audisti.*
Quintus had been *praetor* (not *consul*) in 62.

[2] Referring to the banishment of Cicero in 58 B.C. at the
instigation of Clodius, and his triumphal recall in 57 B.C.

[3] M. Cicero's freedman who followed him into banishment.

[4] *i.e.* as a token of victory.

[5] This was the temple erected by Marius to Jupiter to
commemorate his victory over the Cimbri, 101 B.C. The

often told to me. When I was governor of Asia[1]
I dreamed that I saw you on horseback riding toward
the bank of some large river, when you suddenly
plunged forward, fell into the stream, and wholly
disappeared from sight. I was greatly alarmed
and trembled with fear. But in a moment you
reappeared mounted on the same horse, and with
a cheerful countenance ascended the opposite bank
where we met and embraced each other. The
meaning of the dream was readily explained to me
by experts in Asia who from it predicted those
events which subsequently occurred.[2]

" I come now to your dream. I heard it, of
course, from you, but more frequently from our
Sallustius.[3] In the course of your banishment, which
was glorious for us but disastrous to the State, you
stopped for the night at a certain country-house
in the plain of Atina. After lying awake most of
the night, finally, about daybreak, you fell into a
very profound sleep. And though your journey was
pressing, yet Sallustius gave instructions to maintain
quiet and would not permit you to be disturbed.
But you awoke about the second hour and related
your dream to him. In it you seemed to be wandering sadly about in solitary places when Gaius
Marius, with his fasces wreathed in laurel,[4] asked
you why you were sad, and you replied that you had
been driven from your country by violence. He
then bade you be of good cheer, took you by the right
hand, and delivered you to the nearest lictor to be
conducted to his memorial temple,[5] saying that there
you should find safety. Sallustius thereupon, as he

Senate sat in this temple when the act for Cicero's recall
was passed.

narrat reditum tibi celerem et gloriosum paratum, et
te ipsum visum somnio delectari. Nam illud mihi
ipsi celeriter nuntiatum est ut audivisses in monumento Mari de tuo reditu magnificentissimum illud
senatus consultum esse factum referente optimo et
clarissimo viro consule, idque frequentissimo theatro
incredibili clamore et plausu comprobatum, dixisse
te nihil illo Atinati somnio fieri posse divinius.

60   XXIX. " At multa falso. Immo obscura fortasse
nobis. Sed sint falsa quaedam ; contra vera quid
dicimus ? Quae quidem multo plura evenirent, si ad
quietem integri iremus. Nunc onusti cibo et vino
perturbata et confusa cernimus. Vide, quid Socrates
in Platonis Politia loquatur. Dicit enim :

' Cum dormientibus ea pars animi, quae mentis et
rationis sit particeps, sopita langueat ; illa autem, in
qua feritas quaedam sit atque agrestis immanitas,
cum sit immoderato tumefacta[1] potu atque pastu,
exsultare eam in somno immoderateque iactari.
Itaque huic omnia visa obiciuntur a mente ac
ratione vacua, ut aut cum matre corpus miscere
videatur aut cum quovis alio vel homine vel deo,
saepe belua, atque etiam trucidare aliquem et impie
cruentari multaque facere impure atque taetre cum

---

[1] tumefacta *Dav.* ; obstupefacta *mss.*

---

[1] *i.e.* Publius Lentulus ; *cf.* Cic. *In Pison.* ch. 15 ; *Pro Sest*
55, 63, 69 ; *Ad fam.* i. 9 ; *Red. in senat.* 4. 9.
[2] Plato, *De rep.* ix. p. 571.

relates, cried out, ' a speedy and a glorious return awaits you.' He further states that you too seemed delighted at the dream. Immediately thereafter it was reported to me that as soon as you heard that it was in Marius' temple that the glorious decree of the Senate for your recall had been enacted on motion of the consul, a most worthy and most eminent man,[1] and that the decree had been greeted by unprecedented shouts of approval in a densely crowded theatre, you said that no stronger proof could be given of a divinely inspired dream than this.

XXIX. " ' Ah,' it is objected, ' but many dreams are untrustworthy.' Rather, perhaps, their meaning is hidden from us. But grant that some are untrustworthy, why do we declaim against those that are trustworthy? The fact is the latter would be much more frequent if we went to our rest in proper condition. But when we are burdened with food and drink our dreams are troubled and confused. Observe what Socrates says in Plato's *Republic* :[2]

" ' When a man goes to sleep, having the thinking and reasoning portion of his soul languid and inert, but having that other portion, which has in it a certain brutishness and wild savagery, immoderately gorged with drink and food, then does that latter portion leap up and hurl itself about in sleep without check. In such a case every vision presented to the mind is so devoid of thought and reason that the sleeper dreams that he is committing incest with his mother, or that he is having unlawful commerce indiscriminately with gods and men, and frequently too, with beasts ; or even that he is killing someone and staining his hands with impious bloodshed ; and that he is doing many vile and

61 temeritate et impudentia. At qui salubri et moderato cultu atque victu quieti se tradiderit ea parte animi, quae mentis et consili est, agitata et erecta saturataque bonarum cogitationum epulis, eaque parte animi, quae voluptate alitur, nec inopia enecta nec satietate affluenti (quorum utrumque praestringere aciem mentis solet, sive deest naturae quidpiam sive abundat atque affluit), illa etiam tertia parte animi, in qua irarum existit ardor, sedata atque restincta, tum eveniet duabus animi temerariis partibus compressis, ut illa tertia pars rationis et mentis eluceat et se vegetam ad somniandum acremque praebeat, tum ei visa quietis occurrent tranquilla atque veracia.' Haec verba ipsa Platonis expressi.

62 XXX. " Epicurum igitur audiemus potius ? Namque Carneades concertationis studio modo ait hoc, modo illud. ' At ille ait quod sentit.' Sentit autem nihil umquam elegans, nihil decorum. Hunc ergo antepones Platoni et Socrati qui ut rationem non redderent, auctoritate tamen hos minutos philosophos vincerent? Iubet igitur Plato sic ad somnum proficisci corporibus affectis, ut nihil sit quod errorem animis perturbationemque afferat. Ex quo etiam Pythagoricis interdictum putatur ne faba vescerentur, quod habet inflationem magnam is cibus tranquillitati men-

---

[1] Adopting Hottinger's interpretation : *nihil subtilius cogitatum, nihil philosopho dignum.*
[2] *Cf.* Tertull. *De anima,* ch. 48 ; Plut. *Sympos.* 9. 10 ; Pliny, *H.N.* xviii. 12.

hideous things recklessly and without shame. But, on the other hand, when the man, whose habits of living and of eating are wholesome and temperate, surrenders himself to sleep, having the thinking and reasoning portion of his soul eager and erect, and satisfied by a feast of noble thoughts, and having that portion which feeds on carnal pleasures neither utterly exhausted by abstinence nor cloyed by over-indulgence—for, as a rule, the edge of thought is dulled whether nature is starved or overfed—and, when such a man, in addition, has that third portion of the soul, in which the fire of anger burns, quieted and subdued—thus having the two irrational portions under complete control—then will the thinking and reasoning portion of his soul shine forth and show itself keen and strong for dreaming and then will his dreams be peaceful and worthy of trust.' I have reproduced Plato's very words.

XXX. " Then shall we listen to Epicurus rather than to Plato ? As for Carneades, in his ardour for controversy he asserts now this and now that. ' But,' you retort, ' Epicurus says what he thinks.' But he thinks nothing that is ever well reasoned, or worthy of a philosopher.[1] Will you, then, put this man before Plato or Socrates, who though they gave no reason, would yet prevail over these petty philosophers by the mere weight of their name ? Now Plato's advice to us is to set out for the land of dreams with bodies so prepared that no error or confusion may assail the soul. For this reason, it is thought, the Pythagoreans were forbidden to indulge in beans [2]; for that food produces great flatulence and induces a condition at war

63 tis quaerentis vera contrariam. Cum ergo est somno
sevocatus animus a societate et a contagione corporis, tum meminit praeteritorum, praesentia cernit,
futura praevidet ; iacet enim corpus dormientis ut
mortui, viget autem et vivit animus. Quod multo
magis faciet post mortem, cum omnino corpore
excesserit. Itaque appropinquante morte multo est
divinior. Nam et id ipsum vident, qui sunt morbo
gravi et mortifero affecti, instare mortem ; itaque
eis occurrunt plerumque imagines mortuorum, tumque vel maxime laudi student ; eosque, qui secus
quam decuit, vixerunt, peccatorum suorum tum
maxime paenitet.

64 " Divinare autem morientes illo etiam exemplo
confirmat Posidonius, quod affert, Rhodium quendam
morientem sex aequales nominasse et dixisse, qui
primus eorum, qui secundus, qui deinde deinceps
moriturus esset. Sed tribus modis censet deorum
appulsu homines somniare : uno, quod praevideat
animus ipse per sese, quippe qui deorum cognatione
teneatur ; altero, quod plenus aër sit inmortalium
animorum, in quibus tamquam insignitae notae
veritatis appareant ; tertio, quod ipsi di cum dormientibus colloquantur. Idque, ut modo dixi,
facilius evenit appropinquante morte, ut animi
65 futura augurentur. Ex quo et illud est Callani, de
quo ante dixi, et Homerici Hectoris, qui moriens
propinquam Achilli mortem denuntiat.

---

[1] *Iliad*, xxii. 358.

with a soul in search of truth. When, therefore, the soul has been withdrawn by sleep from contact with sensual ties, then does it recall the past, comprehend the present, and foresee the future. For though the sleeping body then lies as if it were dead, yet the soul is alive and strong, and will be much more so after death when it is wholly free of the body. Hence its power to divine is much enhanced by the approach of death. For example, those in the grasp of a serious and fatal sickness realize the fact that death impends ; and so, visions of dead men generally appear to them and then their desire for fame is strongest ; while those who have lived otherwise than as they should, feel, at such a time, the keenest sorrow for their sins.

" Moreover, proof of the power of dying men to prophesy is also given by Posidonius in his well-known account of a certain Rhodian, who, when on his death-bed, named six men of equal age and foretold which of them would die first, which second, and so on. Now Posidonius holds the view that there are three ways in which men dream as the result of divine impulse : first, the soul is clairvoyant of itself because of its kinship with the gods ; second, the air is full of immortal souls, already clearly stamped, as it were, with the marks of truth ; and third, the gods in person converse with men when they are asleep. And, as I said just now, it is when death is at hand that men most readily discern signs of the future. This is illustrated by the story which I related about Callanus and by Homer's account of Hector, who, as he was dying, prophesied the early death of Achilles.[1]

XXXI. " Neque enim illud verbum temere consuetudo approbavisset, si ea res nulla esset omnino :

praésagibat ánimus frustra me íre, cum exirém domo.

Sagire enim sentire acute est ; ex quo sagae anus,
quia multa scire volunt, et sagaces dicti canes. Is
igitur, qui ante sagit, quam oblata res est, dicitur
praesagire, id est futura ante sentire.

66 " Inest igitur in animis praesagitio extrinsecus
iniecta atque inclusa divinitus. Ea, si exarsit acrius,
furor appellatur, cum a corpore animus abstractus
divino instinctu concitatur.

H. séd quid oculis rábere visa est dérepente ardéntibus ?
úbi illa paulo ante sápiens, vírginalis modéstia ?
C. máter, optimá tu multo múlier melior múlierum,
míssa sum supérstitiosis háriolatiónibus ;
nam mé[1] Apollo fátis fandis démentem invitám ciet.
vírgines vero aéqualis, pátris mei meum factúm pudet,

----

[1] nam me *Giese* ; namque *Müller* ; neque me *Dav.*

----

[1] *Aulular.* ii. 2. 1.
[2] *i.e.* witches.
[3] This quotation and the two succeeding are probably
from the *Hecuba* of Accius, or from the *Alexander* of
Ennius. *Cf.* i. 50. 114.

XXXI. " It is clear that, in our ordinary speech, we should not have made such frequent use of the word *praesagire*, meaning ' to sense in advance, or to presage,' if the power of presaging had been wholly non-existent. An illustration of its use is seen in the following well-known line from Plautus [1] :

My soul presaged as I left home that my leaving was in vain.

Now *sagire* means ' to have a keen perception.' Accordingly certain old women are called *sagae*,[2] because they are assumed to know a great deal, and dogs are said to be ' sagacious.' And so one who has knowledge of a thing before it happens is said to ' presage,' that is, to perceive the future in advance.

" Therefore the human soul has an inherent power of presaging or of foreknowing infused into it from without, and made a part of it by the will of God. If that power is abnormally developed, it is called ' frenzy ' or ' inspiration,' which occurs when the soul withdraws itself from the body and is violently stimulated by a divine impulse, as in the following instance, where Hecuba says to Cassandra [3] :

But why those flaming eyes, that sudden rage ?
And whither fled that sober modesty,
Till now so maidenly and yet so wise ? '

and Cassandra answers :

O mother, noblest of thy noble sex !
I have been sent to utter prophecies :
Against my will Apollo drives me mad
To revelation make of future ills.
O virgins ! comrades of my youthful hours,
My mission shames my father, best of men.

297

óptumi vir. mea mater, túi me miseret, méi piget.
óptumam progéniem Priamo péperisti extra me ; hóc dolet,
méd obesse, illós prodesse, me óbstare, illos óbsequi.

O poëma tenerum et moratum atque molle ! Sed
67 hoc minus ad rem ; illud, quod volumus, expressum
est, ut vaticinari furor vera soleat.

> ádest, adest fax óbvoluta sánguine atque íncendio !
> múltos annos látuit ; cives, férte opem et restínguite.

Deus inclusus corpore humano iam, non Cassandra,
loquitur :

> iámque mari magnó classis cita
> téxitur ; exitium éxamen rapit ;
> adveniet, fera vélivolantibus
> návibus complebít[1] manus litora.

68   XXXII. " Tragoedias loqui videor et fabulas. At
ex te ipso non commenticiam rem, sed factam eiusdem
generis audivi : C. Coponium ad te venisse Dyrrha-
chium,[2] cum praetorio imperio classi Rhodiae prae-
esset, cumprime hominem prudentem atque doctum,
eumque dixisse remigem quendam e quinqueremi
Rhodiorum vaticinatum madefactum iri minus xxx
diebus Graeciam sanguine, rapinas Dyrrhachi et
conscensionem in naves cum fuga fugientibusque
miserabilem respectum incendiorum fore ; sed

    [1] *for* adveniet *Dav. has* advenit et, *and for* complebit,
complevit.
    [2] Dyrrachium *Müller, Moser* ; Dyrrachio *MSS., Dav., and*
Giese.

---

    [1] The reference is to Paris, who, after being exposed on
Ida, lived there a long time as a shepherd.
    [2] *Exitium examen* = *turbam malorum*, Hottinger ; *cf.* Cic.
Orat. 46.
    [3] During the civil war between Caesar and Pompey,
and just before the battle of Pharsalus (Aug. 9, 48 B.C.).

> O mother dear ! great loathing for myself
> And grief for thee I feel. For thou hast borne
> To Priam goodly issue—saving me.
> 'Tis sad that unto thee the rest bring weal,
> I woe ; that they obey, but I oppose.

What a tender and pathetic poem, and how suitable
to her character ! though it is not altogether relevant,
I admit.   However, the point which I wish to press,
that true prophecies are made during frenzy, has
found expression in the following lines :

> It comes ! it comes ! that bloody torch,[1] in fire
> Enwrapped, though hid from sight these many years !
> Bring aid, my countrymen, and quench its flames !

It is not Cassandra who next speaks, but a god in
human form :

> Already, on the mighty deep is built
> A navy swift that hastes with swarms of woe.
> Its ships are drawing nigh with swelling sails,
> And bands of savage men will fill our shores.

XXXII. " I seem to be relying for illustrations
on myths drawn from tragic poets.   But you yourself are my authority for an instance of the same
nature, and yet it is not fiction but a real occurrence.
Gaius Coponius, a man of unusual capacity and
learning, came to you at Dyrrachium [3] while he,
as praetor, was in command of the Rhodian fleet,
and told you of a prediction made by a certain oarsman from one of the Rhodian quinqueremes.   The
prediction was that in less than thirty days Greece
would be bathed in blood ; Dyrrachium would be
pillaged ; its defenders would flee to their ships and,
as they fled, would see behind them the unhappy
spectacle of a great conflagration ; but the Rhodian

Rhodiorum classi propinquum reditum ac domum
itionem dari ; tum neque te ipsum non esse commo‑
tum Marcumque Varronem et M. Catonem, qui tum
ibi erant, doctos homines, vehementer esse perterri‑
tos ; paucis sane post diebus ex Pharsalia fuga
venisse Labienum ; qui cum interitum exercitus
nuntiavisset, reliqua vaticinationis brevi esse confecta.
69 Nam et ex horreis direptum effusumque frumentum
vias omnis angiportusque constraverat, et naves
subito perterriti metu conscendistis, et noctu ad
oppidum respicientes flagrantis onerarias quas incen‑
derant milites, quia sequi noluerant, videbatis ;
postremo a Rhodia classe deserti verum vatem fuisse
sensistis.

70 " Exposui quam brevissime potui somni et furoris
oracula, quae carere arte dixeram. Quorum amborum
generum una ratio est, qua Cratippus noster uti solet ;
animos hominum quadam ex parte extrinsecus esse
tractos et haustos (ex quo intellegitur esse extra
divinum animum, humanus unde ducatur) ; humani
autem animi eam partem, quae sensum, quae motum,
quae appetitum habeat, non esse ab actione corporis
seiugatam ; quae autem pars animi rationis atque
intellegentiae sit particeps, eam tum maxime vigere,
71 cum plurimum absit a corpore. Itaque, expositis
exemplis verarum vaticinationum et somniorum,
Cratippus solet rationem concludere hoc modo :
" ' Si sine oculis non potest exstare officium et
munus oculorum, possunt autem aliquando oculi non

---

[1] *Cf.* ii. 18. 34.

fleet would have a quick passage home. This story gave you some concern, and it caused very great alarm to those cultured men, Marcus Varro and Marcus Cato, who were at Dyrrachium at the time. In fact, a few days later Labienus reached Dyrrachium in flight from Pharsalus, with the news of the loss of the army. The rest of the prophecy was soon fulfilled. For the granaries were pillaged and their contents scattered and strewn all about the streets and alleys. You and your companions, in great alarm, suddenly embarked, and as you looked back at night towards the town you saw the flames of the merchant ships, which the soldiers (not wishing to follow) had set on fire. Finally, when your party had been deserted by the Rhodian fleet you realized that the prophecy had been fulfilled.

" As briefly as I could, I have discussed divination by means of dreams and frenzy, which, as I said,[1] are devoid of art. Both depend on the same reasoning, which is that habitually employed by our friend Cratippus : ' The human soul is in some degree derived and drawn from a source exterior to itself. Hence we understand that outside the human soul there is a divine soul from which the human soul is sprung. Moreover, that portion of the human soul which is endowed with sensation, motion, and carnal desire is inseparable from bodily influence ; while that portion which thinks and reasons is most vigorous when it is most distant from the body.' And so, after giving examples of true prophecies through frenzy and dreams, Cratippus usually concludes his argument in this way :

" ' Though without eyes it is impossible to perform the act and function of sight, and though the eyes

301

fungi suo munere, qui vel semel ita est usus oculis
ut vera cerneret, is habet sensum oculorum vera
cernentium. Item igitur, si sine divinatione non
potest officium et munus divinationis exstare, potest
autem quis, cum divinationem habeat, errare
aliquando nec vera cernere, satis est ad confirmandam
divinationem semel aliquid esse ita divinatum ut
nihil fortuito cecidisse videatur ; sunt autem eius
generis innumerabilia ; esse igitur divinationem
confitendum est.'

72   XXXIII. " Quae vero aut coniectura explicantur
aut eventis animadversa ac notata sunt, ea genera
divinandi, ut supra dixi, non naturalia, sed artificiosa
dicuntur ; in quo haruspices, augures coniectoresque
numerantur. Haec improbantur a Peripateticis, a
Stoicis defenduntur. Quorum alia sunt posita in
monumentis et disciplina, quod Etruscorum declarant
et haruspicini et fulgurales et tonitruales[1] libri, vestri
etiam augurales ; alia autem subito ex tempore
coniectura explicantur, ut apud Homerum Calchas,
qui ex passerum numero belli Troiani annos auguratus
est ; et ut in Sullae scriptum historia videmus, quod te
inspectante factum est, ut, cum ille in agro Nolano
immolaret ante praetorium, ab infima ara subito

---

[1] tonitruales *MSS. Reg., Cantab., Dav.*; rituales *other MSS.*,
Müller.

---

[1] See 6. 12.
[2] *Cf.* Homer's *Il.* ii. 301-329 ; and below ii. 30. 63, where
the verses from Homer are quoted.
[3] Nola is in Campania and still bears the same name.
This campaign was in 91–88 B.C.

sometimes cannot perform their appointed function, yet when a person has even once so employed his eyes as to see things as they are, he has a realization of what correct vision is. Likewise, therefore, although without the power of divination it is impossible for the act and function of divining to exist, and though one with that power may sometimes be mistaken and may make erroneous prophecies, yet it is enough to establish the existence of divination that a single event has been so clearly foretold as to exclude the hypothesis of chance. But there are many such instances ; therefore, the existence of divination must be conceded.'

XXXIII. " But those methods of divination which are dependent on conjecture, or on deductions from events previously observed and recorded, are, as I have said before,[1] not natural, but artificial, and include the inspection of entrails, augury, and the interpretation of dreams. These are disapproved of by the Peripatetics and defended by the Stoics. Some are based upon records and usage, as is evident from the Etruscan books on divination by means of inspection of entrails and by means of thunder and lightning, and as is also evident from the books of your augural college ; while others are dependent on conjecture made suddenly and on the spur of the moment. An instance of the latter kind is that of Calchas in Homer, prophesying the number of years of the Trojan War from the number of sparrows.[2] We find another illustration of conjectural divination in the history of Sulla in an occurrence which you witnessed. While he was offering sacrifices in front of his head-quarters in the Nolan district[3] a snake suddenly came out from

CICERO

anguis emergeret, cum quidem C. Postumius haruspex
oraret illum ut in expeditionem exercitum educeret.
Id cum Sulla fecisset, tum ante oppidum Nolam
fortissima Samnitium castra cepit.

73   " Facta coniectura etiam in Dionysio est paulo
ante quam regnare coepit ; qui, cum per agrum
Leontinum iter faciens, equum ipse demisisset in
flumen, submersus equus voraginibus non exstitit ;
quem cum maxima contentione non potuisset extra-
here, discessit, ut ait Philistus, aegre ferens. Cum
autem aliquantum progressus esset, subito exaudivit
hinnitum respexitque et equum alacrem laetus
aspexit, cuius in iuba examen apium consederat.
Quod ostentum habuit hanc vim, ut Dionysius paucis
post diebus regnare coeperit.

74   XXXIV. " Quid ? Lacedaemoniis paulo ante
Leuctricam calamitatem quae significatio facta est,
cum in Herculis fano arma sonuerunt Herculisque
simulacrum multo sudore manavit ! At eodem tempore Thebis, ut ait Callisthenes, in templo Herculis
valvae clausae repagulis subito se ipsae aperuerunt,
armaque quae fixa in parietibus fuerant ea sunt humi
inventa. Cumque eodem tempore apud Lebadiam
Trophonio res divina fieret, gallos gallinaceos in eo
loco sic assidue canere coepisse, ut nihil intermit-
terent ; tum augures dixisse Boeotios Thebanorum
esse victoriam, propterea quod avis illa victa silere
soleret, canere, si vicisset.

---

¹ Leuctra was a small town in Boeotia, memorable for
the victory won there in 371 B.C. by the Thebans under
Epaminondas over the Spartans.
² The oracle of Zeus Trophonius was located in a cave
in Lebadia and was much resorted to. *Cf.* Aristoph.
Nubes 508 ; Athenaeus, 614 A.

beneath the altar. The soothsayer, Gaius Postumius, begged Sulla to proceed with his march at once. Sulla did so and captured the strongly fortified camp of the Samnites which lay in front of the town of Nola.

" Still another instance of conjectural divination occurred in the case of Dionysius, a little while before he began to reign. He was travelling through the Leontine district, and led his horse down into a river. The horse was engulfed in a whirlpool and disappeared. Dionysius did his utmost to extricate him but in vain and, so Philistus writes, went away greatly troubled. When he had gone on a short distance he heard a whinny, looked back and, to his joy, saw his horse eagerly following and with a swarm of bees in its mane. The sequel of this portent was that Dionysius began to reign within a few days.

XXXIV. " Again : what a warning was given to the Spartans just before the disastrous battle of Leuctra,[1] when the armour clanked in the temple of Hercules and his statue dripped with sweat ! But at the same time, according to Callisthenes, the folding doors of Hercules' temple at Thebes, though closed with bars, suddenly opened of their own accord, and the armour which had been fastened on the temple walls, was found on the floor. And, at the same time, at Lebadia, in Boeotia, while divine honours were being paid to Trophonius,[2] the cocks in the neighbourhood began to crow vigorously and did not leave off. Thereupon the Boeotian augurs declared that the victory belonged to the Thebans, because it was the habit of cocks to keep silence when conquered and to crow when victorious.

305

CICERO

75 " Eademque tempestate multis signis Lacedaemoniis Leuctricae pugnae calamitas denuntiabatur.
Namque et Lysandri, qui Lacedaemoniorum cla-
rissimus fuerat, statuae, quae Delphis stabat, in
capite corona subito exstitit ex asperis herbis et
agrestibus ; stellaeque aureae, quae Delphis erant
a Lacedaemoniis positae post navalem illam victoriam
Lysandri, qua Athenienses conciderunt, qua in pugna
quia Castor et Pollux cum Lacedaemoniorum classe
visi esse dicebantur. Eorum insignia deorum, stellae
aureae, quas dixi, Delphis positae paulo ante Leuctricam pugnam deciderunt, neque repertae sunt.
76 Maximum vero illud portentum isdem Spartiatis fuit,
quod, cum oraculum ab Iove Dodonaeo petivissent de
victoria sciscitantes legatique vas illud in quo inerant
sortes collocavissent, simia, quam rex Molossorum
in deliciis habebat, et sortes ipsas et cetera, quae
erant ad sortem parata, disturbavit et aliud alio
dissipavit. Tum ea, quae praeposita erat oraculo,
sacerdos dixisse dicitur de salute Lacedaemoniis esse
non de victoria cogitandum.
77 XXXV. " Quid ? bello Punico secundo nonne C.
Flaminius consul iterum neglexit signa rerum
futurarum magna cum clade rei publicae ? Qui
exercitu lustrato cum Arretium versus castra movisset
et contra Hannibalem legiones duceret, et ipse et
equus eius ante signum Iovis Statoris sine causa
repente concidit, nec eam rem habuit religioni obiecto
signo, ut peritis videbatur, ne committeret proelium.

---

[1] At Aegospotami 405 B.C.
[2] Gaius Flaminius Nepos was defeated and slain 217 B.C.,
by Hannibal at Lake Trasimenus with the loss of 15,000
troops. *Cf.* Livy xxi. 57, 63.

"The Spartans received many warnings given at that time of their impending defeat at Leuctra. For example, a crown of wild, prickly herbs suddenly appeared on the head of the statue erected at Delphi in honour of Lysander, the most eminent of the Spartans. Furthermore, the Spartans had set up some golden stars in the temple of Castor and Pollux at Delphi to commemorate the glorious victory [1] of Lysander over the Athenians, because, it was said, those gods were seen accompanying the Spartan fleet in that battle. Now, just before the battle of Leuctra these divine symbols—that is, the golden stars at Delphi, already referred to— fell down and were never seen again. But the most significant warning received by the Spartans was this : they sent to consult the oracle of Jupiter at Dodona as to the chances of victory. After their messengers had duly set up the vessel in which were the lots, an ape, kept by the king of Molossia for his amusement, disarranged the lots and everything else used in consulting the oracle, and scattered them in all directions. Then, so we are told, the priestess who had charge of the oracle said that the Spartans must think of safety and not of victory.

XXXV. " Again, did not Gaius Flaminius [2] by his neglect of premonitory signs in his second consulship in the Second Punic War cause great disaster to the State ? For, after a review of his army, he had moved his camp and was marching towards Arretium to meet Hannibal, when his horse, for no apparent reason, suddenly fell with him just in front of the statue of Jupiter Stator. Although the soothsayers considered this a divine warning not to join battle, he did not so regard it. Again, after the

Idem cum tripudio auspicaretur, pullarius diem proeli
committendi differebat. Tum Flaminius ex eo
quaesivit, si ne postea quidem pulli pascerentur,
quid faciendum censeret. Cum ille quiescendum
respondisset, Flaminius : ' Praeclara vero auspicia,
si esurientibus pullis res geri poterit, saturis nihil
geretur ! ' Itaque signa convelli et se sequi iussit.
Quo tempore cum signifer primi hastati signum non
posset movere loco, nec quicquam proficeretur, plures
cum accederent, Flaminius, re nuntiata, suo more,
neglexit. Itaque tribus eis horis concisus exercitus
78 atque ipse interfectus est. Magnum illud etiam,
quod addidit Coelius, eo tempore ipso, cum hoc
calamitosum proelium fieret, tantos terrae motus in
Liguribus, Gallia compluribusque insulis totaque in
Italia factos esse, ut multa oppida conruerint, multis
locis labes factae sint terraeque desederint fluminaque
in contrarias partes fluxerint atque in amnes mare
influxerit.

XXXVI. " Fiunt certae divinationum coniecturae
a peritis. Midae illi Phrygi, cum puer esset, dormienti formicae in os tritici grana congesserunt.
Divitissimum fore praedictum est ; quod evenit.
At Platoni cum in cunis parvulo dormienti apes in
labellis consedissent, responsum est singulari illum
suavitate orationis fore. Ita futura eloquentia provisa
79 in infante est. Quid ? amores ac deliciae tuae,

---

[1] *Cf.* i. 15. 28, and ii. 34. 72.

auspices by means of the *tripudium*[1] had been taken, the keeper of the sacred chickens advised the postponement of battle. Flaminius then asked, 'Suppose the chickens should never eat, what would you advise in that case?' 'You should remain in camp,' was the reply. 'Fine auspices indeed!' said Flaminius, 'for they counsel action when chickens' crops are empty and inaction when chickens' crops are filled.' So he ordered the standards to be plucked up and the army to follow him. Then, when the standard-bearer of the first company could not loosen his standard, several soldiers came to his assistance, but to no purpose. This fact was reported to Flaminius, and he, with his accustomed obstinacy, ignored it. The consequence was that within three hours his army was cut to pieces and he himself was slain. Coelius has added the further notable fact that, at the very time this disastrous battle was going on, earthquakes of such violence occurred in Liguria, in Gaul, on several islands, and in every part of Italy, that a large number of towns were destroyed, landslips took place in many regions, the earth sank, rivers flowed upstream, and the sea invaded their channels.

XXXVI. "Trustworthy conjectures in divining are made by experts. For instance, when Midas, the famous king of Phrygia, was a child, ants filled his mouth with grains of wheat as he slept. It was predicted that he would be a very wealthy man; and so it turned out. Again, while Plato was an infant, asleep in his cradle, bees settled on his lips and this was interpreted to mean that he would have a rare sweetness of speech. Hence in his infancy his future eloquence was foreseen. And what about your

Roscius, num aut ipse aut pro eo Lanuvium totum
mentiebatur ? Qui cum esset in cunabulis educare-
turque in Solonio, qui est campus agri Lanuvini,
noctu lumine apposito experrecta nutrix animadvertit
puerum dormientem circumplicatum serpentis am-
plexu. Quo aspectu exterrita clamorem sustulit.
Pater autem Rosci ad haruspices rettulit, qui
responderunt nihil illo puero clarius, nihil nobilius
fore. Atque hanc speciem Pasiteles[1] caelavit
argento et noster expressit Archias versibus.

" Quid igitur expectamus ? an dum in foro nobis-
cum di immortales, dum in viis versentur, dum domi ?
qui quidem ipsi se nobis non offerunt, vim autem
suam longe lateque diffundunt, quam tum terrae
cavernis includunt, tum hominum naturis implicant.
Nam terrae vis Pythiam Delphis incitabat, naturae
Sibyllam. Quid enim ? non videmus quam sint
varia terrarum genera ? ex quibus et mortifera
quaedam pars est, ut et Ampsancti in Hirpinis et
in Asia Plutonia, quae vidimus, et sunt partes
agrorum aliae pestilentes, aliae salubres, aliae, quae
acuta ingenia gignant, aliae, quae retusa ; quae
omnia fiunt et ex caeli varietate et ex disparili
80 aspiratione terrarum. Fit etiam saepe specie quadam, saepe vocum gravitate et cantibus ut pellan-

---

[1] Pasiteles *Winckelman* ; Praxiteles MSS.

---

[1] The famous actor.
[2] The divine afflatus was supposed to be connected with
an exhalation (*spiritus*) from a chasm.
[3] Lake Ampsanctus was in Samnium and reputed to be an
entrance to the infernal regions. *Cf.* Virgil, *Aen.* vii. 563.

beloved and charming friend Roscius[1]? Did he lie
or did the whole of Lanuvium lie for him in telling
the following incident : In his cradle days, while he
was being reared in Solonium, a plain in the Lanuvian
district, his nurse suddenly awoke during the night
and by the light of a lamp observed the child asleep
with a snake coiled about him. She was greatly
frightened at the sight and gave an alarm. His
father referred the occurrence to the soothsayers,
who replied that the boy would attain unrivalled
eminence and glory. Indeed, Pasiteles has engraved
the scene in silver and our friend Archias has
described it in verse.

"Then what do we expect ? Do we wait for
the immortal gods to converse with us in the forum,
on the street, and in our homes ? While they do
not, of course, present themselves in person, they
do diffuse their power far and wide — sometimes
enclosing it in caverns of the earth and sometimes
imparting it to human beings. The Pythian priestess
at Delphi was inspired by the power of the earth[2]
and the Sibyl by that of nature. Why need you
marvel at this ? Do we not see how the soils of
the earth vary in kind ? Some are deadly, like that
about Lake Ampsanctus[3] in the country of the Hir-
pini and that of Plutonia in Asia, both of which I
have seen. Even in the same neighbourhood, some
parts are salubrious and some are not ; some produce
men of keen wit, others produce fools. These
diverse effects are all the result of differences in
climate and differences in the earth's exhalations.
It often happens, too, that the soul is violently
stirred by the sight of some object, or by the deep
tones of a voice, or by singing. Frequently anxiety

311

tur animi vehementius, saepe etiam cura et timore, qualis est illa

> flexánima tamquam lýmphata aut Bacchí sacris
> commóta in tumulis Teúcrum commemoráns suum.

XXXVII. " Atque etiam illa concitatio declarat vim in animis esse divinam. Negat enim sine furore Democritus quemquam poëtam magnum esse posse, quod idem dicit Plato. Quem, si placet, appellet furorem, dum modo is furor ita laudetur, ut in Phaedro Platonis laudatus est. Quid ? vestra oratio in causis, quid ipsa actio potest esse vehemens et gravis et copiosa, nisi est animus ipse commotior ? Equidem etiam in te saepe vidi et, ut ad leviora veniamus, in Aesopo, familiari tuo, tantum ardorem vultuum atque motuum, ut eum vis quaedam abstraxisse a sensu mentis videretur.

81   " Obiciuntur etiam saepe formae quae reapse nullae sunt, speciem autem offerunt ; quod contigisse Brenno dicitur eiusque Gallicis copiis, cum fano Apollinis Delphici nefarium bellum intulisset. Tum enim ferunt ex oraclo ecfatam esse Pythiam :

> ego próvidebo rem ístam et albae vírgines.

Ex quo factum ut viderentur virgines ferre arma contra et nive Gallorum obrueretur exercitus.

XXXVIII. " Aristoteles quidem eos etiam, qui valetudinis vitio furerent et melancholici dicerentur,

---

[1] The verses are from the *Teucer* of Pacuvius. Hesione was mother of Teucer.

[2] Plato, *Phaedr*. p. 244 A.

[3] This was not the Brennus who captured Rome, but a later one who invaded Macedonia and perished there in 278 B.C.

[4] Athena and Artemis. The Greek line is ἐμοὶ μελήσει ταῦτα καὶ λευκαῖς κόραις.

[5] *Cf.* Aristot. *Prob*. xxx. p. 471.

[6] Lit. ' sufferers from black bile ' (μέλαινα χολή).

or fear will have that effect, as it did in the case of Hesione, who

> Did rave like one by Bacchic rites made mad
> And mid the tombs her Teucer called aloud.[1]

XXXVII. "And poetic inspiration also proves that there is a divine power within the human soul. Democritus says that no one can be a great poet without being in a state of frenzy, and Plato says the same thing. Let Plato call it ' frenzy ' if he will, provided he praises it as it was praised in his *Phaedrus*.[2] And what about your own speeches in law suits ? Can the delivery of you lawyers be impassioned, weighty, and fluent unless your soul is deeply stirred ? Upon my word, many a time have I seen in you such passion of look and gesture that I thought some power was rendering you unconscious of what you did ; and, if I may cite a less striking example, I have seen the same in your friend Aesopus.

" Frequently, too, apparitions present themselves and, though they have no real substance, they seem to have. This is illustrated by what is said to have happened to Brennus[3] and to his Gallic troops after he had made an impious attack on the temple of Apollo at Delphi. The story is that the Pythian priestess, in speaking from the oracle, said to Brennus :

> To this the virgins white[4] and I will see.

The result was that the virgins were seen fighting against the Gauls, and their army was overwhelmed with snow.

XXXVIII. "Aristotle thought[5] that even the people who rave from the effects of sickness and are called ' hypochondriacs '[6] have within their souls some power

313

censebat habere aliquid in animis praesagiens atque
divinum. Ego autem haud scio an nec cardiacis hoc
tribuendum sit nec phreneticis ; animi enim integri
82 non vitiosi est corporis divinatio. Quam quidem
esse re vera hac Stoicorum ratione concluditur :

" ' Si sunt di neque ante declarant hominibus quae
futura sint, aut non diligunt homines, aut quid
eventurum sit ignorant ; aut existimant nihil
interesse hominum scire quid sit futurum, aut non
censent esse suae maiestatis praesignificare hominibus quae sunt futura ; aut ea ne ipsi quidem di
significare possunt. At neque non diligunt nos (sunt
enim benefici generique hominum amici) ; neque
ignorant ea quae ab ipsis constituta et designata
sunt ; neque nostra nihil interest scire ea, quae
eventura sunt (erimus enim cautiores si sciemus) ;
neque hoc alienum ducunt maiestate sua (nihil est
enim beneficentia praestantius) ; neque non possunt
83 futura praenoscere ; non igitur sunt di nec significant
futura ; sunt autem di, significant ergo ; et non,
si significant, nullas vias dant nobis ad significationis
scientiam (frustra enim significarent) ; nec, si dant
vias, non est divinatio ; est igitur divinatio.'

of foresight and of prophecy. But, for my part, I am inclined to think that such a power is not to be attributed either to a diseased stomach or to a disordered brain. On the contrary, it is the healthy soul and not the sickly body that has the power of divination. The Stoics, for example, establish the existence of divination by the following process of reasoning:

" ' If there are gods and they do not make clear to man in advance what the future will be, then they do not love man ; or, they themselves do not know what the future will be ; or, they think that it is of no advantage to man to know what it will be ; or, they think it inconsistent with their dignity to give man forewarnings of the future ; or, finally, they, though gods, cannot give intelligible signs of coming events. But it is not true that the gods do not love us, for they are the friends and benefactors of the human race ; nor is it true that they do not know their own decrees and their own plans ; nor is it true that it is of no advantage to us to know what is going to happen, since we should be more prudent if we knew   nor is it true that the gods think it inconsistent with their dignity to give forecasts, since there is no more excellent quality than kindness ; nor is it true that they have not the power to know the future ; therefore it is not true that there are gods and yet that they do not give us signs of the future ; but there are gods, therefore they give us such signs ; and if they give such signs, it is not true that they give us no means to understand those signs—otherwise their signs would be useless ; and if they give us the means, it is not true that there is no divination ; therefore there is divination.'

315

84 XXXIX. " Hac ratione et Chrysippus et Diogenes et Antipater utitur. Quid est igitur cur dubitandum sit quin sint ea quae disputavi verissima, si ratio mecum facit, si eventa, si populi, si nationes, si Graeci, si barbari, si maiores etiam nostri, si denique hoc semper ita putatum est, si summi philosophi, si poëtae, si sapientissimi viri, qui res publicas constituerunt, qui urbes condiderunt ? An, dum bestiae loquantur exspectamus ? hominum consentiente auc-

85 toritate contenti non sumus ? Nec vero quicquam aliud affertur cur ea quae dico divinandi genera nulla sint, nisi, quod difficile dictu videtur, quae cuiusque divinationis ratio, quae causa sit. ' Quid enim habet haruspex, cur pulmo incisus etiam in bonis extis dirimat tempus et proferat diem?' Quid augur, cur a dextra corvus, a sinistra cornix, faciat ratum ? ' ' Quid astrologus cur stella Iovis aut Veneris coniuncta cum luna ad ortus puerorum salutaris sit, Saturni Martisve contraria ? ' ' Cur autem deus dormientes nos moneat, vigilantes neglegat ? ' ' Quid deinde causae est cur Cassandra furens futura prospiciat, Priamus sapiens hoc idem facere non queat ? '

86 " Cur fiat quidque, quaeris. Recte omnino ; sed non nunc id agitur ; fiat necne fiat, id quaeritur. Ut, si magnetem lapidem esse dicam qui ferrum ad se adliciat et attrahat, rationem cur id

XXXIX. "Chrysippus, Diogenes, and Antipater employ the same reasoning. Then what ground is there to doubt the absolute truth of my position? For I have on my side reason, facts, peoples, and races, both Greek and barbarian, our own ancestors, the unvarying belief of all ages, the greatest philosophers, the poets, the wisest men, the builders of cities, and the founders of republics. Are we not satisfied with the unanimous judgement of men, and do we wait for beasts to give their testimony too? The truth is that no other argument of any sort is advanced to show the futility of the various kinds of divination which I have mentioned except the fact that it is difficult to give the cause or reason of every kind of divination. You ask, ' Why is it that the soothsayer, when he finds a cleft in the lung of the victim, even though the other vitals are sound, stops the execution of an undertaking and defers it to another day?' 'Why does an augur think it a favourable omen when a raven flies to the right, or a crow to the left?' 'Why does an astrologer consider that the moon's conjunction with the planets Jupiter and Venus at the birth of children is a favourable omen, and its conjunction with Saturn or Mars unfavourable?' Again, 'Why does God warn us when we are asleep and fail to do so when we are awake?' Finally, 'Why is it that mad Cassandra foresees coming events and wise Priam cannot do the same?'

"You ask why everything happens. You have a perfect right to ask, but that is not the point at issue now. The question is, Does it happen, or does it not? For example, if I were to say that the magnet attracted iron and drew it to itself, and I could not

317

fiat, afferre nequeam, fieri omnino neges. Quod idem facis in divinatione, quam et cernimus ipsi et audimus et legimus et a patribus accepimus. Neque ante philosophiam patefactam, quae nuper inventa est, hac de re communis vita dubitavit, et, posteaquam philosophia processit, nemo aliter philosophus sensit, 87 in quo modo esset auctoritas. Dixi de Pythagora, de Democrito, de Socrate, excepi de antiquis praeter Xenophanem neminem; adiunxi veterem Academiam, Peripateticos, Stoicos; unus dissentit Epicurus. Quid vero hoc turpius, quam quod idem nullam censet gratuitam esse virtutem?

XL. "Quis est autem quem non moveat clarissimis monumentis testata consignataque antiquitas? Calchantem augurem scribit Homerus longe optimum, eumque ducem classium fuisse ad Ilium, auspiciorum 88 credo scientia, non locorum. Amphilochus et Mopsus Argivorum reges fuerunt, sed eidem augures, eique urbis in ora maritima Ciliciae Graecas condiderunt; atque etiam ante hos Amphiaraus et Tiresias non humiles et obscuri neque eorum similes, ut apud Ennium est,

quí sui quaestus caúsa fictas súscitant senténtias.

tell you why, then I suppose you would utterly deny that the magnet had any such power. At least that is the course you pursue in regard to the existence of the power of divination, although it is established by our own experience and that of others, by our reading and by the traditions of our forefathers. Why, even before the dawn of philosophy, which is a recent discovery, the average man had no doubt about divination, and, since its development, no philosopher of any sort of reputation has had any different view. I have already cited Pythagoras, Democritus, and Socrates and, of the ancients, I have excluded no one except Xenophanes. To them I have added the Old Academy, the Peripatetics; and the Stoics. The only dissenter is Epicurus. But why wonder at that ? for is his opinion of divination any more discreditable than his view that there is no such thing as a disinterested virtue ?

XL. " But is there a man anywhere who is un-influenced by clear and unimpeachable records signed and sealed by the hand of Time ? For example, Homer writes that Calchas was by far the best augur among the Greeks and that he com-manded the Greek fleet before Troy. His command of the fleet I suppose was due to his skill as an augur and not to his skill in seamanship. Amphilochus and Mopsus were kings of Argos, but they were augurs too, and they founded Greek cities on the coasts of Cilicia. And even before them were Amphiaraus and Tiresias. They were no lowly and unknown men, nor were they like the persons described by Ennius,

Who, for their own gain, uphold opinions that are false,

319

sed clari et praestantes viri, qui avibus et signis
admoniti futura dicebant ; quorum de altero etiam
apud inferos Homerus ait ' solum sapere, ceteros
umbrarum vagari modo ' ; Amphiaraum autem sic
honoravit fama Graeciae, deus ut haberetur, atque ut
ab eius solo, in quo est humatus, oracla peterentur.

89 " Quid ? Asiae rex Priamus nonne et Helenum
filium et Cassandram filiam divinantes habebat,
alterum auguriis, alteram mentis incitatione et
permotione divina ? Quo in genere Marcios quosdam
fratres, nobili loco natos, apud maiores nostros fuisse
scriptum videmus. Quid ? Polyidum Corinthium
nonne Homerus et aliis multa et filio ad Troiam proficiscenti mortem praedixisse commemorat ? Omnino
apud veteres, qui rerum potiebantur, iidem auguria
tenebant ; ut enim sapere, sic divinare regale ducebant. Ut testis est nostra civitas, in qua et reges
augures et postea privati eodem sacerdotio praediti
rem publicam religionum auctoritate rexerunt.

90 XLI. " Eaque divinationum ratio ne in barbaris
quidem gentibus neglecta est, siquidem et in Gallia
Druidae sunt, e quibus ipse Divitiacum Aeduum,
hospitem tuum laudatoremque, cognovi, qui et
naturae rationem, quam φυσιολογίαν Graeci appellant, notam esse sibi profitebatur et partim

---

[1] Cf. Homer, Od. x. 492.
[2] Mentioned by Servius in Aen. vi. 70 and 72 as having
their oracles preserved along with the Sibylline books.
[3] Cf. Homer, Il. xiii. 663.
[4] The priestly functions of the " king " were afterwards
exercised by a rex sacrorum.
[5] Cf. Caes. B.G. vi. 13 ; Pomp. Mel. iii. 2 ; Strabo iv
p. 302.

but they were eminent men of the noblest
type and foretold the future by means of augural
signs. In speaking of Tiresias, even when in the
infernal regions, Homer says that he alone was
wise, that the rest were mere wandering shadows.[1]
As for Amphiaraus, his reputation in Greece was
such that he was honoured as a god, and oracular
responses were sought in the place where he was
buried.

" Furthermore, did not Priam, the Asiatic king,
have a son, Helenus, and a daughter, Cassandra,
who prophesied, the first by means of auguries and
the other when under a heaven-inspired excitement
and exaltation of soul ? In the same class, as we
read in the records of our forefathers, were those
famous Marcian brothers,[2] men of noble birth. And
does not Homer relate that Polyidus of Corinth [3]
not only made many predictions to others, but
that he also foretold the death of his own son, who
was setting out for Troy ? As a general rule among
the ancients the men who ruled the state had
control likewise of augury, for they considered
divining, as well as wisdom, becoming to a king.
Proof of this is afforded by our State wherein the
kings were augurs ; and, later, private citizens
endowed with the same priestly office ruled the
republic by the authority of religion.[4]

XLI. " Nor is the practice of divination disregarded even among uncivilized tribes, if indeed
there are Druids [5] in Gaul—and there are, for I
knew one of them myself, Divitiacus, the Aeduan,
your guest and eulogist. He claimed to have that
knowledge of nature which the Greeks call ' physio-
logia,' and he used to make predictions, sometimes

auguriis, partim coniectura, quae essent futura,
dicebat. Et in Persis augurantur et divinant magi,
qui congregantur in fano commentandi causa atque
inter se conloquendi, quod etiam idem vos quondam
91 facere Nonis solebatis. Nec quisquam rex Persarum
potest esse, qui non ante magorum disciplinam
scientiamque perceperit. Licet autem videre et
genera quaedam et nationes huic scientiae deditas.
Telmessus in Caria est, qua in urbe excellit haruspicum disciplina ; itemque Elis in Peloponneso familias
duas certas habet, Iamidarum unam, alteram Cluti-
darum, haruspicinae nobilitate praestantes. In Syria
Chaldaei cognitione astrorum sollertiaque ingeniorum
antecellunt.

92 "Etruria autem de caelo tacta scientissime
animadvertit eademque interpretatur, quid quibusque ostendatur monstris atque portentis. Quocirca
bene apud maiores nostros senatus tum, cum florebat
imperium, decrevit, ut de principum filiis sex[1]
singulis Etruriae populis in disciplinam traderentur,
ne ars tanta propter tenuitatem hominum a religionis
auctoritate abduceretur ad mercedem atque quaestum. Phryges autem et Pisidae et Cilices et Arabum
natio avium significationibus plurimum obtemperant,
quod idem factitatum in Umbria accepimus.

93 XLII. "Ac mihi quidem videntur e locis quoque
ipsis, qui a quibusque incolebantur, divinationum
opportunitates esse ductae. Etenim Aegyptii et

[1] sex MSS., Dav. ; x. ex Müller.

---

[1] Cf. Herod. ix. 33.
[2] Val. Max. i. 1 says that ten (not six) were handed over.
Editors differ as to whether the youths set apart were Roman
or Etruscan. See Moser, De div. p. 106, note; Wissowa,
Relig. und Kult.[2] p. 548.

by means of augury and sometimes by means of conjecture. Among the Persians the augurs and diviners are the magi, who assemble regularly in a sacred place for practice and consultation, just as formerly you augurs used to do on the Nones. Indeed, no one can become king of the Persians until he has learned the theory and the practice of the magi. Moreover, you may see whole families and tribes devoted to this art. For example, Telmessus in Caria is a city noted for its cultivation of the soothsayer's art, and there is also Elis in Peloponnesus, which has permanently set aside two families as soothsayers, the Iamidae and the Clutidae,[1] who are distinguished for superior skill in their art. In Syria the Chaldeans are pre-eminent for their knowledge of astronomy and for their quickness of mind.

" Again, the Etrurians are very skilful in observing thunderbolts, in interpreting their meaning and that of every sign and portent. That is why, in the days of our forefathers, it was wisely decreed by the Senate, when its power was in full vigour, that, of the sons of the chief men, six should be handed over to each of the Etruscan tribes[2] for the study of divination, in order that so important a profession should not, on account of the poverty of its members, be withdrawn from the influence of religion, and converted into a means of mercenary gain. On the other hand the Phrygians, Pisidians, Cilicians, and Arabians rely chiefly on the signs conveyed by the flights of birds, and the Umbrians, according to tradition, used to do the same.

XLII. " Now, for my part, I believe that the character of the country determined the kind of divination which its inhabitants adopted. For

Babylonii in camporum patentium aequoribus habi·
tantes, cum ex terra nihil emineret, quod contem-
plationi caeli officere posset, omnem curam in siderum
cognitione posuerunt. Etrusci autem, quod religione
imbuti studiosius et crebrius hostias immolabant,
extorum cognitioni se maxime dediderunt, quodque
propter aëris crassitudinem de caelo apud eos multa
fiebant, et quod ob eandem causam multa inusitata
partim e caelo, alia ex terra oriebantur, quaedam
etiam ex hominum pecudumve conceptu et satu,
ostentorum exercitatissimi interpretes exstiterunt.
Quorum quidem vim, ut tu soles dicere, verba
ipsa prudenter a maioribus posita declarant. Quia
enim ostendunt, portendunt, monstrant, praedicunt,
ostenta, portenta, monstra, prodigia dicuntur.
94 Arabes autem et Phryges et Cilices, quod pastu
pecudum maxime utuntur campos et montes, hieme
et aestate peragrantes, propterea facilius cantus
avium et volatus notaverunt ; eademque et Pisidiae
causa fuit et huic nostrae Umbriae. Tum Caria tota
praecipueque Telmesses, quos ante dixi, quod agros
uberrimos maximeque fertiles incolunt, in quibus
multa propter fecunditatem fingi gignique possunt.
in ostentis animadvertendis diligentes fuerunt.

---

[1] *Cf.* Cic. *N.D.* ii. 3. 7, which the present passage almost
repeats.

example, the Egyptians and Babylonians, who live on the level surface of open plains, with no hills to obstruct a view of the sky, have devoted their attention wholly to astrology. But the Etruscans, being in their nature of a very ardent religious temperament and accustomed to the frequent sacrifice of victims, have given their chief attention to the study of entrails. And as on account of the density of the atmosphere signs from heaven were common among them, and furthermore since that atmospheric condition caused many phenomena both of earth and sky and also certain prodigies that occur in the conception and birth of men and cattle—for these reasons the Etruscans have become very proficient in the interpretation of portents. Indeed, the inherent force of these means of divination, as you like to observe,[1] is clearly shown by the very words so aptly chosen by our ancestors to describe them. Because they ' make manifest ' (*ostendunt*), ' portend ' (*portendunt*), ' intimate ' (*monstrant*), ' predict ' (*praedicunt*), they are called ' manifestations,' ' portents,' ' intimations,' and ' prodigies.' But the Arabians, Phrygians, and Cilicians, being chiefly engaged in the rearing of cattle, are constantly wandering over the plains and mountains in winter and summer and, on that account, have found it quite easy to study the songs and flights of birds. The same is true of the Pisidians and of our fellow-countrymen, the Umbrians. While the Carians, and especially the Telmessians, already mentioned, because they live in a country with a very rich and prolific soil, whose fertility produces many abnormal growths, have turned their attention to the study of prodigies.

95 XLIII. " Quis vero non videt in optima quaque re publica plurimum auspicia et reliqua divinandi genera valuisse ? Quis rex umquam fuit, quis populus, qui non uteretur praedictione divina ? neque solum in pace, sed in bello multo etiam magis, quo maius erat certamen et discrimen salutis. Omitto nostros, qui nihil in bello sine extis agunt, nihil sine auspiciis domi externa videamus : namque et Athenienses omnibus semper publicis consiliis divinos quosdam sacerdotes, quos μάντεις vocant, adhibuerunt, et Lacedaemonii regibus suis augurem assessorem dederunt, itemque senibus (sic enim consilium publicum appellant) augurem interesse voluerunt, iidemque de rebus maioribus semper aut Delphis oraclum aut ab 96 Hammone aut a Dodona petebant. Lycurgus quidem, qui Lacedaemoniorum rem publicam temperavit, leges suas auctoritate Apollinis Delphici confirmavit ; quas cum vellet Lysander commutare, eadem est prohibitus religione. Atque etiam qui praeerant Lacedaemoniis, non contenti vigilantibus curis, in Pasiphaae fano, quod est in agro propter urbem, somniandi causa excubabant, quia vera quietis oracla ducebant.

97 " Ad nostra iam redeo. Quoties senatus decemviros ad libros ire iussit ! quantis in rebus quamque saepe responsis haruspicum paruit ! Nam et cum

326

XLIII. "But who fails to observe that auspices and all other kinds of divination flourish best in the best regulated states? And what king or people has there ever been who did not employ divination? I do not mean in time of peace only, but much more even in time of war, when the strife and struggle for safety is hardest. Passing by our own countrymen, who do nothing in war without examining entrails and nothing in peace without taking the auspices, let us look at the practice of foreign nations. The Athenians, for instance, in every public assembly always had present certain priestly diviners, whom they call *manteis*. The Spartans assigned an augur to their kings as a judicial adviser, and they also enacted that an augur should be present in their Council of Elders, which is the name of their Senate. In matters of grave concern they always consulted the oracle at Delphi, or that of Jupiter Hammon or that of Dodona. Lycurgus himself, who once governed the Spartan state, established his laws by authority of Apollo's Delphic oracle, and Lysander, who wished to repeal them, was prevented from doing so by the religious scruples of the people. Moreover, the Spartan rulers, not content with their deliberations when awake, used to sleep in a shrine of Pasiphaë which is situated in a field near the city, in order to dream there, because they believed that oracles received in repose were true.

"I now return to instances at home. How many times the Senate has ordered the decemvirs to consult the Sibylline books! How often in matters of grave concern it has obeyed the responses of the soothsayers! Take the following examples: When

duo visi soles sunt et cum tres lunae et cum faces,
et cum sol nocte visus est, et cum e caelo fremitus
auditus, et cum caelum discessisse visum est atque
in eo animadversi globi, delata etiam ad senatum
labe agri Privernatis, cum ad infinitam altitudinem
terra desedisset Apuliaque maximis terrae motibus
conquassata esset—quibus portentis magna populo
Romano bella perniciosaeque seditiones denuntia-
bantur. Inque his omnibus responsa haruspicum
cum Sibyllae versibus congruebant.

98   " Quid ? cum Cumis Apollo sudavit, Capuae
Victoria ? quid ? ortus androgyni nonne fatale quoddam monstrum fuit ? quid ? cum fluvius Atratus
sanguine fluxit ? quid ? cum saepe lapidum, san-
guinis non numquam, terrae interdum, quondam
etiam lactis imber affluxit ? quid ? cum in Capitolio
ictus Centaurus e caelo est, in Aventino portae et
homines, Tusculi aedes Castoris et Pollucis, Romae-
que Pietatis : nonne et haruspices ea responderunt,
quae evenerunt, et in Sibyllae libris eaedem repertae
praedictiones sunt ?

99   XLIV. " Caeciliae Q. filiae somnio modo Marsico
bello templum est a senatu Iunoni Sospitae restitu-
tum. Quod quidem somnium Sisenna cum disputa-
visset mirifice ad verbum cum re convenisse, tum

---

¹ The word *ignei* may have dropped out ; *cf.* Sen. *Nat.
Quaest.* i. 14 " caelum visum discedere cuius hiatu vertices
flammae apparuerunt." Davies suggests *ignei animadversi
globi.*
² Nothing is known of this river.   ³ 91–89 B.C.
328

at one time, two suns and, at another, three moons, were seen ; when meteors appeared ; when the sun shone at night ; when rumblings were heard in the heavens ; when the sky seemed to divide, showing balls of fire [1] enclosed within ; again, on the occasion of the landslip in Privernum, report of which was made to the Senate ; and when Apulia was shaken by a most violent earthquake and the land sank to an incredible depth—in all these cases of portents which warned the Roman people of mighty wars and deadly revolutions, the responses of the soothsayers were in agreement with the Sibylline verses.

" And what of those other instances ? As when, for example, the statue of Apollo at Cumae and that of Victory at Capua dripped with sweat ; when that unlucky prodigy, the hermaphrodite, was born ; when the river Atratus [2] ran with blood ; when there were showers frequently of stone, sometimes of blood, occasionally of earth and even of milk ; and finally, when lightning struck the statue of the Centaur on the Capitoline hill, the gates and some people on the Aventine and the temples of Castor and Pollux at Tusculum and of Piety at Rome— in each of these cases did not the soothsayers give prophetic responses which were afterwards fulfilled ? And were not these same prophecies found in the Sibylline books ?

XLIV. " In recent times, during the Marsian war,[3] the temple of Juno Sospita was restored because of a dream of Caecilia, the daughter of Quintus Caecilius Metellus. This is the same dream that Sisenna discussed as marvellous, in that its prophecies were fulfilled to the letter, and yet later

insolenter, credo ab Epicureo aliquo inductus, disputat somniis credi non oportere. Idem contra ostenta nihil disputat exponitque initio belli Marsici et deorum simulacra sudavisse, et sanguinem fluxisse, et discessisse caelum, et ex occulto auditas esse voces, quae pericula belli nuntiarent, et Lanuvi clipeos, quod haruspicibus tristissimum visum esset, a muribus esse derosos.

100 "Quid, quod in annalibus habemus Veienti bello, cum lacus Albanus praeter modum crevisset, Veientem quendam ad nos hominem nobilem perfugisse, eumque dixisse ex fatis, quae Veientes scripta haberent, Veios capi non posse, dum lacus is redundaret; et, si lacus emissus lapsu et cursu suo ad mare profluxisset, perniciosum populo Romano; sin autem ita esset eductus, ut ad mare pervenire non posset, tum salutare nostris fore? Ex quo illa admirabilis a maioribus Albanae aquae facta deductio est. Cum autem Veientes bello fessi legatos ad senatum misissent, tum ex eis quidam dixisse dicitur non omnia illum transfugam ausum esse senatui dicere; in isdem enim fatis scriptum Veientes habere fore ut brevi a Gallis Roma caperetur, quod quidem sexennio post Veios captos factum esse videmus.

---

[1] After a siege of ten years, 406–396 B.C., Veii was captured by Camillus. *Cf.* Livy v. 15; Plutarch, *Camil.* 4.

[2] For an account of how this irrigation project was begun *cf.* Plutarch, *Camillus*, ch. 3. ff.

—influenced no doubt by some petty Epicurean—
he goes on inconsistently to maintain that dreams
are not worthy of belief. This writer, however, has
nothing to say against prodigies ; in fact he relates
that, at the outbreak of the Marsian War, the
statues of the gods dripped with sweat, rivers ran
with blood, the heavens opened, voices from unknown
sources were heard predicting dangerous wars, and
finally—the sign considered by the soothsayers the
most ominous of all—the shields at Lanuvium were
gnawed by mice.

" And what do you say of the following story
which we find in our annals ? During the Veientian
War,[1] when Lake Albanus had overflowed its banks, a
certain nobleman of Veii deserted to us and said
that, according to the prophecies of the Veientian
books, their city could not be taken while the lake
was at flood, and that if its waters were permitted
to overflow and take their own course to the sea
the result would be disastrous to the Roman people ;
on the other hand, if the waters were drained off
in such a way that they did not reach the sea the
result would be to our advantage. In consequence
of this announcement our forefathers dug that
marvellous canal to drain off the waters from the
Alban lake.[2] Later when the Veientians had grown
weary of war and had sent ambassadors to the
Senate to treat for peace, one of them is reported
to have said that the deserter had not dared to
tell the whole of the prophecy contained in the
Veientian books, for those books, he said, also foretold the early capture of Rome by the Gauls. And
this, as we know, did occur six years after the fall
of Veii.

101   XLV. "Saepe etiam et in proeliis fauni auditi et
in rebus turbidis veridicae voces ex occulto missae
esse dicuntur ; cuius generis duo sint ex multis
exempla, sed maxima : nam non multo ante urbem
captam exaudita vox est a luco Vestae, qui a Palati
radice in novam viam devexus est, ut muri et portae
reficerentur ; futurum esse, nisi provisum esset, ut
Roma caperetur. Quod neglectum tum, cum caveri
poterat, post acceptam illam maximam cladem
expiatum[1] est ; ara enim Aio Loquenti, quam saep-
tam videmus, exadversus eum locum consecrata est.
Atque etiam scriptum a multis est, cum terrae motus
factus esset, ut sue plena procuratio fieret, vocem
ab aede Iunonis ex arce extitisse ; quocirca Iunonem
illam appellatam Monetam. Haec igitur et a dis
significata et a nostris maioribus iudicata contem-
nimus ?

102   " Neque solum deorum voces Pythagorei observita-
verunt, sed etiam hominum, quae vocant omina.
Quae maiores nostri quia valere censebant, idcirco
omnibus rebus agendis, ' Quod bonum, faustum,
felix fortunatumque esset ' praefabantur ; rebusque
divinis, quae publice fierent, ut ' faverent linguis,'
imperabatur ; inque feriis imperandis, ut ' litibus

---

[1] expiatum *Dav.* ; explicatum MSS.

---

[1] *Cf.* Livy v. 32 and 50.

XLV. " Again, we are told that fauns have often been heard in battle and that during turbulent times truly prophetic messages have been sent from mysterious places. Out of many instances of this class I shall give only two, but they are very striking. Not long before the capture of the city by the Gauls, a voice, issuing from Vesta's sacred grove, which slopes from the foot of the Palatine Hill to the New Road, was heard to say, ' the walls and gates must be repaired ; unless this is done the city will be taken.' [1] Neglect of this warning, while it was possible to heed it, was atoned for after the supreme disaster had occurred ; for, adjoining the grove, an altar, which is now to be seen enclosed with a hedge, was dedicated to Aius the Speaker. The other illustration has been reported by many writers. At the time of the earthquake a voice came from Juno's temple on the citadel commanding that an expiatory sacrifice be made of a pregnant sow. From this fact the goddess was called Juno the Adviser. Are we, then, lightly to regard these warnings which the gods have sent and our forefathers adjudged to be trustworthy ?

" Nor is it only to the voices of the gods that the Pythagoreans have paid regard but also to the utterances of men which they term ' omens.' Our ancestors, too, considered such ' omens ' worthy of respect, and for that reason, before entering upon any business enterprise, used to say, ' May the issue be prosperous, propitious, lucky, and successful.' At public celebrations of religious rites they gave the command, ' Guard your tongues ' ; and in issuing the order for the Latin festival the customary injunction was, ' Let the people refrain from strife

et iurgiis se abstinerent.' Itemque in lustranda
colonia ab eo qui eam deduceret, et cum imperator
exercitum, censor populum, lustraret, bonis nominibus, qui hostias ducerent, eligebantur. Quod idem
in dilectu consules observant, ut primus miles fiat
103 bono nomine. Quae quidem a te scis et consule et
imperatore summa cum religione esse servata.
Praerogativam etiam maiores omen iustorum comitiorum esse voluerunt.

XLVI. " Atque ego exempla ominum nota proferam : L. Paulus consul iterum, cum ei bellum ut
cum rege Perse gereret obtigisset, ut ea ipsa die
domum ad vesperum rediit, filiolam suam Tertiam,
quae tum erat admodum parva, osculans animum ad-
vertit tristiculam. ' Quid est,' inquit, ' mea Tertia ?
quid tristis es ? ' ' Mi pater,' inquit, ' Persa periit.'
Tum ille arctius puellam complexus, ' Accipio,' inquit,
' mea filia, omen.' Erat autem mortuus catellus eo
104 nomine. L. Flaccum, flaminem Martialem, ego
audivi, cum diceret Caeciliam Metelli, cum vellet
sororis suae filiam in matrimonium collocare, exisse
in quoddam sacellum ominis capiendi causa, quod
fieri more veterum solebat. Cum virgo staret et Caecilia in sella sederet neque diu ulla vox exstitisset,

---

¹ *Cf. Pro Murena* 18. 38 *omen praerogativae.* " The
order of voting being determined by lot, the vote of the first
century was taken as an omen of the vote to follow."
—Heitland.
² Probably L. Valerius Flaccus, praetor 63 **b.c.,** and defended for embezzlement by Cicero in 60.

and quarrelling.' So too, when the sacred ceremony of purification was held by one starting on an expedition to found a colony, or when the commander-in-chief was reviewing his army, or the censor was taking his census, it was the rule to choose men with names of good omen to lead the victims. Furthermore, the consuls in making a levy of troops take pains to see that the first soldier enlisted is one with a lucky name. You, of course, are aware that you, both as consul at home and later as commander in the field, employed the same precaution with the most scrupulous care. In the case, too, of the prerogative tribe or century, our forefathers determined that it should be the ' omen ' of a proper election.[1]

XLVI. " Now let me give some well-known examples of omens : When Lucius Paulus was consul the second time, and had been chosen to wage war against King Perses, upon returning home on the evening of the day on which he had been appointed, he noticed, as he kissed his little daughter Tertia (at that time a very small child), that she was rather sad. ' What is the matter, Tertia, my dear ? Why are you sad ? ' ' Oh ! father, Persa is dead.' Paulus clasped the child in a closer embrace and said, ' Daughter, I accept that as an omen.' Now ' Persa ' was the name of a little dog that had died. I heard Lucius Flaccus,[2] the high priest of Mars, relate the following story : Metellus' daughter, Caecilia, who was desirous of arranging a marriage for her sister's daughter, went, according to the ancient custom, to a small chapel to receive an omen. A long time passed while the maiden stood and Caecilia was seated on a chair without

puellam defatigatam petisse a matertera, ut sibi con
cederet, paulisper ut in eius sella requiesceret ;
illam autem dixisse : ' Vero, mea puella, tibi concedo
meas sedes.' Quod omen res consecuta est ; ipsa
enim brevi mortua est, virgo autem nupsit, cui Caecilia nupta fuerat. Haec posse contemni vel etiam
rideri praeclare intellego, sed id ipsum est deos non
putare, quae ab eis significantur, contemnere.

105   XLVII. " Quid de auguribus loquar ? Tuae partes
sunt, tuum, inquam, auspiciorum patrocinium debet
esse.   Tibi App. Claudius augur consuli nuntiavit
addubitato Salutis augurio bellum domesticum triste
ac turbulentum fore ; quod paucis post mensibus
exortum paucioribus a te est diebus oppressum. Cui
quidem auguri vehementer assentior ; solus enim
multorum annorum memoria non decantandi auguri,
sed divinandi tenuit disciplinam. Quem irridebant
collegae tui eumque tum Pisidam, tum Soranum
augurem esse dicebant ; quibus nulla videbatur in
auguriis aut praesensio aut scientia veritatis futurae ;
sapienter aiebant ad opinionem imperitorum esse
fictas religiones. Quod longe secus est ; neque enim
in pastoribus illis, quibus Romulus praefuit, nec in
ipso Romulo haec calliditas esse potuit, ut ad errorem
multitudinis religionis simulacra fingerent. Sed
difficultas laborque discendi disertam neglegentiam

---

¹ For the augury of safety *cf.* Dio Cass. xxxvii. p. 40 ; Tac.
Annal. xii. 23 ; it could be made only in time of peace, and
decided (apparently) whether prayers could be made on behalf of the state.   Catiline's conspiracy is referred to here.
    ² *Cf.* ii. 34. 71-72.
    ³ The Pisidians devoted themselves to auspices, *cf.* i. 2 ;
the Sorans, who lived in Sora, a small town in Latium, were
noted for their superstition.

any word being spoken. Finally, the former grew weary and said to her aunt : ' Let me sit awhile on your chair.' ' Certainly, my child,' said Caecilia, ' you may have my place.' And this was an omen of what came to pass, for in a short time Caecilia died and the girl married her aunt's husband. I realize perfectly well that the foregoing omens may be lightly regarded and even be laughed at, but to make light of signs sent by the gods is nothing less than to disbelieve in the existence of the gods.

XLVII. " Why need I speak of augurs ? That is your rôle ; the duty to defend auspices, I maintain, is yours. For it was to you, while you were consul, that the augur Appius Claudius declared that because the augury of safety [1] was unpropitious a grievous and violent civil war was at hand. That war began a few months later, but you brought it to an end in still fewer days. Appius is one augur of whom I heartily approve, for not content merely with the sing-song ritual of augury,[2] he, alone, according to the record of many years, has maintained a real system of divination. I know that your colleagues used to laugh at him and call him at one time ' a Pisidian ' and at another ' a Soran.' [3] They did not concede to augury any power of prevision or real knowledge of the future, and used to say that it was a superstitious practice shrewdly invented to gull the ignorant. But the truth is far otherwise, for neither those herdsmen whom Romulus governed, nor Romulus himself, could have had cunning enough to invent miracles with which to mislead the people. It is the trouble and hard work involved in mastering the art that has induced this

reddidit; malunt enim disserere nihil esse in
auspiciis quam quid sit ediscere.

106 "Quid est illo auspicio divinius quod apud te in
Mario est? ut utar potissimum auctore te:

> hic Iovis altisoni subito pinnata satelles
> arboris e trunco serpentis saucia morsu
> subigit ipsa feris transfigens unguibus anguem
> semianimum et varia graviter cervice micantem;
> quem se intorquentem lanians rostroque cruentans,
> iam satiata animos, iam duros ulta dolores,
> abicit ecflantem et laceratum adfligit in unda,
> seque obitu a solis nitidos convertit ad ortus.
> hanc ubi praepetibus pinnis lapsuque volantem
> conspexit Marius, divini numinis augur,
> faustaque signa suae laudis reditusque notavit;
> partibus intonuit caeli pater ipse sinistris.
> sic aquilae clarum firmavit Iuppiter omen.

107 XLVIII. "Atque ille Romuli auguratus pastoralis,
non urbanus fuit, nec fictus ad opiniones inperitorum,
sed a certis acceptus et posteris traditus. Itaque
Romulus augur, ut apud Ennium est, cum fratre item
augure

> curantes magna cum cura tum concupientes
> regni dant operam simul auspicio augurioque.
> hinc Remus auspicio se devovet atque secundam
> solus avem servat. at Romulus pulcher in alto

---

[1] This poem, written by Cicero in his early youth, eulogizes
Marius, who like Cicero, was born at Arpinum. *Cf.* Cic.
De leg. i. 1.

[2] *Annales*, i. 94 *et seq.*

[3] According to other accounts, Romulus stood on the
Palatine and Remus on the Aventine. *Cf.* Livy i. 5;
Dionys. Halicar. i. 86; Florus i. 6.

eloquent contempt; for men prefer to say glibly that there is nothing in auspices rather than to learn what auspices are.

"Now—to employ you as often as I can as my authority—what could be more clearly of divine origin than the auspice which is thus described in your *Marius*[1] ?

> Behold, from out the tree, on rapid wing,
> The eagle that attends high-thundering Jove
> A serpent bore, whose fangs had wounded her :
> And as she flew her cruel talons pierced
> Quite through its flesh.   The snake, tho' nearly dead,
> Kept darting here and there its spotted head ;
> And, as it writhed, she tore with bloody beak
> Its twisted folds.   At last, with sated wrath
> And grievous wounds avenged, she dropped her prey,
> Which, dead and mangled, fell into the sea ;
> And from the West she sought the shining East.
> When Marius, reader of divine decrees,
> Observed the bird's auspicious, gliding course,
> He recognized the goodly sign foretold
> That he in glory would return to Rome ;
> Then, on the left, Jove's thunder pealed aloud
> And thus declared the eagle's omen true.

XLVIII. " As for that augural art of Romulus of which I spoke, it was pastoral and not city-bred, nor was it 'invented to gull the ignorant,' but received by trustworthy men, who handed it on to their descendants.   And so we read in Ennius[2] the following story of Romulus, who was an augur, and of his brother Remus, who also was an augur :

> When each would rule they both at once appealed
> Their claims, with anxious hearts, to augury.
> Then Remus took the auspices alone
> And waited for the lucky bird ; while on
> The lofty Aventine[3] fair Romulus

339

quaerit Aventino, servat genus altivolantum.
certabant, urbem Romam Remoramne vocarent.
omnibus cura viris, uter esset induperator.
exspectant ; veluti, consul quom mittere signum
volt, omnes avidi spectant ad carceris oras,
108   quam mox emittat pictis e faucibus currus,
sic exspectabat populus atque ore timebat
rebus utri magni victoria sit data regni.
interea sol albus recessit in infera noctis.
exin candida se radiis dedit icta foras lux,
et simul ex alto longe pulcherrima praepes
laeva volavit avis ; simul aureus exoritur sol,
cedunt de caelo ter quattuor corpora sancta
avium, praepetibus sese pulchrisque locis dant.
conspicit inde sibi data Romulus esse priora,
auspicio regni stabilita scamna solumque.

109   XLIX. " Sed ut, unde huc digressa est, eodem
redeat oratio. Si nihil queam disputare quam ob
rem quidque fiat, et tantum modo fieri ea quae
commemoravi, doceam, parumne Epicuro Carneadive
respondeam ? Quid, si etiam ratio exstat artificiosae
praesensionis facilis, divinae autem paulo obscurior ?
Quae enim extis, quae fulgoribus, quae portentis,
quae astris praesentiuntur, haec notata sunt observatione diuturna. Affert autem vetustas omnibus in
rebus longinqua observatione incredibilem scientiam ;
quae potest esse etiam sine motu atque impulsu
deorum, cum, quid ex quoque eveniat, et quid quam-

His quest did keep to wait the soaring tribe:
Their contest would decide the city's name
As Rome or Remora. The multitude
Expectant looked to learn who would be king.
As, when the consul is about to give
The sign to start the race, the people sit
With eyes intent on barrier doors from whose
Embellished jaws the chariots soon will come;
So now the people, fearful, looked for signs
To know whose prize the mighty realm would be.
Meantime the fading sun into the shades
Of night withdrew and then the shining dawn
Shot forth its rays. 'Twas then an augury,
The best of all, appeared on high—a bird
That on the left did fly. And, as the sun
Its golden orb upraised, twelve sacred birds
Flew down from heaven and betook themselves
To stations set apart for goodly signs.
Then Romulus perceived that he had gained
A throne whose source and prop was augury.

XLIX. "But let us bring the discussion back to the point from which it wandered. Assume that I can give no reason for any of the instances of divination which I have mentioned and that I can do no more than show that they did occur, is that not a sufficient answer to Epicurus and to Carneades? And what does it matter if, as between artificial and natural divination, the explanation of the former is easy and of the latter is somewhat hard? For the results of those artificial means of divination, by means of entrails, lightnings, portents, and astrology, have been the subject of observation for a long period of time. But in every field of inquiry great length of time employed in continued observation begets an extraordinary fund of knowledge, which may be acquired even without the intervention or inspiration of the gods, since repeated observa-

que rem significet, crebra animadversione perspectum est.

110 " Altera divinatio est naturalis, ut ante dixi ; quae physica disputandi subtilitate referenda est ad naturam deorum, a qua, ut doctissimis sapientissimisque placuit, haustos animos et libatos habemus ; cumque omnia completa et referta sint aeterno sensu et mente divina, necesse est contagione divinorum animorum animos humanos commoveri. Sed vigilantes animi vitae necessitatibus serviunt diiunguntque se a societate divina vinclis corporis impediti.

111 " Rarum est quoddam genus eorum, qui se a corpore avocent et ad divinarum rerum cognitionem cura omni studioque rapiantur. Horum sunt auguria non divini impetus, sed rationis humanae ; nam et natura futura praesentiunt, ut aquarum eluviones[1] et deflagrationem futuram aliquando caeli atque terrarum ; alii autem in re publica exercitati, ut de Atheniensi Solone accepimus, orientem tyrannidem multo ante prospiciunt ; quos prudentes possumus dicere, id est providentes, divinos nullo modo possumus ; non plus quam Milesium Thalem, qui, ut obiurgatores suos convinceret ostenderetque etiam philosophum, si ei commodum esset, pecuniam facere posse, omnem oleam ante quam florere

---

[1] eluviones *Lambinus, Turneb., Dav.* ; fluxiones MSS.

---

[1] i. 18. 34.
[2] *Cf.* Diog. Laert. i. 48 ; Val. Max. v. 3. 3.

tion makes it clear what effect follows any given cause, and what sign precedes any given event.

" The second division of divination, as I said before,[1] is the natural; and it, according to the exact teaching of physics, must be ascribed to divine Nature, from which, as the wisest philosophers maintain, our souls have been drawn and poured forth. And since the universe is wholly filled with the Eternal Intelligence and the Divine Mind, it must be that human souls are influenced by their contact with divine souls. But when men are awake their souls, as a rule, are subject to the demands of everyday life and are withdrawn from divine association because they are hampered by the chains of the flesh.

" However, there is a certain class of men, though small in number, who withdraw themselves from carnal influences and are wholly possessed by an ardent concern for the contemplation of things divine. Some of these men make predictions, not as the result of direct heavenly inspiration, but by the use of their own reason. For example, by means of natural law, they foretell certain events, such as a flood, or the future destruction of heaven and earth by fire Others, who are engaged in public life, like Solon of Athens,[2] as history describes him, discover the rise of tyranny long in advance. Such men we may call ' foresighted '—that is, ' able to foresee the future '; but we can no more apply the term ' divine ' to them than we can apply it to Thales of Miletus, who, as the story goes, in order to confound his critics and thereby show that even a philosopher, if he sees fit, can make money, bought up the entire olive crop in the district of Miletus

112 coepisset, in agro Milesio, coëmisse dicitur. Ani-
madverterat fortasse quadam scientia olearum ubertatem fore. Et quidem idem primus defectionem
solis, quae Astyage regnante facta est, praedixisse
fertur.

L. " Multa medici, multa gubernatores, agricolae
etiam multa praesentiunt, sed nullam eorum divinationem voco, ne illam quidem qua ab Anaximandro
physico moniti Lacedaemonii sunt ut urbem et tecta
linquerent armatique in agro excubarent, quod
terrae motus instaret, tum cum et urbs tota corruit
et e monte Taygeto extrema montis quasi puppis
avulsa est. Ne Pherecydes quidem, ille Pythagorae
magister, potius divinus habebitur quam physicus,
quod, cum vidisset haustam aquam de iugi puteo,
terrae motus dixit instare.

113 " Nec vero umquam animus hominis naturaliter
divinat, nisi cum ita solutus est et vacuus ut ei
plane nihil sit cum corpore, quod aut vatibus contingit
aut dormientibus. Itaque ea duo genera a Dicaearcho
probantur et, ut dixi, a Cratippo nostro ; si propterea,
quod ea proficiscuntur a natura, sint summa sane,
modo ne sola ; sin autem nihil esse in observatione
putant, multa tollunt quibus vitae ratio continetur.

---

[1] Cf. Aristot. Polit. i. 11. Pliny tells this story of
Democritus, Hist. Nat. xviii. 28.
[2] The appearance of the water indicated the internal
disturbance. Cf. Pliny, Hist. Nat. ii. 83.

before it had begun to bloom.[1] Perhaps he had observed, from some special knowledge he had on the subject, that the crop would be abundant. And, by the way, he is said to have been the first man to predict the solar eclipse which took place in the reign of Astyages.

L. " There are many things foreseen by physicians, pilots, and also by farmers, but I do not call the predictions of any of them divination. I do not even call that a case of divination when Anaximander, the natural philosopher, warned the Spartans to leave the city and their homes and to sleep in the fields under arms, because an earthquake was at hand. Then the whole city fell down in ruins and the extremity of Mount Taygetus was torn away like the stern of a ship in a storm. Not even Pherecydes, the famous teacher of Pythagoras, will be considered a prophet rather than a natural philosopher, because he predicted an earthquake from the appearance of some water drawn from an unfailing well.[2]

" In fact, the human soul never divines naturally, except when it is so unrestrained and free that it has absolutely no association with the body, as happens in the case of frenzy and of dreams. Hence both these kinds of divination have been sanctioned by Dicaearchus and also, as I said, by our friend Cratippus. Let us grant that these two methods (because they originate in nature) take the highest rank in divination ; but we will not concede that they are the only kind. But if, on the other hand, Dicaearchus and Cratippus believe that there is nothing in observation, they hold a doctrine destructive of the foundation on which many things in every-

345

Sed quoniam dant aliquid, idque non parvum,
vaticinationes cum somniis, nihil est quod cum his
magnopere pugnemus, praesertim cum sint qui
omnino nullam divinationem probent.

114 " Ergo et ei, quorum animi spretis corporibus
evolant atque excurrunt foras, ardore aliquo inflam-
mati atque incitati, cernunt illa profecto quae vati-
cinantes pronuntiant ; multisque rebus inflammantur
tales animi qui corporibus non inhaerent, ut ei qui
sono quodam vocum et Phrygiis cantibus incitantur.
Multos nemora silvaeque, multos amnes aut maria
commovent. Credo etiam anhelitus quosdam fuisse
terrarum quibus inflatae mentes oracla funderent.
Quorum furibunda mens videt ante multo, quae sint
futura. Quo de genere illa sunt :

> eheu videte ! iudicabit inclytum iudicium
> inter deas tres aliquis ; quo iudicio Lacedaemonia
> mulier, furiarum una, adveniet.

Eodem enim modo multa a vaticinantibus saepe
praedicta sunt, neque solum verbis, sed etiam

> versibus quos olim Fauni vatesque canebant.

115 Similiter Marcius et Publicius vates cecinisse dicuntur ; quo de genere Apollinis operta prolata sunt.

---

[1] In i. 50. 114, after *commovent* and before *quorum*,
I insert the last two lines of chapter 50 (i. 50. 115) *credo
etiam . . . funderent*, and strike them out of their present
place in the ms. Hottinger suggested the transposition,
which Giese and Moser approved, though they did not make
it in their texts.
[2] Cassandra is speaking of the judgement of Paris and
the coming of Helen. The author of the lines is not known.
[3] From Ennius, *Annales*, vii. 2.

day life depend. However, since these men make us some concession—and that not a small one—in granting us divination by frenzy and dreams, I see no cause for any great war with them, especially in view of the fact that there are some philosophers who do not accept any sort of divination whatever.

" Those then, whose souls, spurning their bodies, take wings and fly abroad—inflamed and aroused by a sort of passion—these men, I say, certainly see the things which they foretell in their prophecies. Such souls do not cling to the body and are kindled by many different influences. For example, some are aroused by certain vocal tones, as by Phrygian songs, many by groves and forests, and many others by rivers and seas. I believe, too, that there were certain subterranean vapours which had the effect of inspiring persons to utter oracles.[1] In all these cases the frenzied soul sees the future long in advance, as Cassandra did in the following instance :

> Alas ! behold ! some mortal will decide
> A famous case between three goddesses :
> Because of that decision there will come
> A Spartan woman, but a Fury too.[2]

It is in this state of exaltation that many predictions have been made, not only in prose but also

> In verse which once the fauns and bards did sing.[3]

Likewise Marcius and Publicius,[4] according to tradition, made their prophecies in verse, and the cryptic utterances of Apollo were expressed in the same form.

[4] Publicius is mentioned again in ii. 55. 113. Nothing else is known of him.

LI. " Atque haec quidem vatium ratio est, nec dissimilis sane somniorum. Nam quae vigilantibus accidunt vatibus, eadem nobis dormientibus. Viget enim animus in somnis liberque est sensibus omni ac[1] impeditione curarum iacente et mortuo paene corpore. Qui quia vixit ab omni aeternitate versatusque est cum innumerabilibus animis, omnia, quae in natura rerum sunt, videt, si modo temperatis escis modicisque potionibus ita est affectus ut sopito corpore ipse vigilet. Haec somniantis est divinatio.

116   " Hic magna quaedam exoritur, neque ea naturalis, sed artificiosa somniorum Antiphontis interpretatio; eodemque modo et oraculorum et vaticinationum, sunt enim explanatores omnium horum,[2] ut grammatici poëtarum. Nam ut aurum et argentum, aes, ferrum frustra natura divina genuisset, nisi eadem docuisset quem ad modum ad eorum venas perveniretur; nec fruges terrae bacasve arborum cum utilitate ulla generi humano dedisset, nisi earum cultus et conditiones tradidisset; materia deinde quid iuvaret, nisi consectionis eius fabricam haberemus; sic cum omni utilitate quam di hominibus dederunt, ars aliqua coniuncta est per quam illa utilitas percipi possit. Item igitur somniis, vaticina-

---

[1] liberque est sensibus omni ac *Dav. for* liber ab sensibus omnique MSS.
[2] omnium horum MSS. om.

---

[1] *Cf.* i. 20. 39.

LI. "Such is the rationale of prophecy by means of frenzy, and that of dreams is not much unlike it. For the revelations made to seers when awake are made to us in sleep. While we sleep and the body lies as if dead, the soul is at its best, because it is then freed from the influence of the physical senses and from the worldly cares that weigh it down. And since the soul has lived from all eternity and has had converse with numberless other souls, it sees everything that exists in nature, provided that moderation and restraint have been used in eating and in drinking, so that the soul is in a condition to watch while the body sleeps. Such is the explanation of divination by dreams.

"At this point it is pertinent to mention Antiphon's [1] well-known theory of the interpretation of dreams. His view is that the interpreters of dreams depend upon technical skill and not upon inspiration. He has the same view as to the interpretation of oracles and of frenzied utterances; for they all have their interpreters, just as poets have their commentators. Now it is clear that divine nature would have done a vain thing if she had merely created iron, copper, silver, and gold and had not shown us how to reach the veins in which those metals lie; the gift of field crops and orchard fruits would have been useless to the human race without a knowledge of how to cultivate them and prepare them for food; and building material would be of no service without the carpenter's art to convert it into lumber. So it is with everything that the gods have given for the advantage of mankind, there has been joined some art whereby that advantage may be turned to account. The same is true

tionibus, oraclis, quod erant multa obscura, multa
ambigua, explanationes adhibitae sunt interpretum.

117　‥Quo modo autem aut vates aut somniantes ea
videant, quae nusquam etiam tunc sint, magna
quaestio est. Sed explorata si sint ea, quae ante
quaeri debeant, sint haec, quae quaerimus, faciliora.
Continet enim totam hanc quaestionem ea ratio,
quae est de natura deorum, quae a te secundo libro
est explicata dilucide. Quam si obtinemus, stabit
illud, quod hunc locum continet, de quo agimus,
'esse deos, et eorum providentia mundum administrari, eosdemque consulere rebus humanis, nec solum
universis, verum etiam singulis.' Haec si tenemus,
quae mihi quidem non videntur posse convelli,
profecto hominibus a dis futura significari necesse est.

118　LII. "Sed distinguendum videtur quonam modo.
Nam non placet Stoicis singulis iecorum fissis aut
avium cantibus interesse deum; neque enim decorum
est nec dis dignum nec fieri ullo pacto potest; sed
ita a principio inchoatum esse mundum, ut certis
rebus certa signa praecurrerent, alia in extis, alia in
avibus, alia in fulgoribus, alia in ostentis, alia in
stellis, alia in somniantium visis, alia in furentium
vocibus. Ea quibus bene percepta sunt, ei non saepe
350

of dreams, prophecies, and oracles : since many of
them were obscure and doubtful, resort was had to
the skill of professional interpreters.

" Now there is a great problem as to how prophets
and dreamers can see things, which, at the time,
have no actual existence anywhere. But that
question would be solved quite readily if we were to
investigate certain other questions which demand
consideration first. For the theory in regard to the
nature of the gods, so clearly developed in the second
book of your work on that subject, includes this
whole question. If we maintain that theory we
shall establish the very point which I am trying
to make : namely, ' that there are gods ; that
they rule the universe by their foresight ; and
that they direct the affairs of men—not merely of
men in the mass, but of each individual.' If
we succeed in holding that position—and for my
part I think it impregnable—then surely it must
follow that the gods give to men signs of coming
events.

LII. " But it seems necessary to settle the principle on which these signs depend. For, according
to the Stoic doctrine, the gods are not directly
responsible for every fissure in the liver or for every
song of a bird ; since, manifestly, that would not
be seemly or proper in a god and furthermore is
impossible. But, in the beginning, the universe was
so created that certain results would be preceded
by certain signs, which are given sometimes by
entrails and by birds, sometimes by lightnings, by
portents, and by stars, sometimes by dreams, and
sometimes by utterances of persons in a frenzy.
And these signs do not often deceive the persons

351

falluntur ; male coniecta maleque interpretata falsa
sunt non rerum vitio, sed interpretum inscientia.

" Hoc autem posito atque concesso, esse quandam
vim divinam hominum vitam continentem, non
difficile est, quae fieri certe videmus, ea qua ratione
fiant, suspicari. Nam et ad hostiam deligendam
potest dux esse vis quaedam sentiens, quae est toto
confusa mundo, et tum ipsam, cum immolare velis,
extorum fieri mutatio potest, ut aut absit aliquid
aut supersit ; parvis enim momentis multa natura
119 aut affingit aut mutat aut detrahit. Quod ne
dubitare possimus, maximo est argumento quod
paulo ante interitum Caesaris contigit. Qui cum
immolaret illo die quo primum in sella aurea sedit
et cum purpurea veste processit, in extis bovis
opimi cor non fuit. Num igitur censes ullum animal,
quod sanguinem habeat, sine corde esse posse ?
Qua ille rei novitate non[1] perculsus cum Spurinna
diceret timendum esse ne et consilium et vita
deficeret ; earum enim rerum utramque a corde
proficisci. Postero die caput in iecore non fuit.
Quae quidem illi portendebantur a dis immortalibus
ut videret interitum, non ut caveret. Cum igitur
eae partes in extis non reperiuntur sine quibus
victuma illa vivere nequisset, intellegendum est in

---

[1] *I insert* non *because the story contradicts* Suet. Iul.
Caesar, *ch.* 77 . . . nec pro ostento ducendum, si pecudi
cor defuisset (*sc.* Caesar dixit), *and is inconsistent with
Caesar's character.*

---

[1] *Cf.* Pliny, *Hist. Nat.* xi. 71 ; Val. Max. i. 6. 13 ; Plut.
Caes.
[2] Spurinna was the soothsayer who warned Caesar to
beware of the Ides of March. *Cf.* Suet. *Iul. Caes.* 81.

who observe them properly. If prophecies, based on erroneous deductions and interpretations, turn out to be false, the fault is not chargeable to the signs but to the lack of skill in the interpreters.

" Assuming the proposition to be conceded that there is a divine power which pervades the lives of men, it is not hard to understand the principle directing those premonitory signs which we see come to pass. For it may be that the choice of a sacrificial victim is guided by an intelligent force, which is diffused throughout the universe ; or, it may be that at the moment when the sacrifice is offered, a change in the vitals occurs and something is added or taken away ; for many things are added to, changed, or diminished in an instant of time. Conclusive proof of this fact, sufficient to put it beyond the possibility of doubt, is afforded by incidents which happened just before Caesar's death. While he was offering sacrifices on the day when he sat for the first time on a golden throne and first appeared in public in a purple robe, no heart was found in the vitals of the votive ox.¹ Now do you think it possible for any animal that has blood to exist without a heart ? Caesar was unmoved by this occurrence, even though Spurinna ² warned him to beware lest thought and life should fail him—both of which, he said, proceeded from the heart. On the following day there was no head to the liver of the sacrifice. These portents were sent by the immortal gods to Caesar that he might foresee his death, not that he might prevent it. Therefore, when those organs, without which the victim could not have lived, are found wanting in the vitals, we should understand that the absent

ipso immolationis tempore eas partes quae absint interisse.

120   LIII. " Eademque efficit in avibus divina mens, ut tum huc, tum illuc volent alites, tum in hac, tum in illa parte se occultent, tum a dextra, tum a sinistra parte canant oscines. Nam si animal omne, ut vult, ita utitur motu sui corporis, prono, obliquo, supino, membraque, quocumque vult, flectit, contorquet, porrigit, contrahit eaque ante efficit paene, quam cogitat, quanto id deo est facilius, cuius numini

121   parent omnia ! Idemque mittit et signa nobis eius generis, qualia permulta historia tradidit, quale scriptum illud videmus : si luna paulo ante solis ortum defecisset in signo Leonis, fore ut armis Dareus et Persae ab Alexandro et Macedonibus vincerentur Dareusque moreretur ; et si puella nata biceps esset, seditionem in populo fore, corruptelam et adulterium domi ; et si mulier leonem peperisse visa esset, fore ut ab exteris gentibus vinceretur ea res publica in qua id contigisset.

" Eiusdem generis etiam illud est, quod scribit Herodotus, Croesi filium, cum esset infans, locutum ; quo ostento regnum patris et domum funditus concidisse. Caput arsisse Servio Tullio dormienti quae historia non prodidit ? Ut igitur, qui se tradit quieti praeparato animo cum bonis cogitationibus,

---

[1] *Alites* were birds, like the eagle, hawk, and osprey, that gave omens by their flight ; *oscines* were birds, like the raven, crow, and owl, that gave omens by their voices. *Cf.* Festus, p. 193.

[2] Herod. i. 85.

[3] *Cf.* Flor. i. 6. 1 ; Livy i. 39. 1 ; Pliny, *Hist. Nat.* ii. 110 ; xxxvi. 27.

organs disappeared at the very moment of immolation.

LIII. " The Divine Will accomplishes like results in the case of birds, and causes those known as *alites*,[1] which give omens by their flight, to fly hither and thither and disappear now here and now there, and causes those known as *oscines*, which give omens by their cries, to sing now on the left and now on the right. For if every animal moves its body forward, sideways, or backward at will, it bends, twists, extends, and contracts its members as it pleases, and performs these various motions almost mechanically ; how much easier it is for such results to be accomplished by a god, whose divine will all things obey ! The same power sends us signs, of which history has preserved numerous examples. We find the following ones recorded : when just before sunrise the moon was eclipsed in the sign of Leo, this indicated that Darius and the Persians would be overcome in battle by the Macedonians under Alexander, and that Darius would die. Again, when a girl was born with two heads, this foretold sedition among the people and seduction and adultery in the home. When a woman dreamed that she had been delivered of a lion, this signified that the country in which she had the dream would be conquered by foreign nations.

" Another instance of a similiar kind is related by Herodotus :[2] Croesus's son, when an infant, spoke, and this prodigy foretold the utter overthrow of his father's family and kingdom. What history has failed to record the fact that while Servius Tullius slept his head burst into flame ?[3] Therefore, just as a man has clear and trustworthy dreams, provided he

tum rebus ad tranquillitatem accommodatis, certa et
vera cernit in somnis ; sic castus animus purusque
vigilantis et ad astrorum et ad avium reliquorumque
signorum et ad extorum veritatem est paratior.

122 LIV. " Hoc nimirum est illud quod de Socrate
accepimus, quodque ab ipso in libris Socraticorum
saepe dicitur : esse divinum quiddam, quod δαιμόνιον
appellat, cui semper ipse paruerit numquam impel-
lenti, saepe revocanti. Et Socrates quidem (quo
quem auctorem meliorem quaerimus ?) Xenophonti
consulenti sequereturne Cyrum, posteaquam exposuit, quae ipsi videbantur : ' Et nostrum quidem,'
inquit, ' humanum est consilium ; sed de rebus et
obscuris et incertis ad Apollinem censeo referendum,'
ad quem etiam Athenienses publice de maioribus
rebus semper rettulerunt.

123 " Scriptum est item, cum Critonis, sui familiaris,
oculum alligatum vidisset, quaesivisse, quid esset ;
cum autem ille respondisset in agro ambulanit
ramulum adductum, ut remissus esset, in oculum
suum recidisse, tum Socrates : ' Non enim paruisti
mihi revocanti, cum uterer, qua soleo, praesagitione
divina.' Idem etiam Socrates, cum apud Delium
male pugnatum esset Lachete praetore fugeretque
cum ipso Lachete, ut ventum est in trivium, eadem,

---

[1] *Cf.* Xen. *Anab.* iii. 1. 4.

goes to sleep, not only with his mind prepared by noble thoughts, but also with every precaution taken to induce repose; so, too, he, when awake, is better prepared to interpret truly the messages of entrails, stars, birds, and all other signs, provided his soul is pure and undefiled.

LIV. " It is this purity of soul, no doubt, that explains that famous utterance which history attributes to Socrates and which his disciples in their books often represent him as repeating : ' There is some divine influence '—δαιμόνιον, he called it— ' which I always obey, though it never urges me on, but often holds me back.' And it was the same Socrates—and what better authority can we quote ? —who was consulted by Xenophon [1] as to whether he should join Cyrus. Socrates, after stating what seemed to him the best thing to do, remarked : ' But my opinion is only that of a man. In matters of doubt and perplexity I advise that Apollo's oracle be consulted.' This oracle was always consulted by the Athenians in regard to the more serious public questions.

" It is also related of Socrates that one day he saw his friend Crito with a bandage on his eye. ' What's the matter, Crito ? ' he inquired. ' As I was walking in the country the branch of a tree, which had been bent, was released and struck me in the eye.' ' Of course,' said Socrates, ' for, after I had had divine warning, as usual, and tried to call you back, you did not heed.' It is also related of him that after the unfortunate battle was fought at Delium under command of Laches, he was fleeing in company with his commander, when they came to a place where three roads met. Upon his refusal

357

qua ceteri, fugere noluit. Quibus quaerentibus, cur
non eadem via pergeret, deterreri se a deo dixit;
cum quidem ei, qui alia via fugerant, in hostium
equitatum inciderunt. Permulta collecta sunt ab
Antipatro quae mirabiliter a Socrate divinata sunt,
quae praetermittam, tibi enim nota sunt, mihi ad
124 commemorandum non necessaria. Illud tamen eius
philosophi magnificum ac paene divinum, quod, cum
impiis sententiis damnatus esset, aequissimo animo
se dixit mori ; neque enim domo egredienti neque
illud suggestum, in quo causam dixerat, ascendenti
signum sibi ullum, quod consuesset, a deo quasi mali
alicuius impendentis datum.

LV. " Equidem sic arbitror, etiamsi multa fallant
eos, qui aut arte aut coniectura divinare videantur,
esse tamen divinationem ; homines autem, ut in
ceteris artibus, sic in hac posse falli. Potest accidere,
ut aliquod signum dubie datum pro certo sit acceptum,
potest aliquod latuisse aut ipsum, aut quod esset illi
contrarium. Mihi autem ad hoc, de quo disputo, pro-
bandum satis est non modo plura, sed etiam pauciora
125 divine praesensa et praedicta reperiri. Quin etiam
hoc non dubitans dixerim, si unum aliquid ita sit
praedictum praesensumque, ut, cum evenerit, ita
cadat ut praedictum sit, neque in eo quicquam casu
et fortuito factum esse appareat, esse certe divinationem, idque esse omnibus confitendum.

---

[1] *Cf.* Plato, *Apol.* ch. 31.

to take the road that the others had chosen he was asked the reason and replied : ' The god prevents me.' Those who fled by the other road fell in with the enemy's cavalry. Antipater has gathered a mass of remarkable premonitions received by Socrates, but I shall pass them by, for you know them and it is useless for me to recount them. However, the following utterance [1] of that philosopher, made after he had been wickedly condemned to death, is a noble one—I might almost call it ' divine ' : ' I am very content to die,' he said ; ' for neither when I left my home nor when I mounted the platform to plead my cause, did the god give any sign, and this he always does when some evil threatens me.'

LV. " And so my opinion is that the power of divination exists, notwithstanding the fact that those who prophesy by means of art and conjecture are oftentimes mistaken. I believe that, just as men may make mistakes in other callings, so they may in this. It may happen that a sign of doubtful meaning is assumed to be certain or, possibly, either a sign was itself unobserved or one that annulled an observed sign may have gone unnoticed. But, in order to establish the proposition for which I contend it is enough for me to find, not many, but even a few instances of divinely inspired prevision and prophecy. Nay, if even one such instance is found and the agreement between the prediction and the thing predicted is so close as to exclude every semblance of chance or of accident, I should not hesitate to say in such a case, that divination undoubtedly exists and that everybody should admit its existence.

" Quocirca primum mihi videtur, ut Posidonius facit, a deo, de quo satis dictum est, deinde a fato, deinde a natura, vis omnis divinandi ratioque repetenda. Fieri igitur omnia fato ratio cogit fateri. Fatum autem id appello, quod Graeci εἱμαρμένην, id est ordinem seriemque causarum, cum causae causa nexa rem ex se gignat. Ea est ex omni aeternitate fluens veritas sempiterna. Quod cum ita sit, nihil est factum, quod non futurum fuerit, eodemque modo nihil est futurum, cuius non causas 126 id ipsum efficientes natura contineat. Ex quo intellegitur, ut fatum sit non id, quod superstitiose, sed id, quod physice dicitur, causa aeterna rerum, cur et ea, quae praeterierunt, facta sint et, quae instant, fiant et, quae sequuntur, futura sint. Ita fit, ut et observatione notari possit, quae res quamque causam plerumque consequatur, etiamsi non semper (nam id quidem affirmare difficile est), easdemque causas veri simile est rerum futurarum cerni ab eis, qui aut per furorem eas aut in quiete videant.

127 LVI. " Praeterea cum fato omnia fiant, id quod alio loco ostendetur, si quis mortalis possit esse, qui colligationem causarum omnium perspiciat animo, nihil eum profecto fallat. Qui enim teneat causas rerum futurarum, idem necesse est omnia teneat, quae futura sint. Quod cum nemo facere nisi deus possit, relinquendum est homini, ut signis quibusdam

---

[1] The genuineness of the words, *id quod . . . ostendetur*, is doubted because (1) in the extant portions of Cicero's work on Fate the opposite of the position here contended for is taken ; and (2) they indicate that Marcus, forgetting for the moment that Quintus is talking, imagines that he himself is the speaker. However, the MSS. support the reading adopted.

" Wherefore, it seems to me that we must do as Posidonius does and trace the vital principle of divination in its entirety to three sources : first, to God, whose connexion with the subject has been sufficiently discussed ; secondly to Fate ; and lastly, to Nature. Reason compels us to admit that all things happen by Fate. Now by Fate I mean the same that the Greeks call εἱμαρμένη, that is, an orderly succession of causes wherein cause is linked to cause and each cause of itself produces an effect. That is an immortal truth having its source in all eternity. Therefore nothing has happened which was not bound to happen, and, likewise, nothing is going to happen which will not find in nature every efficient cause of its happening. Consequently, we know that Fate is that which is called, not ignorantly, but scientifically, ' the eternal cause of things, the wherefore of things past, of things present, and of things to come.' Hence it is that it may be known by observation what effect will in most instances follow any cause, even if it is not known in all ; for it would be too much to say that it is known in every case. And it is probable that these causes of coming events are perceived by those who see them during frenzy or in sleep.

LVI. " Moreover, since, as will be shown elsewhere,[1] all things happen by Fate, if there were a man whose soul could discern the links that join each cause with every other cause, then surely he would never be mistaken in any prediction he might make. For he who knows the causes of future events necessarily knows what every future event will be. But since such knowledge is possible only to a god, it is left to man to presage the future by means of certain

consequentia declarantibus futura praesentiat. Non
enim illa, quae futura sunt, subito exsistunt, sed est
quasi rudentis explicatio sic traductio temporis nihil
novi efficientis et primum quidque replicantis. Quod
et ei vident, quibus naturalis divinatio data est, et
ei, quibus cursus rerum observando notatus est. Qui
etsi causas ipsas non cernunt, signa tamen causarum
et notas cernunt; ad quas adhibita memoria et
diligentia et monumentis superiorum efficitur ea
divinatio, quae artificiosa dicitur, extorum, fulgorum,
ostentorum signorumque caelestium.

128   " Non est igitur ut mirandum sit ea praesentiri a
divinantibus, quae nusquam sint; sunt enim omnia,
sed tempore absunt. Atque ut in seminibus vis
inest earum rerum, quae ex eis progignuntur, sic
in causis conditae sunt res futurae, quas esse futuras
aut concitata mens aut soluta somno cernit aut ratio
aut coniectura praesentit. Atque ut ei qui solis et
lunae reliquorumque siderum ortus, obitus motusque
cognorunt, quo quidque tempore eorum futurum sit,
multo ante praedicunt, sic, qui cursum rerum
eventorumque consequentiam diuturnitate pertractata notaverunt, aut semper aut, si id difficile est,
plerumque, quodsi ne id quidem conceditur, non
numquam certe, quid futurum sit, intellegunt. Atque

signs which indicate what will follow them. Things which are to be do not suddenly spring into existence, but the evolution of time is like the unwinding of a cable : it creates nothing new and only unfolds each event in its order. This connexion between cause and effect is obvious to two classes of diviners : those who are endowed with natural divination and those who know the course of events by the observation of signs. They may not discern the causes themselves, yet they do discern the signs and tokens of those causes. The careful study and recollection of those signs, aided by the records of former times, has evolved that sort of divination, known as artificial, which is divination by means of entrails, lightnings, portents, and celestial phenomena.

" Therefore it is not strange that diviners have a presentiment of things that exist nowhere in the material world : for all things ' are,' though, from the standpoint of ' time,' they are not present. As in seeds there inheres the germ of those things which the seeds produce, so in causes are stored the future events whose coming is foreseen by reason or conjecture, or is discerned by the soul when inspired by frenzy, or when it is set free by sleep. Persons familiar with the rising, setting, and revolutions of the sun, moon, and other celestial bodies, can tell long in advance where any one of these bodies will be at a given time. And the same thing may be said of men who, for a long period of time, have studied and noted the course of facts and the connexion of events, for they always know what the future will be ; or, if that is putting it too strongly, they know in a majority of cases ; or, if that will not be conceded either, then, surely, they sometimes know what the future will be.

haec quidem et quaedam eiusdem modi argumenta,
cur sit divinatio, ducuntur a fato.

129   LVII. " A natura autem alia quaedam ratio est,
quae docet quanta sit animi vis seiuncta a corporis
sensibus, quod maxime contingit aut dormientibus
aut mente permotis.   Ut enim deorum animi sine
oculis, sine auribus, sine lingua sentiunt inter se,
quid quisque sentiat (ex quo fit, ut homines, etiam
cum taciti optent quid aut voveant, non dubitent,
quin di illud exaudiant), sic animi hominum, cum aut
somno soluti vacant corpore aut mente permoti per
se ipsi liberi incitati moventur, cernunt ea quae
permixti cum corpore animi videre non possunt.

130 Atque hanc quidem rationem naturae difficile est
fortasse traducere ad id genus divinationis, quod ex
arte profectum dicimus, sed tamen id quoque rimatur,
quantum potest, Posidonius.   Esse censet in natura
signa quaedam rerum futurarum.   Etenim Ceos
accepimus ortum Caniculae diligenter quotannis
solere servare coniecturamque capere, ut scribit
Ponticus Heraclides, salubrisne an pestilens annus
futurus sit.   Nam si obscurior et quasi caliginosa
stella extiterit, pingue et concretum esse caelum, ut
eius asspiratio gravis et pestilens futura sit ; sin
illustris et perlucida stella apparuerit, significari
caelum esse tenue purumque et propterea salubre.

131   " Democritus autem censet sapienter instituisse

These and a few other arguments of the same kind for the existence of divination are derived from Fate.

LVII. " Moreover, divination finds another and a positive support in nature, which teaches us how great is the power of the soul when it is divorced from the bodily senses, as it is especially in sleep, and in times of frenzy or inspiration. For, as the souls of the gods, without the intervention of eyes or ears or tongue, understand each other and what each one thinks (hence men, even when they offer silent prayers and vows, have no doubt that the gods understand them), so the souls of men, when released by sleep from bodily chains, or when stirred by inspiration and delivered up to their own impulses, see things that they cannot see when they are mingled with the body. And while it is difficult, perhaps, to apply this principle of nature to explain that kind of divination which we call artificial, yet Posidonius, who digs into the question as deep as one can, thinks that nature gives certain signs of future events. Thus Heraclides of Pontus records that it is the custom of the people of Ceos, once each year, to make a careful observation of the rising of the Dog-star and from such observation to conjecture whether the ensuing year will be healthy or pestilential. For if the star rises dim and, as it were enveloped in a fog, this indicates a thick and heavy atmosphere, which will give off very unwholesome vapours ; but if the star appears clear and brilliant, this is a sign that the atmosphere is light and pure and, as a consequence, will be conducive to good health.

" Again, Democritus expresses the opinion that the ancients acted wisely in providing for the

veteres, ut hostiarum immolatarum inspicerentur
exta ; quorum ex habitu atque ex colore tum
salubritatis, tum pestilentiae signa percipi, non
numquam etiam, quae sit vel sterilitas agrorum vel
fertilitas futura. Quae si a natura profecta observatio
atque usus agnovit, multa afferre potuit dies quae
animadvertendo notarentur, ut ille Pacuvianus, qui
in *Chryse* physicus inducitur, minime naturam rerum
cognosse videatur :

> . . . nam istis quí linguam avium intéllegunt
> plusque éx alieno iécore sapiunt quam éx suo,
> magis aúdiendum quam aúscultandum cénseo.

Cur ? quaeso, cum ipse paucis interpositis versibus
dicas satis luculente :

> quicquid est hoc, ómnia animat, fórmat, alit, augét, creat,
> sépelit recipitque ín sese omnia ómniumque idémst pater,
> índidemque eademque oriuntur de íntegro atque eodem
> óccidunt.

Quid est igitur, cur, cum domus sit omnium una,
eaque communis, cumque animi hominum semper
fuerint futurique sint, cur ei, quid ex quoque eveniat ,
et quid quamque rem significet, perspicere non possint ?
" Haec habui," inquit, " de divinatione quae
dicerem."

---

[1] Often spoken of as the seat of the emotions, but here
of the intelligence.

[2] The earth is meant and is personified as Dis or Pluto ;
cf. Cic. *N.D.* ii. 26. 66 *Terrena autem vis omnis atque
natura Diti patri dedicata est, qui Dives, ut apud Graecos*
Πλούτων, *quia et recidunt omnia in terras et oriuntur e
terris.*

inspection of the entrails of sacrifices ; because, as
he thinks, the colour and general condition of the
entrails are prophetic sometimes of health and
sometimes of sickness and sometimes also of whether
the fields will be barren or productive. Now, if it
is known by observation and experience that these
means of divination have their source in nature, it
must be that the observations made and records
kept for a long period of time have added much
to our knowledge of this subject. Hence, that
natural philosopher introduced by Pacuvius into his
play of *Chryses*, seems to show very scanty apprehension of the laws of nature when he speaks as
follows :

> The men who know the speech of birds and more
> Do learn from other livers [1] than their own—
> 'Twere best to hear, I think, and not to heed.

I do not know why this poet makes such a statement
when only a few lines further on he says clearly
enough :

> Whate'er the power may be, it animates,
> Creates, gives form, increase, and nourishment
> To everything ; of everything the sire,
> It takes all things unto itself and hides
> Within its breast ; and as from it all things
> Arise, likewise to it all things return.[2]

Since all things have one and the same and that a
common home, and since the human soul has always
been and will always be, why, then, should it not be
able to understand what effect will follow any cause,
and what sign will precede any event ?

" This," said Quintus, " is all that I had to say
on divination."

132   LVIII. " Nunc illa testabor, non me sortilegos
neque eos, qui quaestus causa hariolentur, ne
psychomantia quidem, quibus Appius, amicus tuus,
uti solebat, agnoscere :

> non habeo denique nauci Marsum augurem ;
> non vicanos haruspices, non de circo astrologos ;
> non Isiacos coniectores, non interpretes sómnium ;

—non enim sunt ei aut scientia aut arte divini—

> séd superstitiósi vates ímpudentesque hárioli
> aút inertes aút insani aut quíbus egestas ímperat,
> quí sibi semitám non sapiunt, álteri monstránt viam ;
> quíbus divitias póllicentur, áb iis drachmam ipsí petunt.
> de hís divitiis síbi deducant dráchmam, reddant cétera.

Atque haec quidem Ennius, qui paucis ante versibus
esse deos censet, sed eos non curare opinatur, quid
agat humanum genus. Ego autem, qui et curare
arbitror et monere etiam ac multa praedicere,
levitate, vanitate, malitia exclusa divinationem
probo."

Quae cum dixisset Quintus, " Praeclare tu quidem,"
inquam, " paratus, Quinte, venisti . . ." [1]

[1] quinte, venisti *cod. R.*

---

[1] Appius Claudius, colleague of Cicero in the augural
college ; *cf.* i. 47. 105.

[2] The words *non habeo . . . arte divini* are written in
verse form in four lines by Giese, Davies, and Moser, and
in prose form by Müller.

[3] *Cf.* ii. 50. 104 ; Cic. *N.D.* iii. 32. 79.

LVIII. " I will assert, however, in conclusion, that I do not recognize fortune-tellers, or those who prophesy for money, or necromancers, or mediums, whom your friend Appius[1] makes it a practice to consult.

> In fine, I say, I do not care a fig
> For Marsian augurs, village mountebanks,
> Astrologers who haunt the circus grounds,
> Or Isis-seers, or dream interpreters :

—for they are not diviners either by knowledge or skill,[2]—

> But superstitious bards, soothsaying quacks,
> Averse to work, or mad, or ruled by want,
> Directing others how to go, and yet
> What road to take they do not know themselves ;
> From those to whom they promise wealth they beg
> A coin. From what they promised let them take
> Their coin as toll and pass the balance on.

Such are the words of Ennius who only a few lines further back[3] expresses the view that there are gods and yet says that the gods do not care what human beings do. But for my part, believing as I do that the gods do care for man, and that they advise and often forewarn him, I approve of divination which is not trivial and is free from falsehood and trickery."

When Quintus had finished I remarked, " My dear Quintus, you have come admirably well prepared."

LIBER SECUNDUS

I. Quaerenti mihi multumque et diu cogitanti quanam re possem prodesse quam plurimis, ne quando intermitterem consulere rei publicae, nulla maior occurrebat quam si optimarum artium vias traderem meis civibus ; quod compluribus iam libris me arbitror consecutum. Nam et cohortati sumus, ut maxime potuimus, ad philosophiae studium eo libro, qui est inscriptus *Hortensius,* et, quod genus philosophandi minime arrogans maximeque et constans et elegans arbitraremur, quattuor *Academicis* 2 libris ostendimus. Cumque fundamentum esset philosophiae positum in finibus bonorum et malorum, perpurgatus est is locus a nobis quinque libris, ut, quid a quoque, et quid contra quemque philosophum diceretur, intellegi posset. Totidem subsecuti libri *Tusculanarum disputationum* res ad beate vivendum maxime necessarias aperuerunt. Primus enim est de contemnenda morte, secundus de tolerando dolore, de aegritudine lenienda tertius, quartus de reliquis animi perturbationibus, quintus eum locum complexus est, qui totam philosophiam maxime illustrat ; docet enim ad beate vivendum virtutem se ipsa esse contentam.

---

[1] *Cf.* August. *Confess.* iii. 4. 7 *ille vero liber* (Hortensius) *mutavit affectum meum et ad te ipsum, Domine, mutavit preces meas et vota ac desideria mea fecit alia.*

[2] *De finibus bonorum et malorum.*

BOOK II

I. After serious and long continued reflection as to how I might do good to as many people as possible and thereby prevent any interruption of my service to the State, no better plan occurred to me than to conduct my fellow-citizens in the ways of the noblest learning—and this, I believe, I have already accomplished through my numerous books. For example, in my work entitled *Hortensius*,[1] I appealed as earnestly as I could for the study of philosophy. And in my *Academics*, in four volumes, I set forth the philosophic system which I thought least arrogant, and at the same time most consistent and refined. And, since the foundation of philosophy rests on the distinction between good and evil, I exhaustively treated that subject in five volumes [2] and in such a way that the conflicting views of the different philosophers might be known. Next, and in the same number of volumes, came the *Tusculan Disputations*, which made plain the means most essential to a happy life. For the first volume treats of indifference to death, the second of enduring pain, the third of the alleviation of sorrow, the fourth of other spiritual disturbances ; and the fifth embraces a topic which sheds the brightest light on the entire field of philosophy since it teaches that virtue is sufficient of itself for the attainment of happiness.

3 Quibus rebus editis tres libri perfecti sunt *de Natura Deorum*, in quibus omnis eius loci quaestio continetur. Quae ut plane esset cumulateque perfecta, *de Divinatione* ingressi sumus his libris scribere ; quibus, ut est in animo, *de Fato* si adiunxerimus, erit abunde satis factum toti huic quaestioni. Atque his libris adnumerandi sunt sex *de Re publica*, quos tum scripsimus, cum gubernacula rei publicae tenebamus. Magnus locus philosophiaeque proprius a Platone, Aristotele, Theophrasto totaque Peripateticorum familia tractatus uberrime. Nam quid ego *de Consolatione* dicam ? quae mihi quidem ipsi sane aliquantum medetur, ceteris item multum illam profuturam puto. Interiectus est etiam nuper liber is, quem ad nostrum Atticum *de Senectute* misimus ; in primisque, quoniam philosophia vir bonus efficitur et fortis, *Cato* noster in horum librorum numero

4 ponendus est. Cumque Aristoteles itemque Theophrastus, excellentes viri cum subtilitate, tum copia, cum philosophia dicendi etiam praecepta coniunxerint, nostri quoque oratorii libri in eundem librorum numerum referendi videntur. Ita tres erunt *de Oratore*, quartus *Brutus*, quintus *Orator*.

II. Adhuc haec erant ; ad reliqua alacri tendebamus animo sic parati, ut, nisi quae causa gravior

---

[1] The lost *Laus Catonis*, to which Caesar wrote a reply ; *cf. Ad Att*. xii. 40.

[2] Cicero refers to the chaotic condition of public affairs following the death of Caesar.

After publishing the works mentioned I finished three volumes *On the Nature of the Gods*, which contain a discussion of every question under that head. With a view of simplifying and extending the latter treatise I started to write the present volume *On Divination*, to which I plan to add a work on *Fate*; when that is done every phase of this particular branch of philosophy will be sufficiently discussed. To this list of works must be added the six volumes which I wrote while holding the helm of state, entitled *On the Republic*—a weighty subject, appropriate for philosophic discussion, and one which has been most elaborately treated by Plato, Aristotle, Theophrastus, and the entire Peripatetic school. What need is there to say anything of my treatise *On Consolation*? For it is the source of very great comfort to me and will, I think, be of much help to others. I have also recently thrown in that book *On Old Age*, which I sent my friend Atticus; and, since it is by philosophy that a man is made virtuous and strong, my *Cato*[1] is especially worthy of a place among the foregoing books. Inasmuch as Aristotle and Theophrastus, too, both of whom were celebrated for their keenness of intellect and particularly for their copiousness of speech, have joined rhetoric with philosophy, it seems proper also to put my rhetorical books in the same category; hence we shall include the three volumes *On Oratory*, the fourth entitled *Brutus*, and the fifth called *The Orator*.

II. I have named the philosophic works so far written: to the completion of the remaining books of this series I was hastening with so much ardour that if some most grievous cause[2] had not inter-

obstitisset, nullum philosophiae locum esse pateremur, qui non Latinis litteris illustratus pateret. Quod enim munus rei publicae afferre maius meliusve possumus, quam si docemus atque erudimus iuventutem, his praesertim moribus atque temporibus, quibus ita prolapsa est, ut omnium opibus refrenanda

5 atque coërcenda sit ? Nec vero id effici posse confido, quod ne postulandum quidem est, ut omnes adulescentes se ad haec studia convertant. Pauci utinam ! quorum tamen in re publica late patere poterit industria. Equidem ex eis etiam fructum capio laboris mei, qui iam aetate provecti in nostris libris adquiescunt ; quorum studio legendi meum scribendi studium vehementius in dies incitatur ; quos quidem plures, quam rebar, esse cognovi. Magnificum illud etiam Romanisque hominibus gloriosum, ut Graecis

6 de philosophia litteris non egeant ; quod adsequar profecto, si instituta perfecero.

Ac mihi quidem explicandae philosophiae causam adtulit casus gravis civitatis, cum in armis civilibus nec tueri meo more rem publicam nec nihil agere poteram nec, quid potius, quod quidem me dignum esset, agerem, reperiebam. Dabunt igitur mihi veniam mei cives vel gratiam potius habebunt, quod, cum esset in unius potestate res publica, neque ego me abdidi neque deserui neque afflixi neque ita gessi,

vened there would not now be any phase of philosophy which I had failed to elucidate and make easily accessible in the Latin tongue. For what greater or better service can I render to the commonwealth than to instruct and train the youth—especially in view of the fact that our young men have gone so far astray because of the present moral laxity that the utmost effort will be needed to hold them in check and direct them in the right way? Of course, I have no assurance—it could not even be expected—that they will all turn to these studies. Would that a few may! Though few, their activity may yet have a wide influence in the state. In fact, I am receiving some reward for my labour even from men advanced in years; for they are finding comfort in my books, and by their ardour in reading are raising my eagerness for writing to a higher pitch every day. Their number, too, I learn, is far greater than I had expected. Furthermore, it would redound to the fame and glory of the Roman people to be made independent of Greek writers in the study of philosophy, and this result I shall certainly bring about if my present plans are accomplished.

The cause of my becoming an expounder of philosophy sprang from the grave condition of the State during the period of the Civil War, when, being unable to protect the Republic, as had been my custom, and finding it impossible to remain inactive, I could find nothing else that I preferred to do that was worthy of me. Therefore my countrymen will pardon me — rather they will thank me — because, when the State was in the power of one man, I refused to hide myself, to quit my place, or to be cast down; I did not bear

quasi homini aut temporibus iratus, neque porro ita
aut adulatus aut admiratus fortunam sum alterius,
ut me meae paeniteret.

Id enim ipsum a Platone philosophiaque didiceram,
naturales esse quasdam conversiones rerum publicarum, ut eae tum a principibus tenerentur, tum a
7 populis, aliquando a singulis. Quod cum accidisset
nostrae rei publicae, tum pristinis orbati muneribus
haec studia renovare coepimus, ut et animus molestiis
hac potissimum re levaretur et prodessemus civibus
nostris, qua re cumque possemus. In libris enim
sententiam dicebamus, contionabamur, philosophiam
nobis pro rei publicae procuratione substitutam
putabamus. Nunc quoniam de re publica consuli
coepti sumus, tribuenda est opera rei publicae, vel
omnis potius in ea cogitatio et cura ponenda, tantum
huic studio relinquendum, quantum vacabit a publico
officio et munere. Sed haec alias pluribus ; nunc ad
institutam disputationem revertamur.

8 III. Nam cum de divinatione Quintus frater ea
disseruisset, quae superiore libro scripta sunt,
satisque ambulatum videretur, tum in bibliotheca,
quae in Lycio est, assedimus. Atque ego :

" Accurate tu quidem," inquam, " Quinte, et Stoice

---

[1] Plato, *Rep.* viii. 2. 545.

myself like one enraged at the man or at the times; and, further, I neither so fawned upon nor admired another's fortune as to repent me of my own.

For one thing in particular I had learned from Plato [1] and from philosophy, that certain revolutions in government are to be expected; so that states are now under a monarchy, now under a democracy, and now under a tyranny. When the last-named fate had befallen my country, and I had been debarred from my former activities, I began to cultivate anew these present studies that by their means, rather than by any other, I might relieve my mind of its worries and at the same time serve my fellow-countrymen as best I could under the circumstances. Accordingly, it was in my books that I made my senatorial speeches and my forensic harangues; for I thought that I had permanently exchanged politics for philosophy. Now, however, since I have begun to be consulted again about public affairs, my time must be devoted to the State, or, rather, my undivided thought and care must be fixed upon it; and only so much time can be given to philosophy as will not be needed in the discharge of my duty to the commonwealth. But more of this at another time; now let us return to the discussion with which we started.

III. After my brother Quintus had delivered his views on divination, as set out in the preceding volume, and we had walked as much as we wished, we took our seats in the library in my "Lyceum," and I remarked:

"Really, my dear Quintus, you have defended

Stoicorum sententiam defendisti, quodque me maxime
delectat, plurimis nostris exemplis usus es, et iis
quidem claris et illustribus.   Dicendum est mihi
igitur ad ea, quae sunt a te dicta, sed ita nihil ut
affirmem, quaeram omnia, dubitans plerumque et
mihi ipse diffidens.   Si enim aliquid certi haberem
quod dicerem, ego ipse divinarem, qui esse divinationem nego.

9   " Etenim me movet illud, quod in primis Carneades
quaerere solebat, quarumnam rerum divinatio esset,
earumne, quae sensibus perciperentur.   At eas
quidem cernimus, audimus, gustamus, olfacimus,
tangimus.   Num quid ergo in his rebus est, quod
provisione aut permotione mentis magis quam natura
ipsa sentiamus ?   aut num nescio qui ille divinus, si
oculis captus sit, ut Tiresias fuit, possit, quae alba
sint, quae nigra, dicere aut, si surdus sit, varietates
vocum aut modos noscere ?   Ad nullam igitur earum
rerum, quae sensu accipiuntur, divinatio adhibetur.

"Atqui ne in eis quidem rebus, quae arte tractantur,
divinatione opus est.   Etenim ad aegros non vates
aut hariolos, sed medicos solemus adducere, nec
vero, qui fidibus aut tibiis uti volunt, ab haruspicibus accipiunt earum tractationem, sed a musicis.
10 Eadem in litteris ratio est reliquisque rebus,

---

[1] This was the characteristic mental attitude in which the
disciples of the New Academy approached every question.

the Stoic doctrine with accuracy and like a Stoic.
But the thing that delights me most is the fact
that you illustrated your argument with many
incidents taken from Roman sources—incidents, too,
of a distinguished and noble type. I must now
reply to what you said, but I must do so with great
diffidence and with many misgivings, and in such
a way as to affirm nothing and question everything.[1]
For if I should assume anything that I said to be
certain I should myself be playing the diviner while
saying that no such thing as divination exists!

"I am impressed with the force of the questions
with which Carneades used to begin his discussions :
' What are the things within the scope of divination ?
Are they things that are perceived by the senses? But
those are things that we see, hear, taste, smell, and
touch. Is there, then, in such objects some quality
that we can better perceive with the aid of prophecy
and inspiration than we can with the aid of the
senses alone ? And is there any diviner, anywhere,
who, if blind, like Tiresias, could tell the difference
between white and black ? Or, who, if deaf, could
distinguish between different voices and different
tones ? Now you must admit that divination is not
applicable in any case where knowledge is gained
through the senses.

"Nor is there any need of divination even in
matters within the domain of science and of art.
For, when people are sick, we, as a general rule,
do not summon a prophet or a seer, but we call in
a physician. Again, persons who want to learn to
play on the harp or on the flute take lessons, not
from a soothsayer, but from a musician. The same
rule applies in literature and in other departments

quarum est disciplina. Num censes eos, qui divinare
dicuntur, posse respondere, sol maiorne quam terra
sit an tantus, quantus videatur ? lunaque suo lumine
an solis utatur ? sol, luna quem motum habeat ?
quem quinque stellae, quae errare dicuntur ? Nec
haec, qui divini habentur, profitentur se esse dicturos,
nec eorum, quae in geometria describuntur, quae
vera, quae falsa sint ; sunt enim ea mathematicorum,
non hariolorum.

IV. " De illis vero rebus, quae in philosophia
versantur, num quid est, quod quisquam divinorum
aut respondere soleat aut consuli, quid bonum sit,
quid malum, quid neutrum ? sunt enim haec propria
11 philosophorum. Quid ? de officio num quis haruspicem consulit, quem ad modum sit cum parentibus,
cum fratribus, cum amicis vivendum ? quem ad
modum utendum pecunia, quem ad modum honore,
quem ad modum imperio ? Ad sapientes haec, non
ad divinos referri solent.

" Quid ? quae a dialecticis aut a physicis tractantur, num quid eorum divinari potest ? unusne
mundus sit an plures, quae sint initia rerum, ex
quibus nascuntur omnia ? Physicorum est ista
prudentia. Quo modo autem ' mentientem,' quem
ψευδόμενον vocant, dissolvas, aut quem ad modum
' soriti ' resistas (quem, si necesse sit, Latino verbo

---

¹ The form of this fallacy best known was this : " Epimenides calls the Cretans liars, but he is himself a Cretan ;
does he then lie or tell the truth ? " *Cf.* Cic. *Acad.* ii. 29.
95 ; Gellius xviii. 2. 10.

of learning. And do you really believe that those who are credited with powers of divining, can, for that reason, tell whether the sun is larger than the earth, and whether it is as big as it seems to be ? Or whether the moon shines by its own light or by that of the sun ? Or do you think that they understand the motions of the sun and moon and of the five stars, which are called ' planets ' ? Your reputed diviners do not claim that they can answer any of these questions ; nor will they profess to tell whether geometrical figures are correctly drawn or not, for that is the business of mathematicians, not of seers.

IV. " Now let us consider matters within the purview of philosophy : When the question is as to what is morally right, or morally wrong, or as to what is neither the one nor the other, do we usually have our doubts resolved by diviners ? In fact, do we often consult them in such a case ? Certainly not, for problems of this kind belong to philosophers. Again, where the question is one of duty : who ever consults a soothsayer as to how he should demean himself towards his parents, his brothers, or his friends ? or as to how he should use his wealth, his office, or his power ? Such matters are usually referred to sages, not to diviners.

" Furthermore, can any of the questions of dialectic or of physics be solved by divination ? For example, is there one world, or are there many worlds ? What are the primary elements from which all things are derived ? Such problems belong to the science of physics. Again, suppose one should wish to know how to resolve the ' liar ' fallacy,[1] which the Greeks call ' ψευδόμενον ' ; or how to meet the ' heap ' fallacy, known in Greek as *sorites* (which,

381

liceat ' acervalem ' appellare ; sed nihil opus est ; **ut
enim ipsa philosophia et multa verba Graecorum, sic
' sorites ' satis Latino sermone tritus est),**—ergo haec
quoque dialectici dicent, non divini.

"Quid ? cum quaeritur, qui sit optimus rei
publicae status, quae leges, qui mores aut utiles aut
inutiles, haruspicesne ex Etruria arcessentur, an
principes statuent et delecti viri periti rerum
12 civilium ? Quodsi nec earum rerum, quae subiectae
sensibus sunt, ulla divinatio est nec earum, quae
artibus continentur, nec earum, quae in philosophia
disseruntur, nec earum, quae in re publica versantur,
quarum rerum sit, nihil prorsus intellego ; nam aut
omnium debet esse, aut aliqua ei materia danda est,
in qua versari possit. Sed nec omnium divinatio est,
ut ratio docuit, nec locus nec materia invenitur, cui
divinationem praeficere possimus. V. Vide igitur,
ne nulla sit divinatio. Est quidam Graecus vulgaris
in hanc sententiam versus :

bene quí coniciet, vátem hunc perhibebo óptumum.

Num igitur aut, quae tempestas impendeat, vates
melius coniciet quam gubernator ? aut morbi naturam
acutius quam medicus ? aut belli administrationem
prudentius quam imperator coniectura assequetur ?

---

[1] The original form of this fallacy began with the question
"Does one grain make a heap ? " The answer was " no."
One grain after another was added until there were, say,
n grains, when it would be admitted that $n+1$ grains made
a heap. Hence the difference between $n+1$ and n grains,
or one grain, made a heap, which was contrary to the first
answer. *Cf.* Reid's *Acad.* ii. 16. 49 note.

if a Latin equivalent were needed, could be represented by the word *acervalis*, but none is needed ;
for, just as the word ' philosophy ' and many other
words are of Greek origin and are in general use
as Latin words, so it is with *sorites*),[1]—in both these
cases the logician, and not the diviner, would speak.

" Assume, next, that the inquiry is as to the best
form of government, or as to what laws or what
customs are beneficial and what are harmful, will
you call soothsayers out of Etruria to settle the
question, or will you accept the decision of men of
eminence chosen for their knowledge of statecraft ?
But if there is no place for divination in things perceived by the senses, or in those included among
the arts, or in those discussed by philosophers, or
in those which have to do with government, I see
absolutely no need for it anywhere. For either it
ought to be of use in every case, or, at least, some
department in which it may be employed should be
found. But divination is not of use in every case,
as my reasoning has shown ; nor can any field or
subject matter be found over which it may exercise
control. V. Therefore I am inclined to think that
there is no such thing as divination. There is a
much-quoted Greek verse to this effect :

> The best diviner I maintain to be
> The man who guesses or conjectures best.[2]

Now do you think that a prophet will ' conjecture '
better whether a storm is at hand than a pilot ?
or that he will by ' conjecture ' make a more accurate diagnosis than a physician, or conduct a war with
more skill than a general ?

[2] From Euripides and quoted in Plutarch, *De orac.
defect.* 432 c μάντις δ' ἄριστος ὅστις εἰκάζει καλῶς.

13   " Sed animadverti, Quinte, te caute et ab eis
coniecturis quae haberent artem atque prudentiam,
et ab eis rebus quae sensibus aut artificiis perciperentur, abducere divinationem eamque ita definire :
' divinationem esse earum rerum praedictionem et
praesensionem, quae essent fortuitae.'   Primum
eodem revolveris. Nam et medici et gubernatoris et
imperatoris praesensio est rerum fortuitarum. Num
igitur aut haruspex aut augur aut vates quis aut
somnians melius coniecerit aut e morbo evasurum
aegrotum aut e periculo navem aut ex insidiis
exercitum, quam medicus, quam gubernator, quam
imperator ?

14   " Atqui ne illa quidem divinantis esse dicebas,
ventos aut imbres impendentes quibusdam praesentire
signis (in quo nostra quaedam Aratea memoriter a
te pronuntiata sunt), etsi haec ipsa fortuita sunt ;
plerumque enim, non semper eveniunt. Quae est
igitur aut ubi versatur fortuitarum rerum praesensio,
quam divinationem vocas ? Quae enim praesentiri
aut arte aut ratione aut usu aut coniectura possunt,
ea non divinis tribuenda putas, sed peritis. Ita
relinquitur, ut ea fortuita divinari possint, quae nulla
nec arte nec sapientia provideri possunt ; ut, si quis
M. Marcellum illum, qui ter consul fuit, multis annis
ante dixisset naufragio esse periturum, divinasset

---

[1] *Cf.* i. 49. 111 *seq.*
[2] *Cf.* i. 5. 9.

" But I observed, Quintus, that you prudently withdrew divination from conjectures based upon skill and experience in public affairs, from those drawn from the use of the senses and from those made by persons in their own callings.[1] I observed, also, that you defined divination to be ' the foreknowledge and foretelling of things which happen by chance.' [2] In the first place, that is a contradiction of what you have admitted. For the foreknowledge possessed by a physician, a pilot, and a general is of ' things which happen by chance.' Then can any soothsayer, augur, prophet, or dreamer conjecture better than a physician, a pilot, or a general that an invalid will come safely out of his sickness, or that a ship will escape from danger, or that an army will avoid an ambuscade ?

" And you went on to say that even the foreknowledge of impending storms and rains by means of certain signs was not divination, and, in that connexion, you quoted a number of verses from my translation of Aratus. Yet such coincidences ' happen by chance,' for though they happen frequently they do not happen always. What, then, is this thing you call divination—this ' foreknowledge of things that happen by chance '—and where is it employed ? You think that ' whatever can be foreknown by means of science, reason, experience, or conjecture is to be referred, not to diviners, but to experts.' It follows, therefore, that divination of ' things that happen by chance ' is possible only of things which cannot be foreseen by means of skill or wisdom. Hence, if someone had declared many years in advance that the famous Marcus Marcellus, who was consul three times, would perish in a shipwreck,

profecto ; nulla enim arte alia id nec sapientia scire potuisset. Talium ergo rerum, quae in fortuna positae sunt, praesensio divinatio est.

15 VI. " Potestne igitur earum rerum, quae nihil habent rationis, quare futurae sint, esse ulla praesensio ? Quid est enim aliud fors, quid fortuna, quid casus, quid eventus, nisi cum sic aliquid cecidit, sic evenit, ut vel non cadere atque evenire, ut vel aliter cadere atque evenire potuerit ? Quo modo ergo id, quod temere fit caeco casu et volubilitate fortunae, 16 praesentiri et praedici potest ? Medicus morbum ingravescentem ratione providet, insidias imperator, tempestates gubernator ; et tamen ei ipsi saepe falluntur, qui nihil sine certa ratione opinantur ; ut agricola, cum florem oleae videt, bacam quoque sese visurum putat, non sine ratione ille quidem ; sed non numquam tamen fallitur. Quodsi falluntur ei qui nihil sine aliqua probabili coniectura ac ratione dicunt, quid existimandum est de coniectura eorum, qui extis aut avibus aut ostentis aut oraclis aut somniis futura praesentiunt ? Nondum dico, quam haec signa nulla sint, fissum iecoris, corvi cantus, volatus aquilae, stellae traiectio, voces furentium, sortes, somnia ; de quibus singulis dicam suo loco ; nunc de universis.

this, by your definition, undoubtedly would have been a case of divination, since that calamity could not have been foreseen by means of any other skill or by wisdom. That is why you say that divination is the foreknowledge of such things as depend upon chance.

VI. " Can there, then, be any foreknowledge of things for whose happening no reason exists ? For we do not apply the words ' chance,' ' luck,' ' accident,' or ' casualty ' except to an event which has so occurred or happened that it either might not have occurred at all, or might have occurred in any other way. How, then, is it possible to foresee and to predict an event that happens at random, as the result of blind accident, or of unstable chance ? By the use of reason the physician foresees the progress of a disease, the general anticipates the enemy's plans and the pilot forecasts the approach of bad weather. And yet even those who base their conclusions on accurate reasoning are often mistaken : for example, when the farmer sees his olive-tree in bloom he expects also, and not unreasonably, to see it bear fruit, but occasionally he is disappointed. If then mistakes are made by those who make no forecasts not based upon some reasonable and probable conjecture, what must we think of the conjectures of men who foretell the future by means of entrails, birds, portents, oracles, or dreams ? I am not ready yet to take up one by one the various kinds of divination and show that the cleft in the liver, the croak of a raven, the flight of an eagle, the fall of a star, the utterances of persons in a frenzy, lots, and dreams have no prophetic value whatever ; I shall discuss each of them in its turn— now I am discussing the subject as a whole.

17 " Qui potest provideri quicquam futurum esse,
quod neque causam habet ullam neque notam cur
futurum sit ? Solis defectiones itemque lunae
praedicuntur in multos annos ab eis qui siderum cursus
et motus numeris persequuntur ; ea praedicunt enim
quae naturae necessitas perfectura est. Vident ex
constantissimo motu lunae, quando illa e regione solis
facta incurrat in umbram terrae, quae est meta noctis,
ut eam obscurari necesse sit, quandoque eadem luna
subiecta atque opposita soli nostris oculis eius lumen
obscuret, quo in signo quaeque errantium stellarum
quoque tempore futura sit, qui exortus quoque die
signi alicuius aut qui occasus futurus sit. Haec qui
ante dicunt, quam rationem sequantur, vides.

18 VII. " Qui thesaurum inventum iri aut hereditatem
venturam dicunt, quid sequuntur ? aut in qua rerum
natura inest id futurum ? Quodsi haec eaque, quae
sunt eiusdem generis, habent aliquam talem necessita-
tem, quid est tandem, quod casu fieri aut forte fortuna
putemus ? Nihil enim est tam contrarium rationi et
constantiae quam fortuna, ut mihi ne in deum quidem
cadere videatur, ut sciat, quid casu et fortuito futurum
sit. Si enim scit, certe illud eveniet ; sin certe

---

¹ *Cf.* Pliny, *N.H.* ii. 7 *manifestum est . . . neque aliud
esse noctem, quam terrae umbram ; figuram autem similem
metae, ac turbini inverso.*

" How can anything be foreseen that has no cause and no distinguishing mark of its coming? Eclipses of the sun and also of the moon are predicted for many years in advance by men who employ mathematics in studying the courses and movements of the heavenly bodies; and the unvarying laws of nature will bring their predictions to pass. Because of the perfectly regular movements of the moon the astronomers calculate when it will be opposite the sun and in the earth's shadow — which is ' the cone of night '[1] — and when, necessarily, it will become invisible. For the same reason they know when the moon will be directly between the earth and the sun and thus will hide the light of the sun from our eyes. They know in what sign each planet will be at any given time and at what time each day any constellation will rise and set. You see the course of reasoning followed in arriving at these predictions.

VII. " But what course of reasoning is followed by men who predict the finding of a treasure or the inheritance of an estate? On what law of nature do such prophecies depend? But, on the other hand, if the prophecies just mentioned and others of the same class are controlled by some natural and immutable law such as regulates the movements of the stars, pray, can we conceive of anything happening by accident, or chance? Surely nothing is so at variance with reason and stability as chance. Hence it seems to me that it is not in the power even of God himself to know what event is going to happen accidentally and by chance. For if He knows, then the event is certain to happen; but if it is certain to happen, chance does not exist.

eveniet, nulla fortuna est; est autem fortuna;
rerum igitur fortuitarum nulla praesensio est.

19   " Aut si negas esse fortunam et omnia, quae fiunt
quaeque futura sunt, ex omni aeternitate definita
dicis esse fataliter, muta definitionem divinationis,
quam dicebas ' praesensionem esse rerum fortuitarum.' Si enim nihil fieri potest, nihil accidere, nihil
evenire, nisi quod ab omni aeternitate certum fuerit
esse futurum rato tempore, quae potest esse fortuna ?
qua sublata qui locus est divinationi ? Quae a te
fortuitarum rerum est dicta praesensio ? Quamquam
dicebas omnia, quae fierent futurave essent, fato
contineri. Anile sane et plenum superstitionis fati
nomen ipsum ; sed tamen apud Stoicos de isto fato
multa dicuntur ; de quo alias ; nunc quod necesse est.

20   VIII. " Si omnia fato, quid mihi divinatio prodest ?
Quod enim is, qui divinat, praedicit, id vero futurum
est ; ut ne illud quidem sciam quale sit, quod Deiotarum, familiarem nostrum et necessarium, ex itinere
aquila revocavit ; ' qui, nisi revertisset, in eo conclavi
ei cubandum fuisset, quod proxima nocte corruit ;
ruina igitur oppressus esset.' At id neque, si fatum
fuerat, effugisset nec, si non fuerat, in eum casum
incidisset.

    " Quid ergo adiuvat divinatio ? aut quid est, quod

---

[1] *Cf.* i. 55. 125.
[2] *i.e.* in the *De fato*.
[3] *Cf.* i. 8. 20.

390

And yet chance does exist, therefore there is no foreknowledge of things that happen by chance.

"But if you deny the existence of chance and assert that the course of everything present or future has been inevitably determined from all eternity, then you must change your definition of divination, which you said was 'the foreknowledge of things that happen by chance.' For if nothing can happen, nothing befall, nothing come to pass, except what has been determined from all eternity as bound to happen at a fixed time, how can there be such a thing as chance? And if there is no such thing as chance, what room is there for that divination, which you termed 'a foreknowledge of things that happen by chance'? And you were inconsistent enough, too, to say that everything that is or will be is controlled by Fate![1] Why, the very word 'Fate' is full of superstition and old women's credulity, and yet the Stoics have much to say of this Fate of yours. A discussion on Fate[2] is reserved for another occasion; at present I shall speak of it only in so far as it is necessary.

VIII. "Of what advantage to me is divination if everything is ruled by Fate? On that hypothesis what the diviner predicts is bound to happen. Hence I do not know what to make of the fact that an eagle recalled our intimate friend Deiotarus from his journey[3]; for if he had not turned back he must have been sleeping in the room when it was destroyed the following night, and, therefore, have been crushed in the ruins. And yet, if Fate had willed it, he would not have escaped that calamity; and *vice versa*. Hence, I repeat, what is the good of divination? Or what is it that lots, entrails, or any

me moneant aut sortes aut exta aut ulla praedictio ? Si enim fatum fuit classes populi Romani bello Punico primo, alteram naufragio, alteram a Poenis depressam, interire, etiamsi tripudium solistimum pulli fecissent L. Iunio et P. Claudio consulibus, classes tamen interissent. Sin, cum auspiciis obtemperatum esset, interiturae classes non fuerunt, non interierunt fato ; vultis autem omnia fato ; nulla igitur est divinatio.

21   " Quodsi fatum fuit bello Punico secundo exercitum populi Romani ad lacum Trasimenum interire, num id vitari potuit, si Flaminius consul eis signis eisque auspiciis, quibus pugnare prohibebatur, paruisset ? Certe non potuit.[1] Aut igitur non fato interiit exercitus, aut, si fato (quod certe vobis ita dicendum est), etiamsi obtemperasset auspiciis, idem eventurum fuisset ; mutari[2] enim fata non possunt. Ubi est igitur ista divinatio Stoicorum ? quae, si fato omnia fiunt, nihil nos admonere potest, ut cautiores simus ; quoquo enim modo nos gesserimus, fiet tamen illud, quod futurum est ; sin autem id potest flecti, nullum est fatum ; ita ne divinatio quidem, quoniam ea rerum futurarum est. Nihil autem est pro certo futurum, quod potest aliqua procuratione accidere ne fiat.

[1] certe non potuit *Pearcius* ; certe potuit *Müller* ; *Dav. om.*
[2] *Dav. has* mutari . . . possunt *following* interiit exercitus.

---

[1] *Cf.* i. 16. 29.
[2] *Cf.* i. 25. 77.
[3] *Procuratio* is a technical term for using means, by sacrifice or otherwise, to avert some evil omen or portent.

other means of prophecy warn me to avoid ? For, if it was the will of Fate that the Roman fleets in the First Punic War should perish—the one by shipwreck and the other at the hands of the Carthaginians—they would have perished just the same even if the sacred chickens had made a *tripudium solistimum* in the consulship of Lucius Junius and Publius Claudius ! [1] On the other hand, if obedience to the auspices would have prevented the destruction of the fleets, then they did not perish in accordance with Fate. But you insist that all things happen by Fate ; therefore there is no such thing as divination.

" Again, if it was the will of Fate that the Roman army should perish at Lake Trasimenus in the Second Punic War, could that result have been avoided if the consul Flaminius had obeyed the signs and the auspices which forbade his joining battle ? [2] Assuredly not. Therefore, either the army did not perish by the will of Fate, or, if it did (and you are certainly bound as a Stoic to say that it did), the same result would have happened even if the auspices had been obeyed ; for the decrees of Fate are unchangeable. Then what becomes of that vaunted divination of you Stoics ? For if all things happen by Fate, it does us no good to be warned to be on our guard, since that which is to happen, will happen regardless of what we do. But if that which is to be can be turned aside, there is no such thing as Fate ; so, too, there is no such thing as divination—since divination deals with things that are going to happen. But nothing is ' certain to happen ' which there is some means of dealing with [3] so as to prevent its happening.

22   IX. "Atque ego ne utilem quidem arbitror esse
nobis futurarum rerum scientiam.   Quae enim vita
fuisset Priamo, si ab adulescentia scisset, quos eventus
senectutis esset habiturus ?   Abeamus a fabulis,
propiora videamus.   Clarissimorum hominum nostrae
civitatis gravissimos exitus in *Consolatione* collegi-
mus. Quid igitur ? ut omittamus superiores, Marcone
Crasso putas utile fuisse tum, cum maximis opibus
fortunisque florebat, scire sibi interfecto Publio filio
exercituque deleto trans Euphratem cum ignominia
et dedecore esse pereundum ?   An Cn. Pompeium
censes tribus suis consulatibus, tribus triumphis,
maximarum rerum gloria laetaturum fuisse, si sciret
se in solitudine Aegyptiorum trucidatum iri amisso
exercitu, post mortem vero ea consecutura, quae sine
lacrimis non possumus dicere ?

23   " Quid vero Caesarem putamus, si divinasset fore
ut in eo senatu, quem maiore ex parte ipse cooptasset,
in curia Pompeia, ante ipsius Pompei simulacrum, tot
centurionibus suis inspectantibus, a nobilissimis
civibus, partim etiam a se omnibus rebus ornatis,
trucidatus ita iaceret ut ad eius corpus non modo
amicorum, sed ne servorum quidem quisquam accederet, quo cruciatu animi vitam acturum fuisse ?

   " Certe igitur ignoratio futurorum malorum utilior

---

[1] Built by Pompey and used as a meeting-place for the
Senate.

IX. " And further, for my part, I think that a knowledge of the future would be a disadvantage. Consider, for example, what Priam's life would have been if he had known from youth what dire events his old age held in store for him ! But let us leave the era of myths and come to events nearer home. In my work *On Consolation* I have collected instances of very grievous deaths that befell some of the most illustrious men of our commonwealth. Passing by men of earlier day, let us take Marcus Crassus. What advantage, pray, do you think it would have been to him, when he was at the very summit of power and wealth, to know that he was destined to perish beyond the Euphrates in shame and dishonour, after his son had been killed and his own army had been destroyed ? Or do you think that Gnaeus Pompey would have found joy in his three consul-ships, in his three triumphs, and in the fame of his transcendent deeds, if he had known that he would be slain in an Egyptian desert, after he had lost his army, and that following his death those grave events would occur of which I cannot speak without tears ?

" Or what do we think of Caesar ? Had he fore-seen that in the Senate, chosen in most part by himself, in Pompey's hall,[1] aye, before Pompey's very statue, and in the presence of many of his own centurions, he would be put to death by most noble citizens, some of whom owed all that they had to him, and that he would fall to so low an estate that no friend—no, not even a slave—would approach his dead body, in what agony of soul would he have spent his life !

" Of a surety, then, ignorance of future ills is more

24 est quam scientia. Nam illud quidem dici, praesertim
Stoicis, nullo modo potest : Non isset ad arma
Pompeius, non transisset Crassus Euphratem, non
suscepisset bellum civile Caesar. Non igitur fatalis
exitus habuerunt ; vultis autem evenire omnia fato ;
nihil ergo illis profuisset divinare ; atque etiam
omnem fructum vitae superioris perdidissent ; quid
enim posset eis esse laetum exitus suos cogitantibus ?
Ita, quoquo sese verterint Stoici, iaceat necesse est
omnis eorum sollertia. Si enim id quod eventurum
est vel hoc, vel illo, modo potest evenire, fortuna
valet plurimum ; quae autem fortuita sunt, certa
esse non possunt. Sin autem certum est quid quaque
de re quoque tempore futurum sit, quid est quod
me adiuvent haruspices cum res tristissimas portendi
dixerunt ?

25 X. " Addunt ad extremum, ' omnia levius casura
rebus divinis procuratis.' Si autem nihil fit extra
fatum, nihil levari re divina potest. Hoc sentit
Homerus cum querentem Iovem inducit quod
Sarpedonem filium a morte contra fatum eripere non
posset. Hoc idem significat Graecus ille in eam
sententiam versus :

---

[1] *Il.* xvi. 433.
[2] It is not known from whom this line is taken. The
same thought is often found. *Cf.* Aesch. *Prom.* 527 ;
Herod. i. 91 ; Plato, *De leg.* v. 10.

profitable than the knowledge of them. For, assuming that men knew the future it cannot in any wise be said—certainly not by the Stoics—that Pompey would not have taken up arms, that Crassus would not have crossed the Euphrates, or that Caesar would not have embarked upon the civil war. If so, then, the deaths that befell these men were not determined by Fate. But you will have it that everything happens by Fate; consequently, knowledge of the future would have done these men no good. In reality it would have entirely deprived the earlier portion of their lives of enjoyment; for how could they have been happy in reflecting what their ends would be? And so, however the Stoics turn and twist, all their shrewdness must come to naught. For, if a thing that is going to happen, may happen in one way or another, indifferently, chance is predominant; but things that happen by chance cannot be certain. But if it is certain what is going to befall me in reference to any matter and on every occasion, how do the soothsayers help me by saying that the greatest misfortunes await me?

X. " To the last point the Stoics make the rejoinder that ' every evil which is going to befall us is made lighter by means of religious rites.' But if nothing happens except in accordance with Fate, no evil can be made lighter by means of religious rites. Homer shows his appreciation of this fact when he represents Jupiter as complaining because he could not snatch his son Sarpedon from death [1] when Fate forbade. The same thought is expressed in the following verses translated from a Greek poet [2]:

quod fóre paratum est, íd summum exsuperát Iovem.

Totum omnino fatum etiam Atellanio versu iure mihi esse irrisum videtur ; sed in rebus tam severis non est iocandi locus. Concludatur igitur ratio : Si enim provideri nihil potest futurum esse eorum, quae casu fiunt, quia esse certa non possunt, divinatio nulla est ; sin autem idcirco possunt provideri, quia certa sunt et fatalia, rursus divinatio nulla est ; eam 26 enim tu fortuitarum rerum esse dicebas. Sed haec fuerit nobis tamquam levis armaturae prima orationis excursio ; nunc comminus agamus experiamurque, si possimus cornua commovere disputationis tuae.

XI. " Duo enim genera divinandi esse dicebas, unum ' artificiosum,' alterum ' naturale.' Artificiosum constare partim ex coniectura, partim ex observatione diuturna. Naturale quod animus arriperet aut exciperet extrinsecus ex divinitate, unde omnes animos haustos aut acceptos aut libatos haberemus. Artificiosae divinationis illa fere genera ponebas : extispicum eorumque qui ex fulguribus ostentisque praedicerent, tum augurum eorumque qui signis aut ominibus uterentur, omneque genus coniecturale 27 in hoc fere genere ponebas. Illud autem naturale aut concitatione mentis edi et quasi fundi

---

[1] The *Fabulae Atellanae* originated in Atella, a town between Capua and Naples. They are often called *Osci Ludi*. *Cf.* Livy vii. 2, x. 208 ; Cic. *Ad fam.* ix. 16. 7.
[2] *Cf.* i. 6. 12 ; i. 18. 34.

That which has been decreed by Fate to be
Almighty Jove himself cannot prevent.

The whole idea of Fate in every detail is justly, as I
think, the subject of derision even in Atellan farces,[1]
but in a discussion as serious as ours joking is out of
place. So then let us sum up our argument: If it is
impossible to foresee things that happen by chance
because they are uncertain, there is no such thing as
divination; if, on the contrary, they can be foreseen
because they are preordained by Fate, still there
is no such thing as divination, which, by your definition, deals with 'things that happen by chance.'
But this introductory part of my discussion has been
mere skirmishing with light infantry; now let me
come to close quarters and see if I cannot drive in
both wings of your argument.

XI. "You divided divination into two kinds, one
artificial and the other natural.[2] 'The artificial,' you
said, 'consists in part of conjecture and in part of
long-continued observation; while the natural is that
which the soul has seized, or, rather, has obtained,
from a source outside itself—that is, from God,
whence all human souls have been drawn off,
received, or poured out.' Under the head of artificial divination you placed predictions made from
the inspection of entrails, those made from lightnings and portents, those made by augurs, and
by persons who depend entirely upon premonitory
signs. Under the same head you included practi-
cally every method of prophecy in which conjecture
was employed. Natural divination, on the other
hand, according to your view, is the result—'the
effusion,' as it were—of mental excitement, or it
is the prophetic power which the soul has during

399

videbatur aut animo per somnum sensibus et curis
vacuo provideri. Duxisti autem divinationem omnem
a tribus rebus, a deo, a fato, a natura. Sed tamen
cum explicare nihil posses, pugnasti commenticiorum
exemplorum mirifica copia. De quo primum hoc
libet dicere : Hoc ego philosophi non esse arbitror
testibus uti, qui aut casu veri aut malitia falsi
fictique esse possunt ; argumentis et rationibus
oportet, quare quidque ita sit, docere, non eventis,
eis praesertim quibus mihi liceat non credere.

28   XII. " Ut ordiar ab haruspicina, quam ego rei
publicae causa communisque religionis colendam
censeo. Sed soli sumus ; licet[1] verum exquirere sine
invidia, mihi praesertim de plerisque dubitanti.
Inspiciamus, si placet, exta primum. Persuaderi
igitur cuiquam potest ea, quae significari dicuntur
extis, cognita esse a haruspicibus observatione
diuturna ? Quam diuturna ista fuit ? aut quam
longinquo tempore observari potuit ? aut quo modo
est collatum inter ipsos, quae pars inimica, quae pars
familiaris esset, quod fissum periculum, quod com-

----

¹ quibus licet *Reid, Ac. n. 8, p.* 11, *making* soli sumus
refer to the Academicians.

----

¹ *Cf.* i. 55. 125.
² *e.g.* i. 21. 42, 43, 44, etc.
³ Cicero was a disciple of the New Academy and as such
reserved the right to question any proposition without
giving adherence to any. *Cf.* i. 4. 7.

sleep while free from bodily sensation and worldly cares. Moreover, you derived every form of divination from three sources—God, Fate, and Nature.[1] And although you could not give a reason for any kind of divination, still you carried on the war by marshalling an astonishing array of examples from fiction.[2] Of such a course I wish to say emphatically that it is not becoming in a philosopher to introduce testimony which may be either true by accident, or false and fabricated through malice. You ought to have employed arguments and reason to show that all your propositions were true and you ought not to have resorted to so-called occurrences—certainly not to such occurrences as are unworthy of belief.

XII. " In discussing separately the various methods of divination, I shall begin with soothsaying, which, according to my deliberate judgement, should be cultivated from reasons of political expediency and in order that we may have a state religion. But we are alone and for that reason we may, without causing ill-will, make an earnest inquiry into the truth of soothsaying—certainly I can do so, since in most things my philosophy is that of doubt.[3] In the first place, then, if you please, let us make ' an inspection ' of entrails ! Now can anybody be induced to believe that the things said to be predicted by means of entrails were learned by the soothsayers through ' long-continued observation ' ? How long, pray, did the observations last ? How could the observations have continued for a long time ? How did the soothsayers manage to agree among themselves what part of the entrails was unfavourable, and what part favourable ; or what cleft in the liver indicated danger and what promised some

modum aliquod ostenderet? An haec inter se
haruspices Etrusci, Elii, Aegyptii, Poeni contulerunt?
At id, praeterquam quod fieri non potuit, ne fingi
quidem potest; alios enim alio more videmus exta
interpretari, nec esse unam omnium disciplinam.

29   " Et certe, si est in extis aliqua vis, quae declaret
futura, necesse est eam aut cum rerum natura esse
coniunctam aut conformari quodam modo numine
deorum. Divina cum rerum natura tanta tamque
praeclara in omnes partes motusque diffusa quid
habere potest commune non dicam gallinaceum fel
(sunt enim, qui vel argutissima haec exta esse dicant),
sed tauri opimi iecur aut cor aut pulmo? quid habet
naturale, quod declarare possit, quid futurum sit?

30   XIII. " Democritus tamen non inscite nugatur, ut
physicus, quo genere nihil adrogantius:

> quód est ante pedes, némo spectat, caéli scrutantúr plagas.

Verum is tamen habitu extorum et colore declarari
censet haec dumtaxat: pabuli genus et earum rerum
quas terra procreet, vel ubertatem vel tenuitatem;
salubritatem etiam aut pestilentiam extis significari
putat. O mortalem beatum! cui certo scio ludum
numquam defuisse. Huncine hominem tantis delecta-
tum esse nugis, ut non videret tum futurum id veri
simile, si omnium pecudum exta eodem tempore in

---

[1] This is the third of three verses quoted by Cicero from
the *Iphigenia* of Ennius in *De rep.* i. 18. 30, but the apo-
phthegm is common. It is sometimes attributed to Thales.

advantage? Are the soothsayers of Etruria, Elis, Egypt, and of Carthage in accord on these matters? Apart from such an agreement being impossible in fact, it is impossible even to imagine; and, moreover, we see some nations interpreting entrails in one way and some in another; hence there is no uniformity of practice.

"Surely if entrails have any prophetic force, necessarily that force either is in accord with the laws of nature, or is fashioned in some way by the will and power of the gods. But between that divine system of nature whose great and glorious laws pervade all space and regulate all motion what possible connexion can there be with—I shall not say the gall of a chicken, whose entrails, some men assert, give very clear indications of the future, but—the liver, heart, and lungs of a sacrificial ox? And what natural quality is there in the entrails which enables them to indicate the future?

XIII. "Nevertheless Democritus jests rather prettily for a natural philosopher—and there is no more arrogant class—when he says:

> No one regards the things before his feet,
> But views with care the regions of the sky.[1]

And yet Democritus gives his approval to divination by means of entrails only to the extent of believing that their condition and colour indicate whether hay and other crops will be abundant or the reverse, and he even thinks that the entrails give signs of future health or sickness. O happy mortal! He never failed to have his joke—that is absolutely certain. But was he so amused with petty trifles as to fail to see that his theory would be plausible only on the assumption that the entrails of all cattle

eundem habitum se coloremque converterent? Sed
si eadem hora aliae pecudis iecur nitidum atque
plenum est, aliae horridum et exile, quid est, quod
declarari possit habitu extorum et colore?

31 " An hoc eiusdem modi est, quale Pherecydeum
illud quod est a te dictum? qui cum aquam ex
puteo vidisset haustam, terrae motum dixit futurum.
Parum, credo, impudenter, quod, cum factus est
motus, dicere audent, quae vis id effecerit; etiamne
futurum esse aquae iugis colore praesentiunt?
Multa istius modi dicuntur in scholis, sed credere
32 omnia vide ne non sit necesse. Verum sint sane ista
Democritea vera; quando ea nos extis exquirimus?
aut quando aliquid eius modi ab haruspice inspectis
extis audivimus? Ab aqua aut ab igni pericula
monent; tum hereditates, tum damna denuntiant;
fissum familiare et vitale tractant; caput iecoris ex
omni parte diligentissime considerant; si vero id
non est inventum, nihil putant accidere potuisse
tristius.

33 XIV. " Haec observari certe non potuerunt, ut
supra docui. Sunt igitur artis inventa, non vetustatis,
si est ars ulla rerum incognitarum. Cum rerum
autem natura quam cognationem habent? quae ut

---

[1] *Cf.* i. 50. 112.

changed to the same colour and condition at the same time ? But if at the same instant the liver of one ox is smooth and full and that of another is rough and shrunken, what inference can be drawn from ' the condition and colour of the entrails ' ?

" Equally amusing is your story about Pherecydes, who, after looking at some water just drawn from a well, foretold an earthquake.[1] It would be presumptuous enough, I think, for natural philosophers to attempt to explain the cause of an earthquake after it had happened; but can they actually tell, from looking at fresh water, that an earthquake is going to happen ? Such nonsense is often heard in the schools, but one does not have to believe everything one hears. But grant that these absurdities of Democritus are true — when do we ever consult entrails to learn about crops or health, or when have we acquired information on these particulars from a soothsayer after he had made an inspection of entrails ? The soothsayers warn us of dangers by fire and flood and sometimes they prophesy the inheritance, sometimes the loss, of money ; they discuss the favourable and the unfavourable cleft ; they view the head of the liver with the utmost care from every side. If, perchance, the liver's head should be wanting they regard it as the most unpropitious sign that could have happened.

XIV. " Such signs, as I have shown before, certainly could not come within your classification of the kinds of divination ' dependent on observation.' Therefore they are not the result of immemorial usage, but they are the inventions of art— if there can be any art in the occult. But what relationship have they with the laws of nature ?

uno consensu iuncta sit et continens, quod video
placuisse physicis, eisque maxime, qui omne quod
esset, unum esse dixerunt, quid habere mundus
potest cum thesauri inventione coniunctum ? Si
enim extis pecuniae mihi amplificatio ostenditur
idque fit natura, primum exta sunt coniuncta mundo,
deinde meum lucrum natura rerum continetur.
Nonne pudet physicos haec dicere ? Ut enim iam
sit aliqua in natura rerum cognatio, quam esse
concedo. Multa enim Stoici colligunt. Nam et
musculorum iecuscula bruma dicuntur augeri, et
puleium aridum florescere brumali ipso die, et
inflatas rumpi vesiculas, et semina [malorum], quae
in eis mediis inclusa sint, in contrarias partis se
vertere ; iam nervos in fidibus aliis pulsis resonare
alios ; ostreisque et conchyliis omnibus contingere,
ut cum luna pariter crescant pariterque decrescant ;
arboresque ut hiemali tempore cum luna simul
senescente, quia tum exsiccatae sint, tempestive
caedi putentur.

34 " Quid de fretis aut de marinis aestibus plura
dicam ? quorum accessus et recessus lunae motu
gubernantur. Sescenta licet eiusdem modi proferri,
ut distantium rerum cognatio naturalis appareat.

---

[1] Cicero has in mind, among others, Xenophanes of
Colophon. *Cf.* Cic. *Acad.* ii. 37. 118.
[2] See valuable discussion by Pease in his *De div.* ii. 33, 34.

Assuming that all the works of nature are firmly bound together in a harmonious whole (which, I observe, is the view of the natural philosophers and especially of those men[1] who maintain that the universe is a unit), what connexion can there be between the universe and the finding of a treasure? For instance, if the entrails foretell an increase in my fortune and they do so in accordance with some law of nature, then, in the first place, there is some relationship between them and the universe, and in the second place, my financial gain is regulated by the laws of nature. Are not the natural philosophers ashamed to utter such nonsense? And yet a certain contact between the different parts of nature may be admitted and I concede it. The Stoics have collected much evidence to prove it. They claim, for example, that the livers of mice become larger in winter; that the dry pennyroyal[2] blooms the very day of the winter solstice, and that its seed-pods become inflated and burst and the seeds enclosed therein are sent in various directions; that at times when certain strings of the lyre are struck others sound; that it is the habit of oysters and of all shell-fish to grow with the growth of the moon and to become smaller as it wanes; and that trees are considered easiest to cut down in winter and in the dark of the moon, because they are then free from sap.

"There is no need to go on and mention the seas and straits with their tides, whose ebb and flow are governed by the motion of the moon. Innumerable instances of the same kind may be given to prove that some natural connexion does exist between objects apparently unrelated. Concede

Demus hoc ; nihil enim huic disputationi adversatur ;
num etiam, si fissum cuiusdam modi fuerit in iecore,
lucrum ostenditur ? qua ex coniunctione naturae et
quasi concentu atque consensu, quam συμπάθειαν
Graeci appellant, convenire potest aut fissum iecoris
cum lucello meo aut meus quaesticulus cum caelo,
terra rerumque natura ?

XV. " Concedam hoc ipsum, si vis, etsi magnam
iacturam causae fecero, si ullam esse convenientiam
35 naturae cum extis concessero ; sed tamen eo concesso
qui evenit, ut is, qui impetrire velit, convenientem
hostiam rebus suis immolet ? Hoc erat, quod ego
non rebar posse dissolvi. At quam festive dissolvitur !
Pudet me non tui quidem, cuius etiam memoriam
admiror, sed Chrysippi, Antipatri, Posidonii, qui
idem istuc quidem dicunt, quod est dictum a te, ad
hostiam deligendam ducem esse vim quandam
sentientem atque divinam, quae toto confusa
mundo sit.

" Illud vero multo etiam melius, quod et a te
usurpatum est et dicitur ab illis : cum immolare
quispiam velit, tum fieri extorum mutationem, ut
aut absit aliquid aut supersit ; deorum enim numini
36 parere omnia. Hoc iam, mihi crede, ne aniculae
quidem existimant. An censes eundem vitulum, si
alius delegerit, sine capite iecur inventurum ; si
alius, cum capite ? Haec decessio capitis aut accessio

that it does exist; it does not contravene the point I make, that no sort of a cleft in a liver is prophetic of financial gain. What natural tie, or what 'symphony,' so to speak, or association, or what 'sympathy,' as the Greeks term it, can there be between a cleft in a liver and a petty addition to my purse? Or what relationship between my miserable money-getting, on the one hand, and heaven, earth, and the laws of nature on the other?

XV. "However, I will concede even this if you wish, though it will greatly weaken my case to admit that there is any connexion between nature and the condition of the entrails; yet, suppose the concession made, how is it brought about that the man in search of favourable signs will find a sacrifice suited to his purpose? I thought the question insoluble. But what a fine solution is offered! I am not ashamed of you—I am actually astonished at your memory; but I am ashamed of Chrysippus, Antipater, and Posidonius who say exactly what you said: 'The choice of the sacrificial victim is directed by the sentient and divine power which pervades the entire universe.'

"But even more absurd is that other pronouncement of theirs which you adopted: 'At the moment of sacrifice a change in the entrails takes place; something is added or something taken away; for all things are obedient to the Divine Will.' Upon my word, no old woman is credulous enough now to believe such stuff! Do you believe that the same bullock, if chosen by one man, will have a liver without a head, and if chosen by another will have a liver with a head? And is it possible that this sudden going or coming of the liver's head occurs

subitone fieri potest, ut se exta ad immolatoris
fortunam accommodent? Non perspicitis aleam
quandam esse in hostiis deligendis, praesertim cum
res ipsa doceat? Cum enim [tristissima] exta sine
capite fuerint, quibus nihil videtur esse dirius,
proxima hostia litatur saepe pulcherrime. Ubi
igitur illae minae superiorum extorum? aut quae
tam subito facta est deorum tanta placatio?

XVI. " Sed affers in tauri opimi extis immolante
Caesare cor non fuisse; id quia non potuerit accidere
ut sine corde victima illa viveret, iudicandum esse
37 tum interisse cor cum immolaretur. Qui fit, ut
alterum intellegas, sine corde non potuisse bovem
vivere, alterum non videas, cor subito non potuisse
nescio quo avolare? Ego enim possum vel nescire,
quae vis sit cordis ad vivendum, vel suspicari contac-
tum aliquo morbo bovis exile et exiguum et vietum
cor et dissimile cordis fuisse. Tu vero quid habes,
quare putes, si paulo ante cor fuerit in tauro opimo,
subito id in ipsa immolatione interisse? An quod
aspexit vestitu purpureo excordem Caesarem, ipse
corde privatus est?

" Urbem philosophiae, mihi crede, proditis, dum
castella defenditis; nam, dum haruspicinam veram

---

[1] *Cf.* i. 52. 119.
[2] Cicero plays on the common use of *cor* as = intelligence;
cf. Caesar's remark on a like occasion (Suet. *Iul. Caesar*
77) that it was no prodigy *si pecudi cor defuisset,* " if a
brute wanted wits."

so that the entrails may adapt themselves to the situation of the person who offers the sacrifice? Do you Stoics fail to see in choosing the victim it is almost like a throw of the dice, especially as facts prove it? For when the entrails of the first victim have been without a head, which is the most fatal of all signs, it often happens that the sacrifice of the next victim is altogether favourable. Pray what became of the warnings of the first set of entrails? And how was the favour of the gods so completely and so suddenly gained?

XVI. " But, you say, ' Once, when Caesar was offering a sacrifice, there was no heart in the entrails of the sacrificial bull;[1] and, since it would have been impossible for the victim to live without a heart, the heart must have disappeared at the moment of immolation.' How does it happen that you understand the one fact, that the bull could not have lived without a heart and do not realize the other, that the heart could not suddenly have vanished I know not where? As for me, possibly I do not know what vital function the heart performs; if I do I suspect that the bull's heart, as the result of a disease, became much wasted and shrunken and lost its resemblance to a heart. But, assuming that only a little while before the heart was in the sacrificial bull, why do you think it suddenly disappeared at the very moment of immolation? Don't you think, rather, that the bull lost his heart when he saw that Caesar in his purple robe had lost his head?[2]

" Upon my word you Stoics surrender the very city of philosophy while defending its outworks! For, by your insistence on the truth of soothsaying,

esse vultis, physiologiam totam pervertitis. Caput
est in iecore, cor in extis ; iam abscedet, simul ac
molam et vinum insperseris ; deus id eripiet, vis
aliqua conficiet aut exedet! Non ergo omnium ortus
atque obitus natura conficiet, et erit aliquid, quod
aut ex nihilo oriatur aut in nihilum subito occidat.
Quis hoc physicus dixit umquam ? 'Haruspices dicunt.' His igitur quam physicis credendum potius
existumas ?

38   XVII. " Quid ? cum pluribus deis immolatur, qui
tandem evenit, ut litetur aliis, aliis non litetur ? quae
autem inconstantia deorum est, ut primis minentur
extis, bene promittant secundis ? aut tanta inter eos
dissensio, saepe etiam inter proximos, ut Apollinis
exta bona sint, Dianae non bona ? Quid est tam
perspicuum quam, cum fortuito hostiae adducantur,
talia cuique exta esse, qualis cuique obtigerit hostia ?
'At enim id ipsum habet aliquid divini, quae cuique
hostia obtingat, tamquam in sortibus, quae cui
ducatur.' Mox de sortibus ; quamquam tu quidem
non hostiarum causam confirmas sortium similitudine,
39 sed infirmas sortis collatione hostiarum. An, cum

you utterly overthrow physiology. There is a head
to the liver and a heart in the entrails, presto! they
will vanish the very second you have sprinkled
them with meal and wine! Aye, some god will
snatch them away! Some invisible power will
destroy them or eat them up! Then the creation
and destruction of all things are not due to nature,
and there are some things which spring from nothing
or suddenly become nothing. Was any such statement ever made by any natural philosopher? 'It
is made,' you say, 'by soothsayers.' Then do you
think that soothsayers are worthier of belief than
natural philosophers?

XVII. "Again, when sacrifices are offered to
more than one god at the same time, how does it
happen that the auspices are favourable in one case
and unfavourable in another? Is it not strange
fickleness in the gods to threaten disaster in the
first set of entrails and to promise a blessing in the
next? Or is there such discord among the gods—
often even among those who are nearest of kin—
that the entrails of the sacrifice you offer to Apollo,
for example, are favourable and of those you offer
at the same time to Diana are unfavourable? When
victims for the sacrifice are brought up at haphazard
it is perfectly clear that the character of entrails
that you will receive will depend on the victim
chance may bring. Oh! but someone will say,
'The choice itself is a matter of divine guidance,
just as in the case of lots the drawing is directed by
the gods!' I shall speak of lots presently; although
you really do not strengthen the cause of sacrifices
by comparing them to lots; but you do weaken
the cause of lots by comparing them with sacrifices.

in Aequimaelium misimus, qui afferat agnum, quem
immolemus, is mihi agnus affertur, qui habet exta
rebus accommodata, et ad eum agnum non casu, sed
duce deo servus deducitur ! Nam si casum in eo
quoque dicis esse quasi sortem quandam cum deorum
voluntate coniunctam, doleo tantam Stoicos nostros
Epicureis irridendi sui facultatem dedisse ; non enim
ignoras quam ista derideant.

40 " Et quidem illi facilius facere possunt ; deos enim
ipsos iocandi causa induxit Epicurus perlucidos et
perflabilis et habitantis tamquam inter duos lucos
sic inter duos mundos propter metum ruinarum,
eosque habere putat eadem membra quae nos, nec
usum ullum habere membrorum. Ergo hic circum-
itione quadam deos tollens recte non dubitat divinationem tollere ; sed non, ut hic sibi constat, item
Stoici. Illius enim deus nihil habens nec sui nec
alieni negoti non potest hominibus divinationem
impertire. Vester autem deus potest non impertire
ut nihilo minus mundum regat et hominibus consulat.

41 Cur igitur vos induitis in eas captiones, quas numquam explicetis ? Ita enim, cum magis properant,
concludere solent : ' Si di sunt, est divinatio ; sunt
autem di ; est ergo divinatio.' Multo est probabilius :
' Non est autem divinatio ; non sunt ergo di.' Vide,

---

[1] *i.e.* in the *intermundia*, μετακόσμια, where they were
safe when a world fell to pieces.

[2] The depression between the two peaks of the Capitoline
Hill was called *Asylum* or *Inter Duos Lucos*. According to
tradition it was there that Romulus established his asylum
or place of refuge for criminals. The groves were originally
on the summits. See Platner, *Topography and Monuments
of Ancient Rome*, p. 305.

When I send a slave to Aequimaelium to bring me a lamb for a sacrifice and he brings me the lamb which has entrails suited to the exigencies of my particular case, it was not chance, I suppose, but a god that led the slave to that particular lamb! If you say that in this case too chance is, as it were, a sort of lot in accordance with the divine will, then I am sorry that our Stoic friends have given the Epicureans so great an opportunity for laughter, for you know how much fun they make of statements like that.

"And they can laugh with the better grace because Epicurus, to make the gods ridiculous, represents them as transparent, with the winds blowing through them, and living between two worlds[1] (as if between our two groves[2]) from fear of the downfall. He further says that the gods have limbs just as we have, but make no use of them. Hence, while he takes a roundabout way to destroy the gods, he does not hesitate to take a short road to destroy divination. At any rate Epicurus is consistent, but the Stoics are not; for his god, who has no concern for himself or for anybody else, cannot impart divination to men. And neither can your Stoic god impart divination, although he rules the world and plans for the good of mankind. Why then do you Stoics involve yourselves in these sophistries, which you can never explain? Members of your school, when they are more hurried than usual, generally give us this syllogism: 'If there are gods, there is divination; but there are gods, therefore there is divination.' A more logical one would be this: 'There is no divination, therefore there are no gods.' Observe how rashly they

415

quam temere committant, ut, si nulla sit divinatio, nulli sint di. Divinatio enim perspicue tollitur, deos esse retinendum est.

42   XVIII. "Atque hac extispicum divinatione sublata omnis haruspicina sublata est. Ostenta enim sequuntur et fulgura. Valet autem in fulguribus observatio diuturna, in ostentis ratio plerumque coniecturaque adhibetur. Quid est igitur, quod observatum sit in fulgure? Caelum in sedecim partis diviserunt Etrusci. Facile id quidem fuit, quattuor, quas nos habemus, duplicare, post idem iterum facere, ut ex eo dicerent, fulmen qua ex parte venisset. Primum id quid interest? deinde quid significat? Nonne perspicuum est ex prima admiratione hominum, quod tonitrua iactusque fulminum extimuissent, credidisse ea efficere rerum omnium praepotentem Iovem? Itaque in nostris commentariis scriptum habemus: 'Iove tonante, fulgurante comitia populi habere
43 nefas.' Hoc fortasse rei publicae causa constitutum est; comitiorum enim non habendorum causas esse voluerunt. Itaque comitiorum solum vitium est fulmen, quod idem omnibus rebus optimum auspicium habemus, si sinistrum fuit. Sed de auspiciis alio loco, nunc de fulguribus.

XIX. "Quid igitur minus a physicis dici debet

commit themselves to the proposition, ' if there is no divination, there are no gods.' I say ' rashly,' for it is evident that divination has been destroyed and yet we must hold on to the gods.

XVIII. " In demolishing divination by means of entrails we have utterly demolished the soothsayer's art ; for the same fate awaits divination by means of lightnings and portents. According to your view, long-continued observation is employed in the case of lightnings, and reason and conjecture are generally employed in the case of portents. But what is it that has been observed in the case of lightnings ? The Etruscans divided the sky into sixteen parts. Of course it was easy enough for them to double the four parts into which we divide it and then double that total and tell from which one of those divisions a bolt of lightning had come. In the first place, what difference does its location make ? and, in the second place, what does it foretell ? It is perfectly evident that, out of the wonder and fear excited in primitive man by lightning and thunderbolts, sprang his belief that those phenomena were caused by omnipotent Jove. And so we find it recorded in our augural annals : ' When Jove thunders or lightens it is impious to hold an election.' This was ordained, perhaps, from reasons of political expediency ; for our ancestors wished to have some excuse for not holding elections sometimes. And so lightning is an unfavourable sign only in case of an election ; in all other cases we consider it the best of auspices, if it appears on the left side. But I shall speak of auspices in another connexion— now I am going to discuss lightnings.

XIX. " There is, then, no statement less worthy

quam quicquam certi significari rebus incertis ? Non
enim te puto esse eum, qui Iovi fulmen fabricatos
44 esse Cyclopas in Aetna putes ; nam esset mirabile,
quo modo id Iuppiter toties iaceret, cum unum
haberet ; nec vero fulminibus homines quid aut
faciendum esset aut cavendum moneret. Placet enim
Stoicis eos anhelitus terrae, qui frigidi sint, cum fluere
coeperint, ventos esse ; cum autem se in nubem
induerint eiusque tenuissimam quamque partem
coeperint dividere atque dirrumpere idque crebrius
facere et vehementius, tum et fulgores et tonitrua
existere ; si autem nubium conflictu ardor expressus
se emiserit, id esse fulmen. Quod igitur vi naturae,
nulla constantia, nullo rato tempore videmus effici,
ex eo significationem rerum consequentium quaerimus ? Scilicet, si ista Iuppiter significaret, tam
45 multa frustra fulmina emitteret ! Quid enim proficit,
cum in medium mare fulmen iecit ? quid, cum in
altissimos montis, quod plerumque fit ? quid, cum in
desertas solitudines ? quid, cum in earum gentium
oras, in quibus haec ne observantur quidem ?

XX. " At 'inventum est caput in Tiberi.' Quasi
ego artem aliquam istorum esse negem! divinationem
nego. Caeli enim distributio, quam antę dixi, et
certarum rerum notatio docet, unde fulmen venerit,

---

[1] *Cf.* i. 10. 16.
[2] *Cf.* ii. 18. 42.

of a natural philosopher than that anything can be
foretold with a certainty by uncertain signs. Of
course I do not think you are credulous enough to
believe that Jove's thunderbolt was made on Mount
Aetna by the Cyclopes. For if he had but one bolt
his hurling it so often would be strange Nor would
he be able to give men so many advices by thunderbolts as to what they should or should not do. But
the Stoics account for the thunderbolt thus : ' When
the cold exhalations from the earth begin to circu-
late they become winds ; when these winds enter a
cloud they begin to break-up and scatter its thinnest
portions ; if they do this very rapidly and with great
violence, thunder and lightning are thereby produced.
Again, when clouds collide their heat is forcibly
driven out and the thunderbolt is the result.' Realizing, then, that these phenomena are due to natural
causes, and happen without regularity and at no
certain time, shall we look to them for signs of future
events ? It is passing strange, if Jupiter warns us
by means of thunderbolts, that he sends so many
to no purpose ! What, for example, is his object
in hurling them into the middle of the sea ? or, as
he so often does, on to the tops of lofty mountains ?
Why, pray, does he waste them in solitary deserts ?
And why does he fling them on the shores of peoples
who do not take any notice of them?

XX. " Oh ! but you say, ' the head was found in
the Tiber.'[1] As if I contended that your soothsayers were devoid of art ! My contention is that
there is no divination. By dividing the heavens in
the manner already indicated [2] and by noting what
happened in each division the soothsayers learn
whence the thunderbolt comes and whither it goes,

quo concesserit ; quid significet autem, nulla ratio
docet. Sed urges me meis versibus :

> nam pater altitonans stellanti nixus Olympo
> ipse suos quondam tumulos ac templa petivit
> et Capitolinis iniecit sedibus ignis.

'Tum statua Nattae, tum simulacra deorum Romu-
lusque et Remus cum altrice belua vi fulminis icti
conciderunt, deque his rebus haruspicum extiterunt
46 responsa verissima.' Mirabile autem illud, quod eo
ipso tempore, quo fieret indicium coniurationis in
senatu, signum Iovis biennio post, quam erat
locatum, in Capitolio collocabatur.

"'Tu igitur animum induces (sic enim mecum
agebas) 'causam istam et contra facta tua et contra
scripta defendere?' Frater es ; eo vereor. Verum
quid tibi hic tandem nocet? resne, quae talis est,
an ego, qui verum explicari volo? Itaque nihil
contra dico, a te rationem totius haruspicinae peto.
Sed te mirificam in latebram coniecisti ; quod enim
intellegeres fore ut premerere, cum ex te causas
unius cuiusque divinationis exquirerem, multa verba

---

[1] Orelli interprets thus : *eo vereor dicere, te vel desipere,
vel iniquius mecum agere ; id quod v.c. Epicureo alicui
exprobrarem apertius.* Moser with a few MSS. reads *non
vereor* and explains, *eo non vereor, sc. fateri, quod sentio ;
quamquam alibi aliter locutus sum, nimirum publice, et rei
pub. causa.*

but no method can show that the thunderbolt has
any prophetic value. However, you array those
verses of mine against me :

For high-thundering Jove, as he stood on starry Olympus,
Hurtled his blows at the temples and monuments raised
    in his honour,
And on the Capitol's site unloosed the bolts of his light-
    ning.

' Then,' the poem goes on to say, ' the statue of
Natta, the images of the gods and the piece representing Romulus and Remus, with their wolf-nurse,
were struck by a thunderbolt and fell to the ground.
The prophecies made by the soothsayers from these
events were fulfilled to the letter.' Besides, you
quote me as authority for the remarkable fact that,
at the very time when proof of the conspiracy was
being presented to the Senate, the statue of Jupiter,
which had been contracted for two years before, was
being erected on the Capitol.

" ' Will you then '—for thus you pleaded with
me—' will you then persuade yourself to take sides
against me in this discussion, in the face of your
own writings and of your own practice ? ' You are
my brother and on that account I shrink from recri-
mination.[1] But what, pray, is causing you distress
in this matter ? Is it the nature of the subject ?
Or is it my insistence on finding out the truth ?
And so I waive your charge of my inconsistency—
I am asking *you* for an explanation of the entire
subject of soothsaying. But you betook yourself to
a strange place of refuge. You knew that you
would be in straits when I asked your reason for
each kind of divination, and, hence, you had much

fecisti te, cum res videres, rationem causamque non
quaerere ; quid fieret, non cur fieret, ad rem pertinere. Quasi ego aut fieri concederem aut esset
philosophi causam cur quidque fieret, non quaerere !
47 Et eo quidem loco et *Prognostica* nostra pronuntiabas
et genera herbarum, scammoniam aristolochiamque
radicem, quarum causam ignorares, vim et effectum
videres.

XXI. " Dissimile totum ; nam et prognosticorum
causas persecuti sunt et Boëthus Stoicus, qui est a
te nominatus, et noster etiam Posidonius, et, si causae
non reperiantur istarum rerum, res tamen ipsae
observari animadvertique possunt. Nattae vero
statua aut aera legum de caelo tacta quid habent
observatum ac vetustum ? 'Pinarii Nattae nobiles ; a
nobilitate igitur periculum.' Hoc tam callide Iuppiter
cogitavit ! ' Romulus lactens fulmine ictus ; urbi
igitur periculum ostenditur, ei quam ille condidit.'
Quam scite per notas nos certiores facit Iuppiter !
' At eodem tempore signum Iovis collocabatur, quo
coniuratio indicabatur.' Et tu scilicet mavis numine
deorum id factum quam casu arbitrari, et redemptor,
qui columnam illam de Cotta et de Torquato con-

---

[1] *Cf.* i. 8. 13.
[2] *Cf.* i. 10. 16.
[3] *Cf.* i. 12. 19.
[4] The Pinarian gens was one of the most ancient patrician
families at Rome.
[5] i. 12. 21.

to say to this effect : ' Since I see what divination does I do not ask the reason or the cause why it does it. The question is, what does it do ? not, why does it do it ? ' As if I would grant either that divination accomplished anything, or that it was permissible for a philosopher not to ask why anything happened ! It was in that same connexion that you brought forth my *Prognostics*[1] and some samples of herbs—the scammony and aristolochia[2] root—saying that you could see their virtue and effect but did not know the cause.

XXI. " But your illustrations are not pertinent at all. For example, the causes of meteorological phenomena have been investigated by Boëthus[1] the Stoic, whom you mentioned, and by our friend Posidonius ; and even if the causes are not discovered by them, yet the phenomena themselves are capable of observation and study. But what opportunity was there for long-continued observation in the case where Natta's statue and the brazen tablets of laws were struck by lightning ?[3] ' The Nattas,' you say, ' were of the Pinarian gens[4] and of noble birth, therefore danger was to be expected from the nobility.' So clever of Jupiter to devise such a means to warn us of danger ! ' The statue of the infant Romulus,' you observe, ' was struck by a thunderbolt ; hence danger was thereby predicted to the city which he founded.' How wise of Jupiter to use signs in conveying information to us ! Again, you say, ' Jupiter's statue was being set up at the very time the conspiracy was being exposed.'[5] You, of course, prefer to attribute this coincidence to a divine decree rather than to chance. The man to whom Cotta and Torquatus let the contract for the

duxerat faciendam, non inertia aut inopia tardior
fuit, sed a deis immortalibus ad istam horam reserva-
tus est!

48 " Non equidem plane despero ista esse vera, sed
nescio et discere a te volo. Nam cum mihi quaedam
casu viderentur sic evenire, ut praedicta essent a
divinantibus, dixisti multa de casu ; ut ' Venerium
iaci posse casu quattuor talis iactis, sed quadringentis
centum Venerios non posse casu consistere.' Primum
nescio cur non possint, sed non pugno ; abundas
enim similibus. Habes et respersionem pigmentorum
et rostrum suis et alia permulta. Item Carneadem
fingere dicis de capite Panisci ; quasi non potuerit
id evenire casu et non in omni marmore necesse sit
inesse vel Praxitelia capita ! Illa enim ipsa efficiuntur
detractione, necque quicquam illuc affertur a Praxi-
tele; sed cum multa sunt detracta et ad lineamenta
oris perventum est, tum intellegas illud quod iam ex-
49 politum sit intus fuisse. Potest igitur tale aliquid
etiam sua sponte in lapicidinis Chiorum extitisse. Sed
sit hoc fictum. Quid ? in nubibus numquam

---

[1] i. 13. 23.

statue did not, I presume, delay the completion of
his work either from lack of energy or from lack
of funds, but his hand was stayed till the appointed
hour by the immortal gods !

" I am not a hopeless sceptic on the subject of
such warnings really being sent by the gods ; however, I do not know that they are and I want to
learn the actual facts from you. Again, when
certain other events occurred as they had been
foretold by diviners and I attributed the coincidence
to chance, you talked a long time about chance.
You said, for example, ' For the Venus-throw to
result from one cast of the four dice might be due
to chance ; but if a hundred Venus-throws resulted
from one hundred casts this could not be due to
chance.'[1]   In the first place I do not know why it
could not ; but I do not contest the point, for you
are full of the same sort of examples—like that
about the scattering of the paints and that one
about the hog's snout,[1] and you had very many
other examples besides. You also mentioned that
myth from Carneades about the head of Pan[1]—as if
the likeness could not have been the result of chance !
and as if every block of marble did not necessarily
have within it heads worthy of Praxiteles ! For his
masterpieces were made by chipping away the
marble, not by adding anything to it ; and when,
after much chipping, the lineaments of a face were
reached, one then realized that the work now
polished and complete had always been inside the
block. Therefore, it is possible that some such
figure as Carneades described did spontaneously
appear in the Chian quarries. On the other hand,
the story may be untrue. Again, you have often

animadvertisti leonis formam aut hippocentauri ¡
Potest igitur, quod modo negabas, veritatem casus
imitari.

XXII. " Sed quoniam de extis et de fulgoribus
satis est disputatum, ostenta restant, ut tota
haruspicina sit pertractata. Mulae partus prolatus
est a te. Res mirabilis, propterea quia non saepe
fit ; sed si fieri non potuisset, facta non esset. Atque
hoc contra omnia ostenta valeat numquam, quod
fieri non potuerit, esse factum ; sin potuerit non esse
mirandum. Causarum enim ignoratio in re nova
mirationem facit ; eadem ignoratio si in rebus usitatis
est, non miramur. Nam qui mulam peperisse miratur,
is, quo modo equa pariat, aut omnino quae natura
partum animantis faciat, ignorat. Sed quod crebro
videt, non miratur, etiamsi cur fiat nescit ; quod ante
non vidit, id si evenit, ostentum esse censet. Utrum
igitur, cum concepit mula, an cum peperit, ostentum
50 est ? Conceptio contra naturam fortasse, sed partus
prope necessarius.

XXIII. " Sed quid plura ? ortum videamus haruspicinae ; sic facillime quid habeat auctoritatis
iudicabimus. Tages quidam dicitur in agro Tar-
quiniensi, cum terra araretur et sulcus altius esset
impressus, extitisse repente et eum affatus esse, qui
arabat. Is autem Tages, ut in libris est Etruscorum,

---

[1] *Cf.* i. 13. 23 *ad fin.*
[2] *Cf.* i. 18. 36.

noticed clouds take the form of a lion or a hippo-
centaur. Therefore it is possible for chance to
imitate reality, and this you just now denied.[1]

XXII. " But since entrails and lightnings have
been sufficiently discussed it remains for us to
examine portents, if we are to treat soothsaying in
its entirety. You spoke of a mule bearing a colt.[2]
Such an event excites wonder because it seldom
occurs ; but if it had been impossible it would not
have occurred. And it may be urged with effect
against all portents that the impossible never has
happened and that the possible need not excite any
wonder. Now, in case of some new occurrence,
ignorance of its cause is what excites our wonder ;
whereas, the same ignorance as to things of frequent
occurrence does not. For the man who marvels that
a mule has foaled does not understand how a mare
foals and is ignorant of animal parturition in general.
What he sees frequently causes him no astonishment
even though he does not know how it happened. If
something happens which he never saw before he
considers it a portent. Then, which is the portent—
the mule's conception or its parturition ? The conception, it may be, is contrary to the usual course
of nature, but the parturition follows as a necessary
sequel of conception.

XXIII. " It seems useless to say more about
soothsaying. However, let us examine its origin
and thus we shall very readily determine its value.
The tradition is that, once upon a time, in the district
of Tarquinii, while a field was being ploughed, the
ploughshare went deeper than usual and a certain
Tages suddenly sprang forth and spoke to the
ploughman. Now this Tages, according to the

puerili specie dicitur visus, sed senili fuisse prudentia.
Eius aspectu cum obstupuisset bubulcus clamorem-
que maiorem cum admiratione edidisset, concursum
esse factum, totamque brevi tempore in eum locum
Etruriam convenisse ; tum illum plura locutum
multis audientibus, qui omnia verba eius exceperint
litterisque mandarint ; omnem autem orationem
fuisse eam, qua haruspicinae disciplina contineretur ;
eam postea crevisse rebus novis cognoscendis et ad
eadem illa principia referendis.

51 " Haec accepimus ab ipsis, haec scripta conservant,
hunc fontem habent disciplinae. Num ergo opus est
ad haec refellenda Carneade ? Num Epicuro ? Estne
quisquam ita desipiens, qui credat exaratum esse—
deum dicam an hominem ? Si deus, cur se contra
naturam in terram abdiderat, ut patefactus aratro
lucem aspiceret ? Quid ? Idem nonne poterat deus
hominibus disciplinam superiore e loco tradere ? Si
autem homo ille Tages fuit, quonam modo potuit
terra oppressus vivere ? Unde porro illa potuit, quae
docebat alios, ipse didicisse ? Sed ego insipientior
quam illi ipsi, qui ista credunt, qui quidem contra
eos tam diu disputem.

XXIV. " Vetus autem illud Catonis admodum
scitum est, qui mirari se aiebat quod non rideret
52 haruspex haruspicem cum vidisset. Quota enim quaque res evenit praedicta ab istis ? Aut, si evenit quip-

---

[1] *Cf.* Ovid, *Met.* xv. 553.

Etruscan annals, is said to have had the appearance
of a boy, but the wisdom of a seer. Astounded and
much frightened at the sight, the rustic raised a
great cry ; a crowd gathered and, indeed, in a short
time, the whole of Etruria assembled at the spot.
Tages[1] then spoke at length to his numerous hearers,
who received with eagerness all that he had to say,
and committed it to writing. His whole address
was devoted to an exposition of the science of soothsaying. Later, as new facts were learned and tested
by reference to the principles imparted by Tages,
they were added to the original fund of knowledge.

" This is the story as we get it from the Etruscans
themselves and as their records preserve it, and
this, in their own opinion, is the origin of their art.
Now do we need a Carneades or an Epicurus to
refute such nonsense ? Who in the world is stupid
enough to believe that anybody ever ploughed up
—which shall I say—a god or a man ? If a god,
why did he, contrary to his nature, hide himself in
the ground to be uncovered and brought to the
light of day by a plough ? Could not this so-called
god have delivered this art to mankind from a more
exalted station ? But if this fellow Tages was a
man, pray, how could he have lived covered with
earth ? Finally, where had he himself learned the
things he taught others ? But really in spending
so much time in refuting such stuff I am more absurd
than the very people who believe it.

XXIV. " But indeed, that was quite a clever
remark which Cato made many years ago : ' I
wonder,' said he, ' that a soothsayer doesn't laugh
when he sees another soothsayer.' For how many
things predicted by them really come true ? If any

piam, quid afferri potest, cur non casu id evenerit?
Rex Prusias, cum Hannibali apud eum exsulanti
depugnari placeret, negabat se audere, quod exta
prohiberent. 'An tu,' inquit, ' carunculae vitulinae
mavis quam imperatori veteri credere?' Quid?
Ipse Caesar cum a summo haruspice moneretur,
ne in Africam ante brumam transmitteret, nonne
transmisit? quod ni fecisset, uno in loco omnes
adversariorum copiae convenissent. Quid ego haruspicum responsa commemorem (possum equidem
innumerabilia) quae aut nullos habuerint exitus aut
53 contrarios? Hoc civili bello, di immortales! quam
multa luserunt! Quae nobis in Graeciam Roma
responsa haruspicum missa sunt! Quae dicta
Pompeio! etenim ille admodum extis et ostentis
movebatur. Non lubet commemorare, nec vero
necesse est, tibi praesertim qui interfuisti; vides
tamen omnia fere contra ac dicta sint evenisse. Sed
haec hactenus; nunc ad ostenta veniamus.

54 XXV. "Multa me consule a me ipso scripta
recitasti, multa ante Marsicum bellum a Sisenna
collecta attulisti, multa ante Lacedaemoniorum
malam pugnam in Leuctricis a Callisthene com-

---

do come true, then what reason can be advanced why the agreement of the event with the prophecy was not due to chance? While Hannibal was in exile at the court of King Prusias he advised the king to go to war, but the king replied, ' I do not dare, because the entrails forbid.' ' And do you,' said Hannibal, ' put more reliance in pieces of ox-meat than you do in a veteran commander ? ' Again, when Caesar himself was warned by a most eminent soothsayer not to cross over to Africa before the winter solstice, did he not cross ? If he had not done so all the forces opposed to him would have effected a junction. Why need I give instances—and, in fact, I could give countless ones—where the prophecies of soothsayers either were without result or the issue was directly the reverse of the prophecy ? Ye gods, how many times they were mistaken in the late civil war! What oracular messages the soothsayers sent from Rome to our Pompeian party then in Greece ! What assurances they gave to Pompey ! For he placed great reliance in divination by means of entrails and portents. I have no wish to call these instances to mind, and indeed it is unnecessary —especially to you, since you had personal knowledge of them. Still, you are aware that the result was nearly always contrary to the prophecy. But enough on this point : let us now come to portents.

XXV. " You have cited many instances of portents from the verses which I wrote during my consulship[1]; you adduced many others which occurred prior to the Marsian War[2] and which are included in Sisenna's compilation, and you mentioned a great number which are recorded by Callisthenes and which preceded the unfortunate battle of the

memorata dixisti ; de quibus dicam equidem singulis,
quoad videbitur, sed dicendum etiam est de universis.
Quae est enim ista a deis profecta significatio et
quasi denuntiatio calamitatum ? Quid autem volunt
di immortales primum ea significantes, quae sine
interpretibus non possimus intellegere, deinde ea,
quae cavere nequeamus ? At hoc ne homines quidem
probi faciunt, ut amicis impendentis calamitates
praedicant quas illi effugere nullo modo possint ; ut
medici, quamquam intellegunt saepe, tamen numquam aegris dicunt illo morbo eos esse morituros ;
omnis enim praedictio mali tum probatur, cum ad
55 praedictionem cautio adiungitur. Quid igitur aut
ostenta aut eorum interpretes vel Lacedaemonios
olim vel nuper nostros adiuverunt ? Quae si signa
deorum putanda sunt, cur tam obscura fuerunt ? si
enim, ut intellegeremus quid esset eventurum, aperte
declarari oportebat, aut ne occulte quidem, si ea
sciri nolebant.

XXVI. " Iam vero coniectura omnis, in qua
nititur divinatio, ingeniis hominum in multas aut
diversas aut etiam contrarias partis saepe deducitur.
Ut enim in causis iudicialibus alia coniectura est
accusatoris, alia defensoris et tamen utriusque
credibilis, sic in omnibus eis rebus, quae coniectura
investigari videntur, anceps reperitur oratio. Quas

---

[1] i. 34. 74.

Spartans at Leuctra.[1] I shall, of course, speak of each of these instances separately, in so far as they require notice ; but I must first discuss portents generally. Now, what is the nature of these intimations, or of this advance-information, as it were, sent out by the gods to apprise us of coming disasters ? In the first place, why do immortal gods see fit to give us warnings which we can't understand without the aid of interpreters ? In the next place, why do they warn us of things which we cannot avoid ? Why, even a mortal, if he has a proper sense of duty, does not warn his friends of imminent disasters which can in no way be escaped. Physicians, for example, although they know many times that their patients are going to die of a present disease, yet never tell them so ; for a forewarning of an evil is justified only when to the warning is joined a means of escape. How, then, did portents or their interpreters help the Spartans of long ago, or our Pompeian friends in more recent times ? If these signs you speak of are to be considered as sent by the gods, why were they so obscure ? For, if we had the right to know what was going to happen, it should have been stated to us clearly : or, if the gods did not wish us to know, they should not have told us—even in riddles.

XXVI. " Now every sort of conjecture—and divination depends on conjecture—is often applied by the wit of man to many different and even contradictory uses. As in judicial causes the prosecutor draws one inference and the lawyer for the defendant another from the same set of facts, and yet the inferences of both are plausible ; so, in all investigations in which it is customary to employ conjecture, ambiguity is found. Moreover, in the case of things

autem res tum natura, tum casus affert (non numquam etiam errorem creat similitudo), magna stultitia
est earum rerum deos facere effectores, causas rerum
non quaerere.

56 "Tu vates Boeotios credis Lebadiae vidisse ex
gallorum gallinaceorum cantu victoriam esse Thebanorum, quia galli victi silere solerent, canere victores.
Hoc igitur per gallinas Iuppiter tantae civitati
signum dabat? An illae aves, nisi cum vicerunt,
canere non solent? At tum canebant nec vicerant.
Id enim est, inquies, ostentum. Magnum vero!
quasi pisces, non galli cecinerint! Quod autem est
tempus, quo illi non cantent, vel nocturnum vel
diurnum? Quodsi victores alacritate et quasi
laetitia ad canendum excitantur, potuit accidisse
alia quoque laetitia, qua ad cantum moverentur.

57 Democritus quidem optimis verbis causam explicat
cur ante lucem galli canant; depulso enim de
pectore et in omne corpus diviso et mitificato cibo
cantus edere quiete satiatos; qui quidem ' silentio
noctis,' ut ait Ennius,

> favent faucíbus russis
> cantú plausuque premúnt alas.

Cum igitur hoc animal tam sit canorum sua sponte,
quid in mentem venit Callistheni dicere deos gallis

---

[1] i. 34. 74.

that happen now by chance now in the usual course of nature (sometimes too mistakes are caused by taking appearance for reality), it is the height of folly to hold the gods as the direct agents and not to inquire into the causes of such things.

" You believe that the Boeotian bards at Lebadia foretold victory for the Thebans from the crowing of cocks ; for cocks, you say, are wont to be silent when defeated and to crow when victorious.[1] Do you really believe that Jupiter would have employed chickens to convey such a message to so great a state ? And is it true that these fowls are not accustomed to crow except when they are victorious ? But at that time they did crow and they had not been victorious. ' Oh ! that was a " portent," ' you say. A fine portent indeed ! you talk as if a fish and not a cock had done the crowing ! But come ; is there any time, day or night, when they are not liable to crow ? And if the pleasant sensation—or ' joy ' if you will—which comes from victory causes them to crow, then, possibly, joy springing from some other source may have the same effect. By the way, Democritus gives a very good explanation of why cocks crow before day. ' Their food,' he says, ' after it has been digested, is expelled from the craw and is distributed over the entire body. By the time that process is completed they have had sleep enough and begin to crow.' And then, ' in the silence of the night,' as Ennius says, ' they indulge their russet throats in song and beat their flapping wings.' In view, then, of the fact that this creature is prone to crow of its own volition at any time, and may be made to crow either by nature or by chance, how did it ever occur to Callisthenes to say

signum dedisse cantandi, cum id vel natura vel casus
efficere potuisset ?

58   XXVII. " ' Sanguinem pluisse senatui nuntiatum
est, Atratum etiam fluvium fluxisse sanguine, deorum
sudasse simulacra.' Num censes his nuntiis Thalen
aut Anaxagoran aut quemquam physicum crediturum
fuisse ? nec enim sanguis nec sudor nisi e corpore.
Sed et decoloratio quaedam ex aliqua contagione
terrena maxime potest sanguini similis esse, et umor
adlapsus extrinsecus, ut in tectoriis videmus austro,
sudorem videtur imitari. Atque haec in bello plura
et maiora videntur timentibus, eadem non tam
animadvertuntur in pace ; accedit illud etiam, quod
in metu et periculo cum creduntur facilius, tum
59 finguntur impunius. Nos autem ita leves atque
inconsiderati sumus, ut, si mures corroserint aliquid,
quorum est opus hoc unum, monstrum putemus ?
' Ante vero Marsicum bellum quod clipeos Lanuvi,'
ut a te dictum est, ' mures rosissent, maximum id
portentum haruspices esse dixerunt.' Quasi vero
quicquam intersit, mures diem noctem aliquid
rodentes scuta an cribra corroserint ! Nam si ista
sequimur, quod Platonis *Politian* nuper apud me
mures corroserunt de re publica debui pertimescere,
aut, si Epicuri *de Voluptate* liber rosus esset, putarem
annonam in macello cariorem fore !

---

[1] *Cf.* i. 43. 98.
[2] *Cf.* i. 44. 99.
[3] Cicero habitually refers to Epicurus as an apostle of
physical gratification. Here, he playfully assumes that
the treatise *On Pleasure* had a tendency to increase the
number of gourmands : the more gourmands, whether men
or mice, the higher the price of food.

that the gods conveyed prophecies to men by the crowing of cocks ?

XXVII. " ' Reports,' you say, ' were made to the Senate that there was a shower of blood, that the river Atratus actually flowed with blood and that the statues of the gods dripped with sweat.'[1] You do not think for a moment that Thales, Anaxagoras, or any other natural philosopher would have believed such reports ? Sweat and blood you may be sure do not come except from animate bodies. An effect strikingly like blood is produced by the admixture of water with certain kinds of soil ; and the moisture which forms on the outside of objects, as we see it on our plastered walls when the south wind blows, seems to resemble sweat. Such occurrences, which in time of war appear to the timid to be most frequent and most real, are scarcely noticed in times of peace. Moreover, in periods of fear and of danger stories of portents are not only more readily believed, but they are invented with greater impunity. But are we simple and thoughtless enough to think it a portent for mice to gnaw something, when gnawing is their one business in life ? ' But,' you say, ' the fact that just before the Marsian War mice gnawed the shields at Lanuvium was pronounced by the soothsayers to be a very direful portent.'[2] As if it mattered a whit whether mice, which are gnawing something day and night, gnawed shields or sieves ! Hence, by the same token, the fact that, at my house, mice recently gnawed my Plato's *Republic* should fill me with alarm for the Roman republic ; or if they had gnawed my Epicurus *On Pleasure* I should have expected a rise in the market price of food ![3]

60 XXVIII. " An vero illa nos terrent, si quando
aliqua portentosa aut ex pecude aut ex homine nata
dicuntur ? Quorum omnium, ne sim longior, una
ratio est. Quicquid enim oritur, qualecumque est,
causam habeat a natura necesse est, ut, etiamsi
praeter consuetudinem extiterit, praeter naturam
tamen non possit existere. Causam igitur investigato
in re nova atque admirabili, si poteris ; si nullam
reperies, illud tamen exploratum habeto, nihil fieri
potuisse sine causa, eumque terrorem, quem tibi
rei novitas attulerit, naturae ratione depellito. Ita
te nec terrae fremitus, nec caeli discessus, nec
lapideus aut sanguineus imber, nec traiectio stellae,
nec faces visae terrebunt.

61 " Quorum omnium causas si a Chrysippo quaeram,
ipse ille divinationis auctor numquam illa dicet facta
fortuito naturalemque rationem omnium reddet :
' Nihil enim fieri sine causa potest ; nec quicquam fit,
quod fieri non potest ; nec, si id factum est, quod
potuit fieri, portentum debet videri ; nulla igitur
portenta sunt.' Nam si, quod raro fit, id portentum
putandum est, sapientem esse portentum est ; saepius
enim mulam peperisse arbitror quam sapientem
fuisse. Illa igitur ratio concluditur : ' Nec id, quod
non potuerit fieri, factum umquam esse, nec, quod

XXVIII. " Are we going to be frightened at these tales of portents, whether of animal or of human birth ? Not to be too verbose, all portents have one and the same explanation and it is this : whatever comes into existence, of whatever kind, must needs find its cause in nature ; and hence, even though it may be contrary to experience, it cannot be contrary to nature. Therefore, explore the cause, if you can, of every strange thing that excites your astonishment. If you do not' find the cause be assured, nevertheless, that nothing could have happened without a cause, and employ the principles of natural philosophy to banish the fear which the novelty of the apparition may have occasioned. Then no earthquake or opening of the heavens, no showers of stones or blood, no shooting stars, or comets, will fill you with alarm.

" If I were to ask Chrysippus the causes of all the phenomena just mentioned, that distinguished writer on divination would never say that they happened by chance, but he would find an explanation for each of them in the laws of nature. For he would say : ' Nothing can happen without a cause ; nothing actually happens that cannot happen ; if that has happened which could have happened, then it should not be considered a portent ; therefore there are no such things as portents.' Now if a thing is to be considered a portent because it is seldom seen, then a wise man is a portent ; for, as I think, it oftener happens that a mule brings forth a colt than that nature produces a sage. Chrysippus, in this connexion, gives the following syllogism : ' That which could not have happened never did happen ; and that which could have

potuerit, id portentum esse ; ita omnino nullum esse
62 portentum.' Quod etiam coniector quidam et interpres portentorum non inscite respondisse dicitur ei,
qui quondam ad eum retulisset quasi ostentum,
quod anguis domi vectem circumiectus fuisset : ' Tum
esset,' inquit, ' ostentum, si anguem vectis circum-
plicavisset.' Hoc ille responso satis aperte declaravit
nihil habendum esse portentum quod fieri posset.

XXIX. " ' C. Gracchus ad M. Pomponium scripsit
duobus anguibus domi comprehensis haruspices a
patre convocatos.' Qui magis anguibus quam
lacertis, quam muribus ? ' Quia sunt haec cotidiana,
angues non item.' Quasi vero referat, quod fieri
potest, quam id saepe fiat. Ego tamen miror, si
emissio feminae anguis mortem afferebat Ti. Graccho,
emissio autem maris anguis erat mortifera Corneliae,
cur alteram utram emiserit ; nihil enim scribit
respondisse haruspices, si neuter anguis emissus esset,
quid esset futurum. ' At mors insecuta Gracchum
est.' Causa quidem, credo, aliqua morbi gravioris,
non emissione serpentis ; neque enim tanta est
infelicitas haruspicum, ut ne casu quidem umquam
fiat, quod futurum illi esse dixerint !
63 XXX. " Nam illud mirarer — si crederem — quod
apud Homerum Calchantem dixisti ex passerum

---

[1] *Cf.* i. 18. 36.

happened is no portent; therefore, in any view, there is no such thing as a portent.' This is illustrated by the story of a clever response made by a certain diviner and interpreter of portents. A man referred to him for interpretation as a portent the fact that a snake was seen at his house, coiled about a beam. ' That was not a portent,' said the diviner ; ' it would have been if the beam had been wrapped around the snake.' By this answer he said plainly enough : ' Nothing that can happen is to be considered a portent.'

XXIX. " You refer to a letter, written by Gaius Gracchus to Marcus Pomponius, stating that Tiberius Gracchus, father of Gaius, caught two snakes in his house and called together the soothsayers.[1] And why a conference about snakes rather than about lizards or mice ? You answer, ' Because we see lizards and mice every day ; snakes we do not.' As if it makes any difference how often a thing happens if it can happen at all ! And yet what surprises me is this : If the release of the female snake was to be fatal to Tiberius Gracchus and that of the male was to be the death of Cornelia, why in the world did he let either snake escape ? For Gaius in his letter does not state that the soothsayers expressed any opinion as to the result if neither snake had been released. ' Be that as it may,' you reply, ' death overtook Gracchus.' That is granted, but his death was caused by some very serious illness and not by the release of the snake. Besides, soothsayers are not so unlucky that their predictions never come true—even by accident !

XXX. " I should, of course, marvel at that famous story you got out of Homer about Calchas predicting the years of the Trojan War from the number of

numero belli Troiani annos auguratum ; de cuius
coniectura sic apud Homerum, ut nos otiosi converti-
mus, loquitur Agamemnon :

ferte, viri, et duros animo tolerate labores,
auguris ut nostri Calchantis fata queamus
scire ratosne habeant an vanos pectoris orsus.
namque omnes memori portentum mente retentant,
qui non funestis liquerunt lumina fatis.
Argolicis primum ut vestita est classibus Aulis,
quae Priamo cladem et Troiae pestemque ferebant,
nos circum latices gelidos fumantibus aris,
aurigeris divom placantes numina tauris,
sub platano umbrifera, fons unde emanat aquaï,
vidimus immani specie tortuque draconem
terribilem, Iovis ut pulsu penetrabat ab ara ;
qui platani in ramo foliorum tegmine saeptos
corripuit pullos ; quos cum consumeret octo,
nona super tremulo genetrix clangore volabat ;
cui ferus immani laniavit viscera morsu.
64   hunc, ubi tam teneros volucris matremque peremit,
qui luci ediderat, genitor Saturnius idem
abdidit et duro formavit tegmina saxo.
nos autem timidi stantes mirabile monstrum
vidimus in mediis divom versarier aris.
tum Calchas haec est fidenti voce locutus :
' quidnam torpentes subito obstipuistis, Achivi ?
nobis haec portenta deum dedit ipse creator
tarda et sera nimis, sed fama ac laude perenni.
nam quot avis taetro mactatas dente videtis,
tot nos ad Troiam belli exanclabimus annos ;
quae decimo cadet et poena satiabit Achivos.'
edidit haec Calchas ; quae iam matura videtis.

---

[1] *Cf.* i. 33 72.

sparrows—if I believed it![1]   In a leisure moment I
thus translated what Agamemnon [2] in Homer says
about this prophecy :

> Be patient, men ; with fortitude endure
> Your grievous tasks till we can ascertain
> If what our Calchas prophesies be true,
> Or only idle fancies of his breast.
> For all who have not left the light of day,
> In gloomy shades to dwell, retain these signs
> Imprinted on their minds. When Aulis first
> Was decked with Grecian fleets, which carried death
> For Priam, ruin for Troy, we stood about
> The fountains cool and sought to please the gods
> With gold-crowned bulls on smoking altars laid.
> Beneath the plane-tree's shade, whence gushed a spring,
> We saw a frightful dragon, huge of size,
> With mighty folds, forth from an altar come,
> By Jove impelled. It seized some sparrows hid
> Within the plane-tree's leafy boughs and eight
> Devoured ; the ninth—the mother bird—began
> To flutter round and utter plaintive cries :
> From her the cruel beast her vitals tore.
> Now when the mother and her tender brood
> Were slain, the son of Saturn who had sent
> The dragon forth, took it away ; and then
> Did change its form into enduring stone.
> In fear we stood and watched the monster strange,
> As midst the altars of the gods it moved.
> Then Calchas, full of courage, thus did speak :
> ' Why paralysed with sudden fear, O Greeks ?
> These signs divine were sent by Jove himself.
> And though these tardy signs were long delayed,
> Their fame and glory will for ever live.
> The number of the birds ye saw destroyed
> By horrid tooth, portends how many years
> Of war we shall endure in front of Troy.
> The tenth year Troy will fall and then her fate
> Will satisfy the Greeks.' Thus Calchas spoke
> And what he prophesied ye see fulfilled.

[2] It was Ulysses, not Agamemnon ; *cf. Il.* ii. 299.

65 Quae tandem ista auguratio est ex passeribus
annorum potius quam aut mensuum aut dierum ?
Cur autem de passerculis coniecturam facit, in quibus
nullum erat monstrum, de dracone silet, qui, id quod
fieri non potuit, lapideus dicitur factus ? postremo
quid simile habet passer annis ?   Nam de angue illo
qui Sullae apparuit immolanti, utrumque memini et
Sullam, cum in expeditionem educturus esset,
immolavisse, et anguem ab ara extitisse, eoque die
rem praeclare esse gestam non haruspicis consilio,
sed imperatoris.

66   XXXI. " Atque haec ostentorum genera mirabile
nihil habent ; quae cum facta sunt, tum ad coniecturam aliqua interpretatione revocantur, ut illa tritici
grana in os pueri Midae congesta, aut apes quas
dixisti in labris Platonis consedisse pueri—non tam
mirabilia sint quam coniecta belle ; quae tamen
vel ipsa falsa esse, vel ea quae praedicta sunt,
fortuito cecidisse potuerunt.   De ipso Roscio potest
illud quidem esse falsum, ut circumligatus fuerit
angui, sed ut in cunis fuerit anguis, non tam est
mirum, in Solonio praesertim, ubi ad focum angues
nundinari solent.   Nam quod haruspices responderint
nihil illo clarius, nihil nobilius fore, miror deos

---

[1] *Cf.* i. 33. 72.
[2] *Cf.* i. 36. 78.
[3] *Cf.* i. 36. 79.

But, pray, by what principle of augury does he deduce years rather than months or days from the number of sparrows? Again, why does he base his prophecy on little sparrows which are not abnormal sights and ignore the alleged fact—which is impossible —that the dragon was turned to stone? Finally, what is there about a sparrow to suggest 'years'? In connexion with your story of the snake which appeared to Sulla when he was offering sacrifices,[1] I recall two facts: first, that when Sulla offered sacrifices, as he was about to begin his march against the enemy, a snake came out from under the altar; and, second, that the glorious victory won by him that day was due not to the soothsayer's art, but to the skill of the general.

XXXI. "There is nothing remarkable about the so-called portents of the kind just mentioned; but after they have happened they are brought within the field of prophecy by some interpretation. Take, for example, your stories of the grains of wheat heaped into the mouth of Midas when a boy,[2] and of the bees which settled on the lips of Plato,[2] when he was a child—they are more remarkable as guesses than as real prophecies. Besides, the incidents may have been fictitious; if not, then the fulfilment of the prophecy may have been accidental. As to that incident about Roscius it may, of course, be untrue that a snake coiled itself around him;[3] but it is not so surprising that a snake was in his cradle—especially in Solonium where snakes are attracted in large numbers by the heat of the fireplaces. As to your statement that the soothsayers prophesied a career of unrivalled brilliancy for Roscius, it is a strange thing to me that the immortal gods foretold

immortales histrioni futuro claritatem ostendisse, nullam ostendisse Africano !

67 " Atque etiam a te Flaminiana ostenta collecta sunt : quod ipse et equus eius repente conciderit ; non sane mirabile hoc quidem ! Quod evelli primi hastati signum non potuerit ; timide fortasse signifer evellebat, quod fidenter infixerat. Nam Dionysi equus quid attulit admirationis, quod emersit e flumine quodque habuit apes in iuba ? Sed quia brevi tempore regnare coepit, quod acciderat casu, vim habuit ostenti ! ' At Lacedaemoniis in Herculis fano arma sonuerunt, eiusdemque dei Thebis valvae clausae subito se aperuerunt, eaque scuta, quae fuerant sublime fixa, sunt humi inventa.' Horum cum fieri nihil potuerit sine aliquo motu, quid est, cur divinitus ea potius quam casu facta esse dicamus ?

68 XXXII. " At in Lysandri statuae capite Delphis extitit corona ex asperis herbis, et quidem subita. Itane ? Censes ante coronam herbae extitisse quam conceptum esse semen ? Herbam autem asperam credo avium congestu, non humano satu ; iam, quicquid in capite est, id coronae simile videri potest. Nam quod eodem tempore stellas aureas Castoris et Pollucis Delphis positas decidisse, neque eas usquam repertas esse dixisti,—furum id magis

---

[1] *Cf.* i. 35. 77.   [2] *Cf.* i. 33. 73.
[3] *Cf.* i. 34. 74.   [4] *Cf.* i. 34. 75.

446

the glory of a future actor and did not foretell that of Africanus !

" And you have even collected the portent-stories connected with Flaminius : [1] ' His horse,' you say, ' stumbled and fell with him.' That is very strange, isn't it ? And, ' The standard of the first company could not be pulled up.' Perhaps the standard-bearer had planted it stoutly and pulled it up timidly. What is astonishing in the fact that the horse of Dionysius [2] came up out of the river, or that it had bees in its mane ? And yet, because Dionysius began to reign a short time later—which was a mere coincidence—the event referred to is considered a portent ! ' The arms sounded,' you say, ' in the temple of Hercules in Sparta ; the folding-doors of the same god at Thebes, though securely barred, opened of their own accord, and the shields hanging upon the walls of that temple fell to the ground.' [3] Now since none of these things could have happened without some exterior force, why should we say that they were brought about by divine agency rather than by chance ?

XXXII. " You mention the appearance—a ' sudden ' appearance it was—of a crown of wild herbs on the head of Lysander's statue at Delphi.[4] Really ? And do you think the crown of herbs appeared before their seeds were formed ? Besides, the wild herbs, in my opinion, came from seeds brought by birds and were not planted by human agency. Again, imagination can make anything on top of a head look like a crown. ' At the same time,' you say, ' the golden stars in the temple of Castor and Pollux at Delphi fell down and were nowhere to be found.' [4] That appears to me to have been the

447

69 factum quam deorum videtur. Simiae vero Dodo-
naeae improbitatem historiis Graecis mandatam
esse demiror. Quid minus mirum quam illam mon-
struosissimam bestiam urnam evertisse, sortes
dissupavisse ? Et negant historici Lacedaemoniis
ullum ostentum hoc tristius accidisse !

" Nam illa praedicta Veientium, ' si lacus Albanus
redundasset isque in mare fluxisset, Romam peri-
turam ; si repressus esset, Veios.' Ita aqua Albana
deducta ad utilitatem agri suburbani, non ad arcem
urbemque retinendam. ' At paulo post audita vox
est monentis ut providerent ne a Gallis Roma
caperetur ; ex eo Aio Loquenti aram in nova via
consecratam.' Quid ergo ? Aius iste Loquens, cum
eum nemo norat, et aiebat et loquebatur et ex eo
nomen invenit ; posteaquam et sedem et aram et
nomen invenit, obmutuit ? Quod idem dici de
Moneta potest ; a qua praeterquam de sue plena
quid umquam moniti sumus ?

70 XXXIII. " Satis multa de ostentis; auspicia restant
et sortes eae, quae ducuntur, non illae, quae vatici-
natione funduntur, quae oracula verius dicimus ; de
quibus tum dicemus, cum ad naturalem divinationem
venerimus. Restat etiam de Chaldaeis ; sed primum
auspicia videamus. ' Difficilis auguri locus ad contra
dicendum.' Marso fortasse, sed Romano facillimus.

---

[1] *Cf.* i. 34. 76.   [2] *Cf.* i. 44. 100.
                [3] *Cf.* i. 45. 101.

work of thieves rather than of gods. I am indeed astonished that Greek historians should have recorded the mischievous pranks of the Dodonean ape.[1] For what is less strange than for this hideous beast to have turned over the vase and scattered the lots ? And yet the historians declare that no portent more direful than this ever befell the Spartans !

"You spoke also of the Veientine prophecy [2] that 'if Lake Albanus overflowed and emptied into the sea, Rome would fall, but if held in check Veii would fall.' Well, it turned out that the water from the lake was drawn off—but it was drawn off through irrigation ditches—not to save the Capitol and the city, but to improve the farming lands. 'And, not long after this occurred, a voice was heard,' you say, 'warning the people to take steps to prevent the capture of Rome by the Gauls. Therefore an altar was erected on the *Nova Via* in honour of Aius the Speaker.' But why ? Did your 'Aius the Speaker,' before anybody knew who he was, both speak and talk and from that fact receive his name ? And after he had secured a seat, an altar, and a name did he become mute ? Your Juno Moneta [3] may likewise be dismissed with a question : What did she ever admonish us about except the pregnant sow ?

XXXIII. "Enough has been said of portents ; auspices remain and so do lots—I mean 'lots' that are drawn, and not those uttered by prophets, and more correctly styled 'oracles.' I shall speak of oracles when I get to natural divination. In addition I must discuss the Chaldeans. But first let us consider auspices. 'To argue against auspices is a hard thing,' you say, 'for an augur to do.' Yes, for a Marsian, perhaps ; but very easy for a Roman.

449

Non enim sumus ei nos augures, qui avium reli-
quorumve signorum observatione futura dicamus.
Et tamen credo Romulum, qui urbem auspicato
condidit, habuisse opinionem esse in providendis
rebus augurandi scientiam (errabat enim multis in
rebus antiquitas), quas, vel usu iam, vel doctrina,
vel vetustate immutatam videmus ; retinetur autem
et ad opinionem vulgi et ad magnas utilitates rei
publicae mos, religio, disciplina, ius augurium,
collegi auctoritas.

71   " Nec vero non omni supplicio digni P. Claudius
L. Iunius consules, qui contra auspicia navigaverunt ;
parendum enim fuit religioni, nec patrius mos tam
contumaciter repudiandus.   Iure igitur alter populi
iudicio damnatus est, alter mortem sibi ipse conscivit.
' Flaminius non paruit auspiciis, itaque periit cum
exercitu.'   At anno post Paulus paruit ; num minus
cecidit in Cannensi pugna cum exercitu ?   Etenim,
ut sint auspicia, quae nulla sunt, haec certe, quibus
utimur, sive tripudio, sive de caelo, simulacra sunt
auspiciorum, auspicia nullo modo.

XXXIV. " ' Q. Fabi, te mihi in auspicio esse volo.'
Respondet : ' audivi.'   (Hic apud maiores nostros

---

¹ Cicero now proceeds to illustrate his point by giving
the empty formulae used by the magistrates in taking the
auspices.   He represents himself as the celebrant and
addresses his assistant, the augur, as " Quintus Fabius "—
the name of any free man you please and as indefinite and
impersonal as " John Doe," or " Richard Roe."

For we Roman augurs are not the sort who foretell the future by observing the flights of birds and other signs. And yet, I admit that Romulus, who founded the city by the direction of auspices, believed that augury was an art useful in seeing things to come— for the ancients had erroneous views on many subjects. But we see that the art has undergone a change, due to experience, education, or the long lapse of time. However, out of respect for the opinion of the masses and because of the great service to the State we maintain the augural practices, discipline, religious rites and laws, as well as the authority of the augural college.

" In my opinion the consuls, Publius Claudius and Lucius Junius, who set sail contrary to the auspices, were deserving of capital punishment; for they should have respected the established religion and should not have treated the customs of their forefathers with such shameless disdain. Therefore it was a just retribution that the former was condemned by a vote of the people and that the latter took his own life. ' Flaminius,' you say, ' did not obey the auspices, therefore he perished with his army.' But a year later Paulus did obey them ; and did he not lose his army and his life in the battle of Cannae ? Granting that there are auspices (as there are not), certainly those which we ordinarily employ—whether by the *tripudium* or by the observation of the heavens— are not auspices in any sense, but are the mere ghosts of auspices.[1]

XXXIV. " ' Quintus Fabius, I wish you to assist me at the auspices.' He answers, ' I will.' (In our forefathers' time the magistrates on such occasions used to call in some expert person to take the

adhibebatur peritus, nunc quilibet. Peritum autem
esse necesse est eum, qui, silentium quid sit, intellegat;
id enim silentium dicimus in auspiciis, quod omni
72 vitio caret. Hoc intellegere perfecti auguris est.)
Illi autem, qui in auspicium adhibetur, cum ita
imperavit is, qui auspicatur, ' Dicito, si silentium esse
videbitur,' nec suspicit nec circumspicit; statim
respondet ' silentium esse videri.' Tum ille : ' Dicito,
si pascentur.' ' Pascuntur.' Quae aves ? aut ubi ?
' Attulit,' inquit, ' in cavea pullos is qui, ex eo ipso,
nominatur pullarius.' Haec sunt igitur aves inter-
nuntiae Iovis ! Quae pascantur necne quid refert ?
Nihil ad auspicia ; sed quia, cum pascuntur, necesse
est aliquid ex ore cadere et terram pavire—' terripavium ' primo, post ' terripudium ' dictum est ; hoc
quidem iam ' tripudium ' dicitur. Cum igitur offa
cecidit ex ore pulli, tum auspicanti tripudium solistimum nuntiatur.

73 XXXV. " Ergo hoc auspicium divini quicquam
habere potest, quod tam sit coactum et expressum ?
Quo antiquissimos augures non esse usos argumento
est, quod decretum collegi vetus habemus omnem
avem tripudium facere posse. Tum igitur esset
auspicium si modo esset ei liberum se ostendisse ;
tum avis illa videri posset interpres et satelles Iovis.
Nunc vero inclusa in cavea et fame enecta, si in offam

---

[1] "The celebrant" is here intended to translate *is*, *qui
auspicatur*, *i.e.* the magistrate who directs and presides
at the taking of the auspices ; while *qui in auspicium
adhibetur* is the expert (the augur, the assistant), who actually
takes the auspices.

[2] *Cf.* i. 15. 28.

[3] *Cf.* i. 47. 106 ; Hom. *Od.* **xv.** 525.

auspices—but in these days anyone will do. But one must be an expert to know what constitutes 'silence,' for by that term we mean 'free of every augural defect.' To understand that belongs to a perfect augur.) After the celebrant [1] has said to his assistant, 'Tell me when silence appears to exist,' the latter, without looking up or about him, immediately replies, 'Silence appears to exist.' Then the celebrant says, 'Tell me when the chickens begin to eat.' 'They are eating now,' is the answer. But what are these birds they are talking about, and where are they? Someone replies, 'It's poultry. It's in a cage and the person who brought it is called "a poulterer," because of his business.' These, then, are the messengers of Jove! What difference does it make whether they eat or not? None, so far as the auspices are concerned. But, because of the fact that, while they eat, some food must necessarily fall from their mouths and strike upon the ground (*terram pavire*),— this at first was called *terripavium*, and later, *terripudium*; now it is called *tripudium*—therefore, when a crumb of food falls from a chicken's mouth a *tripudium solistimum* is announced to the celebrant.[2]

XXXV. "Then, how can there be anything divine about an auspice so forced and so extorted? That such a practice did not prevail with the augurs of ancient times is proven by an old ruling of our college which says, 'Any bird may make a *tripudium*.' There might be an auspice if the bird were free to show itself outside its cage. In that case it might be called 'the interpreter and satellite of Jove.'[3] But now, when shut up inside a cage and tortured by hunger, if it seizes greedily upon its morsel of

pultis invadit, et si aliquid ex eius ore cecidit, hoc
tu auspicium aut hoc modo Romulum auspicari
74 solitum putas ? Iam de caelo servare non ipsos
censes solitos, qui auspicabantur ? Nunc imperant
pullario ; ille renuntiat. Fulmen sinistrum auspicium
optimum habemus ad omnis res praeterquam ad
comitia ; quod quidem institutum rei publicae causa
est, ut comitiorum vel in iudiciis populi vel in iure
legum vel in creandis magistratibus principes civitatis
essent interpretes.

" ' At Ti. Gracchi litteris Scipio et Figulus consules,
cum augures iudicassent eos vitio creatos esse,
magistratu se abdicaverunt.' Quis negat augurum
disciplinam esse ? divinationem nego. ' At haruspices divini quos, cum Ti. Gracchus, propter mortem
repentinam eius qui in praerogativa referenda
subito concidisset, in senatum introduxisset, non
75 iustum rogatorem fuisse dixerunt.' Primum vide
ne in eum dixerint qui rogator centuriae fuisset ; is
enim erat mortuus ; id autem sine divinatione
coniectura poterant dicere. Deinde fortasse casu,
qui nullo modo est ex hoc genere tollendus. Quid

---

[1] Apparently Cicero ridicules the idea of a " poulterer "
and not the " celebrant " taking the auspices.
[2] See this incident more fully describied in Cic. *N.D.* ii.
chap. 4. ; *cf.* i. 17. 33. The prerogative century—or the
one which voted first at the election—had its *rogator*, or
president, who collected the votes ; and the entire assembly,
made up of all the electors voting by centuries, had its
rogator, usually the consul who received the reports of the
subordinate presidents.

pottage and something falls from its mouth, do you consider that is an auspice ? Or do you believe that this was the way in which Romulus used to take the auspices ? Again, do you not think that formerly it was the habit of the celebrants themselves to make observation of the heavens ? Now they order the poulterer, and he gives responses ! [1] We regard lightning on the left as a most favourable omen for everything except for an election, and this exception was made, no doubt, from reasons of political expediency so that the rulers of the State would be the judges of the regularity of an election, whether held to pass judgements in criminal cases, or to enact laws, or to elect magistrates.

" ' The consuls, Scipio and Figulus,' you say, ' resigned their office when the augurs rendered a decision based on a letter written by Tiberius Gracchus, to the effect that those consuls had not been elected according to augural law.' Who denies that augury is an art ? What I deny is the existence of divination. But you say : ' Soothsayers have the power of divination ' ; and you mention the fact that, on account of the unexpected death of the person who had suddenly fallen while bringing in the report of the vote of the prerogative century, Tiberius Gracchus introduced the soothsayers into the Senate and they declared that ' the president ' had violated augural law. [2] Now, in the first place, do not understand that by ' the president ' they meant the president of the prerogative century, for he was dead ; and, moreover, they could have told that by conjecture without the use of divination ; or, in the second place, perhaps, they said so by accident which is in no wise to be left out of account

enim scire Etrusci haruspices aut de tabernaculo recte capto aut de pomeri iure potuerunt ? Equidem assentior C. Marcello potius quam App. Claudio, qui ambo mei collegae fuerunt, existimoque ius augurum, etsi divinationis opinione principio constitutum sit, tamen postea rei publicae causa conservatum ac 76 retentum. XXXVI. Sed de hoc loco plura in aliis, nunc hactenus.

" Externa enim auguria, quae sunt non tam artificiosa quam superstitiosa, videamus. Omnibus fere avibus utuntur, nos admodum paucis ; alia illis sinistra sunt, alia nostris. Solebat ex me Deiotarus percontari nostri auguri disciplinam, ego ex illo sui. Di immortales ! quantum differebat ! ut quaedam essent etiam contraria. Atque ille eis semper utebatur, nos, nisi dum a populo auspicia accepta habemus, quam multum eis utimur ? Bellicam rem administrari maiores nostri nisi auspicato noluerunt ; quam multi anni sunt, cum bella a proconsulibus et a propraetoribus administrantur, qui auspicia non 77 habent ! Itaque nec amnis transeunt auspicato nec tripudio auspicantur.[1] Ubi ergo avium divinatio ? quae, quoniam ab eis, qui auspicia nulla habent, bella

---

[1] MSS., Dav., Giese, Moser, have Nam ex acuminibus . . . optimus following auspicantur.

---

[1] As to *tabernaculum* and *pomerium* see i. 17. 33 and note

in cases of this kind. For what could the Etruscan soothsayers have known, either as to whether the *tabernaculum* had been properly placed, or as to whether the regulations pertaining to the *pomerium* [1] had been observed ? For my part, I agree with Gaius Marcellus, rather than with Appius Claudius —both of whom were my colleagues—and I think that, although in the beginning augural law was established from a belief in divination, yet later it was maintained and preserved from considerations of political expediency. XXXVI. But we shall discuss the latter point at greater length in other discourses ; let us dismiss it for the present.

" Now let us examine augury as practised among foreign nations, whose methods are not so artificial as they are superstitious. They employ almost all kinds of birds, we only a few ; they regard some signs as favourable, we, others. Deiotarus used to question me a great deal about our system of augury, and I him about that of his country. Ye gods ! how much they differed ! So much that in some cases they were directly the reverse of each other. He employed auspices constantly, we never do except when the duty of doing so is imposed by a vote of the people. Our ancestors would not undertake any military enterprise without consulting the auspices ; but now, for many years, our wars have been conducted by pro-consuls and pro-praetors, who do not have the right to take auspices. Therefore they have no *tripudium* and they cross rivers without first taking the auspices. What, then, has become of divining by means of birds ? It is not used by those who conduct our wars, for they have not the right of auspices. Since it has been

administrantur, ad urbanas res retenta videtur, a
bellicis esse sublata.

" Nam ex acuminibus quidem, quod totum auspicium militare est, iam M. Marcellus ille quinquiens
consul totum omisit, idem imperator, idem augur
optimus. Et quidem ille dicebat, ' si quando rem
agere vellet, ne impediretur auspiciis, lectica operta
facere iter se solere.' Huic simile est, quod nos
augures praecipimus, ne iuge auspicium obveniat ut
78 iumenta iubeant diiungere. Quid est aliud nolle
moneri a Iove nisi efficere ut, aut ne fieri possit
auspicium, aut, si fiat, videri ?

XXXVII. " Nam illud admodum ridiculum, quod
negas, ' Deiotarum auspiciorum, quae sibi ad
Pompeium proficiscenti facta sint, paenitere, quod
fidem secutus amicitiamque populi Romani functus
sit officio ; antiquiorem enim sibi fuisse laudem et
gloriam quam regnum et possessiones suas.' Credo
equidem, sed hoc nihil ad auspicia ; nec enim ei
cornix canere potuit recte eum facere, quod populi
Romani libertatem defendere pararet ; ipse hoc
79 sentiebat, sicuti sensit. Aves eventus significant
aut adversos aut secundos. Virtutis auspiciis video
esse usum Deiotarum, quae vetat spectare fortunam,
dum praestetur fides. Aves vero, si prosperos
eventus ostenderunt, certe fefellerunt. Fugit e

---

[1] This is supposed to be a divining by means of electrical
flashes from the points of spears, swords, and javelins.
Cf. Pliny, *H.N.* ii. 37; Seneca, *Q.N.* i. 1; Livy xxii. 1; xliii.
13 ; Cic. *N.D.* ii. 3. 9.

[2] So that he would not see any unpropitious signs.

[3] This occurred when two draught cattle while yoked
together dunged at the same time.

[4] *Cf.* i. 15. 26-27.

withdrawn from use in the field I suppose it is reserved for city use only !

" As to divination *ex acuminibus*,[1] which is altogether military, it was wholly ignored by that famous man, Marcus Marcellus, who was consul five times and, besides, was a commander-in-chief, as well as a very fine augur. In fact, he used to say that, if he wished to execute some manœuvre which he did not want interfered with by the auspices, he would travel in a closed litter.[2] His method is of a kind with the advice which we augurs give, that the draught-cattle be ordered to be unyoked so as to prevent a *iuge auspicium*.[3] What else does a refusal to be warned by Jove accomplish except either to prevent an auspice from occurring, or, if it occurs, to prevent it from being seen ?

XXXVII. " Your story about Deiotarus[4] is utterly absurd : ' He did not regret the auspices given him as he was setting out to join Pompey. They caused him to continue in the path of loyalty and friendship to the Roman people and to perform his duty ; for he valued his reputation and glory more than kingdom and riches.' I dare say ; but that has nothing to do with auspices. For the crow could not tell Deiotarus that he was doing right in preparing to defend the liberty of the Roman people. He ought to have realized that of himself, and in fact he did. Birds indicate that results will be unfavourable or favourable. In my view of the case Deiotarus employed the auspices of virtue, and virtue bids us not to look to fortune until the claims of honour are discharged. However, if the birds indicated that the issue would be favourable to Deiotarus they certainly deceived him. He fled

proelio cum Pompeio — grave tempus ! Discessit
ab eo — luctuosa res ! Caesarem eodem tempore
hostem et hospitem vidit — quid hoc tristius ? Is
cum ei Trocmorum tetrarchiam eripuisset et asseculae
suo Pergameno nescio cui dedisset eidemque
detraxisset Armeniam a senatu datam, cumque ab
eo magnificentissimo hospitio acceptus esset, spolia-
tum reliquit et hospitem et regem. Sed labor longius ; ad propositum revertar. Si eventa quaerimus,
quae exquiruntur avibus, nullo modo prospera
Deiotaro ; sin officia, a virtute ipsius, non ab auspiciis
petita sunt.

80   XXXVIII. " Omitte igitur lituum Romuli, quem
in maximo incendio negas potuisse comburi ; con-
temne cotem Atti Navi. Nihil debet esse in philosophia commenticiis fabellis loci ; illud erat philosophi
potius,[1] totius auguri primum naturam ipsam videre,
deinde inventionem, deinde constantiam. Quae est
igitur natura, quae volucris huc et illuc passim
vagantis efficiat ut significent aliquid et tum vetent
agere, tum iubeant aut cantu aut volatu ? cur autem
aliis a laeva, aliis a dextra datum est avibus ut
ratum auspicium facere possint ? Quo modo autem
haec aut quando aut a quibus inventa dicemus ?

---

[1] potius *Moser, MSS.* ; *Dav. om.*

---

[1] *Cf.* i. 17. 30. Cicero having discussed foreign instances
in Chapters 36 and 37 now returns to Roman illustrations.
[2] *Cf.* i. 17. 32.

from the battle with Pompey—a serious situation!
He separated from Pompey—an occasion of sorrow!
He beheld Caesar at once his enemy and his guest
—what could have been more distressing than that?
Caesar wrested from him the tetrarchy over the
Trocmi and conferred it upon some obscure syco-
phant of his own from Pergamus; deprived him of
Armenia, a gift from the Senate; accepted a most
lavish hospitality at the hands of his royal host
and left him utterly despoiled. But I wander too
far: I must return to the point at issue. If we
examine this matter from the standpoint of the
results—and that was the question submitted to
the determination of the birds—the issue was in
no sense favourable to Deiotarus; but if we examine
it from the standpoint of duty, he sought information
on that score not from the auspices, but from his
own conscience.

XXXVIII. " Then dismiss Romulus's augural staff,[1]
which you say the hottest of fires was powerless to
burn, and attach slight importance to the whetstone of Attus Navius.[2] Myths should have no
place in philosophy. It would have been more in
keeping with your rôle as a philosopher to consider,
first, the nature of divination generally, second, its
origin, and third, its consistency. What, then, is
the nature of an art which makes prophets out of
birds that wander aimlessly about—now here, now
there—and makes the action or inaction of men
depend upon the song or flight of birds? and why
was the power granted to some birds to give a
favourable omen when on the left side and to others
when on the right? Again, how, when, and by
whom, shall we say that the system was invented?

461

Etrusci tamen habent exaratum puerum auctorem
disciplinae suae ; nos quem ?   Attumne Navium ?
At aliquot annis antiquior Romulus et Remus, ambo
augures, ut accepimus.   An Pisidarum aut Cilicum
aut Phrygum ista inventa dicemus ?   Placet igitur
humanitatis expertis habere divinitatis auctores !

81   XXXIX. " ' At omnes reges, populi, nationes
utuntur auspiciis.'   Quasi vero quicquam sit tam
valde quam nihil sapere vulgare, aut quasi tibi ipsi
in iudicando placeat multitudo !   Quotus quisque
est qui voluptatem neget esse bonum ?   plerique
etiam summum bonum dicunt.   Num igitur eorum
frequentia Stoici de sententia deterrentur ?   aut num
plerisque in rebus sequitur eorum auctoritatem
multitudo ?   Quid mirum igitur, si in auspiciis et in
omni divinatione imbecilli animi superstitiosa ista
82 concipiant, verum dispicere non possint ?   Quae
autem est inter augures conveniens et coniuncta
constantia ?   Ad nostri auguri consuetudinem dixit
Ennius :

> tum tonuit laevum bene tempestate serena.

" At Homericus Aiax apud Achillem querens de
ferocitate Troianorum nescio quid hoc modo nuntiat :

> prospera Iuppiter his dextris fulguribus edit.

---

[1] Cicero uses *divinitas* here for *divinatio* to bring out the
contrast with *humanitas* and to add to the sarcastic effect.

[2] From the *Annales*, ii. 5.

[3] *Cf. Iliad*, ix. 236.   Cicero's memory again deceives
him, the reference being to Ulysses.

The Etruscans, it is true, find the author of their
system in the boy who was ploughed up out of the
ground ; but whom have we ? Attus Navius ?
But Romulus and Remus, both of whom, by tradition,
were augurs, lived many years earlier. Are we to
say that it was invented by the Pisidians, Cilicians,
or Phrygians ? It is your judgement, then, that
those devoid of *human* learning are the authors of a
divine science ! [1]

XXXIX. " ' But,' you say, ' all kings, peoples, and
nations employ auspices.' As if there were anything
so absolutely common as want of sense, or as if
you yourself in deciding anything would accept the
opinion of the mob ! How often will you find a man
who will say that pleasure is not a good ! Most
people actually call it the highest good. Then will
the Stoics abandon their views about pleasure because
the crowd is against them ? or do you think that the
multitude follows the lead of the Stoics in very
many matters ? What wonder, then, if in auspices
and in every kind of divination weak minds should
adopt the superstitious practices which you have
mentioned and should be unable to discern the
truth ? Moreover, there is no uniformity, and no
consistent and constant agreement between augurs.
Ennius, speaking with reference to the Roman
system of augury, said :

> Then on the left, from out a cloudless sky,
> Jove's thunder rolled its goodly omen forth. [2]

But Homer's Ajax [3] in complaining to Achilles of
some ferocious deed or other of the Trojans, speaks
in this wise :

> For their success Jove thunders on the right

CICERO

Ita nobis sinistra videntur, Graiis et barbaris dextra
meliora. Quamquam haud ignoro, quae bona sint,
' sinistra ' nos dicere, etiamsi dextra sint ; sed certe
nostri ' sinistrum ' nominaverunt externique ' dex-
83 trum,' quia plerumque id melius videbatur. Haec
quanta dissensio est! Quid? quod aliis avibus
utuntur, aliis signis, aliter observant, alia respondent,
non necesse est fateri partim horum errore susceptum
esse, partim superstitione, multa fallendo ?

XL. "Atque his superstitionibus non dubitasti
etiam omina adiungere. ' Aemilia Paulo Persam
perisse, quod pater omen accepit.' ' Caecilia se
sororis filiae sedes suas tradere.' Iam illa : ' Favete
linguis ' et ' praerogativam,' omen comitiorum. Hoc
est ipsum esse contra se copiosum et disertum !
Quando enim ista observans quieto et libero animo
esse poteris, ut ad rem gerendam non superstitionem
habeas, sed rationem ducem ? Itane ? si quis aliquid
ex sua re atque ex suo sermone dixerit et eius
verbum aliquod apte ceciderit ad id, quod ages aut
cogitabis, ea res tibi aut timorem afferet aut alacri-
84 tatem ? Cum M. Crassus exercitum Brundisi
imponeret, quidam in portu caricas Cauno advectas

---

¹ In taking the auspices Roman augurs faced the south,
Greek augurs faced the north, and hence the left of the
Roman observer would be the right of the Greek. But some
right-hand signs were favourable to the Romans—*e.g.* the
croaking of a crow ; *cf.* i. 7. 12.

² *Cf.* i. 46. 103.

³ *Cf.* i. 45. 102.

⁴ *Cf.* i. 45. 103.

⁵ When he was starting on his fatal expedition against
the Parthians.

So we regard signs on the left as best—Greeks and barbarians, those on the right. And yet I am aware that we call favourable signs *sinistra*, or 'left-hand' signs, even though they may be on the right.[1] Undoubtedly our ancestors in choosing the left side and foreign nations the right were both influenced by what experience had shown them was the more favourable quarter in most cases. What a conflict this is! In view, then, of the differences between different nations in the responses, in the manner in which observations are made and in the kinds of birds and signs employed, need I assert that divination is compounded of a little error, a little superstition, and a good deal of fraud?

XL. " And to these superstitions you have actually joined omens! For example : ' Aemilia told Paulus that Persa was dead and her father accepted this as an omen.'[2] ' Caecilia said that she surrendered her seat to her sister's daughter.' Then you go on and speak of the order of silence, *favete linguis*[3] and the 'prerogative,' or omen of the elections.[4] This is indeed turning the artillery of one's eloquence and learning against oneself! For while on the watch for these ' oracles' of yours could you be so free and calm of mind that you would have reason and not superstition to guide your course? Now, if a person in the course of his own business or conversation should make some remark, and a word spoken by him happened to apply to what you were doing or thinking, do you really believe that such an accident should cause you either fear or joy? When Marcus Crassus was embarking his army at Brundisium[5] a man who was selling Caunian figs at the

465

vendens ' Cauneas ' clamitabat. Dicamus, si placet,
monitum ab eo Crassum, ' caveret ne iret ' ; non fuisse
periturum, si omini paruisset. Quae si suscipiamus,
pedis offensio nobis et abruptio corrigiae et sternu-
menta erunt observanda.

XLI. " Sortes restant et Chaldaei, ut ad vates
85 veniamus et ad somnia. Dicendum igitur putas de
sortibus ? Quid enim sors est ? Idem prope modum,
quod micare, quod talos iacere, quod tesseras, quibus
in rebus temeritas et casus, non ratio nec consilium
valet. Tota res est inventa fallaciis aut ad quaestum
aut ad superstitionem aut ad errorem. Atque ut
in haruspicina fecimus, sic videamus, clarissimarum
sortium quae tradatur inventio. Numerium Suffus-
tium Praenestinorum monumenta declarant, honestum hominem et nobilem, somniis crebris, ad
extremum etiam minacibus, cum iuberetur certo in
loco silicem caedere, perterritum visis irridentibus
suis civibus id agere coepisse ; itaque perfracto saxo
sortis erupisse in robore insculptas priscarum lit-
terarum notis. Is est hodie locus saeptus religiose
propter Iovis pueri, qui lactens[1] cum Iunone Fortunae
in gremio sedens mammam appetens castissime
colitur a matribus.

[1] qui lactens *MSS.*, *Dav.* ; *Ernesti, Hotting. om.* lactens.

---

[1] *i.e.* " Caunian figs," but might be heard as *cave ne
eas.* This illustration of the identity of sound between
cavneas, i.e. cave ne eas, and *cauneas* has been the subject
of some interesting discussion in Latin phonetics. *Cf.*
Moser, *Div., ad loc.*

harbour, repeatedly cried out, ' Cauneas, Cauneas.'[1]
Let us say, if you will, that this was a warning to
Crassus to bid him ' Beware of going,' and that if
he had obeyed the omen he would not have perished.
But if we are going to accept chance utterances of
this kind as omens, we had better look out when
we stumble, or break a shoe-string, or sneeze !

XLI. " Lots and the Chaldean astrologers remain
to be discussed before we come to prophets and to
dreams. And pray what is the need, do you think,
to talk about the casting of lots ? It is much like
playing at morra, dice, or knuckle-bones, in which
recklessness and luck prevail rather than reflection
and judgement. The whole scheme of divination by
lots was fraudulently contrived from mercenary
motives, or as a means of encouraging superstition
and error. But let us follow the method used in
the discussion of soothsaying and consider the
traditional origin of the most famous lots. According
to the annals of Praeneste Numerius Suffustius, who
was a distinguished man of noble birth, was admonished by dreams, often repeated, and finally even
by threats, to split open a flint rock which was lying
in a designated place. Frightened by the visions
and disregarding the jeers of his fellow-townsmen
he set about doing as he had been directed. And
so when he had broken open the stone, the lots
sprang forth carved on oak, in ancient characters.
The site where the stone was found is religiously
guarded to this day. It is hard by the statue of
the infant Jupiter, who is represented as sitting
with Juno in the lap of Fortune and reaching for her
breast, and it is held in the highest reverence by
mothers.

86 " Eodemque tempore in eo loco, ubi Fortunae nunc stat[1] aedes, mel ex olea fluxisse dicunt, haruspicesque dixisse summa nobilitate illas sortis futuras, eorumque iussu ex illa olea arcam esse factam, eoque conditas sortis, quae hodie Fortunae monitu tolluntur. Quid igitur in his potest esse certi, quae Fortunae monitu pueri manu miscentur atque ducuntur ? quo modo autem istae positae in illo loco ? quis robur illud cecidit, dolavit, inscripsit ? ' Nihil est,' inquiunt, ' quod deus efficere non possit.' Utinam sapientis Stoicos effecisset ne omnia cum superstitiosa sollicitudine et miseria crederent ! Sed hoc quidem genus divinationis vita iam communis explosit ; fani pulchritudo et vetustas Praenestinarum etiam nunc retinet sortium nomen, atque id in **87** volgus. Quis enim magistratus aut quis vir illustrior utitur sortibus ? ceteris vero in locis sortes plane refrixerunt. Quod Carneadem Clitomachus scribit dicere solitum, nusquam se fortunatiorem quam Praeneste vidisse Fortunam. Ergo hoc divinationis genus omittamus.

XLII. " Ad Chaldaeorum monstra veniamus ; de quibus Eudoxus, Platonis auditor, in astrologia iudicio doctissimorum hominum facile princeps, sic opinatur, id quod scriptum reliquit, Chaldaeis in

---

[1] stat *conject. Dav.*; MSS. est *and* sit

---

[1] If the statue of the goddess gives a sign by a nod or otherwise.
[2] *i.e.* the reputation of the lots at Praeneste lasted longer than elsewhere.

"There is a tradition that, concurrently with the finding of the lots and in the spot where the temple of Fortune now stands, honey flowed from an olive-tree. Now the soothsayers, who had declared that those lots would enjoy an unrivalled reputation, gave orders that a chest should be made from the tree and the lots placed in the chest. At the present time the lots are taken from their receptacle if Fortune directs.[1] What reliance, pray, can you put in these lots, which at Fortune's nod are shuffled and drawn by the hand of a child? And how did they ever get in that rock? Who cut down the oak-tree? and who fashioned and carved the lots? Oh! but somebody says, 'God can bring anything to pass.' If so, then I wish he had made the Stoics wise, so that they would not be so pitiably and distressingly superstitious and so prone to believe everything they hear! This sort of divining, how-ever, has now been discarded by general usage. The beauty and age of the temple still preserve the name of the lots of Praeneste—that is, among the common people, for no magistrate and no man of any reputation ever consults them; but in all other places lots have gone entirely out of use. And this explains the remark which, according to Clitomachus, Carneades used to make that he had at no other place seen Fortune more fortunate than at Praeneste.[2] Then let us dismiss this branch of divination.

XLII. "Let us come to Chaldean manifestations. In discussing them Plato's pupil, Eudoxus, whom the best scholars consider easily the first in astro-nomy, has left the following opinion in writing: 'No reliance whatever is to be placed in Chaldean

praedictione et in notatione cuiusque vitae ex natali
88 die minime esse credendum. Nominat etiam
Panaetius, qui unus e Stoicis astrologorum praedicta
reiecit, Anchialum et Cassandrum, summos astrologos
illius aetatis, qua erat ipse, cum in ceteris astrologiae
partibus excellerent, hoc praedictionis genere non
usos. Scylax Halicarnassius, familiaris Panaetii
excellens in astrologia idemque in regenda sua
civitate princeps, totum hoc Chaldaicum praedicendi
genus repudiavit.

89 " Sed ut ratione utamur omissis testibus, sic isti
disputant qui haec Chaldaeorum natalicia praedicta
defendunt. Vim quandam esse, aiunt, signifero in
orbe, qui Graece ζωδιακός dicitur, talem ut eius
orbis una quaeque pars alia alio modo moveat
immutetque caelum, perinde ut quaeque stellae in
his finitimisque partibus sint quoque tempore,
eamque vim varie moveri ab eis sideribus, quae
vocantur errantia ; cum autem in eam ipsam partem
orbis venerint, in qua sit ortus eius, qui nascatur,
aut in eam, quae coniunctum aliquid habeat aut consentiens, ea 'triangula' illi et 'quadrata' nominant.
Etenim cum tempestatumque[1] caeli conversiones
commutationesque tantae fiant accessu stellarum et
recessu, cumque ea vi solis efficiantur, quae videmus,
non veri simile solum, sed etiam verum esse censent
perinde, utcumque temperatus sit aër, ita pueros

---

[1] tempore anni tempestatumque *MSS.*; *Dav. om.* tempore
anni.

---

[1] The word *astrologus*=" student of the stars," can mean
either " astronomer " or " astrologer."
[2] See Moser, *Div., ad loc.*, note on "triangle " and
"square"; *cf.* Sext. Empir. *Adv. mathem.* v. 39.

astrologers when they profess to forecast a man's
future from the position of the stars on the day of
his birth.' Panaetius, too, who was the only one
of the Stoics to reject the prophecies of astrologers,[1]
mentions Anchialus and Cassander as the greatest
astronomers of his day and states that they did not
employ their art as a means of divining, though they
were eminent in all other branches of astronomy.
Scylax of Halicarnassus, an intimate friend of Panaetius, and an eminent astronomer, besides being
the head of the government in his own city, utterly
repudiated the Chaldean method of foretelling the
future.

"But let us dismiss our witnesses and employ
reasoning. Those men who defend the natal-day
prophecies of the Chaldeans, argue in this way :
' In the starry belt which the Greeks call the Zodiac
there is a certain force of such a nature that every
part of that belt affects and changes the heavens in a
different way, according to the stars that are in
this or in an adjoining locality at a given time.
This force is variously affected by those stars which
are called ' planets ' or ' wandering ' stars. But
when they have come into that sign of the Zodiac
under which someone is born, or into a sign having
some connexion or accord with the natal sign, they
form what is called a ' triangle ' or ' square.'[2] Now
since, through the procession and retrogression of
the stars, the great variety and change of the
seasons and of temperature take place, and since
the power of the sun produces such results as are
before our eyes, they believe that it is not merely
probable, but certain, that just as the temperature
of the air is regulated by this celestial force, so also

471

orientis animari atque formari, ex eoque ingenia, mores, animum, corpus, actionem vitae, casus cuiusque eventusque fingi.'

90   XLIII. " O delirationem incredibilem ! non enim omnis error stultitia dicenda est. Quibus etiam Diogenes Stoicus concedit aliquid, ut praedicere possint dumtaxat, quali quisque natura et ad quam quisque maxime rem aptus futurus sit ; cetera, quae profiteantur, negat ullo modo posse sciri ; etenim geminorum formas esse similis, vitam atque fortunam plerumque disparem. Procles et Eurysthenes, Lacedaemoniorum reges, gemini fratres fue-

91 runt.   At nec totidem annos vixerunt ; anno enim Procli vita brevior fuit, multumque is fratri rerum gestarum gloria praestitit. At ego id ipsum quod vir optimus, Diogenes, Chaldaeis quasi quadam prae varicatione concedit, nego posse intellegi. Etenim cum, ut ipsi dicunt, ortus nascentium luna moderetur, eaque animadvertant et notent sidera natalicia Chaldaei, quaecumque lunae iuncta videantur, oculorum fallacissimo sensu iudicant ea, quae ratione atque animo videre debebant. Docet enim ratio mathematicorum, quam istis notam esse oportebat,

---

¹ *Praevaricatio* is used of an advocate who acts in collusion with the opposite side.

children at their birth are influenced in soul and body and by this force their minds, manners, disposition, physical condition, career in life and destinies are determined.

XLIII. " What inconceivable madness ! For it is not enough to call an opinion ' foolishness ' when it is utterly devoid of reason. However, Diogenes the Stoic makes some concession to the Chaldeans. He says that they have the power of prophecy to the extent of being able to tell the disposition of any child and the calling for which he is best fitted. All their other claims of prophetic powers he absolutely denies. He says, for example, that twins are alike in appearance, but that they are generally unlike in career and in fortune. Procles and Eurysthenes, kings of the Lacedaemonians, were twin brothers. But they did not live the same number of years, for the life of Procles was shorter by a year than that of his brother and his deeds were far more glorious. But for my part I say that even this concession which our excellent friend Diogenes makes to the Chaldeans in a sort of collusive way,[1] is in itself unintelligible. For the Chaldeans, according to their own statements, believe that a person's destiny is affected by the condition of the moon at the time of his birth, and hence they make and record their observations of the stars which appear to be in conjunction with the moon on his birthday. As a result, in forming their judgements, they depend on the sense of sight, which is the least trustworthy of the senses, whereas they should employ reason and intelligence. For the science of mathematics, which the Chaldeans ought to know, teaches us how close the moon comes to

quanta humilitate luna feratur terram paene contin-
gens, quantum absit a proxima Mercuri stella, multo
autem longius a Veneris, deinde alio intervallo distet a
sole, cuius lumine collustrari putatur. Reliqua vero tria
intervalla infinita et inmensa, a sole ad Martis, inde
ad Iovis, ab eo ad Saturni stellam, inde ad caelum
ipsum, quod extremum atque ultimum mundi est.
92 Quae potest igitur contagio ex infinito paene intervallo pertinere ad lunam vel potius ad terram ?

XLIV. " Quid ? cum dicunt, id quod eis dicere
necesse est, omnis omnium ortus, quicumque gignan-
tur in omni terra, quae incolatur, eosdem esse,
eademque omnibus, qui eodem statu caeli et stellarum
nati sint, accidere necesse esse, nonne eius modi sunt,
ut ne caeli quidem naturam interpretes istos caeli
nosse appareat ? Cum enim illi orbes, qui caelum
quasi medium dividunt et aspectum nostrum defi-
niunt, qui a Graecis ὁρίζοντες nominantur, a nobis
' finientes ' rectissime nominari possunt, varietatem
maximam habeant aliique in aliis locis sint, necesse
est ortus occasusque siderum non fieri eodem tempore
93 apud omnis. Quodsi eorum vi caelum modo hoc
modo illo modo temperatur, qui potest eadem vis
esse nascentium, cum caeli tanta sit dissimilitudo ?
In his locis quae nos incolimus, post solstitium
Canicula exoritur, et quidem aliquot diebus, at apud
Troglodytas, ut scribitur, ante solstitium ; ut, si iam

---

[1] The summer solstice, on June 22nd.

the earth, which indeed it almost touches ; how far it is from Mercury, the nearest star ; how much further yet it is from Venus ; and what a great interval separates it from the sun, which is supposed to give it light. The three remaining distances are beyond computation : from the Sun to Mars, from Mars to Jupiter, from Jupiter to Saturn. Then there is the distance from Saturn to the limits of heaven—the ultimate bounds of space. In view, therefore, of these almost limitless distances, what influence can the planets exercise upon the moon, or rather, upon the earth ?

XLIV. " Again, when the Chaldeans say, as they are bound to do, that all persons born anywhere in the habitable earth under the same horoscope, are alike and must have the same fate, is it not evident that these would-be interpreters of the sky are of a class who are utterly ignorant of the nature of the sky ? For the earth is, as it were, divided in half and our view limited by those circles which the Greeks call ὁρίζοντες, and which we may in all accuracy term *finientes* or *horizons*. Now these horizons vary without limit according to the position of the spectator. Hence, of necessity, the rising and setting of the stars will not occur at the same time for all persons. But if this stellar force affects the heavens now in one way and now in another, how is it possible for this force to operate alike on all persons who are born at the same time, in view of the fact that they are born under vastly different skies ? In those places in which we live the Dog-star rises after the solstice,[1] in fact, several days later. But among the Troglodytes, we read, it sets before the solstice. Hence if we should now admit

concedamus aliquid vim caelestem ad eos, qui in terra gignuntur, pertinere, confitendum sit illis eos, qui nascuntur eodem tempore posse in dissimilis incidere naturas propter caeli dissimilitudinem ; quod minime illis placet ; volunt enim illi omnis eodem tempore ortos, qui ubique sint nati, eadem condicione nasci.

94 XLV. " Sed quae tanta dementia est, ut in maximis motibus mutationibusque caeli nihil intersit, qui ventus, qui imber, quae tempestas ubique sit ! quarum rerum in proximis locis tantae dissimilitudines saepe sunt, ut alia Tusculi, alia Romae eveniat saepe tempestas ; quod, qui navigant, maxime animadvertunt, cum in flectendis promunturiis ventorum mutationes maximas saepe sentiunt. Haec igitur cum sit tum serenitas, tum perturbatio caeli, estne sanorum hominum hoc ad nascentium ortus pertinere non dicere, quod non certe pertinet, illud nescio quid tenue, quod sentiri nullo modo, intellegi autem vix potest, quae a luna ceterisque sideribus caeli temperatio fiat, dicere ad puerorum ortus pertinere ?

" Quid ? quod non intellegunt seminum vim, quae ad gignendum procreandumque plurimum valeat, funditus tolli, mediocris erroris est ? Quis enim non videt et formas et mores et plerosque status ac motus effingere a parentibus liberos ? quod non contingeret,

that some stellar influence affects persons who are born upon the earth, then it must be conceded that all persons born at the same time may have different natures owing to the differences in their horoscopes. This is a conclusion by no means agreeable to the astrologers ; for they insist that all persons born at the same time, regardless of the place of birth, are born to the same fate.

XLV. " But what utter madness in these astrologers, in considering the effect of the vast movements and changes in the heavens, to assume that wind and rain and weather anywhere have no effect at birth ! In neighbouring places conditions in these respects are so different that frequently, for instance, we have one state of weather at Tusculum and another at Rome. This is especially noticeable to mariners who often observe extreme changes of weather take place while they are rounding the capes. Therefore, in view of the fact that the heavens are now serene and now disturbed by storms, is it the part of a reasonable man to say that this fact has no natal influence—and of course it has not—and then assert that a natal influence is exerted by some subtle, imperceptible, well-nigh inconceivable force which is due to the condition of the sky, which condition, in turn, is due to the action of the moon and stars ?

" Again, is it no small error of judgement that the Chaldeans fail to realize the effect of the parental seed which is an essential element in the process of generation ? For, surely, no one fails to see that the appearance and habits, and generally, the carriage and gestures of children are derived from their parents. This would not be

477

si haec non vis et natura gignentium efficeret, sed
95 temperatio lunae caelique moderatio. Quid? quod
uno et eodem temporis puncto nati dissimilis et
naturas et vitas et casus habent, parumne declarat
nihil ad agendam vitam nascendi tempus pertinere?
nisi forte putamus neminem eodem tempore ipso
et conceptum et natum, quo Africanum. Num quis
igitur talis fuit?

96   XLVI. "Quid? illudne dubium est, quin multi,
cum ita nati essent, ut quaedam contra naturam
depravata haberent, restituerentur et corrigerentur
ab natura, cum se ipsa revocasset, aut arte atque
medicina? ut, quorum linguae sic inhaererent, ut
loqui non possent, eae scalpello resectae liberarentur.
Multi etiam naturae vitium meditatione atque
exercitatione sustulerunt, ut Demosthenem scribit
Phalereus, cum rho dicere nequiret, exercitatione
fecisse, ut planissime diceret. Quodsi haec astro
ingenerata et tradita essent, nulla res ea mutare
posset. Quid? dissimilitudo locorum nonne dissimilis hominum procreationes habet? quas quidem
percurrere oratione facile est, quid inter Indos et
Persas et Aethiopas et Syros differat corporibus,
animis, ut incredibilis varietas dissimilitudoque sit.
97 Ex quo intellegitur plus terrarum situs quam lunae
status ad nascendum valere. Nam quod aiunt

the case if the characteristics of children were determined, not by the natural power of heredity, but by the phases of the moon and by the condition of the sky. And, again, the fact that men who were born at the very same instant, are unlike in character, career, and in destiny, makes it very clear that the time of birth has nothing to do in determining man's course in life. That is, unless perchance we are to believe that nobody else was conceived and born at the very same time that Africanus was. For was there ever anyone like him?

XLVI. " Furthermore, is it not a well-known and undoubted fact that many persons who were born with certain natural defects have been restored completely by Nature herself, after she had resumed her sway, or by surgery or by medicine? For example, some, who were so tongue-tied that they could not speak, have had their tongues set free by a cut from the surgeon's knife. Many more have corrected a natural defect by intelligent exertion. Demosthenes is an instance : according to the account given by Phalereus, he was unable to pronounce the Greek letter *rho*, but by repeated effort learned to articulate it perfectly. But if such defects had been engendered and implanted by a star nothing could have changed them. Do not unlike places produce unlike men? It would be an easy matter to sketch rapidly in passing the differences in mind and body which distinguish the Indians from the Persians and the Ethiopians from the Syrians—differences so striking and so pronounced as to be incredible. Hence it is evident that one's birth is more affected by local environment than by the condition of the moon. Of course, the

quadringenta septuaginta milia annorum in pericli-
tandis experiendisque pueris, quicumque essent
nati, Babylonios posuisse, fallunt ; si enim esset
factitatum, non esset desitum ; neminem autem
habemus auctorem, qui aut fieri dicat aut factum
sciat.

XLVII. " Videsne me non ea dicere quae Carneades, sed ea quae princeps Stoicorum Panaetius
dixerit ? Ego autem etiam hoc requiro : omnesne
qui Cannensi pugna ceciderint uno astro fuerint ?
exitus quidem omnium unus et idem fuit. Quid ?
qui ingenio atque animo singulares, num astro
quoque uno ? quod enim tempus, quo non innumera-
98 biles nascantur ? at certe similis nemo Homeri. Et, si
ad rem pertinet, quo modo caelo affecto compositis-
que sideribus quodque animal oriatur, valeat id
necesse est etiam in rebus inanimis ; quo quid dici
potest absurdius ? L. quidem Tarutius Firmanus,
familiaris noster, in primis Chaldaicis rationibus
eruditus, urbis etiam nostrae natalem diem repetebat
ab iis Parilibus, quibus eam a Romulo conditam
accepimus, Romamque, in iugo cum esset luna, natam
99 esse dicebat, nec eius fata canere dubitabat. O vim
maximam erroris ! Etiamne urbis natalis dies ad
vim stellarum et lunae pertinebat ? Fac in puero
referre, ex qua affectione caeli primum spiritum

---

[1] *Cf.* i. 19. 36.
[2] Celebrated on April 21. Pales was the tutelary god
of shepherds.

statement quoted by you that the Babylonians for
470,000 years [1] had taken the horoscope of every child
and had tested it by the results, is untrue ; for if this
had been their habit they would not have abandoned
it. Moreover we find no writer who says that the
practice exists or who knows that it ever did exist.

XLVII. " You observe that I am not repeating
the arguments of Carneades, but those of Panaetius,
the head of the Stoic school. But now on my own
initiative I put the following questions : Did all the
Romans who fell at Cannae have the same horoscope ? Yet all had one and the same end. Were
all the men eminent for intellect and genius born
under the same star ? Was there ever a day when
countless numbers were not born ? And yet there
never was another Homer. Again : if it matters
under what aspect of the sky or combination of
the stars every animate being is born, then necessarily the same conditions affect inanimate things
also : can any statement be more ridiculous
than that ? Be that as it may, our good friend
Lucius Tarutius of Firmum, who was steeped in
Chaldaic lore, made a calculation, based on the
assumption that our city's birthday was on the
Feast of Pales [2] (at which time tradition says it was
founded by Romulus), and from that calculation
Tarutius even went so far as to assert that Rome
was born when the moon was in the sign of Libra
and from that fact unhesitatingly prophesied her
destiny. What stupendous power delusion has !
And was the city's natal day also subject to the
influence of the moon and stars ? Assume, if you
will, that it matters in the case of a child under
what arrangement of the heavenly bodies it draws

duxerit; num hoc in latere aut in caemento, ex quibus urbs effecta est, potuit valere? Sed quid plura? cotidie refelluntur. Quam multa ego Pompeio, quam multa Crasso, quam multa huic ipsi Caesari, a Chaldaeis dicta memini, neminem eorum nisi senectute, nisi domi, nisi cum claritate esse moriturum! ut mihi permirum videatur quemquam exstare, qui etiam nunc credat eis quorum praedicta cotidie videat re et eventis refelli.

100 XLVIII. "Restant duo divinandi genera quae habere dicimur a natura, non ab arte, vaticinandi et somniandi; de quibus, Quinte," inquam, "si placet, disseramus."

"Mihi vero," inquit, "placet; his enim, quae adhuc disputasti, prorsus adsentior, et, vere ut loquar, quamquam tua me oratio confirmavit, tamen etiam mea sponte nimis superstitiosam de divinatione Stoicorum sententiam iudicabam; haec me Peripateticorum ratio magis movebat et veteris Dicaearchi et eius, qui nunc floret, Cratippi, qui censent esse in mentibus hominum tamquam oraclum aliquod, ex quo futura praesentiant, si aut furore divino incitatus animus aut somno relaxatus solute moveatur ac libere. His de generibus quid sentias et quibus ea rationibus infirmes, audire sane velim."

---

[1] At the time of the dialogue, 45 B.C., Cratippus was lecturing in Athens and had as one of his pupils Marcus, the only son of Marcus Cicero.

its first breath, does it also follow that the stars could have had any influence over the bricks and cement of which the city was built ? But why say more against a theory which every day's experience refutes ? I recall a multitude of prophecies which the Chaldeans made to Pompey, to Crassus and even to Caesar himself (now lately deceased), to the effect that no one of them would die except in old age, at home and in great glory. Hence it would seem very strange to me should anyone, especially at this time, believe in men whose predictions he sees disproved every day by actual results.

XLVIII. " There remain the two kinds of divination which we are said to derive from nature and not from art—vaticination and dreams,—these, my dear Quintus, if agreeable to you, let us now discuss."

" Delighted, I assure you," said he, " for I am in entire accord with the views which you have so far expressed. To be quite frank, your argument has merely strengthened the opinion which I already had, for my own reasoning had convinced me that the Stoic view of divination smacked too much of superstition. I was more impressed by the reasoning of the Peripatetics, of Dicaearchus, of ancient times, and of Cratippus,[1] who still flourishes. According to their opinion there is within the human soul some sort of power—' oracular,' I might call it—by which the future is foreseen when the soul is inspired by a divine frenzy, or when it is released by sleep and is free to move at will. I should like very much to learn your views of these two classes of divination and by what arguments you disprove them."

101 XLIX. Quae cum ille dixisset, tum ego rursus quasi ab alio principio sum exorsus dicere :

"Non ignoro," inquam, "Quinte, te semper ita sensisse, ut de ceteris divinandi generibus dubitares, ista duo, furoris et somnii, quae a libera mente fluere viderentur, probares. Dicam igitur de istis ipsis duobus generibus mihi quid videatur, si prius et Stoicorum conclusio rationis et Cratippi nostri quid valeat videro. Dixisti enim et Chrysippum et Diogenem et Antipatrum concludere hoc modo :

' Si sunt di neque ante declarant hominibus quae futura sint, aut non diligunt homines, aut quid eventurum sit ignorant ; aut existimant nihil interesse hominum scire quid sit futurum ; aut non censent esse suae maiestatis praesignificare hominibus quae sunt futura ; aut ea ne ipsi quidem di significare 102 possunt. At neque non diligunt nos (sunt enim benefici generique hominum amici) ; neque ignorant ea quae ab ipsis constituta et designata sunt ; neque nostra nihil interest scire ea quae futura sunt (erimus enim cautiores, si sciemus) ; neque hoc alienum ducunt maiestate sua (nihil est enim beneficentia praestantius) ; neque non possunt futura praenoscere ; non igitur di sunt nec significant

---

[1] *Cf.* i. 38. 82.
[2] All leading Stoics and defenders of divination. *Cf* i. 3. 6.

XLIX. After this statement had been made by Quintus, I began again, making a new start, so to speak :

" I am well aware, my dear Quintus, that, while you have always felt a doubt about all other kinds of divination, you approve of the two you just mentioned — divination by frenzy and divination by dreams, both of which, it is thought, flow from a soul set free. Let me, then, state my opinion of these two kinds of divination. But, first, let me examine that syllogism [1] of the Stoics and of our friend Cratippus and see how sound it is. You stated the syllogism of Chrysippus, Diogenes, and Antipater [2] in this way :

" ' If there are gods and they do not make clear to man in advance what the future will be, then they do not love man, or they themselves do not know what the future will be ; or they think that it is of no advantage to man to know what the future will be ; or they think it inconsistent with their dignity to give to man forewarnings of the future ; or they, though gods, cannot give signs of coming events. But it is not true that the gods do not love us (for they are the friends and benefactors of the human race) ; nor is it true that they do not know what they themselves have determined and planned ; nor is it true that it is of no advantage to us to know what is going to happen (for man would be more prudent if he knew) ; nor is it true that the gods think it inconsistent with their dignity to give forecasts of the future (for there is no more excellent quality than kindness) ; nor is it true that they have not the power to know the future ; therefore, it is not true that there are gods and yet that

nobis futura ; sunt autem di ; significant ergo ; et non, si significant futura, nullas dant vias nobis ad significationum scientiam (frustra enim significarent) ; nec, si dant vias, non est divinatio ; est igitur divinatio.'

103 " O acutos homines ! quam paucis verbis confectum negotium putant ! Ea sumunt ad concludendum quorum eis nihil conceditur. Conclusio autem rationis ea probanda est, in qua ex rebus non dubiis id quod dubitatur efficitur.

L. " Videsne Epicurum, quem hebetem et rudem dicere solent Stoici, quem ad modum, quod in natura rerum omne esse dicimus, id infinitum esse concluserit ? ' Quod finitum est,' inquit, ' habet extremum.' Quis hoc non dederit ? ' Quod autem habet extremum, id cernitur ex alio extrinsecus.' Hoc quoque est concedendum. ' At, quod omne est, id non cernitur ex alio extrinsecus.' Ne hoc quidem negari potest. ' Nihil igitur cum habeat extremum, infini-
104 tum sit necesse est.' Videsne ut ad rem dubiam concessis rebus pervenerit ? Hoc vos dialectici non facitis ; nec solum ea non sumitis ad concludendum quae ab omnibus concedantur, sed ea sumitis, quibus concessis nihilo magis efficiatur quod velitis. Primum enim hoc sumitis : ' Si sunt di, benefici in homines sunt.' Quis hoc vobis dabit ? Epicurusne ? Qui negat quicquam deos nec alieni curare nec sui.

they do not give us signs of the future; but there
are gods; therefore they give us such signs; and
it is not true, if they give us such signs, that
they give us no means of understanding those signs,
otherwise their signs would be useless; nor, if they
give us the means, is it true that there is no divination: therefore divination exists.'

"What keen-witted men! With how very few
words they think the business dispatched! But to
establish their syllogism they take propositions for
granted which are not conceded at all; yet a chain
of reasoning, to be valid, should proceed from premises which are not doubtful to the conclusion
which is in dispute.

L. "Pray observe the neat way in which Epicurus
(whom you Stoics usually call a blundering idiot)
proves that what we term 'the universe' is infinite.
'That,' said he, 'which is finite has an end.' Who
would deny that? Again, 'That which has an end
is seen from some point outside itself.' That, too,
must be granted. 'But the universe is not seen
from without itself.' We cannot question that
proposition either. 'Therefore, since it has no end
the universe must be infinite.' You see how Epicurus proceeds from admitted premises to the proposition to be established. But this you Stoic
logicians do not do; for you not only do not assume
premises which everybody concedes, but you even
assume premises which, if granted, do not tend in
the least to establish what you wish to prove. For
you start with this assumption: 'If there are gods
they are kindly disposed towards men.' Now who
will grant you that? Epicurus? But he says that
the gods do not trouble a whit about themselves or

CICERO

An noster Ennius ? Qui magno plausu loquitur assentiente populo :

> égo deum genus ésse semper díxi et dicam caélitum,
> séd eos non curáre opinor, quíd agat humanúm genus.

Et quidem cur sic opinetur rationem subicit ; sed nihil est necesse dicere quae sequuntur ; tantum sat est intellegi, id sumere istos pro certo, quod dubium controversumque sit.

105   LI. "Sequitur porro, 'nihil deos ignorare, quod omnia sint ab eis constituta.' Hic vero quanta pugna est doctissimorum hominum negantium esse haec a dis inmortalibus constituta ! 'At nostra interest scire ea, quae eventura sunt.' Magnus Dicaearchi liber est nescire ea melius esse quam scire. Negant 'id esse alienum maiestate deorum.' Scilicet casas omnium introspicere ut videant quid cuique conducat !

106 'Neque non possunt futura praenoscere.' Negant posse ei quibus non placet esse certum, quid futurum sit. Videsne igitur, quae dubia sint, ea sumi pro certis atque concessis ? Deinde contorquent et ita concludunt : 'Non igitur et sunt di nec significant futura.' Id enim iam perfectum arbitrantur.— Deinde assumunt : 'Sunt autem di,' quod ipsum

---

    [1] In his *Telamon*. The succeeding line is quoted in Cic. *N.D.* iii. 32. 79 *nam si curent, bene bonis sit, male malis ; quod nunc abest.*

488

about anybody else. Is it our own Ennius? But he says with general approval and applause :[1]

> I always said that there were gods on high,
> And this I never will neglect to say ;
> But my opinion is they do not care
> What destiny befalls the human race.

To be sure he proceeds to give the reason for his opinion in succeeding lines, but there is no need to repeat them. Enough has been shown to make it clear that your Stoic friends assume as certain what is the subject of doubt and discussion.

LI. " But the syllogism goes on to say : ' The gods are not ignorant of anything, for all things were ordained by them.' But what a heavy attack is made on this very point by scholars who deny that such and such things were ordained by the immortal gods ! ' But it is to our interest to know what is going to happen.' Yet Dicaearchus has written a large volume to prove that it is better not to know than to know the future. They say further : ' It is not inconsistent with the dignity of gods to give knowledge of the future.' But entirely consistent, I presume, for them to peer into every man's house to see what he needs ! ' It is not true that the gods cannot know the future.' But their ability to know is denied by those who maintain that it is not certain what the future will be. Now don't you see what doubtful premises they assume to be certain and take for granted ? Next they hurl this dialectical dart : ' Therefore it is not true both that there are gods and yet that they do not give signs of the future.' And of course they think that the matter is now settled. Then they make another assumption : ' But there are gods.' Even that is

489

non ab omnibus conceditur. 'Significant ergo.' Ne
id quidem sequitur ; possunt enim non significare et
tamen esse di. 'Nec, si significent, non dant vias
aliquas ad scientiam significationis.' At id quoque
potest, ut non dent homini, ipsi habeant ; cur enim
Tuscis potius quam Romanis darent ? 'Nec, si
dant vias, nulla est divinatio.' Fac dare deos, quod
absurdum est, quid refert, si accipere non possumus ?
Extremum est : 'Est igitur divinatio.' Sit extremum, effectum tamen non est ; ex falsis enim,
ut ab ipsis didicimus, verum effici non potest. Iacet
igitur tota conclusio.

107   LII. " Veniamus nunc ad optimum virum,
familiarem nostrum, Cratippum :

'Si sine oculis,' inquit, 'non potest exstare
officium et munus oculorum, possunt autem aliquando
oculi non fungi suo munere, qui vel semel ita est
usus oculis, ut vera cerneret, is habet sensum
oculorum vera cernentium. Item igitur, si sine
divinatione non potest officium et munus divinationis exstare, potest autem, cum quis divinationem
habeat, errare aliquando nec vera cernere, satis est
ad confirmandam divinationem, semel aliquid ita
esse divinatum, nihil ut fortuito cecidisse videatur ;
sunt autem eius generis innumerabilia ; esse igitur
divinationem confitendum est.'

" Festive et breviter ; sed cum bis sumpsit quod

------

[1] *Cf.* i. 32. 71.

not conceded by everybody. ' Therefore they give signs of the future.' Not necessarily so : for they may not give us signs of the future and still be gods. ' Nor is it true that, if they give such signs, they give no means of interpreting those signs.' But it may be that they have the means and yet do not impart them to man ; for why would they impart them to the Etruscans rather than to the Romans ? Again, the Stoics say : ' If the gods do impart the means, that is divination.' Grant that they do (which is absurd), what is the good if we do not understand ? Their conclusion is : ' Therefore there is divination.' Suppose that is their conclusion, still they have not proved it ; for, as they themselves have taught us, the truth cannot be proved from false premises. Hence their entire argument falls to the ground.

LII. " Now let us come to the argument of that most worthy gentleman, our intimate friend, Cratippus : [1]

" ' Though without eyes,' he says, ' it is impossible to perform the act and function of sight, and though the eyes sometimes cannot perform their appointed function, yet when a person has once so employed his eyes as to see things as they are, he has a realization of what correct vision is. Likewise, too, although without the power of divination it is impossible for the act and function of divining to exist, and though one with that power may be mistaken and may make erroneous prophecies, yet to establish the existence of divination it is enough that a single event has been so clearly foretold as to exclude the hypothesis of chance. But there are many such instances ; therefore the existence of divination must be conceded.'

" Delightfully and briefly put ; but after he has

491

voluit, etiamsi faciles nos ad concedendum habuerit,
id tamen quod assumit concedi nullo modo potest.
108 ' Si,' inquit, ' aliquando oculi peccent, tamen, quia
recte aliquando viderint, inest in eis vis videndi ;
item si quis semel aliquid in divinatione viderit, is,
etiam cum peccet, tamen existimandus sit habere
vim divinandi.'

LIII. " Vide, quaeso, Cratippe noster, quam sint
ista similia ; nam mihi non videntur. Oculi enim
vera cernentes utuntur natura atque sensu ; animi,
si quando vel vaticinando vel somniando vera viderunt,
usi sunt fortuna atque casu ; nisi forte concessuros
tibi existimas eos, qui somnia pro somniis habent, si
quando aliquod somnium verum evaserit, non id
fortuito accidisse. Sed demus tibi istas duas sumptiones (ea quae λήμματα appellant dialectici, sed
nos Latine loqui malumus), assumptio tamen (quam
πρόσληψιν eidem vocant), non dabitur.

109 " Assumit autem Cratippus hoc modo : ' Sunt
autem innumerabiles praesensiones non fortuitae.'
At ego dico nullam. Vide, quanta sit controversia.
Iam assumptione non concessa nulla conclusio est.
' At impudentes sumus qui, cum tam perspicuum
sit, non concedamus.' Quid est ' perspicuum ' ?
' Multa vera,' inquit, ' evadere.' Quid, quod multo

twice made gratuitous assumptions, even though he has found us quite generous in making concessions, yet his further assumption cannot possibly be conceded. He says in substance, ' If the eyes are sometimes at fault, yet, because they have sometimes seen correctly, the power of sight resides within them ; likewise if a person has once foreseen something by means of divination, yet even when he errs in his predictions, he must be held to have the power of divination.'

LIII. " Pray point out, my dear Cratippus, the similarity in these propositions of yours. I confess that it is not apparent to me. For the eyes in seeing correctly employ a sense conferred by nature ; while the soul, if it ever has a true vision of the future, whether by vaticination or by dreams, relies upon luck or chance. This you must admit unless, perchance, you think that those who consider dreams as dreams and nothing more, are going to concede that the fulfilment of any dream was ever due to anything but luck. While we may grant your two major premises,—these the Greeks call λήμματα, but we prefer to call them by their Latin equivalent *sumptiones*—yet we will not grant your minor premise—which the Greeks call πρόσληψις.

" Cratippus states his minor premise thus : ' But there are countless instances of prophecies being fulfilled without the intervention of luck.' On the contrary, I say there isn't even one. Observe how keen the controversy grows ! Now that the minor premise is denied the conclusion fails. But he retorts : ' You are unreasonable not to grant it, it is so evident.' Why ' evident ' ? ' Because many prophecies come true.' And what of the fact that many more don't

plura falsa ? Nonne ipsa varietas, quae est propria
fortunae, fortunam esse causam, non naturam esse
docet ? Deinde, si tua ista conclusio, Cratippe, vera
est—tecum enim mihi res est—non intellegis eadem
uti posse et haruspices et fulguratores et interpretes
ostentorum et augures et sortilegos et Chaldaeos ?
quorum generum nullum est ex quo non aliquid
sicut praedictum sit evaserit. Ergo aut ea quoque
genera divinandi sunt, quae tu rectissime improbas,
aut, si ea non sunt, non intellego cur haec duo sint
quae relinquis. Qua ergo ratione haec inducis,
eadem illa possunt esse, quae tollis.

110 LIV. " Quid vero habet auctoritatis furor iste,
quem ' divinum ' vocatis ut, quae sapiens non videat,
ea videat insanus, et is qui humanos sensus amiserit
divinos adsecutus sit ? Sibyllae versus observamus,
quos illa furens fudisse dicitur. Quorum interpres
nuper falsa quadam hominum fama dicturus in
senatu putabatur eum, quem re vera regem habeba-
mus, appellandum quoque esse regem, si salvi esse
vellemus. Hoc si est in libris, in quem hominem et
in quod tempus est ? Callide enim, qui illa composuit,
perfecit, ut, quodcumque accidisset, praedictum videretur hominum et temporum definitione sublata.

---

[1] Lucius Cotta, one of the *quindecimviri* who had charge
of the verses. This story is told by Suetonius in his *Iul.
Caesar*, ch. 79. It was said that according to the Sibylline verses the Parthians could only be conquered by a
king and therefore that Caesar should be called king.
Plutarch, *Caesar*, ch. 60 and 64.

come true ? Does not this very uncertainty, which is characteristic of luck, demonstrate that their fulfilment is accounted for by luck and not by any law of nature ? Furthermore, my dear Cratippus—for my controversy is with you—if that argument of yours is sound, don't you see that it is equally available in behalf of the means of divination practised by soothsayers, augurs, Chaldeans and by interpreters of lightnings, portents, and lots ? For each of these classes will furnish you with at least one instance of a prophecy that came to pass. Therefore either they too are all means of divining—and this you very properly deny—or, if they are not, then, so far as I can see, the two classes which you permit to remain are not means of divining. Hence the same reasoning employed by you to establish the two kinds which you accept may be used to establish the others which you reject.

LIV. " But what weight is to be given to that frenzy of yours, which you term ' divine ' and which enables the crazy man to see what the wise man does not see, and invests the man who has lost human intelligence with the intelligence of gods ? We Romans venerate the verses of the Sibyl who is said to have uttered them while in a frenzy. Recently there was a rumour, which was believed at the time, but turned out to be false, that one of the interpreters [1] of those verses was going to declare in the Senate that, for our safety, the man whom we had as king in fact should be made king also in name. If this is in the books, to what man and to what time does it refer ? For it was clever in the author to take care that whatever happened should appear foretold because all reference to persons or time had been

111 Adhibuit etiam latebram obscuritatis, ut eidem versus alias in aliam rem posse accommodari viderentur. Non esse autem illud carmen furentis cum ipsum poëma declarat (est enim magis artis et diligentiae quam incitationis et motus), tum vero ea, quae ἀκρο-στιχίς dicitur, cum deinceps ex primis versuum litteris aliquid conectitur, ut in quibusdam Ennianis : 'Quintus Ennius fecit.' Id certe magis est attenti animi

112 quam furentis. Atque in Sibyllinis ex primo versu cuiusque sententiae primis litteris illius sententiae carmen omne praetexitur. Hoc scriptoris est, non furentis, adhibentis diligentiam, non insani. Quam ob rem Sibyllam quidem sepositam et conditam habeamus, ut, id quod proditum est a maioribus, iniussu senatus ne legantur quidem libri valeantque ad deponendas potius quam ad suscipiendas religiones ;[1] cum antistitibus agamus, ut quidvis potius ex illis libris quam regem proferant, quem Romae posthac nec di nec homines esse patientur.

LV. " At multi saepe vera vaticinati, ut Cassandra :

iamque mari magno . . .

eademque paulo post :

eheu videte . . .

113 Num igitur me cogis etiam fabulis credere ?[2] quae

---

omitted. He also employed a maze of obscurity so that the same verses might be adapted to different situations at different times. Moreover, that this poem is not the work of frenzy is quite evident from the quality of its composition (for it exhibits artistic care rather than emotional excitement), and is especially evident from the fact that it is written in what are termed 'acrostics,' wherein the initial letters of each verse taken in order convey a meaning ; as, for example, in some of Ennius's verses, the initial letters form the words, *Quintus Ennius Fecit*, that is, 'Quintus Ennius wrote it.' That surely is the work of concentrated thought and not of a frenzied brain. And in the Sibylline books, throughout the entire work, each prophecy is embellished with an acrostic, so that the initial letters of each of the lines give the subject of that particular prophecy. Such a work comes from a writer who is not frenzied, who is painstaking, not crazy. Therefore let us keep the Sibyl under lock and key so that in accordance with the ordinances of our forefathers her books may not even be read without permission of the Senate and may be more effective in banishing rather than encouraging superstitious ideas. And let us plead with the priests to bring forth from those books anything rather than a king, whom henceforth neither gods nor men will suffer to exist in Rome.

LV. " But many persons in a frenzy often utter true prophecies, as Cassandra did when she said.

Already on the mighty deep . . . [1]

and when, a little later, she exclaimed,

Alas ! behold ! . . . [2]

Then, I suppose you are going to force me to believe

delectationis habeant, quantum voles, verbis, sententiis, numeris, cantibus adiuventur ; auctoritatem quidem nullam debemus nec fidem commenticiis rebus adiungere. Eodemque modo nec ego Publicio nescio cui, nec Marciis vatibus, nec Apollinis opertis, credendum existimo ; quorum partim ficta aperte, partim effutita temere numquam, ne mediocri quidem cuiquam, non modo prudenti probata sunt.

114   " ' Quid ? ' inquies, ' remex ille de classe Coponi nonne ea praedixit, quae facta sunt ? ' Ille vero, et ea quidem quae omnes eo tempore ne acciderent timebamus. Castra enim in Thessalia castris collata audiebamus, videbaturque nobis exercitus Caesaris et audaciae plus habere, quippe qui patriae bellum intulisset, et roboris propter vetustatem ; casum autem proeli nemo nostrum erat quin timeret ; sed, ita ut constantibus hominibus par erat, non aperte. Ille autem Graecus, quid mirum si, magnitudine timoris, ut plerumque fit, a constantia atque a mente atque a se ipse discessit ? qua perturbatione animi, quae, sanus cum esset, timebat ne evenirent, ea demens eventura esse dicebat. Utrum tandem, per deos atque homines ! magis veri simile est vesanum remigem an aliquem nostrum qui ibi tum eramus,

---

[1] *Cf.* i. 50. 115.
[2] *Cf.* i. 40. 89.
[3] *Cf.* i. 32. 68.

in myths ? Let them be as charming as you please and as finished as possible in language, thought, rhythm, and melody, still we ought not to give credence to fictitious incidents or to quote them as authority. On that principle no reliance, in my opinion, should be placed in the prophecies of your Publicius [1]—whoever he may have been—or in those of the Marcian bards [2] or in those of the hazy oracles of Apollo[1] : some were obviously false and others mere senseless chatter and none of them were ever believed in by any man of ordinary sense, much less by any person of wisdom.

" ' Oh ! but what about that oarsman in Coponius's fleet,' [3] you say, ' didn't he truly foretell what afterwards came to pass ? ' He did indeed, and the very things that all of us at the time feared would happen. For news was coming to us that the armies of Caesar and Pompey were facing each other in Thessaly. We thought that Caesar's troops had more reckless courage because they were fighting against their country and greater strength because of their long military training. Besides there was not one of us who did not dread the outcome of the battle, but our apprehension was not openly shown and was such as not to be discreditable to men of strong character. As for that Greek sailor, is it strange if, in the extremity of his fear, he, as most people do in such cases, lost his courage, reason, and self-control ? In his mental excitement and aberration, he merely stated that things would occur, which, when he was himself, he feared would come to pass. In heaven's name, pray tell me, then, which you think was more likely to have had the power to interpret the decrees of the immortal gods—that crazy sailor,

me, Catonem, Varronem, Coponium ipsum, consilia
deorum immortalium perspicere potuisse ?

115   LVI. " Sed iam ad te venio,

> ó sancte Apollo, qui úmbilicum cértum terrarum óbsides,
> únde superstitiósa primum saéva evasit vóx fera.

Tuis enim oraculis Chrysippus totum volumen
implevit partim falsis, ut ego opinor, partim casu
veris, ut fit in omni oratione saepissime ; partim
flexiloquis et obscuris, ut interpres egeat interprete,
et sors ipsa ad sortes referenda sit ; partim ambiguis,
et quae ad dialecticum deferenda sint. Nam cum
illa sors edita est opulentissimo regi Asiae :

> Croesus Halyn penetrans magnam pervertet opum vim,

hostium vim se perversurum putavit, pervertit autem
116 suam. Utrum igitur eorum accidisset, verum oraclum
fuisset. Cur autem hoc˙ credam umquam editum
Croeso ? aut Herodotum cur veraciorem ducam
Ennio ? Num minus ille potuit de Croeso quam de
Pyrrho fingere Ennius ? Quis enim est qui credat
Apollinis ex oraculo Pyrrho esse responsum :

> aio te, Aeacida, Romanos vincere posse ?

Primum Latine Apollo numquam locutus est ; deinde
ista sors inaudita Graecis est ; praeterea Pyrrhi
temporibus iam Apollo versus facere desierat ;

---

[1] Marcus Varro, the most learned Roman of his time.

[2] The author of these lines is unknown ; *umbilicus terrarum*
(ὀμφαλὸς γῆς), because it was supposed to be the centre of
the earth.

[3] *Cf.* i. 3. 6, i. 19. 37, i. 50. 115.

[4] In Greek Κροῖσος Ἅλυν διαβὰς μεγάλην ἀρχὴν καταλύσει.

[5] Herodotus gives the substance of this story in i. 53.

[6] From the *Annales* of Ennius.

or someone of our party then on the ground—Cato, Varro,[1] Coponius or I ?

LVI. " But now I come to you,

> Apollo, sacred guard of earth's true core,
> Whence first came frenzied, wild prophetic words.[2]

Chrysippus filled a whole volume with your oracles[3]; of these some, as I think, were false ; some came true by chance, as happens very often even in ordinary speech ; some were so intricate and obscure that their interpreter needs an interpreter and the oracles themselves must be referred back to the oracle ; and some so equivocal that they require a dialectician to construe them. For example, when the following oracular response was made to Asia's richest king :

> When Croesus o'er the river Halys goes
> He will a mighty kingdom overthrow,[4]

Croesus thought that he would overthrow his enemy's kingdom, whereas he overthrew his own. But in either event the oracle would have been true. Besides, why need I believe that this oracle was ever given to Croesus ? or why should I consider Herodotus[5] more truthful than Ennius ? and was the former less able to invent stories about Croesus than Ennius was about Pyrrhus ? For instance, nobody believes Ennius when he says that Apollo's oracle gave the following response to Pyrrhus :

> O son of Aeacus, my prediction is
> That you the Roman army will defeat.[6]

In the first place Apollo never spoke in Latin ; second, that oracle is unknown to the Greeks ; third, in the days of Pyrrhus Apollo had already ceased making

postremo, quamquam semper fuit, ut apud Ennium
est,

> stolidum genus Aeacidarum,
> bellipotentes sunt magis quam sapientipotentes,

tamen hanc amphiboliam versus intellegere potuisset,
' vincere te Romanos ' nihilo magis in se quam in
Romanos valere ; nam illa amphibolia quae Croesum
decepit, vel Chrysippum potuisset fallere, haec vero
ne Epicurum quidem !

117   LVII. " Sed, quod caput est, cur isto modo iam
oracla Delphis non eduntur non modo nostra aetate,
sed iam diu, ut modo nihil possit esse contemptius ?
Hoc loco cum urguentur, ' evanuisse,' aiunt, ' vetustate vim loci eius, unde anhelitus ille terrae fieret,
quo Pythia mente incitata oracla ederet.' De vino
aut salsamento putes loqui, quae evanescunt vetustate. De vi loci agitur, neque solum naturali, sed
etiam divina ; quae quo tandem modo evanuit ?
' Vetustate,' inquies. Quae ' vetustas ' est quae
vim divinam conficere possit ? Quid tam divinum
autem quam afflatus e terra mentem ita movens,
ut eam providam rerum futurarum efficiat, ut ea
non modo cernat multo ante, sed etiam numero
versuque pronuntiet ? Quando ista vis autem
evanuit ? an postquam homines minus creduli esse
coeperunt ?

verses, and, finally, although "the sons of Aeacus have ever been," as Ennius says,

a stolid race,
And more for valour than for wisdom famed,

still Pyrrhus would have had sense enough to see that the equivocal line—" You the Roman army will defeat "—was no more favourable to him than to the Romans. As for that equivocal response which deceived Croesus, it might have deceived—Chrysippus, for example; but the one made to Pyrrhus wouldn't have fooled—even Epicurus !

LVII. " However, the main question is this : Why are Delphic oracles (of which I have just given you examples) not uttered at the present time and have not been for a long time ? And why are they regarded with the utmost contempt ? When pressed at this point their apologists affirm that ' the long flight of time has gradually dissipated the virtue of the place whence came those subterranean exhalations which inspired the Pythian priestess to utter oracles.' One might think that they are talking about wine or brine which do evaporate. But the question is about the virtue of a place—a virtue which you call not only ' natural ' but even ' divine,'—pray how did it evaporate ? ' By length of time,' you say. But what length of time could destroy a divine power ? And what is as divine as a subterranean exhalation that inspires the soul with power to foresee the future—a power such that it not only sees things a long time before they happen, but actually foretells them in rhythmic verse ? When did the virtue disappear ? Was it after men began to be less credulous ?

118 " Demosthenes quidem, qui abhinc annos prope
trecentos fuit, iam tum φιλιππίζειν Pythiam
dicebat, id est quasi cum Philippo facere. Hoc
autem eo spectabat, ut eam a Philippo corruptam
diceret. Quo licet existimare in aliis quoque oraculis
Delphicis aliquid non sinceri fuisse. Sed nescio quo
modo isti philosophi superstitiosi et paene fanatici
quidvis malle videntur quam se non ineptos.
Evanuisse mavultis et extinctum esse id quod si
umquam fuisset, certe aeternum esset, quam ea
quae non sunt credenda non credere.

119 LVIII. " Similis est error in somniis ; quorum
quidem defensio repetita quam longe est ! Divinos
animos censent esse nostros, eosque esse tractos
extrinsecus, animorumque consentientium multitudine completum esse mundum ; hac igitur mentis
et ipsius divinitate et coniunctione cum externis
mentibus cerni, quae sint futura. Contrahi autem
animum Zeno et quasi labi putat atque concidere id
ipsum esse dormire. Iam Pythagoras et Plato,
locupletissimi auctores, quo in somnis certiora
videamus, praeparatos quodam cultu atque victu
proficisci ad dormiendum iubent. Faba quidem
Pythagorei utique abstinere, quasi vero eo cibo mens,
non venter, infletur ! Sed nescio quo modo nihil tam
absurde dici potest quod non dicatur ab aliquo
philosophorum.

120 " Utrum igitur censemus dormientium animos per
sene ipsos in somniando moveri, an, ut Democritus

---

[1] *Cf.* Dem. 287. 1 ; Aeschin. 72. 14.

" By the way, Demosthenes, who lived nearly three hundred years ago, used to say even then that the Pythian priestess ' philippized,' [1] in other words, that she was Philip's ally. By this expression he meant to infer that she had been bribed by Philip. Hence we may conclude that in other instances the Delphic oracles were not entirely free of guile. But, for some inexplicable cause, those superstitious and half-cracked philosophers of yours would rather appear absurd than anything else in the world. You Stoics, instead of rejecting these incredible tales, prefer to believe that a power had gradually faded into nothingness, whereas if it ever had existed it certainly would be eternal.

LVIII. " There is a like error in regard to dreams. How far-fetched is the argument in their defence ! ' Our souls ' (according to the view of your school) ' are divine and are derived from an external source ; the universe is filled with a multitude of harmonious souls ; therefore, because of its divinity and its contact with other souls, the human soul during sleep foresees what is to come.' But Zeno thinks that sleep is nothing more than a contraction—a slipping and a collapse, as it were—of the human soul. Then Pythagoras and Plato, who are most respectable authorities, bid us, if we would have trustworthy dreams, to prepare for sleep by following a pre-scribed course in conduct and in eating. The Pythagoreans make a point of prohibiting the use of beans, as if thereby the soul and not the belly was filled with wind ! Somehow or other no statement is too absurd for some philosophers to make.

" Then shall we believe that the souls of sleepers while dreaming are spontaneously moved ? or, as

censet, externa et adventicia visione pulsari? Sive
enim sic est sive illo modo, videri possunt permulta
somniantibus falsa pro veris. Nam et navigantibus
moveri videntur ea quae stant, et quodam obtutu
oculorum duo pro uno lucernae lumina. Quid dicam,
insanis, quid ebriis, quam multa falsa videantur?
Quodsi eius modi visis credendum non est, cur
somniis credatur, nescio. Nam tam licet de his
erroribus, si velis, quam de somniis disputare, ut
ea quae stant, si moveri videantur, terrae motum
significare dicas aut repentinam aliquam fugam;
gemino autem lucernae lumine declarari dissensionem
ac seditionem moveri!

121 LIX. " Iam ex insanorum aut ebriorum visis
innumerabilia coniectura trahi possunt, quae futura
videantur. Quis est enim, qui totum diem iaculans
non aliquando colliniet? Totas noctes dormimus,
neque ulla est fere, qua non somniemus, et miramur
aliquando id quod somniarimus evadere? Quid est
tam incertum quam talorum iactus? tamen nemo
est quin saepe iactans Venerium iaciat aliquando,
non numquam etiam iterum ac tertium. Num igitur,
ut inepti, Veneris id impulsu fieri malumus quam
casu dicere? Quodsi ceteris temporibus falsis visis
credendum non est, non video, quid praecipui
somnus habeat, in quo valeant falsa pro veris.

---

[1] *Visiones*, the equivalent of *spectra*, *simulacra*, εἴδωλα,
phantoms from without which burst upon the mind through
the body. *Cf.* Cic. *Acad.* ii. 15.

Democritus thinks, that they are impelled to action
by phantoms from without[1] ? Whether the one
theory or the other be correct, the fact remains that
men in sleep assume many false apparitions to be
true. Likewise, to men who are sailing, stationary
objects on shore seem to be moving ; and also,
sometimes in looking at a lamp, by some sort of
optical illusion we see two flames instead of one.
Why need I mention how many non-existent things
are seen by men who are drunk or crazy ? And if
we are to put no trust in such apparitions of the
waking man I do not understand why we should put
any trust in dreams. Of course you may argue, if
you will, about these tricks of vision as you would
about dreams, and say, for example, that when
stationary objects appear to be in motion, it foretells
an earthquake or a sudden flight ; and when the
lamp's flame appears to be double it portends that
insurrection and rebellion are afoot !

LIX. " By applying conjecture to the countless
delusions of drunk or crazy men we may sometimes
deduce what appears to be a real prophecy ; for who,
if he shoots at a mark all day long, will not occasionally hit it ? We sleep every night and there is
scarcely ever a night when we do not dream ; then
do we wonder that our dreams come true sometimes ?
Nothing is so uncertain as a cast of dice and yet there
is no one who plays often who does not sometimes
make a Venus-throw and occasionally twice or thrice in
succession. Then are we, like fools, to prefer to say
that it happened by the direction of Venus rather
than by chance ? And if we are to put no trust in
false visions at other times I do not see what especial
virtue there is in sleep to entitle its false visions to

122 Quodsi ita natura paratum esset, ut ea dormientes
agerent, quae somniarent, alligandi omnes essent,
qui cubitum irent ; maiores enim quam ulli insani
efficerent motus somniantes.

"Quodsi insanorum visis fides non est habenda,
quia falsa sunt, cur credatur somniantium visis,
quae multo etiam perturbatiora sunt, non intellego
An quod insani sua visa coniectori non narrant,
narrant, qui somniaverunt ? Quaero etiam, si velim
scribere quid, aut legere, aut canere, vel voce vel
fidibus, aut geometricum quiddam, aut physicum,
aut dialecticum explicare, somniumne exspectandum
sit, an ars adhibenda, sine qua nihil earum rerum
nec fieri nec expediri potest ? Atqui, ne si navigare
quidem velim, ita gubernem ut somniaverim ;
123 praesens enim poena sit. Qui igitur convenit
aegros a coniectore somniorum potius quam a
medico petere medicinam ? An Aesculapius an
Serapis potest nobis praescribere per somnium
curationem valetudinis, Neptunus gubernantibus
non potest ? et si sine medico medicinam dabit
Minerva, Musae scribendi, legendi, ceterarum
artium scientiam somniantibus non dabunt ? At
si curatio daretur valetudinis, haec quoque, quae
dixi, darentur ; quae quoniam non dantur, medicina

---

[1] With the temples of these gods were connected dream-
oracles by means of which remedies were prescribed for
the sick.

[2] ='Aθήνη 'Υγίεια.

be taken as true. On the other hand if nature had intended that sleepers should do what they dreamed, persons on going to bed would always have to be tied, otherwise they would commit more follies in their dreams than any madman ever did.

" And if, because of their unreality, we are to have no faith in the visions of the insane, I do not understand why we place any confidence in dreams, which are far more confused. Is it because the insane do not tell their delusions to interpreters of visions while dreamers do ? I ask you this : suppose I wished to read, write, or sing, or to play on the lute, or to solve some problem in geometry, physics, or logic, must I wait for a dream, or must I depend upon the peculiar knowledge which each of these several arts or sciences requires and without which none of them can be utilized or mastered ? No ; and not even if I wanted to sail a ship, would I pilot it as I might have dreamed I should ; for the punishment would be immediate. What would be the sense in the sick seeking relief from an interpreter of dreams rather than from a physician ? Or do you think that Aesculapius and Serapis [1] have the power to prescribe a cure for our bodily ills through the medium of a dream and that Neptune cannot aid pilots through the same means ? or think you that though Minerva [2] will prescribe physic in a dream without the aid of a physician, yet that the Muses will not employ dreams to impart a knowledge of reading, writing, and of other arts ? If knowledge of a remedy for disease were conveyed by means of dreams, knowledge of the arts just mentioned would also be given by dreams. But since knowledge of these arts is not so conveyed neither is the knowledge

non datur. Qua sublata tollitur omnis auctoritas somniorum.

124   LX. "Sed haec quoque in promptu fuerint, nunc interiora videamus. Aut enim divina vis quaedam consulens nobis somniorum significationes facit ; aut coniectores ex quadam convenientia et coniunctione naturae, quam vocant συμπάθειαν, quid cuique rei conveniat ex somniis, et quid quamque rem sequatur, intellegunt ; aut eorum neutrum est, sed quaedam observatio constans atque diuturna est, cum quid visum secundum quietem sit, quid evenire et quid sequi soleat. Primum igitur intellegendum est nullam vim esse divinam effectricem somniorum. Atque illud quidem perspicuum est, nulla visa somniorum proficisci a numine deorum ; nostra enim causa di id facerent, ut providere futura possemus.

125   " Quotus igitur est quisque, qui somniis pareat, qui intellegat, qui meminerit ? quam multi vero, qui contemnant eamque superstitionem imbecilli animi atque anilis putent ! Quid est igitur cur his hominibus consulens deus somniis moneat eos qui illa non modo cura, sed ne memoria quidem digna ducant ? Nec enim ignorare deus potest, qua mente quisque sit, nec frustra ac sine causa quid facere dignum deo

of medicine. The theory that the medical art was imparted by means of dreams having been disproved, the basis of a belief in dreams is utterly destroyed.

LX. " But, though the conclusion just stated is obvious, let us now look deeper into the question. Surely you must assume, either that there is a Divine Power which, in planning for our good, gives us information by means of dreams ; or that, because of some natural connexion and association — the Greeks call it συμπάθεια — interpreters of dreams know what sort of a dream is required to fit any situation and what sort of a result will follow any dream ; or that neither of these suppositions is true, but that the usual result or consequence of every dream is known by a consistent system of rules based on long-continued observation. In the first place, then, it must be understood that there is no divine power which creates dreams. And indeed it is perfectly clear that none of the visions seen in dreams have their origin in the will of the gods ; for the gods, for our sakes, would so interpose that we might be able to foresee the future.

" But how often, pray, do you find anyone who pays any attention to dreams or who understands or remembers them ? On the other hand, how many treat them with disdain, and regard a belief in them as the superstition of a weak and effeminate mind ! Moreover, why does God, in planning for the good of the human race, convey his warnings by means of dreams which men consider unworthy not only of worrying about, but even of remembering ? For it is impossible that God does not know how people generally regard dreams ; and to do anything needlessly and without a cause

est, quod abhorret etiam ab hominis constantia.
Ita, si pleraque somnia aut ignorantur aut negle-
guntur, aut nescit hoc[1] deus aut frustra somniorum significatione utitur ; sed horum neutrum
in deum cadit ; nihil igitur a deo somniis significari
fatendum est.

126   LXI. " Illud etiam requiro, cur, si deus ista visa
nobis providendi causa dat, non vigilantibus potius
det quam dormientibus ? Sive enim externus et
adventicius pulsus animos dormientium commovet,
sive per se ipsi animi moventur, sive quae causa alia
est cur secundum quietem aliquid videre, audire,
agere videamur, eadem causa vigilantibus esse
poterat ; idque si nostra causa di secundum quietem
facerent, vigilantibus idem facerent, praesertim
cum Chrysippus Academicos refellens permulto
clariora et certiora esse dicat quae vigilantibus
videantur quam quae somniantibus. Fuit igitur
divina beneficentia dignius, cum consulerent nobis,
clariora visa dare vigilantibus quam obscuriora per
somnum. Quod quoniam non fit, somnia divina
127 putanda non sunt. Iam vero quid opus est circumi-
tione et amfractu, ut sit utendum interpretibus
somniorum potius quam directo. Deus, siquidem
nobis consulebat, ' Hoc facito,' ' hoc ne feceris,'
diceret idque visum vigilanti potius quam dormienti
daret.

[1] ea *Davies.*

is unworthy of a god and is inconsistent even with the habits of right-thinking men. And hence, if most dreams are unnoticed and disregarded, either God is ignorant of that fact, or he does a vain thing in conveying information by means of dreams ; but neither supposition accords with the nature of a god, therefore, it must be admitted that God conveys no information by means of dreams.

LXI. " I also ask, if God gives us these visions as forewarnings, why does he not give them to us when we are awake rather than when we are asleep ? For, whether our souls in sleep are impelled by some external and foreign force ; or whether they are self-moved ; or whether there is some other cause why, during sleep, we imagine ourselves seeing or hearing, or doing certain things—whatever the cause, it would apply just as well when we are awake. If the gods did send us warnings in our sleep and for our good they would do the same for us when we are awake, especially since, as Chrysippus says in replying to the Academicians, appearances seen when we are awake are much more distinct and trustworthy than those seen in dreams. It would, therefore, have been more in keeping with the beneficence of gods, in consulting for our good, to send us clear visions in our waking moments rather than unintelligible ones in our dreams. But since that is not the case, dreams ought not to be held divine. And, further, what is the need of a method which, instead of being direct, is so circuitous and roundabout that we have to employ men to interpret our dreams? And if it be true that God consults for our advantage he would say : ' Do this,' ' Don't do that,' and not give us visions when we are awake rather than when we are asleep

LXII. " Iam vero quis dicere audeat vera omnia
esse somnia ? ' Aliquot somnia vera,' inquit Ennius,
' sed omnia non est necesse.' Quae est tandem
ista distinctio ? quae vera, quae falsa habet ? et, si
vera a deo mittuntur, falsa unde nascuntur ? nam
si ea quoque divina quid inconstantius deo ? quid
inscitius autem est quam mentes mortalium falsis
et mendacibus visis concitare ? sin vera visa divina
sunt, falsa autem et inania humana, quae est ista
designandi licentia, ut hoc deus, hoc natura fecerit
potius quam aut omnia deus, quod negatis, aut
omnia natura ? quod quoniam illud negatis, hoc
128 necessario confitendum est. Naturam autem eam
dico, qua numquam animus insistens agitatione et
motu esse vacuus potest. Is cum languore corporis
nec membris uti nec sensibus potest, incidit in visa
varia et incerta ' ex reliquiis,' ut ait Aristoteles,
' inhaerentibus earum rerum, quas vigilans gesserit
aut cogitaverit.' Quarum perturbatione mirabiles
interdum existunt species somniorum ; quae si
alia falsa, alia vera, qua nota internoscantur, scire
sane velim. Si nulla est, quid istos interpretes
audiamus ? sin quaepiam est, aveo audire, quae sit ;
sed haerebunt.
129   LXIII. " Venit enim iam in contentionem, utrum
sit probabilius, deosne immortalis, rerum omnium

---

[1] *Insistens=etiamsi insistit a cogitationis opera*, Giese.
[2] Aristot. Περὶ ἐνυπνίων ch. 3.

LXII. " And further, would anybody dare to say that all dreams are true ? ' Some dreams are true,' says Ennius, ' but not necessarily all.' Pray how do you distinguish between the two ? What mark have the false and what the true ? And if God sends the true, whence come the false ? Surely if God sends the false ones too what is more untrustworthy than God ? Besides what is more stupid than to excite the souls of mortals with false and lying visions ? But if true visions are divine while the false and meaningless ones are from nature, what sort of caprice decided that God made the one and nature made the other, rather than that God made them all, which your school denies, or that nature made them all ? Since you deny that God made them all you must admit that nature made them all. By ' nature,' in this connexion, I mean that force because of which the soul can never be stationary [1] and free from motion and activity. And when, because of the weariness of the body, the soul can use neither the limbs nor the senses, it lapses into varied and untrustworthy visions, which emanate from what Aristotle [2] terms ' the clinging remnants of the soul's waking acts and thoughts.'. These ' remnants,' when aroused, some- times produce strange types of dreams. Now if some of these dreams are true and others false, I should like very much to know by what mark they may be distinguished. If there is none, why should we listen to your interpreters ? But if there is one, I am eager for them to tell me what it is, but they will grow confused when I ask and will not answer.

LXIII. " The question now arises as to which is the more probable : do the immortal gods, who are

praestantia excellentis, cursare omnium mortalium
qui ubique sunt, non modo lectos, verum etiam
grabatos et, cum stertentem aliquem viderint,
obicere eis visa quaedam tortuosa et obscura, quae
illi exterriti somno ad coniectorem mane deferant ?
an natura fieri ut mobiliter animus agitatus, quod
vigilans viderit, dormiens videre videatur ? Utrum
philosophia dignius, sagarum superstitione ista
interpretari an explicatione naturae ? ut, si iam fieri
possit vera coniectura somniorum, tamen isti, qui
profitentur, eam facere non possint ; ex levissimo
enim et indoctissimo genere constant. Stoici
autem tui negant quemquam nisi sapientem divinum
esse posse.

130   " Chrysippus quidem divinationem definit his
verbis : ' vim cognoscentem et videntem et expli-
cantem signa, quae a dis hominibus portendantur ;
officium autem esse eius praenoscere, dei erga
homines mente qua sint quidque significent, quem
ad modumque ea procurentur atque expientur.'
Idemque somniorum coniectionem definit hoc modo :
' esse vim cernentem et explanantem, quae a dis
hominibus significentur in somnis.' Quid ergo ? ad
haec mediocri opus est prudentia an et ingenio prae-
stanti et eruditione perfecta ? Talem autem cognovi-
mus neminem.

131   LXIV. " Vide igitur, ne, etiamsi divinationem tibi
esse concessero, quod numquam faciam, neminem

of surpassing excellence in all things, constantly
flit about, not only the beds, but even the lowly
pallets of mortals, wherever they may be, and when
they find someone snoring, throw at him dark and
twisted visions, which scare him from his sleep and
which he carries in the morning to a dream-expert
to unravel ? or does nature bring it to pass that
the ever-active soul sees in sleep phantoms of
what it saw when the body was awake ? Which is
more consonant with philosophy : to explain these
apparitions by the superstitious theories of fortune-
telling hags, or by an explanation based on natural
causes ? But even if it were possible to draw trustworthy inferences from dreams, it could not be done
by those who profess to have that power ; for their
fraternity is composed of the most shallow and the
most ignorant of men. Yet your Stoics assert that
no one can be a diviner unless he is a 'wise man.'

" Chrysippus, indeed, defines divination in these
words: 'The power to see, understand, and explain premonitory signs given to men by the gods.' 'Its duty,'
he goes on to say, 'is to know in advance the disposition of the gods towards men, the manner in which
that disposition is shown and by what means the gods
may be propitiated and their threatened ills averted.'
And this same philosopher defines the interpretation
of dreams thus : ' It is the power to understand and
explain the visions sent by the gods to men in sleep.'
Then, if that be true, will just ordinary shrewdness
meet these requirements, or rather is there not need
of surpassing intelligence and absolutely perfect
learning ? But I have never seen such a man.

LXIV. " Therefore, even if I granted your contention as to the existence of divination—and this I will

tamen divinum reperire possimus. Qualis autem ista
mens est deorum, si neque ea nobis significant in
somnis quae ipsi per nos intellegamus, neque ea
quorum interpretes habere possimus? similes enim
sunt dei, si ea nobis obiciunt, quorum nec scientiam
neque explanatorem habeamus, tamquam si Poeni aut
Hispani in senatu nostro loquerentur sine interprete.
132 Iam vero quo pertinent obscuritates et aenigmata
somniorum? intellegi enim a nobis di velle debebant
ea quae nostra causa nos monerent. Quid? poëta
nemo physicus obscurus? Illi[1] vero nimis etiam
133 obscurus Euphorion; at non Homerus. Uter
igitur melior? Valde Heraclitus obscurus, minime
Democritus. Num igitur conferendi? Mea causa
me mones, quod non intellegam. Quid me igitur
mones? Ut si quis medicus aegroto imperet, ut sumat

terrigenam, herbigradam, domiportam, sanguine cassam,

potius quam hominum more 'cocleam' diceret.
Nam Pacuvianus Amphio

quadrupes tardigrada, agrestis, humilis, aspera,
capite brevi, cervice anguina, aspecta truci,
eviscerata, inanima, cum animali sono.

Cum dixisset obscurius, tum Attici respondent:

<hr>

[1] illi *Lambinus for* ille

<hr>

[1] Clement of Alexandria classes him in this respect with
Callimachus and Lycophron.
[2] Heraclitus was called ὁ σκοτεινός, " The Obscure." *Cf.*
Cic. *De fin.* ii. 5. 15.
[3] The lines are from his *Antiope* and occur in a discussion
between Amphion and his brother Zethus.

never do—still, you must realize that it would be impossible for us to find a diviner. Then what do the gods mean by sending us in our dreams visions which we cannot understand ourselves and which we cannot find anybody to interpret for us ? If the gods send us these unintelligible and inexplicable dream-messages they are acting as Carthaginians and Spaniards would if they were to address our Senate in their own vernacular without the aid of an interpreter. Besides, what purpose is served by dark and enigmatic dreams ? Surely the gods ought to want us to understand the advice they give us for our good. ' Oh ! ' but you retort, ' Are poets and natural philosophers never obscure ? ' Indeed they are : Euphorion [1] is even too obscure ; but Homer is not. Which of them, pray, is the better poet? Heraclitus [2] is very obscure ; Demo-critus is not so in the least : then are they to be compared ? But you give me advice and for my good in words that I cannot understand. Then why do you advise me at all ? That's like a doctor ordering a patient to take

> A bloodless, earth-engendered thing that crawls
> And bears its habitation on its back,

instead of saying in common, every-day speech, ' a snail.' Amphion, in a play by Pacuvius,[3] speaks to the Athenians of a creature as

> Four-footed, of stature short; rough, shy, and slow;
> Fierce-eyed, with tiny head and serpent's neck;
> When disembowelled and deprived of life,
> It lives for ever in melodious song.

His meaning being too obscure the Athenians replied :

non intellegimus, nisi si aperte dixeris.

Ait ille uno verbo : ' Testudo.' Non potueras hoc igitur a principio, citharista, dicere ?

134 LXV. " Defert ad coniectorem quidam somniasse se ovum pendere ex fascia lecti sui cubicularis— est hoc in Chrysippi libro somnium— ; respondit coniector thesaurum defossum esse sub lecto. Fodit, invenit auri aliquantum, idque circumdatum argento, misit coniectori quantulum visum est de argento. Tum ille : ' Nihilne,' inquit, ' de vitello ? ' id enim ei ex ovo videbatur aurum declarasse reliquum argentum. Nemone igitur umquam alius ovum somniavit ? cur ergo hic nescio qui thesaurum solus invenit ? quam multi inopes digni praesidio deorum nullo somnio ad thesaurum reperiendum admonentur ! Quam autem ob causam tam est obscure admonitus ut ex ovo nasceretur thesauri similitudo, potius quam aperte thesaurum quaerere iuberetur, sicut aperte Simonides vetitus est navi-
135 gare ? Ergo obscura somnia minime consentanea maiestati deorum.

LXVI. " Ad aperta et clara veniamus, quale est de illo interfecto a caupone Megaris ; quale de Simonide, qui ab eo, quem humarat, vetitus est navigare ; quale etiam de Alexandro, quod a te praeteritum esse miror, Quinte. Cum Ptolemaeus, fa- miliaris eius, in proelio telo venenato ictus esset eo-

Speak plainer, else we cannot understand.

Whereupon he described it in a single word—' a tortoise.' Couldn't you have said so at first, you cithara-player ?

LXV. " A diviner was consulted by a man who had dreamed that he saw an egg hanging from the bed-cords of the bed in his sleeping-room—the story is from Chrysippus *On Dreams*—and the diviner answered, ' A treasure is buried under your bed.' The man dug, found a quantity of gold surrounded with silver and sent the diviner as much of the silver as he thought fit. The diviner then inquired, ' Do I get none of the yolk ? ' For, in his view, the yolk meant gold, the white of the egg, silver. Now, did no one else ever dream of an egg ? If so, then why did this fellow, whoever he was, alone find a treasure by dreaming of an egg ? What a lot of poor devils there are, deserving of divine assistance, who never were instructed by a dream how to find a treasure ! Furthermore, why was this man given so obscure an intimation as that contained in the fancied resemblance between an egg and a treasure, instead of being as plainly directed as Simonides[1] was when he was bidden not to go on board the ship ? My conclusion is that obscure messages by means of dreams are utterly inconsistent with the dignity of gods.

LXVI. " Let us now consider dreams that are clear and direct, like the dream of the man who was killed by the innkeeper at Megara ;[2] or like that of Simonides who was warned by the man he had buried not to sail ; and also like Alexander's dream, which, to my surprise, my dear Quintus, you passed by without notice : Alexander's intimate friend, Ptolemaeus, had been struck in battle by a

que vulnere summo cum dolore moreretur, **Alexander**
assidens somno est consopitus. Tum secundum
quietem visus ei dicitur draco is, quem mater
Olympias alebat, radiculam ore ferre et simul dicere,
quo illa loci nasceretur (neque is longe aberat ab eo
loco), eius autem esse vim tantam, ut Ptolomaeum
facile sanaret. Cum Alexander experrectus narras-
set amicis somnium, emissi sunt, qui illam radiculam
quaererent; qua inventa et Ptolomaeus sanatus
dicitur et multi milites, qui erant eodem genere
teli vulnerati.

136 " Multa etiam sunt a te ex historiis prolata
somnia, matris Phalaridis, Cyri superioris, matris
Dionysi, Poeni Hamilcaris, Hannibalis, P. Deci;
pervulgatum iam illud de praesule, C. Gracchi
etiam et recens Caeciliae, Balearici filiae, somnium.
Sed haec externa ob eamque causam ignota nobis
sunt, non nulla etiam ficta fortasse. Quis enim
auctor istorum? De nostris somniis quid habemus
dicere? tu de emerso me et equo ad ripam, ego de
Mario cum fascibus laureatis me in suum deduci
iubente monumentum?

LXVII. Omnium somniorum, Quinte, una ratio
est; quae, per deos immortalis! videamus ne nostra

---

[1] *Cf.* i. 23. 46.   [2] *Cf.* i. 23. 46.   [3] *Cf.* i. 20. 39.
[4] *Cf.* i. 24. 50.   [5] *Cf.* i. 24. 48, 49.   [6] *Cf.* i. 24. 51.
[7] *Cf.* i. 26. 55.   [8] *Cf.* i. 26. 56.   [9] *Cf.* i. 44. 99.
[10] So Moser, Giese, and Kühner explain *haec externa.*
[11] *Cf.* i. 28. 58.   [12] *Cf.* i. 28. 59.

poisoned arrow and was at the point of death from his wound and suffering the most excruciating agony. Alexander, while sitting by the bedside of his friend, fell fast asleep. Thereupon, so the story goes, he dreamed that the pet serpent of his mother Olympias appeared to him carrying a root in its mouth and, at the same time, gave him the name of a place close by where it said the root grew. This root, the serpent told him, was of such great virtue that it would effect the speedy cure of Ptolemaeus. As soon as Alexander awoke he related his dream to his friends and men were sent to find the root. It is said that when the root was found it worked the cure not only of Ptolemaeus, but also of many soldiers who had been wounded by the same kind of arrow.

" You, too, have drawn on history for dreams, a number of which you told. You spoke, for example, of the dreams of the mother of Phalaris,[1] of Cyrus the Elder,[2] of the mother of Dionysius,[3] of the Carthaginians Hamilcar[4] and Hannibal,[5] and of Publius Decius.[6] You mentioned that much-spoken-of dream about the slave who opened the votive games,[7] also the dream of Gaius Gracchus[8] and the recent one of Caecilia,[9] the daughter of Balearicus. But these are other people's dreams[10] and hence we know nothing about them and some of them are fabrications perhaps. For who stands sponsor for them ? And what have we to say of our own dreams ? Of your dream of me and of my horse emerging from the river and appearing on the bank ?[11] and of my dream of Marius, attended by his laurelled fasces, ordering me to be conducted to his monument ?[12]

LXVII. " All dreams, my dear Quintus, have one explanation and, in heaven's name, let us see that it

137 superstitione et depravatione superetur. Quem enim tu Marium visum a me putas? 'Speciem,' credo, eius et 'imaginem,' ut Democrito videtur. Unde profectam 'imaginem'? 'A corporibus' enim solidis et a certis figuris vult fluere 'imagines.' Quod igitur Marii corpus erat? 'Ex eo,' inquit, 'quod fuerat.' Ista igitur me 'imago' Mari in campum Atinatem persequebatur? 'Plena sunt "imaginum" omnia';[1] nulla enim species cogitari

138 potest nisi pulsu 'imaginum.' Quid ergo? istae 'imagines' ita nobis dicto audientes sunt ut, simul atque velimus, accurrant? etiamne earum rerum quae nullae sunt? Quae est enim forma tam invisitata, tam nulla, quam non sibi ipse fingere animus possit? ut, quae numquam vidimus, ea tamen informata habeamus, oppidorum situs, homi-

139 num figuras. Num igitur, cum aut muros Babylonis aut Homeri faciem cogito, 'imago' illorum me aliqua pellit? Omnia igitur, quae volumus, nota nobis esse possunt; nihil est enim, de quo cogitare nequeamus; nullae ergo 'imagines' obrepunt in animos dormientium extrinsecus, nec omnino fluunt ullae, nec cognovi quemquam, qui maiore auctoritate nihil diceret.

"Animorum est ea vis eaque natura, ut vigeant vigilantes nullo adventicio pulsu, sed suo motu incredibili quadam celeritate. Hi cum sustinentur

---

[1] *In* MSS. *and Dav.* Plena . . . omnia *immediately follows* ex eo . . . quod fuerat

---

[1] One of the εἴδωλα, *simulacra*, given off according to the atomic philosophers by all bodies and by their impact causing sight.

is not set at naught by superstition and perversity. Now what Marius do you think it was I saw? His 'likeness' or 'phantom,'[1] I suppose—at least that is what Democritus thinks. Whence did the 'phantom' come? He would have it that 'phantoms' emanate from material bodies and from actual forms. Then, it was the body of Marius from which my 'phantom' came? 'No,' says Democritus, 'but from his body that was.' So that 'phantom' of Marius was pursuing me to the plains of Atina? 'Oh, but the universe is full of "phantoms"; no picture of anything can be formed in the mind except as the result of the impact of "phantoms."' Then are these 'phantoms' of yours so obedient to our beck and call that they come the instant we summon them? And is this true even of the 'phantoms' of things that do not exist? For what is there so unreal and unheard of that we cannot form a mental picture of it? We even shape things which we have never seen—as the sites of towns and the faces of men. Then, by your theory, when I think of the walls of Babylon or of the face of Homer, some 'phantom' of what I have in mind 'strikes upon my brain'! Hence it is possible for us to know everything we wish to know, since there is nothing of which we cannot think. Therefore no 'phantoms' from the outside steal in upon our souls in sleep; nor do 'phantoms' stream forth at all. In fact I never knew anybody who could say nothing with more ponderous gravity than Democritus.

"The soul is of such a force and nature that, when we are awake, it is active, not because of any extraneous impulse, but because of its own inherent power of self-motion and a certain incredible

membris et corpore et sensibus, omnia certiora
cernunt, cogitant, sentiunt. Cum autem haec
subtracta sunt desertusque animus languore corporis,
tum agitatur ipse per sese. Itaque in eo et formae
versantur et actiones, et multa audiri, multa dici
140 videntur. Haec scilicet in imbecillo remissoque
animo multa omnibus modis confusa et variata
versantur, maximeque ' reliquiae ' rerum earum
moventur in animis et agitantur de quibus vigilantes
aut cogitavimus aut egimus ; ut mihi temporibus
illis multum in animo Marius versabatur recordanti,
quam ille gravem suum casum magno animo, quam
constanti tulisset. Hanc credo causam de illo
somniandi fuisse.

LXVIII. " Tibi autem de me cum sollicitudine
cogitanti subito sum visus emersus e flumine. Inerant enim in utriusque nostrum animis ' vigilantium
cogitationum vestigia.' At quaedam adiuncta sunt,
ut mihi de monumento Mari, tibi, quod equus, in
quo ego vehebar, mecum una demersus rursus
141 apparuit. An tu censes ullam anum tam deliram
futuram fuisse ut somniis crederet, nisi ista casu non
numquam forte temere concurrerent ? Alexandro
draco loqui visus est. Potest omnino hoc esse falsum,
potest verum ; sed utrum est non est mirabile ;
non enim audivit ille draconem loquentem, sed est
visus audire ; et quidem, quo maius sit, cum radicem

---

[1] This same view (which is also expressed in Cic. *C.M.*
21. 78, *Tusc.* i. 43), was held by the ancient philosophers
generally.
[2] During Cicero's banishment.

swiftness.[1] When the soul is supported by the bodily
members and by the five senses its powers of perception, thought, and apprehension are more trustworthy. But when these physical aids are removed
and the body is inert in sleep, the soul then moves
of itself. And so, in that state, visions flit about
it, actions occur and it seems to hear and say many
things. When the soul itself is weakened and
relaxed many such sights and sounds, you may
be sure, are seen and heard in all manner of
confusion and diversity. Then especially do the
' remnants ' of our waking thoughts and deeds move
and stir within the soul. For example, in the time
of my banishment Marius was often in my mind as
I recalled with what great fortitude and courage he
had borne his own heavy misfortunes, and this I
think is the reason why I dreamed about him.

LXVIII. " As for your dream, it occurred while
you were thinking and worrying about me [2] and
then you had the vision of me as I suddenly arose
from the river. For in the souls of us both were
'traces of our waking thoughts,' but with some
added features, of course : as, for example, my
dreaming of Marius's monument and your dreaming
that the horse on which I rode sank with me and
then reappeared. But do you suppose that there
ever would have been any old woman crazy enough
to believe in dreams, if by some lucky accident or
chance they had not come true sometimes ? But
let us consider Alexander's dream of the talking
serpent. The story may be true ànd it may be
wholly false. In either case it is no miracle ; for
he did not hear the serpent speak, but thought he
heard it and, strangest thing of all, he thought it

ore teneret locutus est. Sed nihil est magnum
somnianti. Quaero autem cur Alexandro tam
illustre somnium, tam certum, nec huic eidem alias,
nec multa ceteris? Mihi quidem praeter hoc
Marianum nihil sane, quod meminerim. Frustra
igitur consumptae tot noctes tam longa in aetate!
142 Nunc quidem propter intermissionem forensis operae
et lucubrationes detraxi et meridiationes addidi,
quibus uti antea non solebam, nec tam multum
dormiens ullo somnio sum admonitus, tantis praesertim de rebus, nec mihi magis umquam videor,
quam cum aut in foro magistratus aut in curia
senatum video, somniare.

LXIX. Etenim—ex divisione hoc secundum est—
quae est continuatio coniunctioque naturae quam,
ut dixi, vocant συμπάθειαν, eius modi, ut thesaurus
ex ovo intellegi debeat? Nam medici ex quibusdam
rebus et advenientis et crescentis morbos intellegunt, non nullas etiam valetudinis significationes, ut
hoc ipsum, pleni enectine simus, ex quodam genere
somniorum intellegi posse dicunt. Thesaurus vero
et hereditas et honos et victoria et multa generis
eiusdem qua cum somniis naturali cognatione
143 iunguntur? Dicitur quidam, cum in somnis com-
plexu Venerio iungeretur, calculos eiecisse. Video

---

[1] The turmoil and chaos which followed Caesar's death.
[2] Because they were mere shadows, without real authority.
[3] *i.e.* between dreams and things seen in dreams.
[4] *Cf.* ii. 14. 34.

spoke while it held the root in its mouth ! But nothing seems strange to a man when he is dreaming. Now, if Alexander ever had such a vivid and trustworthy dream as this, I want to ask why he never had another one like it and why other men have not had many of the same kind ? As for me, except for that dream about Marius, I really never had one that I can recall. Think then how many nights in my long life I have spent in vain ! Moreover, at the present time, owing to the interruption of my public labours, I have ceased my nocturnal studies, and (contrary to my former practice) I have added afternoon naps. Yet despite all this time spent in sleep I have not received a single prophecy in a dream, certainly not one about the great events [1] now going on. Indeed, I never seem to be dreaming more than when I see the magistrates in the forum and the Senate in its chamber.[2]

LXIX. "Coming now to the second branch of the present topic, is there some such natural connecting link,[3] which, as I said before,[4] the Greeks call συμπάθεια, that the finding of a treasure must be deduced from dreaming of an egg ? Of course physicians, from certain symptoms, know the incipiency and progress of a disease ; and it is claimed that from some kinds of dreams they even can gather certain indications as to a patient's health, as whether the internal humours of the body are excessive or deficient. But what natural bond of union is there between dreams, on the one hand, and treasures, legacies, public office, victory and many other things of the same kind, on the other ? A person, it is said, while dreaming of coition, ejected gravel. In this case I can see a relation between the dream and

sympathian; visum est enim tale obiectum dormienti,
ut id, quod evenit naturae vis, non opinio erroris
effecerit. Quae igitur natura obtulit illam speciem
Simonidi a qua vetaretur navigare? aut quid naturae
copulatum habuit Alcibiadis quod scribitur somnium?
qui paulo ante interitum visus est in somnis amicae
esse amictus amiculo. Is cum esset proiectus
inhumatus ab omnibusque desertus iaceret, amica
corpus eius texit suo pallio. Ergo hoc inerat in
rebus futuris et causas naturalis habebat, an, et ut
videretur et ut eveniret, casus effecit?

144   LXX. " Quid? ipsorum interpretum coniecturae
nonne magis ingenia declarant eorum quam vim
consensumque naturae? Cursor, ad Olympia proficisci cogitans, visus est in somnis curru quadrigarum
vehi. Mane ad coniectorem. At ille: ' Vinces,'
inquit; ' id enim celeritas significat et vis equorum.'
Post idem ad Antiphontem. Is autem: ' Vincare,'
inquit, ' necesse est; an non intellegis quattuor ante
te cucurrisse?' Ecce alius cursor—atque horum
somniorum et talium plenus est Chrysippi liber,
plenus Antipatri—sed ad cursorem redeo: ad
interpretem detulit aquilam se in somnis visum
esse factum. At ille: ' Vicisti; ista enim avi
volat nulla vehementius.' Huic eidem Antipho:

---

¹ The translation adopts the interpretation of Hottinger,
De div. p. 541. What is implied is that the dream was the
effect and not the cause *eiectionis calculorum.*

the result ; for the vision presented to the sleeper was such as to make it clear that what happened was due to natural causes and not to the delusion.[1] But by what law of nature did Simonides receive that vision which forbade him to sail ? or what was the connexion between the laws of nature and the dream of Alcibiades in which, according to history, shortly before his death, he seemed to be enveloped in the cloak of his mistress ? Later, when his body had been cast out and was lying unburied and universally neglected, his mistress covered it with her mantle. Then do you say that this dream was united by some natural tie with the fate that befell Alcibiades, or did chance cause both the apparition and the subsequent event ?

LXX. " Furthermore, is it not a fact that the conjectures of the interpreters of dreams give evidence of their authors' sagacity rather than afford any proof of a relation between dreams and the laws of nature ? For example, a runner, who was planning to set out for the Olympic games, dreamed that he was riding in a chariot drawn by four horses. In the morning he went to consult an interpreter, who said to him, ' You will win, for that is implied in the speed and strength of horses.' Later the runner went to Antipho, who said, ' You are bound to lose, for do you not see that four ran ahead of you ? And behold another runner !—for the books of Chrysippus and Antipater are full of such dreams— but to return to the runner : he reported to an interpreter that he had dreamed of having been changed into an eagle. The interpreter said to him, ' You are the victor, for no bird flies faster than the eagle.' This runner also consulted Antipho.

'Baro,' inquit, 'victum te esse non vides? ista enim avis insectans alias avis et agitans semper ipsa postrema est.'

145 "Parere quaedam matrona cupiens. dubitans essetne praegnans, visa est in quiete obsignatam habere naturam. Rettulit. Negavit eam, quoniam obsignata fuisset, concipere potuisse. At alter praegnantem esse dixit; nam inane obsignari nihil solere. Quae est ars coniectoris eludentis ingenio? an ea, quae dixi, et innumerabilia, quae collecta habent Stoici, quicquam significant nisi acumen hominum ex similitudine aliqua coniecturam modo huc, modo illuc ducentium? Medici signa quaedam habent ex venis et spiritu aegroti multisque ex aliis futura praesentiunt; gubernatores cum exsultantis lolligines viderunt aut delphinos se in portum conicientes, tempestatem significari putant. Haec ratione explicari et ad naturam revocari facile possunt, ea vero, quae paulo ante dixi, nullo modo.

146 LXXI. "At enim observatio diuturna (haec enim pars una restat) notandis rebus fecit artem. An tandem? somnia observari possunt? quonam modo? sunt enim innumerabiles varietates; nihil tam praepostere, tam incondite, tam monstruose cogitari potest, quod non possimus somniare. Quo modo

---

[1] *i.e.* of the three mentioned in ii. 60. 124.

' Simpleton,' said the latter, ' don't you see that you are beaten ? For that bird is always pursuing and driving other birds before it and itself is always last.'

" A married woman who was desirous of a child and was in doubt whether she was pregnant or not, dreamed that her womb had been sealed. She referred the dream to an interpreter. He told her that since her womb was sealed conception was impossible. But another interpreter said, ' You are pregnant, for it is not customary to seal that which is empty.' Then what is the dream-interpreter's art other than a means of using one's wits to deceive ? And those incidents which I have given and the numberless ones collected by the Stoics prove nothing whatever except the shrewdness of men who employ slight analogies in order to draw now one inference and now another. There are certain indications from the condition of the pulse and breath and from many other symptoms in sickness by means of which physicians foretell the course of a disease. When pilots see cuttle-fish leaping or dolphins betaking themselves to a haven they believe that a storm is at hand. In such cases signs are given which are traceable to natural causes and explicable by reason, but that is far from true of the dreams spoken of a little while ago.

LXXI. " In our consideration of dreams we come now to the remaining point [1] left for discussion, which is your contention that ' by long-continued observation of dreams and by recording the results an art has been evolved.' Really ? Then, it is possible, I suppose, to ' observe ' dreams ? If so, how ? For they are of infinite variety and there is no imaginable thing too absurd, too involved, or too abnormal for us to dream about it. How, then, is it possible

igitur, haec infinita et semper nova aut memoria
complecti aut observando notare possumus ? Astro-
logi motus errantium stellarum notaverunt; inventus est enim ordo in eis stellis, qui non putabatur.
Cedo tandem qui sit ordo aut quae concursatio
somniorum ? quo modo autem distingui possunt
vera somnia a falsis, cum eadem et aliis aliter
evadant et eisdem non semper eodem modo ? ut
mihi mirum videatur, cum mendaci homini ne verum
quidem dicenti credere soleamus, quo modo isti, si
somnium verum evasit aliquod, non ex multis potius
uni fidem derogent quam ex uno innumerabilia
confirment.

147 " Si, igitur, neque deus est effector somniorum,
neque naturae societas ulla cum somniis neque
observatione inveniri potuit scientia, effectum est,
ut nihil prorsus somniis tribuendum sit, praesertim
cum illi ipsi qui ea vident nihil divinent, ei qui
interpretantur coniecturam adhibeant, non naturam,
casus autem innumerabilibus paene saeculis in
omnibus plura mirabilia quam in somniorum visis
effecerit, neque coniectura, quae in varias partis

for us either to remember this countless and ever-changing mass of visions or to observe and record the subsequent results ? Astronomers have recorded the movements of the planets and thereby have discovered an orderly course of the stars, not thought of before. But tell me, if you can, what is the orderly course of dreams and what is the harmonious relation between them and subsequent events ? And by what means can the true be distinguished from the false, in view of the fact that the same dreams have certain consequences for one person and different consequences for another and seeing also that even for the same individual the same dream is not always followed by the same result ? As a rule we do not believe a liar even when he tells the truth, but, to my surprise, if one dream turns out to be true, your Stoics do not withdraw their belief in the prophetic value of that one though it is only one out of many ; rather, from the character of the one true dream, they establish the character of countless others that are false.

" Therefore, if God is not the creator of dreams ; if there is no connexion between them and the laws of nature ; and finally, if, by means of observation no art of divining can be found in them, it follows that absolutely no reliance can be placed in dreams. This becomes especially evident when we consider that those who have the dreams deduce no prophecies from them ; that those who interpret them depend upon conjecture and not upon nature ; that in the course of the almost countless ages, chance has worked more miracles through all other agencies than through the agency of dreams ; and, finally, that nothing is more uncertain than conjecture,

duci possit, non numquam etiam in contrarias,
quicquam sit incertius.

148 LXXII. Explodatur igitur haec quoque somniorum
divinatio pariter cum ceteris. Nam, ut vere loqua-
mur, superstitio, fusa per gentis, oppressit omnium
fere animos atque hominum imbecillitatem occupavit.
Quod et in eis libris dictum est qui sunt *de Natura
Deorum*, et hac disputatione id maxime egimus.
Multum enim et nobismet ipsis et nostris profuturi
videbamur, si eam funditus sustulissemus. Nec
vero—id enim diligenter intellegi volo—superstitione tollenda religio tollitur. Nam et maiorum
instituta tueri sacris caerimoniisque retinendis
sapientis est, et esse praestantem aliquam aeter-
namque naturam, et eam suspiciendam admiran-
damque hominum generi pulchritudo mundi ordoque
rerum caelestium cogit confiteri.

149 " Quam ob rem, ut religio propaganda etiam est,
quae est iuncta cum cognitione naturae, sic superstitionis stirpes omnes eiiciendae.[1] Instat enim et
urget et, quo te cumque verteris, persequitur, sive
tu vatem sive tu omen audieris, sive immolaris sive
avem aspexeris, si Chaldaeum, si haruspicem videris,
si fulserit, si tonuerit, si tactum aliquid erit de
caelo, si ostenti simile natum factumve quippiam;

[1] eiiciendae *MSS.*; eligendae *Madv.*, *Müller.*

which may be led not only into varying, but sometimes even into contradictory, conclusions.

LXXII. " Then let dreams, as a means of divination, be rejected along with the rest. Speaking frankly, superstition, which is widespread among the nations, has taken advantage of human weakness to cast its spell over the mind of almost every man. This same view was stated in my treatise *On the Nature of the Gods* ; and to prove the correctness of that view has been the chief aim of the present discussion. For I thought that I should be rendering a great service both to myself and to my countrymen if I could tear this superstition up by the roots. But I want it distinctly understood that the destruction of superstition does not mean the destruction of religion. For I consider it the part of wisdom to preserve the institutions of our forefathers by retaining their sacred rites and ceremonies. Furthermore, the celestial order and the beauty of the universe compel me to confess that there is some excellent and eternal Being, who deserves the respect and homage of men.

" Wherefore, just as it is a duty to extend the influence of true religion, which is closely associated with the knowledge of nature, so it is a duty to weed out every root of superstition. For superstition is ever at your heels to urge you on ; it follows you at every turn. ·It is with you when you listen to a prophet, or an omen ; when you offer sacrifices or watch the flight of birds ; when you consult an astrologer or a soothsayer ; when it thunders or lightens or there is a bolt from on high ; or when some so-called prodigy is born or is made. And since necessarily some of these signs

quorum necesse est plerumque aliquid eveniat, ut numquam liceat quieta mente consistere.

150   "Perfugium videtur omnium laborum et sollicitudinum esse somnus.   At ex eo ipso plurimae curae metusque nascuntur ; qui quidem ipsi per se minus valerent et magis contemnerentur, nisi somniorum patrocinium philosophi suscepissent, nec ei quidem contemptissimi, sed in primis acuti et consequentia et repugnantia videntes, qui prope iam absoluti et perfecti putantur. - Quorum licentiae nisi Carneades restitisset, haud scio an soli iam philosophi iudicarentur.   Cum quibus omnis fere nobis disceptatio contentioque est, non quod eos maxime contemnamus, sed quod videntur acutissime sententias suas prudentissimeque defendere.   Cum autem proprium sit Academiae iudicium suum nullum interponere, ea probare quae simillima veri videantur, conferre causas, et quid in quamque sententiam dici possit expromere, nulla adhibita sua auctoritate iudicium audientium relinquere integrum ac liberum. Tenebimus hanc consuetudinem, a Socrate traditam, eaque inter nos, si tibi, Quinte frater, placebit, quam saepissime utemur."

"Mihi vero," inquit ille, "nihil potest esse iucundius."

Quae cum essent dicta, surreximus.

are nearly always being given, no one who believes in them can ever remain in a tranquil state of mind.

"Sleep is regarded as a refuge from every toil and care ; but it is actually made the fruitful source of worry and fear. In fact dreams would be less regarded on their own account and would be viewed with greater indifference had they not been taken under the guardianship of philosophers—not philosophers of the meaner sort, but those of the keenest wit, competent to see what follows logically and what does not—men who are considered well-nigh perfect and infallible. Indeed, if their arrogance had not been resisted by Carneades, it is probable that by this time they would have been adjudged the only philosophers. While most of my war of words has been with these men, it is not because I hold them in especial contempt, but on the contrary, it is because they seem to me to defend their own views with the greatest acuteness and skill. Moreover, it is characteristic of the Academy to put forward no conclusions of its own, but to approve those which seem to approach nearest to the truth ; to compare arguments ; to draw forth all that may be said in behalf of any opinion ; and, without asserting any authority of its own, to leave the judgement of the inquirer wholly free. That same method, which by the way we inherited from Socrates, I shall, if agreeable to you, my dear Quintus, follow as often as possible in our future discussions."

"Nothing could please me better," Quintus replied.

When this was said, we arose.

INDEX TO THE *DE SENECTUTE*

CICERO

INDEX TO THE DE SENECTUTE

CICERO

Duellius, Gaius (as consul 260 defeated the Carthaginian fleet near Messina), 44.

Ennius, Quintus (b. 239 in Calabria, d. 169 ; brought to Rome by Cato ; one of the greatest of the early Roman poets ; wrote *Annales*, a poetical history of Rome, also tragedies), 1, 10, 14, 16, 50, 73.

Epicurus (Greek philosopher, lived 341-270 B.C. ; founder of the Epicurean school of philosophy), 43.

Fabius, Quintus Maximus (called " Cunctator " ; consul 233, 228, 215, 214, 209 ; censor 230 ; dictator 217 ; he wore out Hannibal by refusing battle ; died 203), 10-13, 15, 39, 61.

Fabius ; Quintus Fabius Maximus (son of the Cunctator ; consul 213, died before his father), 12.

Fabricius, Gaius Luscinus (consul 282, 278 ; censor 275 ; distinguished in the war against Pyrrhus, but best known for his virtue and integrity), 15, 43.

Flaccus, Marcus Valerius (friend and colleague of Cato as consul and censor, see Introduction), 42.

Flaminian law, 11.

Flamininus, Lucius Quinctius (brother of Titus Flamininus ; legate in Greece under his brother ; consul 192 ; expelled from the Senate by Cato as Censor, 184), 42.

Flamininus, Titus Quinctius (consul 198 ; censor 189 ; conquered Philip V. of Macedon in 197 at Cynoscephalae in Thessaly ; he was distinguished for his learning), 1, 42.

Flamininus, Titus Quinctius (son of the victor over Philip ; consul 150 B.C.), 14.

Flaminius, Gaius (tribune of the plebs and author of the Flaminian law, 232 ; consul 223 and 217 ; censor 220 ; builder of the Flaminian Way ; entrapped and killed in battle with Hannibal at Lake Trasimene, 217), 11.

Gallus, Sulpicius (consul 166; orator, writer, astronomer; predicted the eclipse which occurred the day before the battle of Pydna, in 168, where Paulus defeated Perseus), 49.

Glabrio, see Acilius.

Gorgias (a famous sophist and rhetorician of Leontini in Sicily, b. about 485 ; his death is variously given as 380, 378, 377), 13, 23.

INDEX TO THE DE SENECTUTE

545

INDEX TO THE DE SENECTUTE

INDEX TO THE *DE AMICITIA*

CICERO

Brutus, Decimus Iunius (consul with Scipio Nasica Serapio 138 ; conquered Lusitania 137 and the Gallaeci in 136), 7.

Capitolium (comprises the citadel ; site of the temple of Jupiter in Rome), 37.

Carbo, Gaius Papirius (a noted orator, b. about 164, d. 119 ; a partisan of Tib. Gracchus ; tribune 131 ; consul 120 ; was suspected of the murder of Scipio), 39, 41, 96.

Cassian law, 41 *n*.

Cassius ; Lucius Cassius Longinus Ravilla (tribune in 137), 41.

Cassius ; Spurius Cassius Vecellinus (consul 502, 493, and 486 ; author of an agrarian law ; accused of aiming at despotic power and killed in 486), 28.

Cato, C. Porcius (grandson of the Censor ; consul 114 ; condemned for extortion), 39.

Cato, Marcus Porcius (the Censor, b. at Tusculum 234, d. 149 ; consul 195 ; censor 184), 4, 5, 9, 10, 76, 90.

Coriolanus, Gaius Marcius (defeated the Corioli in 493 ; a patrician, hated the plebs ; was exiled and went to the Volsci whom he led to attack Rome, but abandoned at the entreaty of his mother), 36, 42.

Crassus, Gaius Licinius (author of the Licinian law regulating the election of augurs ; tribune, 145), 96.

Cumae (an ancient Greek colony in Campania, Italy), 37.

Curius ; Manius Curius Dentanus (consul 290, 275, 274 ; defeated the Samnites and Sabines 290, Pyrrhus 274 ; a type of old-fashioned Roman honour and simplicity), 18, 28, 39.

Empedocles, see Agrigentum.

Ennius, Quintus (b. in Calabria 239, d. 169 ; wrote *Annales*, a history of Rome in verse and tragedies and other poetical works), 22, 64.

Epiclerus (or *The Heiress*, a play of Caecilius Statius), 99 *n*.

Fabricius ; Gaius Fabricius Luscinus (consul 282, 278 ; envoy in 280 to Pyrrhus, who tried in vain to bribe and frighten him ; he was a typical old-fashioned Roman), 18, 28.

INDEX TO THE DE AMICITIA

551

INDEX TO THE DE AMICITIA

INDEX TO THE *DE DIVINATIONE*

Note.—The references are to tne volume and section.

554

INDEX TO THE DE DIVINATIONE

561

INDEX TO THE DE DIVINATIONE

CICERO

565

INDEX TO THE DE DIVINATIONE